Timothy Taylor

slay the
Sicilian!

EVERYMAN CHESS

Gloucester Publishers plc www.everymanchess.com

First published in 2012 by Gloucester Publishers Limited, Northburgh House, 10 Northburgh Street, London EC1V 0AT

British Library Cataloguing-in-Publication Data
A catalogue record for this book is available from the British Library.

ISBN: 978 1 85744 684 5

Distributed in North America by The Globe Pequot Press, P.O Box 480, 246 Goose Lane, Guilford, CT 06437-0480.

All other sales enquiries should be directed to Everyman Chess, Northburgh House, 10 Northburgh Street, London EC1V 0AT
tel: 020 7253 7887 fax: 020 7490 3708
email: info@everymanchess.com; website: www.everymanchess.com

To my wonderful children Vanessa, Aileen, Suzanne, Nikolay and Kennedy.

Everyman Chess Series
Chief advisor: Byron Jacobs
Commissioning editor: John Emms
Assistant editor: Richard Palliser

Typeset and edited by First Rank Publishing, Brighton.
Cover design by Horatio Monteverde.
Printed and bound in Great Britain by Clays, Bungay, Suffolk.

Contents

Bibliography

Books

Anti-Sicilians: A Guide for Black, Dorian Rogozenko (Gambit 2003)

Art of Attack in Chess, Vladimir Vukovic (Everyman Chess 2009)

The Art of Chess Analysis, Jan Timman (RHM 1980)

The Book of the Nottingham International Chess Tournament, Alexander Alekhine (Dover 1962)

Dangerous Weapons: Anti-Sicilians, John Emms, Richard Palliser & Peter Wells (Everyman Chess 2009)

Dangerous Weapons: The Sicilian, John Emms & Richard Palliser (Everyman Chess 2007)

The Games of Robert J. Fischer, Robert Wade & Kevin O'Connell (Batsford 1972)

How to Beat the Sicilian Defence, Gawain Jones (Everyman Chess 2011)

The Life and Games of Mikhail Tal, Mikhail Tal (Everyman Chess 2003)

My Best Games, Anatoly Karpov (RHM 1978)

My Best Games of Chess, Vassily Smyslov (Constable and Co. 1958)

My Sixty Memorable Games, Robert J. Fischer (Simon and Schuster 1969)

The New Sicilian Dragon, Simon Williams (Everyman Chess 2009)

New World Chess Champion, Garry Kasparov (Pergamon 1986)

New York 1985: The Manhattan Chess Club International, Timothy Taylor (Chess Enterprises 1987)

Play the Najdorf, Scheveningen Style, John Emms (Everyman Chess 2003)

Play the Sicilian Kan, Johan Hellsten (Everyman Chess 2008)

Sicilian: Najdorf, Michael Stean (Batsford 1976)

Starting Out: Accelerated Dragon, Andrew Greet (Everyman Chess 2008)

Starting Out: Classical Sicilian, Alex Raetsky & Maxim Chetverik (Everyman Chess 2007)

Starting Out: Sicilian Najdorf, Richard Palliser (Everyman Chess 2006)

Starting Out: Sicilian Sveshnikov, John Cox (Everyman Chess 2007)

Starting Out: The Sicilian, John Emms (Everyman Chess 2009)

World Championship Interzonals, R.G.Wade, L.S.Blackstock & A.Kotov (Batsford 1974)

Computer Programs and Databases

Chessbase.com
Fritz 12
MegaBase 2011

Acknowledgement

Special thanks to my friend and superlative analysis partner, Joe Cepiel.

Introduction

This book came about completely by accident. I had been commissioned by Everyman Chess to write a book on the King's Gambit, which was right up my alley: having written the book *Pawn Sacrifice!*, I loved the idea of starting off with a strong gambit, and moreover a gambit renowned for the attacking chances that could ensue. I had played the King's Gambit off and on through-out my career, with excellent results—but I generally played 1 e4 only when I expected the reply 1...e5. I had very rarely played 1 e4 against "the general public" so to speak.

In any case, I was eager to begin work and, as all my readers know, I won't recommend what I don't play—so the next tournament I went to I played 1 e4 for the first time in many years—and got the answer, 1...c5! What's this? Next White I play 1 e4: answer, 1...c5! Third time... Sicilian again!

"Help!" I cried to my editor, the un-flappable GM John Emms. "I must learn the Sicilian before I can even begin to find someone who will answer 1 e4 with 1...e5."

My editor and publisher were happy to defer the King's Gambit and agreed to a first book on the Sicilian—but what repertoire would I recommend? What would I, myself, like to play?

In those three games mentioned above I tried an assortment of Anti-Sicilians—and got absolutely nothing out of the opening. I used to play the Sicilian Defence myself and I tended to agree with GM Rogozenko who wrote in his book, *Anti-Sicilians: A Guide for Black*, that after 1 e4 c5 the "most am-bitious" plan for White is 2 ♘f3 fol-lowed, usually on the next move, by d2-d4.

Rogozenko implies, and I will come right out and say it, that Black is by no means certain of equalizing after this bold strategy. Consider the popular position 1 e4 c5 2 ♘f3 d6 3 d4 cxd4 4 ♘xd4—White absolutely owns the centre, and while diverse counter plans are possible for Black, it's clear that at least for the moment he is fighting for equality.

Rogozenko goes on with a corollary, that he puts in bold print: "Anti-Sicilians do not bring an opening advantage for White."

This one I have a slight reservation about, for if Black is bent on the Sveshnikov, he can bend himself right out of positional shape, and there (and only there) I think White can go for the advantage with a specific Anti-Sicilian—see my list of chapter themes below and Chapter Six for specifics.

But if one believes that an Open Sicilian repertoire is objectively strongest, one must wrestle with the myriad possibilities *after* 3 d4.

The basic questions arise again: What can I recommend? What can I *play*? Many of my opponents have probably played the Sicilian all their life, and I have to hit the ground running! Certainly I'm not going to advocate memorizing 30 book moves of the Yugoslav Attack against the Dragon, or 30 moves of the English Attack against the Najdorf. That's a waste of brain cells, takes the fun out of chess, and ultimately becomes a question of "Is my computer better than your computer?"

No, we're not going there!

A glimmer of hope was provided by Tal, who throughout his career remarked how he "very much enjoyed" playing against the Sicilian.

On the other hand, he also sometimes played lines like this:

M.Tal-S.Gligoric
Alekhine Memorial,
Moscow 1963

1 e4 c5 2 ♘f3 d6 3 d4 cxd4 4 ♘xd4 ♘f6 5 ♘c3 a6 6 ♗g5 e6 7 f4 ♗e7 8 ♕f3 ♕c7 9 0-0-0 ♘bd7 10 g4 b5 11 ♗xf6 ♘xf6 12 g5 (I love you Misha, but this razor sharp and incalculable position has over 2,000 games in the database—on move 12!!) 12...♘d7 13 a3 ♗b7 14 ♗h3 0-0-0 15 ♗xe6

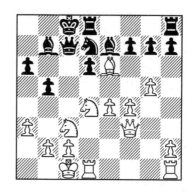

(a wonderful Tal sac—but all this is "theory" now!) 15...fxe6 16 ♘xe6 ♕c4 17 ♘d5 ♗xd5 18 exd5 ♔b7 19 b3 ♕c8 20 ♖d3 ♘b6 21 ♖c3 ♕d7 22 ♖c7+ ♕xc7 23 ♘xc7 ♔xc7 24 ♕c3+ ♔b8 25 ♕xg7 ♘c8 26 ♖e1 ♖dg8 27 ♕d4 ♗d8 28 ♖e6 ♖f8 29 h4 h6 30 g6 ♖hg8 31 h5 ♖f5 32

♕e4 ♖xh5 33 ♖e8 ♖xe8 34 ♕xe8 ♗f6
35 c4 bxc4 36 bxc4 ♖h3 37 ♔d2 ♗c3+
38 ♔c2 ♗d4 39 f5 ♖xa3 40 c5 dxc5 41
d6 ♖a2+ 42 ♔d3 ♖a3+ 43 ♔c4 1-0

While Tal also played some "human" lines (and some of his games will be found in this book), much of his stuff requires either his wizardry (and sometimes even more than that—see the introduction to Chapter Two) or a multi-processor computer! I only wish I had the former, and I don't have the latter, so I was still stuck.

And then I was rescued by a very unexpected benefactor.

I was idly looking at World Champion Anatoly Karpov's book, *My Best Games*—and I came across a line that absolutely stunned me, that I quote in full below:

"I have always felt it completely unnecessary for White to rush headlong into a maelstrom of forced variations with his first moves in the Sicilian. His superiority in the centre gives him the possibility of resolving any problem by solid positional play."

While I have always admired Karpov's positional play and his relentless technique, I've never been a fan in the way I am a fan of the wizard of Riga.

But after being rescued from a desperate situation, I not only became a big fan, I have made Karpov (like Keres in *Slay the Spanish*) the hero of this entire book!

I found Karpov's repertoire to be amazingly human and easy to learn—and absolutely deadly over the board. It seems that no one really plays this way anymore—instead everyone is out there with their laptops rushing headlong into that "maelstrom of forced variations". Thus virtually none of the opponents I encountered were prepared for what I would describe as *solid positional play with a drop of poison*. However (I couldn't help myself!), against the Dragon I also offer an alternative, non-Karpovian method, the Alekhine Attack, which so suited my style I barely had to study it!

In any case, each chapter starts with a Karpov game, and then continues with relevant games from renowned GMs and World Champions, as well as a number of my own efforts from the trenches.

Let's take a look at this repertoire, which I stress is easy to learn and very very effective. The Sicilian naturally divides into six types of opening, according to pawn structure, represented by the first six chapters of this book, with a seventh "catch all" chapter devoted to unusual odds and ends.

Here's a look at what's in store for White:

Chapter One

I start with one of the oldest lines in the Sicilian, played by Paulsen in the 19th century, the Classical Variation: 1 e4 c5 2 ♘f3 d6 3 d4 cxd4 4 ♘xd4 ♘f6 5 ♘c3 ♘c6.

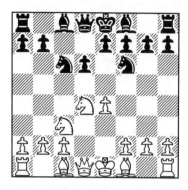

Here I recommend 6 ♗e2, and the Boleslavsky Wall structure is covered in this chapter, where Black answers 6...e5. Although it's unfashionable to say so, I think White maintains a pull in this variation, as it is not at all easy for Black to rid himself of the weakness at d5 without making some concessions. Watch Karpov take down Jan Timman with only the most minute edge—which he carries from opening through middlegame to ending and a full point.

Chapter Two

What World Champion doesn't love the Najdorf Variation that arrives after the inexplicable series of non-developing moves 1 e4 c5 2 ♘f3 d6 3 d4 cxd4 4 ♘xd4 ♘f6 5 ♘c3 a6 - ?

(see following diagram)

Think Fischer, Kasparov, Anand!
Karpov loved the Najdorf too—playing against it that is! Naturally I recommend 6 ♗e2 again, and after the pure Najdorf move 6...e5 (continuing

our exploration of the Boleslavsky Wall structure), one notices that Karpov *never lost this position*. With 22 games in the database, the box score is 14 wins for Karpov and 8 draws for his foes. And Karpov beat people like Kasparov, Bronstein, Polugaevsky—Fish!

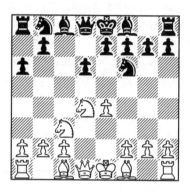

White has many good follow-ups after the natural 7 ♘b3, and my opinion is that once again the hole at d5 is more costly than most Sicilian books will admit.

Chapter Three

The Dragon is so much fun to play... against! By moving his pawn to g6 early, Black offers you a choice of f4-f5 or h4-h5 levers (and sometimes both—see Game 30, Taylor-Casella). I also offer the reader a choice: A Karpov specialty was 1 e4 c5 2 ♘f3 d6 3 d4 cxd4 4 ♘xd4 ♘f6 5 ♘c3 g6 6 ♗e2 ♗g7

(see following diagram)

7 0-0 0-0 followed by the key move of 8 ♗g5! with positional pressure, and

a mating attack often coming into the picture around move 35.

Rather more ferocious is my second recommendation, the Alekhine Attack, which continues like this: 7 ♗e3 ♘c6 8 ♘b3 ♗e6 9 f4 0-0 10 g4!. OK, not too Karpovian, but very little explored in the computer age, and suitable for quick wins (and one quick loss!)

One good point about both my recommendations is that they work against the regular Dragon as well as the Accelerated (with a few slight modifications), as will be pointed out in the text. Furthermore I took the opportunity to box the Dragodorf on its ear a couple of times, when Black attempts to confuse his opponent by playing two systems at once—but more often just confuses himself in the process!

Chapter Four

Black might set up a "little centre" of pawns on e6 and d6 and wait to see what White does—this is the Scheveningen system, most often

reached these days after the sequence 1 e4 c5 2 ♘f3 d6 3 d4 cxd4 4 ♘xd4 ♘f6 5 ♘c3 a6 6 ♗e2 e6.

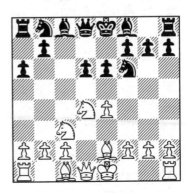

I advocate the solid Karpovian (and Birdian, if that's a word!) method of creating a big centre with pawns at e4 and f4, and then using that centre as the basis of an eventual kingside attack, usually helped out by the manoeuvre ♕e1-g3. White's free hand in the centre makes this line easy to play, though one must watch out for counter punchers!

Chapter Five

If Black plays an early ...e7-e6 but holds off on ...d7-d6, he is playing either a Taimanov or a Kan (or possibly a couple of wacky sidelines!). I thought of breaking up the chapter into various parts, but since all the lines can transpose into each other, I have put all the variations usually reached after 1 e4 c5 2 ♘f3 e6 in one umbrella chapter. I will cover the pure Taimanov, which comes about after 3 d4 cxd4 4 ♘xd4 ♘c6 5 ♘c3 a6,

where I recommend, as usual, 6 ♗e2—and make sure you check out Karpov's stunning victory over Taimanov himself in this line, where our hero sacs two pawns—for a positional advantage!

As usual I don't think it's at all easy for Black to equalize against White's solid but strong play.

Against the pure Kan (3 d4 cxd4 4 ♘xd4 a6 5 ♘c3 ♕c7 I also recommend our ubiquitous 6 ♗e2 (though in the fashionable sideline 5...b5 I suggest the precise 6 ♗d3!—see the explanation in the main text). Once again White's central control and solid positional play give him every chance of an edge.

I also offer recipes against the peculiar Pin (4...♘f6 5 ♘c3 ♗b4), the Four Knights (4...♘f6 5 ♘c3 ♘c6), and the downright odd Gå På (4...♘f6 5 ♘c3 ♕b6), as well as the early 4...♗c5—none of which should trouble White... if he knows what to do!

Chapter Six

Black might go for the bizarre Svesh-

nikov which is reached after 1 e4 c5 2 ♘f3 ♘c6 3 d4 cxd4 4 ♘xd4 ♘f6 5 ♘c3 e5 6 ♘b5 d6 7 ♗g5 a6 8 ♘a3, when I have to borrow a Larsen quote and say: "Both sides stand badly!" Black has a gaping hole at d5, but White has spent four moves to manoeuvre his king's knight to the worst possible square imaginable—a3! Ever helpful, my friend Joe Cepiel said, "The game usually starts around move 17, as all lines are heavily booked up to that point!" Joe also claimed all the moves were logical, but friendship only goes so far—these moves look utterly insane to me!

While Karpov did enter this morass at times, he once again rescued me with a logical and strong positional alternative: after 1 e4 c5 2 ♘f3 ♘c6 White simply plays 3 ♘c3!.

Now the Sveshnikov adherent is thrown completely out of his game, as his opening is no longer playable (and his thirty memorized moves are meaningless!). If he plays 3...e5, White gets an edge with the simple 4 ♗c4 targeting the weak d5-square (Rogozenko claims this is OK for Black, indeed even the "principled" answer—but my feeling is that Black is giving up too much too soon here, as Games 63-65 will show.

Black might also try to transpose to the Svesh by playing 3...♘f6, but then as Karpov—as well as Tal and Adams—has shown, White has excellent chances for an advantage with 4 ♗b5. The first player then reaches a Rossolimo Variation where Black, due to the provocative placement of his king's knight, must constantly watch out for White's e4-e5 thrust.

In practice (after 3 ♘c3) my opponents always played 3...g6, when the Open Sicilian appeared again after 4 d4, with Dragon slaying on the menu.

Chapter Seven
The first six chapters have offered a repertoire solution to all the main lines that can be reached after the big three of second moves: 2...d6, 2...♘c6 or 2...e6. However, these are not the only continuations, just the most popular ones.

White must also be ready for 2...a6, 2...g6 (mostly this will transpose to regular Dragon lines, but not always), 2...b6 and 2...♘f6. Of these, by far the most important is the O'Kelly Variation, 2...a6—not having outlined the last chapter yet, I was surprised by this and lost!—which has been touted in Everyman's *Dangerous Weapons* books

and is a great surprise weapon!

On the other hand, it's really nothing special if you are armed in advance. While Karpov played the approved 3 c3, I also offer the simple yet very strong 3 ♘c3, when if Black wants to stay in a pure O'Kelly he must take probably unsustainable risks—or else he must make the psychologically difficult decision to return to main lines.

Against the other unusual moves I offer simple and strong play where, in general, Black faces the same dilemma as he does in the O'Kelly—return to the main lines where our repertoire gives comfortable play for White, or take extreme risks that can likely be punished right in the opening—see especially Bobby Fischer's demolition of 2...♘f6 in the last game of this book, Game 70.

The reader might wonder, how did I do with this repertoire? It's true I had to learn it fast (and in one case, the O'Kelly, had not learned it *yet*). I was also playing (while researching and writing this book) in a series of strong

Metropolitan Club International events—round robins with an array of titled players, many of whom were higher rated than myself. I also kept busy with a number of Swiss system open events—and I faced a ton of Sicilians (well, 28 to be exact). Every one of these games was an Open Sicilian (as mentioned above, when I offered an Anti-Sicilian—after 1 e4 c5 2 ♘f3 ♘c6 3 ♘c3—I always ended up with the Dragon).

The statistics are quite interesting: first of all, I faced twelve titled players: one GM, ten IMs (I am counting in this group two "IM-elect"s who have made all their norms for the title, and probably will have it by the time this book comes out) and one WGM. I must admit that all twelve of these titled players were higher rated than myself.

My score against this group with my Open Sicilian repertoire was six wins, five draws and only one loss, for a fairly awesome 8½/12 or 71% against higher-rated opposition.

Against non-titled players (usually in the master class, ranging from 1950 to 2350), or in other words against players roughly at my rating level or below, I scored 12 wins and 4 losses for an expected percentage increase to 75%.

Karpov rules!

However, the statistics also have one very strange anomaly—or possibly it's a result of the chosen repertoire. What was the most popular Sicilian variation chosen by my opponents? Go ahead, guess the Najdorf—and you'll be wrong! I did score 4½/5 out of my five games against the Najdorf—but that opening line was dwarfed in popularity by the Dragon Variation!

Out of these twenty-eight recent games, more than half— *seventeen*— featured the Dragon. I found I loved playing against this and scored 13/17 or 76% (and would have scored higher had my technique been better!). In every game but one I got the advantage right out of the opening, playing both Karpov's positional ♗g5 and Alekhine's wild attack with g2-g4.

How does one explain the huge popularity of this variation? Could Los Angeles be a hotbed of Dragon fiends? Yes, some opponents played directly for the Dragon—but the repertoire has something to do with it. When I played 1 e4 c5 2 ♘f3 ♘c6 3 ♘c3 I got 3...g6 (always), and after my recommended 1 e4 c5 2 ♘f3 d6 3 d4 cxd4 4 ♘xd4 ♘f6 5 ♘c3 ♘c6 6 ♗e2 I also (usually) got 6...g6. Apparently there are some "recipes" floating around the internet that advise Black to transpose into the Dragon in such situations—but I say the fire has gone out, and the Dragon can slink back to his cave like Puff after Jackie Paper took away the sealing wax! In any case, if these stats mean anything, the reader would do well to study Chapter Three intensively!

Now let's examine in detail how to *Slay the Sicilian*.

Chapter One
The Classical Variation: The Boleslavsky Wall

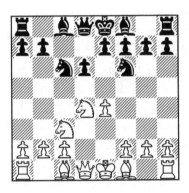

There seems to be some sort of "faith-based" belief that the Boleslavsky system is so strong that White must avoid it—but, as far as I can see, most players have more faith than knowledge of this system. When put to the test they will either avoid the Bole or (as in Game 4) commit ancient errors right in the opening.

After our basic first moves: 1 e4 c5 2 ♘f3 d6 3 d4 cxd4 4 ♘xd4 ♘f6 5 ♘c3 ♘c6 6 ♗e2 Black can play 6...e5, gaining space at the cost of a hole on d5,

which is known as the "Boleslavsky Wall" structure. The exact same Wall also appears in the Najdorf after 1 e4 c5 2 ♘f3 d6 3 d4 cxd4 4 ♘xd4 ♘f6 5 ♘c3 a6 6 ♗e2 e5, although there are important differences due to the substitution of ...a7-a6 for ...♘c6.

Returning to the original Classical Variation/Boleslavsky, after 6...e5 we'll see Karpov stay in his comfort zone and go to b3 with his knight in Game 1; Louma play his pet 7 ♘xc6 in Game 2; and what I consider objectively best, the restraint move 7 ♘f3 (White holds up ...d6-d5 by putting pressure on Black's e-pawn), will be seen in the meat of the chapter, Games 3-8.

Game 1
A.Karpov-J.Timman
Bad Lauterberg 1977

1 e4 c5 2 ♘f3 ♘c6 3 d4 cxd4 4 ♘xd4

♘f6 5 ♘c3 d6 6 ♗e2

Black can of course opt out here (as previously mentioned) with 6...g6 (the Dragon—see Chapter Three) or 6...e6 (the Scheveningen—see Chapter Four).
6...e5

Now I recommend 7 ♘f3 to hold up ...d6-d5 and restrain Black. I also think the rare 7 ♘xc6 is certainly worth a try for surprise value (see next game). But Karpov, not worrying so much about the opening, gets a familiar position (he had great success with such an arrangement in the Najdorf) and banks on his middle and endgame mastery.
7 ♘b3 ♗e7 8 0-0 0-0

9 ♔h1

I was initially attracted to the white side of the Boleslavsky years ago when I annotated the following game for my book *New York 1985: The Manhattan Chess Club International*. White is an IM playing a GM: 9 ♗e3 a6 (Black, evidently unfamiliar with the Boleslavsky, tries to shoehorn the opening into a Najdorf—but loses too much time) 10 f3 b6 11 ♕d2 ♗b7 12 ♖fd1 ♘b8 13 ♗f1 ♘bd7 14 ♕f2 b5 15 a3 ♕c7 16 ♘c1 ♘c5 17 ♘1a2 ♘a4 (this creates permanent weaknesses, but otherwise ♘b4-d5 gives White a huge plus—the GM is already on the ropes!) 18 ♘xa4 bxa4 19 c4 ♗c6 20 ♖ac1 ♖fb8 21 ♘b4 a5 22 ♘d5 ♗xd5 23 cxd5 ♕b7 24 ♖d2 ♘d7 25 ♖c4 (as I pointed out in my book, 25 ♖c6 should win for White) 25...♖c8 26 ♖xc8+ ♖xc8 27 ♖c2 h6 28 ♖xc8+ ♕xc8 29 ♗b5 ♘c5 30 ♕c2 ♕b8 31 ♕c4 ♗d8 32 ♔f2 ♗b6 33 ♔e2 ♘b3 34 ♗xa4 ♗xe3 35 ♕xb3?! (even now 35 ♔xe3 is better for White) ½-½ Di.London-J.Fedorowicz, New York 1985. I found it interesting that the higher-rated player had to struggle so much to, just barely, make a draw!

Unfortunately, there is a serious improvement for Black: showing the dangers for White is the following high-level blitz: 9...a5! (Black must play actively as opposed to Fedorowicz's 9...a6; one reason I prefer 7 ♘f3 is that on b3 the knight is a target for this exact pawn advance) 10 a4 b6 11 ♔h1 ♗b7 (this bishop controls d5 and attacks the white e-pawn) 12 f4 ♘b4 13 ♗f3 ♖c8 14 ♕d2 d5 (Black has not only solved his problems, he already stands better) 15 exd5 e4 16 ♗e2 ♘fxd5 17 ♘xd5 ♘xd5 18 ♗d4 e3 19 ♕d1 ♕c7 20 ♗f3 ♕xc2 21 ♕xc2 ♖xc2 22 ♖ae1 ♗b4 23 ♖c1 e2 0-1 E.Atarov-V.Baklan, Internet (blitz) 2004.

9...♗e6

The bishop aims the wrong way and is a target for White's advancing f-pawn—or in other words, the incredibly strong Timman is out of his element by move 9!

Correct is 9...a5 à la Baklan, which also scores best statistically for Black:

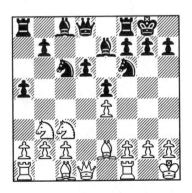

10 a4 (the natural 10 ♗g5 is weak due to 10...♘xe4!—Black equalizes and more with this trick, but note it doesn't work after White's 7 ♘f3 as the g5-bishop will be protected—11 ♘xe4 ♗xg5 12 ♘xd6 a4 13 ♘c5 ♗e7 14 ♘dxb7? ♗xb7 15 ♘xb7 ♕c7 traps the errant white knight, while after 14 ♘ce4 ♗e6 Black was already clearly better in B.Abramovic-M.Tal, Yerevan 1982) 10...♘b4 (Black already stands well with his good knight, which both holds the weakness at d5 and pressures c2, as pointed out long ago by Geller and seconded by *Mr. Fritz*—but note that Black can still go wrong by reverting to 10...♗e6 here; e.g. 11 f4! exf4 12 ♗xf4 d5 13 e5 ♘e4 14 ♗d3 f5 15 exf6 ♘xf6 16 ♘b5 ♖c8 17 ♕e1!—Black is already dead as even if he saves the pawn by 17...♗d7 the infiltration 18 ♘d6 is positionally decisive—17...♕d7 18 ♘xa5 ♘b4 19 ♘d4 ♗g4 20 ♘b5 ♕d8 21 ♘xb7 1-0 V.Ivanchuk-Y.Vovk, Warsaw rapid 2009; one notices how ill prepared modern players are in this line, and we'll see Ivanchuk score stylishly against the Boleslavsky again in the notes to Game 3) 11 f4 ♗d7 12 ♗f3 ♗c6 (since the white e-pawn has been weakened by the f2-f4 advance—obviously f2-f3 will never be possible—Black's light-squared bishop takes up its rightful place on the long diagonal) 13 ♕e2 ♕c7! 14 ♖d1 b6 15 ♗d2 and now not 15...♘xc2 16 ♖ac1 with play against Black's exposed queen, but rather 15...♕b7!, increasing the pres-

sure on the long diagonal, when Black is at least equal.

10 f4 exf4

10...d5 is premature due to 11 f5 ♗c8 12 ♘xd5 ♘xe4 13 ♗e3 and White enjoys good positional pressure.

11 ♗xf4 d5 12 e5 ♘e4 13 ♗d3!

13...♘xc3

Timman wisely eschews greed—Black must not go for a pawn, since White will give a piece! 13...g5?! 14 ♕h5!! (Black's idea is 14 ♗c1 ♘xe5) 14...gxf4 15 ♘xe4 dxe4 16 ♗xe4 f5 17 exf6 ♖xf6 18 ♕xh7+ ♔f8 19 ♖ad1 and the attack goes through; e.g. 19...♕b8 (or 19...♕e8 20 ♖xf4 ♖xf4 21 ♕h6+ ♔g8 22 ♗h7+ ♔f7 23 ♗g6+ ♔f6 24 ♗xe8+ and winning the queen is good enough) 20 ♗g6 ♗d6 (or 20...a5 21 ♕h8+ ♗g8 22 ♕h6 mate) 21 ♕h8+ ♔e7 22 ♕g7+ ♗f7 23 ♖fe1+ ♘e5 24 ♗xf7 ♖xf7 25 ♕g5+ ♔f8 26 ♕h6+ ♔e7 27 ♘d4 ♕h8 (or 27...a5 28 ♘f3 and White recovers his piece with a winning attack—Black's king is simply too exposed) 28 ♘c6+! bxc6 29 ♕xd6+ ♔e8 30 ♖xe5+ and mates soon.

14 bxc3 ♖e8 15 ♘d4 ♕d7 16 ♖b1

Karpov is in the saddle with his trademark small but enduring edge: White has a dominant knight in the centre, which Timman can't stand for long—but when he exchanges it he straightens out White's pawns. Karpov also has more space, due to the advanced central pawn at e5, and pressure down the b-file. Black has a solid but rather passive position, and he has no effective way to attack the doubletons. In short, Timman can only look forward to a long and painful defence, and that's what he gets!

16...♘xd4

This might be too obliging: 16...♖ab8, simply waiting, is *Mr. Fritz's* recommendation, but it's difficult for a human just to remain passive and worse like this.

17 cxd4 ♖ec8 18 ♗d2 ♖c7 19 ♗a5 b6 20 ♗b4

Karpov ticks off another small accomplishment—he exchanges off Black's better bishop.

20...♗xb4 21 ♖xb4 ♗g4 22 ♕e1 ♗h5 23

🜚b3 ♕g4 24 🜚c3!

This trade also favours White, who is left with the only active rook. Imagine playing against this with nothing to hope for but "maybe I can make a draw if I never ever make a mistake in the next 80 moves"!

24...🜚xc3 25 ♕xc3 🜚c8 26 ♕b4 ♗g6 27 ♕e7 a5 28 h3 ♕e6 29 ♕a3 h6 30 🜚f2 🜚c7 31 ♔h2 ♕c6 32 ♗xg6 ♕xg6 33 ♕f3 ♕e6 34 ♕g3 ♔f8

Black must be extra careful, as White's pawn wedge gives him kingside chances; e.g. 34...a4 35 🜚f6!.

35 c3

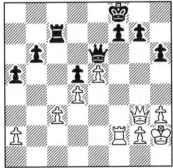

White has consolidated his space advantage—Timman continues his sterling but tiring defence.

35...🜚c6 36 🜚f4 🜚c4 37 🜚g4 g5 38 ♕d3 f5 39 exf6 ♕xf6 40 🜚g3 ♔g7 41 🜚f3 ♕d6+ 42 ♔g1 b5 43 h4! gxh4

The patient Karpov has finally launched his attack and the variation 43...g4?! 44 🜚e3 ♕c6 45 ♕f5 winning shows just how quickly things could go south.

44 ♕f5 ♕e7 45 ♔h2

White has the safe king.

45...🜚c6 46 ♕xd5 ♕d6+?

Timman, only human, finally makes a mistake. Correct is 46...♕c7+ 47 ♔h3 🜚xc3 48 🜚xc3 ♕xc3+ 49 ♔xh4 and it's not clear that White wins the queen ending, despite being first on the block with a passed pawn.

47 ♕xd6 🜚xd6 48 a3 🜚c6 49 ♔h3 🜚c4

Both 49...🜚g6!? ...

50 ♔xh4 ♔g6

And 50...🜚a4 51 🜚f5 🜚xa3 52 🜚xb5 🜚xc3 53 🜚xa5 give Black some drawing chances.

51 ♔h3 ♔g5 52 d5! 🜚c7 53 d6!

Passed pawns must be pushed! Any hope of a draw for Black is gone.

53...🜚d7 54 🜚d3

Karpov wins in classic style.

54...♔f5 55 ♔h4 ♔e4 56 🜚d1 ♔e5 57 ♔h5 1-0

White is faster after 57...🜚xd6 58 🜚xd6 ♔xd6 59 ♔xh6 ♔d5 60 g4 ♔c4 61 g5 ♔xc3 62 g6 b4 63 axb4 axb4 64 g7 b3 65 g8♕ b2 66 ♕h7 and all my chess students can win this one!

Attacking chess doesn't have to

start on move 1! Karpov's patient approach can be equally lethal—the game may be longer, but one point is one point.

As for the opening, 7 ♘b3 can't be recommended whole-heartedly in view of Geller's ...a7-a5 idea—but Black has to know this! Even Ivanchuk scored easily with ♘b3, though he later switched to the more precise 7 ♘f3. However, before we get to that critical line, let's take a look at the sideline 7 ♘xc6.

1 e4 c5 2 ♘f3 ♘c6 3 d4 cxd4 4 ♘xd4 ♘f6 5 ♘c3 d6 6 ♗e2 e5 7 ♘xc6

Generally considered bad in the Sicilian, as it brings a black pawn toward the centre, but very interesting in this precise position: White has a clear d-file for pressure on the somewhat loose d6-pawn and the possibility of kingside play with a later f2-f4.

7...bxc6 8 ♕d3

The Czech master Josef Louma's idea, which is best in my opinion. The queen pressures d6 and might slide across to g3, while f2-f4 will come in later.

Still, this is not the only move. The independent IM, Bjarke Sahl, also featured in *Slay the Spanish*, has tried 8

0-0 and won both by positional play and speculative attack after 8...♗e7 9 ♔h1 0-0 10 f4 ♖b8 and now:

a) 11 ♕e1!? (the speculative attack) 11...exf4 12 ♗xf4 ♖xb2 13 ♗c4 ♖b7 14 ♖d1 and White had pressure for the pawn and eventually won in B.Sahl-I.V.Ivanov, Saint John 1988.

b) 11 b3 (positional—White shuts off Black's b-file play) 11...♕c7 12 ♗e3 exf4 13 ♗xf4 ♘d7 14 ♘a4 ♘b6 15 ♘c5 ♘d7 16 ♘xd7 ♗xd7 17 ♕d2 ♖bd8 18 ♖ad1 ♗e6 19 c4 (Black is tied down to the weakness at d6) 19...c5 20 ♗g3 ♖d7 21 ♖f3 ♕b7 22 ♕e3 ♖e8 23 h3 ♕c7 24 ♗e1 ♗f8 25 ♕f2 ♖de7 26 ♗c3 ♗c8 27 ♖g3! (White switches to a kingside attack and wins stylishly) 27...♖e6 28 ♗g4 ♖g6 29 ♗f5 ♖xg3 30 ♕xg3 h6 31 ♖f1 ♗xf5 32 exf5 ♔h7 33 ♕d3 ♕c6 34 ♖f4 ♕d7 35 ♖g4 f6 36 ♔g1 ♖d8 37 ♕d5 ♖e8 38 ♗xf6! ♖e1+ 39 ♔f2 ♖c1 40 ♗xg7 h5 41 ♖g3 ♕e7 42 ♗e5 1-0 B.Sahl-E.Gausel, Skei 1993.

Given a choice, in this particular case I like 'b'—the positional line—rather than the riskier speculation.

8...♗e7

Black is unable to free himself with 8...d5, as after 9 exd5 cxd5 10 ♗g5! his centre collapses in all variations:

a) 10...♗e7 11 ♗xf6 ♗xf6 12 ♕xd5 snaps off a pawn and no compensation can be found.

b) 10...♗e6 11 0-0-0 ♖b8 (11...d4 12 ♕b5+ ♗d7 13 ♕xe5+ is no better) 12 ♗xf6 gxf6 13 ♘xd5 again snags a button.

c) 10...d4 11 ♕b5+ and the e-pawn goes with check.

d) 10...e4 11 ♕b5+ ♗d7 12 ♗xf6 ♕xf6 13 ♕xd5 and a second pawn will drop as well.

The white queen is ideally posted at d3 in all these lines, setting up both ♕b5+ and 0-0-0.

In general, one of the key factors in the Boleslavsky is whether ...d6-d5 is possible or not. White's policy is restraint, which doesn't necessarily mean prevention: White can often allow this advance in order to obtain some other advantage.

9 0-0

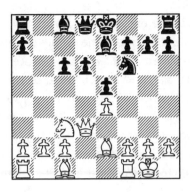

9...0-0

9...d5 still doesn't work: 10 exd5 cxd5 11 ♕g3 with too many threats; e.g. 11...0-0 12 ♕xe5 with a pawn, while 12 ♖d1 might be even stronger.

If Black plays quietly, one must remember that the f2-f4 break is key to Louma's system. Take a look at the following game as a cautionary tale: 9...♘d7 10 ♕g3 (I'd throw in 10 f4 right now!) 10...0-0 11 ♗h6 ♗f6 12 ♖ad1 ♘c5 13 ♗c4 ♘e6 14 ♗c1 ♘d4 15 ♕d3 ♕b6 16 ♔h1 ♗e6 17 ♗xe6 fxe6 (White's game is lifeless because he never broke with f2-f4, which is necessary to create f-file play and often pressure on d6 after ...e5xf4 and ♗xf4) 18 b3 ♖ad8 19 ♗e3 ♕b7 20 ♘a4 ♘b5 21 c4 ♘d4 22 c5 d5 (Black gets this in safely and assumes the advantage) 23 f4 (too late! Black no longer has a weakness at d6) 23...♘b5 24 fxe5 ♗xe5 25 ♗g5 ♖de8 26 g3 ♖f7 27 ♗f4 ♗d4 28 ♗e3 ♗f6 29 ♗f4 ♖ef8 30 ♔g2 ♗d4 31 exd5 exd5 32 ♗d6 ♖f2+ and Black owned the f-file and soon won in E.Bogoljubow-S.Gligoric, Birmingham 1951.

10 ♖d1

Louma experimented with 10 ♗g5 with good effect—the whole system is unexplored: 10...♖b8 11 b3 ♗e6 12 ♖ad1 ♕a5 and now instead of the de-centralizing 13 ♘a4 of J.Louma-A.Gragger, Vienna 1949, White can get some advantage with 13 ♕g3 d5 14 ♗h6 (but not 14 ♕xe5? ♘d7 15 ♕g3 ♗xg5 16 ♕xg5 ♕xc3 and Black wins a piece) 14...♘e8 15 ♗d2 ♕c5 16 b4! ♕d6 (16...♖xb4?! 17 exd5 cxd5 18 ♘xd5 produces winning discoveries) 17 f4! (always key) 17...dxe4 18 a3! with an excellent attack for White.

10...♘d7

If 10...♕c7 then best is 11 ♕g3 (preventing counterplay with ...♘g4 while smiling at the black king) 11...♔h8 12 f4! and White gets his break in with an edge.

11 ♗e3 ♘b6 12 a4

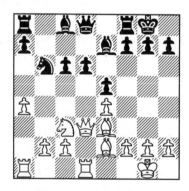

12...♗e6

12...a5 13 b3 is given without comment in *Starting Out: Classical Sicilian*, but what we're looking at here is a weak player unfamiliar with the ideas of the position—against the great Smyslov! Here's that mismatch for a second cautionary tale: 13...f5 14 f3 ♔h8 15 ♔h1 ♗e6 16 ♕d2 ♕c7 17 ♕e1 ♘d7 18 ♖ab1 fxe4 19 ♘xe4 d5 (White is positionally crushed) 20 ♘g5 ♗g8 21 ♕g3 ♖ae8 22 c4 h6 23 ♗d3 d4 24 ♗d2 ♘c5 25 ♗g6 ♗xg5 26 ♗xg5 ♖e6 27 ♗d2 ♖ff6 28 ♗h5 ♗h7 (now things are worse) 29 ♖b2 ♘d3 30 ♖a2 ♕b6 31 b4 axb4 32 a5 ♕a6 33 ♗g4 ♖e8 34 ♖aa1 b3 35 h4 b2 36 ♖ab1 ♕xc4 37 ♔h2 ♕a2 38 h5 c5 39 ♕h4 c4 40 ♗d7 ♖ef8 0-1 R.Ortega-V.Smyslov, Havana 1964.

Of course if you don't play actively against Gligoric or Smyslov, you will be destroyed—again f2-f4 is required, so instead of 13 b3? (my comment!) White should play 13 f4! ♕c7 (Smyslov's 13...f5 doesn't work here, as the simple 14 fxe5 gives White a big plus) 14 ♕d2 with a typical slight edge.

13 b3

White shuts off Black's queenside play and...

13...a5 14 f4

Breaks!

14...f6

Black should probably try to free himself at the cost of one weakness, though that may not cure everything: 14...exf4 15 ♗xf4 d5 16 exd5 ♘xd5 17 ♘xd5 cxd5 18 ♗e3 and White has a Carlsen position where he can play all night—as I will note in a future book, Magnus often wins against a single weakness, not two as old books claim is necessary.

15 f5 ♗f7 16 ♗f3

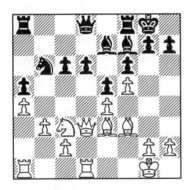

A typical anti-Boleslavsky idea: the black centre is under restraint.

16...♕c7 17 ♕e2 ♖fd8 18 ♕f2 ♖ab8 19 ♖d2 d5

Black can wait with 19...♕b7 but is then under pressure from 20 ♖ad1.

20 ♗xb6 ♕xb6?

Missing the coming tactic! Correct is 20...♖xb6 21 exd5 ♗b4 22 ♖d3 ♗xc3 23 ♖xc3 ♗xd5 24 ♖d1 ♗e4 25 ♖d2, when Black's piece play should balance White's superior pawn structure.

21 ♕xb6 ♖xb6 22 exd5 ♗b4

If 22...cxd5 then 23 ♘xd5 nets a pawn.

23 dxc6!!

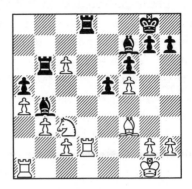

An astonishing Excelsior combination: nothing can be taken without allowing the new passed c-pawn to go through—White is winning.

23...♖c8 24 ♖ad1! ♖bb8

The knight is still immune, since 24...♗xc3 25 ♖d8+ exploits the weak back rank.

25 ♖d3

Not bad, but 25 ♘b5! ♗xd2 26 ♖xd2 wins more quickly, as the c-pawn will cost Black big material.

25...♗e8 26 ♘b5 ♗xc6 27 ♗xc6 ♖xc6 28 ♖d8+ ♖xd8 29 ♖xd8+ ♔f7 30 c4 1-0

Black has no compensation for the extra pawn.

Louma's line is certainly worth a try—though, as we saw, even against good play Black may be able to equalize against White's initiative (see the note to move 20). Still, since White's plan is easy—♕d3 and then some combination of ♖d1 and f2-f4—and Black is under early pressure, I think this would be a terrific surprise weapon.

However, from a repertoire standpoint, given the rareness of the Boleslavsky system, having two lines against it is a bit of an overkill: over 28 games I faced this system exactly once—and when I finally got my one Boleslavsky I just went straight for the objectively best 7 ♘f3, and that's what we will look at in the remaining six games of this chapter.

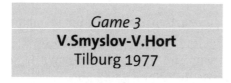

1 e4 c5 2 ♘f3 ♘c6 3 d4 cxd4 4 ♘xd4 ♘f6 5 ♘c3 d6 6 ♗e2 e5 7 ♘f3

Best! White doesn't make this knight a target for ...a5-a4 (♘b3) and doesn't improve Black's centre (♘xc6). White simply prevents ...d6-d5 for the moment by pressuring e5, and threatens 8 ♗g5 which takes over the d5-square.

7...♗e7?!

The top GM Hort overlooks or ignores White's threat! 7...h6 is necessary, as all the books say, and is played about six times more often—but there are about 300 games in the database with this mistake, and Black immediately reaches a deplorable situation where he can only hope to draw.

Against top opposition Black really has to grovel: after White's follow-up 8 ♗g5 we see that the top twenty of the "Elo White" brigade scores 12 wins against 8 draws in this line (not a win for Black can be found in this entire group).

In this game Hort undergoes awesome suffering, yet nonetheless defends like a lion and makes his draw—against a less redoubtable foe in the next game, I enjoy a brisk 29-move walk-over.

8 ♗g5

That's it for any ...d6-d5 breaks! Note too that ...♘xe4 combinations (we saw Tal play one of these in a note to Game 1) generally fail here as the g5-bishop is protected by the f3-knight.

8...♗e6 9 0-0 0-0

Black can try to avoid the following exchange by 9...♘d7, but this loss of time gives White interesting tactical opportunities; e.g. 10 ♕d2 f6 11 ♗e3 ♘c5 12 ♘h4 g6 13 ♗f3 f5 14 exf5 ♗c4 (a drastic attack is seen after 14...gxf5 15 ♗h5+ ♔f8 16 ♗xc5 dxc5 17 ♕h6+ ♔g8 18 ♕xe6+ ♔g7 19 ♘xf5+ ♔f8 20 ♕f7 mate) 15 ♖fe1 ♗xh4 16 ♗xc5 dxc5 17 ♗xc6+ bxc6 18 ♕f4! with a surprising and decisive fork.

10 ♗xf6

This simple move gives White an enduring edge and, against a lesser defender than Hort, would have been good enough to win. Nonetheless, a modern GM has found an improvement: 10 a3!—Ivanchuk scores with this: he waits and makes a useful move, with the plan of keeping the queens on, no doubt well aware of the present game, where opposite-coloured bishops ultimately saved Black. As we'll see, if the queens are on, the opposite bishops may actually be a liability for Black, as White enjoys excellent attacking chances: 10...h6 11 ♗xf6 ♗xf6 12 ♘d5 ♗xd5 13 ♕xd5 ♕b6 14 ♕a2 (the point of a2-a3!) 14...♘e7 15 c3 ♕c6 16 ♗d3 ♖fd8 17 ♖fe1 ♖ac8 18 ♖ad1 b5 19 ♗c2 ♖c7 20 ♗b3 (White has full control of the weakness at d5 and the much better bishop: Ivanchuk can grind away until death—of his opponent that is!) 20...♘c8 21 g3 g6 22 h4 ♔g7 23 ♘h2 ♘b6 24 ♘g4 ♕d7 25 ♘e3 ♕h3 26 ♖d3 ♖f8 27 ♕b1 ♗e7 28 ♕d1 ♕c8 29 ♖d2 ♖d8 30 ♕f3 (with queens

on, Black can hardly hold all his weaknesses) 30...♖f8 31 ♖ed1 h5 32 ♕e2 a6 33 ♖a1 ♖c5 34 ♔h2 ♘d7 35 ♘d5 ♗d8 36 a4 ♕b7 37 axb5 axb5 38 ♖ad1 ♖c8 39 ♗c2 ♘f6 40 ♘xf6 ♗xf6 41 ♖xd6 ♗e7 42 ♖6d5 b4 43 c4 ♕b8 44 ♗a4 ♖fd8 45 ♗d7 ♖c5 46 ♗b5 ♖cc8 47 ♕d2 ♕b6 48 ♔g2 ♖a8 49 b3 ♖xd5 50 exd5 ♗d6 51 ♗a4 ♖a7 52 ♖e1 ♖e7 53 ♕b2 ♗c5 54 ♖xe5! (ultimately mobilizing the passed pawns) 54...♗d4 55 ♕xd4 ♕xd4 56 ♖xe7 ♔f6 57 ♖e3 ♔g7 58 ♗d7 ♔f8 (58...f5 is the last hope for a draw, but in a one-session game Black is unlikely to be defending at full strength by this point in the game!) 59 ♗h3! ♔g7 60 ♔g1 f5 61 ♗f1 ♔f7 62 ♖d3! (with the rook behind the passed pawn, Black has no hope) 62...♕a7 63 d6 ♔e8 64 ♖d5 ♕a8 65 ♖e5+ ♔d8 66 c5 ♕a1 67 ♖e7 ♕c1 68 ♖c7 f4 69 gxf4 ♕d1 70 c6 ♕g4+ 71 ♗g2 ♕xf4 72 ♗h3 1-0 V.Ivanchuk-N.Delgado Ramirez, Havana 2005.

10...♗xf6

11 ♘d5 ♗xd5

The best practical try: after 11...♖c8

12 c3 ♗g5 13 ♘xg5 ♕xg5 14 ♕d3
White has the usual annoying plus, but
Black has no hope of a saving opposite
bishop ending.

12 ♕xd5 ♕b6 13 ♕b3

White doesn't have the a2-square!

13...♘d4! 14 ♘xd4 exd4 15 ♕xb6 axb6

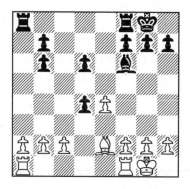

Black's pawn structure is a mess,
but Hort got the queens off and opposite bishops are a powerful drawing
tool. I doubt this would be held in sudden death today though.

**16 ♗c4 ♖fc8 17 ♗b3 b5 18 f4 ♖c7 19
♖ae1 ♖e8 20 ♖e2 d3!**

Passive play would ultimately be
hopeless against Smyslov, so Hort sacrifices the almost worthless doubleton to
activate his bishop.

**21 cxd3 ♗d4+ 22 ♔h1 ♖ec8 23 h4 ♖c1
24 ♖xc1 ♖xc1+**

Hort chops wood at every opportunity and tries to make it to move 40—
when he can analyze overnight (what
luxury!).

**25 ♔h2 h5 26 e5 dxe5 27 fxe5 ♖c5 28
e6 fxe6 29 ♖xe6 ♔f8 30 ♖b6 ♗xb2 31
♖xb7 ♗f6 32 g3 ♗c3 33 ♔g2 b4 34 ♖d7**

♖e5 35 d4 ♖e7 36 ♖d8+

36 ♖xe7 ♔xe7 is most likely an objective draw, even though the black
pawn on h5 makes the second player's
defence difficult.

**36...♖e8 37 ♖d5 ♖e3 38 ♖f5+ ♔e8 39
d5 ♖e5 40 ♖f3 ♖e2+**

White has consolidated with a good
extra pawn, but Black has made move
40 and can now go to work with his
second!

41 ♔f1 ♖e5 42 a4!

A nice trick that would blow your
opponent's mind in a one-session sud-
den-death game—but Hort was no
doubt prepared and has his defence
ready.

**42...♔e7 43 ♗c4 ♖e4 44 ♖f4 ♖xf4+ 45
gxf4 ♗f6 46 a5 ♔d6 47 a6 ♔c7 ½-½**

Black's king arrives just in time.

I believe the main game would win
for White nine times out of ten in one-
session play, and Ivanchuk's improvement makes Black's task even more
difficult!

Yes, at the GM level Black *might*

make a draw, but what about a somewhat less exalted rating plain? Let's see the next game.

Game 4 B58
T.Taylor-J.Gutman
SCCF Championship,
Los Angeles 2011

1 e4 c5 2 ♘f3 d6 3 d4 cxd4 4 ♘xd4 ♘f6 5 ♘c3 ♘c6 6 ♗e2 e5 7 ♘f3

I considered playing Louma's 7 ♘xc6, but I thought I might never get another 6...e5, so I should play the objectively best move...

7...♗e7

And was immediately rewarded! People don't know their Boleslavsky!

8 ♗g5 ♗e6 9 0-0 a6

If 9...0-0, I was ready with 10 a3!.

10 ♗xf6 ♗xf6 11 ♘d5

White has conquered d5 and one can't see anything Black got out of it: the white knight looks better than both black bishops!

11...♘e7

So Black tries to get rid of it! If instead 11...0-0, then 12 ♘xf6+ (12 c3 is possible with a typical plus-equals squeeze position) 12...♕xf6 (12...gxf6 is ugly but necessary) 13 ♕xd6 ♕f4 14 ♖fe1 and no compensation for the pawn can be found, as 14...♕xe4 fails to 15 ♗xa6.

Another try is 11...♗xd5 12 ♕xd5 ♕c7 13 c3 0-0 14 ♘d2 ♖ad8 15 ♗f3 ♗g5 16 ♖fd1, but then White had the typical annoying pull with Black having no compensation for the weaknesses at d5 and d6—White converted in 36 moves in W.Kobese-Cho.Stanley, African Championship, Cairo 1998.

12 ♘xf6+ gxf6

13 ♕d2

I spotlight the pawns at d6 and f6.

13...♕c7

Black can't free himself: 13...d5 14 ♕h6! dxe4 15 ♖ad1 ♘d5 (or 15...♕c7 16 ♕xf6 with destruction) 16 c4! exf3 17 ♗xf3 and White recovers his piece with an overwhelming positional advantage, as Black is unlikely ever to castle in this game.

14 ♖fd1 ♖d8

14...0-0-0 is relatively best, but after 15 c4 White has locked down d5 and retains the safer king.

15 c4!

Since the c-pawn is immune, Black will not be getting ...d6-d5 in any time soon!

15...♘g6 16 ♖ac1 ♖d7 17 g3 h5 18 h4 f5 19 ♘g5

Perhaps 19 exf5 ♗xf5 20 ♖e1 ♖g8 21 ♘g5 f6 22 ♕d5 is simpler, when Black's position is full of holes.

19...f4 20 ♘xe6 fxe6 21 ♖c3

Another way is 21 c5 dxc5 22 ♕xd7+ ♕xd7 23 ♖xd7 ♔xd7 24 ♖xc5 ♔d6 25 ♖c3 with a big endgame plus, but I wanted to "Fracture him!" Fischer-style in the middlegame.

21...♕c5 22 ♔g2 fxg3

22...♔e7 is necessary, but White follows with something like ♗f3 and a2-a3/b2-b4—ultimately Black is fighting a losing battle, in view of his weaknesses at d6 and h5 and unsafe king in the middle.

23 fxg3 ♖g7 24 ♕xd6!

24...♕xd6

White refutes the demonstration 24...♘xh4+ 25 ♔h3 ♕f2 with 26 ♗xh5+! ♖xh5 27 ♕xe6+ ♖e7 (27...♔f8 28 ♖d8 mate is drastic) 28 ♕g8+ ♕f8 29 ♖d8+ ♔xd8 30 ♕xf8+, winning the queen.

25 ♖xd6

So I got an ending after all—but Black's pawns are so weak, there is no doubt White has a winning position.

25...♔e7

The same counter also fails here: 25...♘xh4+ 26 ♔h3 ♘g6 27 ♖cd3!, when White forces the exchange of rooks and wins cleanly; e.g. 27...♖h6 28 ♖d8+ ♔e7 29 ♖3d7+ ♔f6 30 ♖xg7 ♔xg7 31 ♖d7+ etc.

26 ♖b6 ♘f4+ 27 ♔f1

27 ♔f3? ♖xg3+ was evidently Black's hope.

27...♘xe2 28 ♔xe2 ♔f6

The simple variation 28...♖b8 29 ♖cb3 ♔f6 30 c5 ♖c7 31 c6 demonstrates that Black's position is indefensible.

29 ♖f3+ 1-0

Pawns start dropping, the first with check.

It's interesting how the same mistake (7...♗e7) is still being played today at every level—despite the warnings against same in every opening book, with this being one more! Bronstein called the Boleslavsky a "well-rutted road" in his Zürich 1953 book, but it seems today everyone is on the Najdorf superhighway and they don't remember that rutted road at all!

Game 5 B58
E.Geller-J.Gast
Bern 1987

---

1 e4 c5 2 ♘f3 d6 3 d4 cxd4 4 ♘xd4 ♘f6 5 ♘c3 ♘c6 6 ♗e2 e5 7 ♘f3 h6!

Correct!

8 0-0 ♗e7

How should White proceed, now that Black has managed eight correct moves? It's not an exaggeration to say that the entire game revolves around the d5-square. This hole is both Black's problem and White's jumping-off point. Black wants to play ...d6-d5 "for free". White wants to restrain this break, either by physically preventing it, or by allowing it in return for some other advantage.

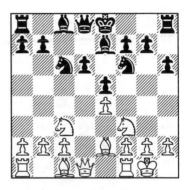

Now what about jumping into this square? White can usually do this with his knight, but must weigh the benefits of the exchange that can ensue. If White must take back with the pawn, Black's weak square disappears—but White may get an alternate advantage of an advanced d-pawn and a strong queenside majority. Geller scores here with this plan and also uses a similar strategy to defeat Fischer in Game 12.

While White can play across the whole board (see Kamsky's 10 ♘h2 below), he must always keep the d5 battleground uppermost in his mind.

9 ♖e1

By far the most popular move: by indirectly pressuring Black's e5-pawn, White makes the ...d6-d5 advance even harder to achieve.

Of course this restraining move is not the only one or only plan in the position—Kamsky shows a very interesting alternate idea: 9 h3 0-0 10 ♘h2 (aiming to exchange a defender of d5) 10...♘d4 11 ♘g4 ♘xe2+ 12 ♕xe2 ♘xg4 (I think Black should risk 12...♗xg4 13 hxg4 d5!? 14 ♘xd5 ♘xd5 15 ♖d1 ♘c3 16 bxc3 ♕c7 with some compensation for White's extra doubled pawn; for after the played...) 13 hxg4 ♗e6 14 ♖d1

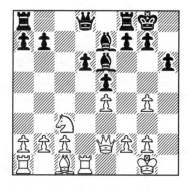

(he was condemned to a joyless defence where ...d6-d5 was never possible) 14...♕d7 15 ♘d5 ♖fc8 16 ♗e3 ♗g5 17 ♗xg5 hxg5 18 ♘e3 b5 19 a3 a5 20 ♖d2 ♖ab8 21 ♖ad1 ♖b6 22 ♘f5 ♗xf5 23 gxf5 ♖c4 24 ♖d5 ♕e7 25 ♖1d3 g6 26 fxg6 fxg6 27 b3 ♖cc6 28 ♖g3 ♔g7 29 c3 b4 30 axb4 axb4 31 c4 (lock the door and throw away the key: ...d6-d5 just isn't happening!) 31...♖a6 32 ♕d2 ♖c8 33 ♔f1 ♖f8 34 ♖e3 g4 35 g3 ♕f6 36 ♔g2 ♖b6 37 ♖ed3 g5 38 ♖xd6 ♖xd6 39 ♖xd6 ♕f3+ 40 ♔g1 ♔h7 41 ♖d3 ♕xe4 42 ♕xb4 ♕xd3 43 ♕xf8 ♕b3 44 ♕f5+ ♔h6 45 ♕xg4 ♕c2 46 ♕e6+ ♔h5 47 ♕f7+ ♔h6 48 ♕d5 e4 49 c5 ♔h5 50

♔g2 ♔h6 51 ♕e6+ ♔g7 52 ♕f5 ♔h6 53 ♕f6+ ♔h5 54 ♕g7 g4 55 ♕f7+ ♔h6 56 ♕f6+ 1-0 G.Kamsky-A.Zhigalko, European Cup, Plovdiv 2010.

After you go through this appalling grind, you will realize why I think Black should have broken out while he could!
9...0-0

Since we'll see White prevent the ...♗g4 pin on the next move, one might wonder if that move is good here: 9...♗g4 10 h3 and it turns out the answer is "No!", for if 10...♗h5 (10...♗e6 is just a loss of tempo) White wins a pawn as follows: 11 ♘xe5! ♗xe2 (or 11...dxe5 12 ♗xh5) 12 ♘xc6 ♗xd1 13 ♘xd8 ♗xc2 14 ♘xb7 0-0 (14...♖b8 15 ♘xd6+ ♗xd6 16 e5 wins by fork) 15 ♗f4 ♖fb8 16 ♘xd6 ♖xb2 17 ♖e2 and Black has no real compensation.
10 h3 ♖e8 11 ♗f1

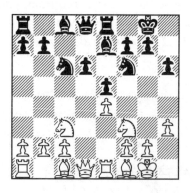

This set-up is what White is aiming for: ...d6-d5 is prevented, the e5-pawn is pressured indirectly, the pin ...♗g4 is prevented and so the d4-square is held—all in all a slight edge for those who enjoy Karpovian grinding!

11...&f8 12 b3

Often in the Sicilian Black can play ...♞a5-c4 with a good outpost on his half open file, but not here!

12...a6 13 &b2 b5 14 ♕d2 &b7

In this and the following game Black fianchettoes his queen's bishop, while in Games 7 and 8 we'll see ...&e6.

15 ♖ad1

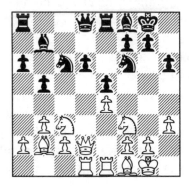

White is better: our friend *Mr. Fritz* gives White a solid plus-equals. In human terms the advantage is easy to explain: White can improve his position (the break a2-a4, the advance ♘d5, even Kamsky manoeuvres like ♘h2-g4—whereas Black is bereft of active play. If this is the best Black can do with the Boleslavsky, then no wonder so many switch to the Dragon on move six!

15...♖c8 16 a4 bxa4

This slight weakening of the pawn structure increases White's edge: better is the more active 16...b4 17 ♘d5 ♘xd5 18 ♕xd5 (but not 18 exd5 ♘e7 19 ♕xb4 &xd5 and Black stands well, as the tactic 20 ♘xe5?! dxe5 21 c4 fails to 21...♘c6) 18...♕b6 19 &c4 ♘d8 20

♕d3, when White still owns d5, but the advanced b-pawn gives Black some hope of c-file counterplay.

17 ♘xa4 ♕c7 18 c4!

As in my game against Gutman, and Kamsky's grind above, this "lockdown" move, securing d5, is often very strong for White in the Boleslavsky.

18...♘d8 19 ♘c3 ♕b6 20 ♖b1 ♘e6

Of course not 20...♕xb3 21 &c1, winning at least a piece.

21 ♘d5!

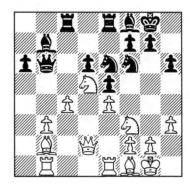

Geller always liked this plan: his knight is too strong and so will be exchanged, when a transition of advantages occurs: the weak d5-square vanishes, but White obtains space and a dangerous queenside majority.

21...&xd5

If 21...♘xd5 22 exd5 ♘f4 then 23 ♖a1 &e7 (not 23...♕xb3 24 ♖eb1 with a deadly discovery coming) 24 ♖a4 and White activates the queenside pawns.

22 exd5 ♘c5 23 b4!?

A little impetuous, as Black now has a tactical opportunity. I would prefer the more solid 23 ♖e3 ♖b8 24 &a3 a5

(24...♘xb3 25 ♕d1 wins by pin) 25 ♕c2 g6 26 ♘d2 ♗g7 27 ♖be1 ♖e7 28 ♗d3 ♘fd7 29 ♖g3, when White retains his queenside plus while also threatening a dangerous kingside sac on g6.

23...♘cd7?!

This retreat is fatal. Given White's alarming positional advantages—two bishops, queenside majority, Black weaknesses at a6, d6, etc—Black's only hope is tactical counterplay. Therefore the bold 23...♘ce4! must be tried:

a) 24 ♕e3 ♕xb4 (not 24...♕xe3? 25 ♖xe3, when White retains his positional advantages at no cost) 25 ♗xe5 dxe5! (Black's point) 26 ♖xb4 ♗xb4 27 ♖a1 ♗c5 28 ♕e2 ♗xf2+ 29 ♔h2 ♗g3+ 30 ♔h1 ♗f4 31 ♔g1 ♘g3 and in this case Black's rook, knight and pawn are compensation for the queen.

b) 24 ♕c2 ♘g3 25 ♕b3 ♘xf1 26 ♔xf1 a5 27 b5 ♘d7 and Black holds.

24 ♗a3

I'm sorry, my friend, but you do not get another chance.

24...♕b7 25 ♖ed1 ♘b6 26 ♕a2 ♕a8 27 ♗c1 ♘bd7 28 ♗e3

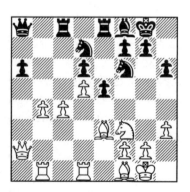

28...a5

If Black continues to play quietly, then something like this will occur: 28...g6 29 ♘d2 ♗g7 30 ♘b3 ♘e4 31 ♕c2 f5 32 ♘a5 and White's coming ♘c6 gives him a decisive positional advantage; Black will have to sac the ox on c6 and still not get enough—but I doubt the game's pawn sac is any better: Black simply had to go into the mêlée with the potential queen sac on move 23.

29 bxa5

Just take it!

29...♘e4 30 ♕c2 ♘ec5 31 ♖b5 ♖b8 32 ♖a1 ♕a6 33 ♘d2 ♕c8 34 ♘b3 ♘a6 35 ♖c1 ♕c7 36 ♕b1 g6 37 ♗d3 ♔h7 38 g4!

White takes over the entire board.

38...♖a8 39 ♔g2 ♖eb8 40 h4 ♔g8 41 g5!

This positionally binding move prevents ....♗f6 in the future: Geller sees that his d-pawn will become passed.

41...hxg5 42 hxg5 ♗g7 43 ♗e4 ♕d8 44 ♖c3 ♘c7 45 ♖xb8 ♕xb8 46 ♖c1 ♘a6 47 c5! dxc5 48 d6 ♖a7 49 ♘xc5 ♕xb1 50 ♗xb1 ♘axc5 51 ♖xc5!

Geller is too cool for school!

51...♖a6

A little demonstration of the crushing nature of White's game is 51...♘xc5 52 ♗xc5 ♖xa5 53 d7 ♖a8 54 ♗b6 etc, as Black can't even defend the queening square with 54...♗f6.

52 ♗d3 ♖xd6 53 ♖c8+ ♗f8 54 ♗c4 1-0

The a-pawn goes through.

This is what happens when Black does not fight back—quiet play just invites White to demonstrate, as here, a positional walk-over.

Game 6
E.Geller-Joe.Benjamin
Moscow 1987

B58

1 e4 c5 2 ♘f3 ♘c6 3 d4 cxd4 4 ♘xd4 ♘f6 5 ♘c3 d6 6 ♗e2 e5 7 ♘f3 h6 8 0-0 ♗e7 9 ♖e1 0-0 10 h3 ♖e8 11 ♗f1 ♗f8 12 b3

12 ♘h2!?, Kamsky-style, can also be played here.

12...a6 13 ♗b2 b6

Mindful of the Geller's a2-a4 break

seen in the previous game, Black plays with restraint—but this also gives White a free hand.

14 ♕d2 ♗b7 15 ♖ad1 ♖c8 16 ♘d5!

You can't get simpler than this: line up and play ♘d5. And yet, despite the simplicity, this plan is very hard to meet—let's watch Geller score again.

16...♘xd5 17 exd5

Geller is not interested in the complications after 17 ♕xd5, though this is also playable: 17...♘b4 18 ♕xb7 ♖e7 19 ♕xc8 ♕xc8 20 c3 ♘c6 21 ♖xd6 ♖e6 22 ♖d5 and White has good play for the queen.

17...♘b8 18 c4

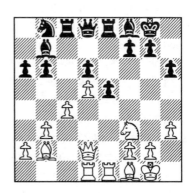

This is what he wants! White gets a clear space advantage, shuts off Black's queenside minor pieces, and obtains his favourite queenside majority.

18...♘d7

19 ♘h2

I think White should take e4 under control and play on the whole board (I also offered the same type of advice in my note to move 23 in the previous game, but Geller didn't listen to me then either!)—anyway, I'll give this a try if I ever get this position: 19 ♗d3!? (aiming at the king while Black is locked down on the queenside) 19...g6 20 h4 f5 (not 20...♘c5 21 h5 ♘xd3 22 ♕xd3 f5 23 hxg6 e4 24 ♕c3 and White wins on the long diagonal, or 22...g5 23 ♘d2 with a positional advantage due to the hole at f5) 21 h5! e4 22 hxg6 exd3 23 ♕c3 ♘e5 24 ♘xe5 ♗g7 25 ♕xd3 dxe5 26 ♕xf5 and White has a terrific attack for the piece.

19...♖c7 20 ♔h1 ♗c8 21 f4 exf4?

Now Black has no resource against White's pressure on the long diagonal and e-file. Better was 21...e4 with coun-

terplay; e.g. 22 ♘g4 ♘c5 and Black has both ...♕h4 and a possible vacating sac with ...e4-e3 on the agenda.

22 ♖xe8 ♕xe8 23 ♖e1 ♘e5 24 ♕xf4 f6

Painful but necessary.

25 a4 ♕g6 26 ♕f2 ♘d3 27 ♗xd3 ♕xd3 28 ♕f3 ♕c2 29 ♗d4

29...b5?!

Black can't afford to give his opponent a passed pawn. Instead 29...♕d2 30 ♖d1 ♕b4 31 ♕d3 is of course good for White, but Black is still playing.

30 axb5 axb5 31 cxb5 ♕d2 32 ♖d1 ♕g5 33 b6

This pawn will win the game—Benjamin's desperate kingside counterplay falls short.

33...♖e7 34 ♘f1 f5 35 ♘e3 f4 36 ♘c4 h5 37 ♖f1 ♖f7 38 ♗e3 ♕h4 39 ♗f2 ♕e7 40 ♖e1 ♕g5 41 ♖e8 ♗g4 42 ♕d3!

Precise: White is only willing to take the bishop if the recapture does not gain a tempo on the queen.

42...♗f5 43 ♕e2 ♕g6

Now 43...♗g4 fails to 44 hxg4! hxg4 45 ♕e6 g3 46 ♘xd6 gxf2 (or 46...♕h4+ 47 ♔g1 gxf2+ 48 ♔f1 ♕h1+ 49 ♔xf2

♕h4+ 50 ♔g1 and Black runs out of checks) 47 ♖xf8+ ♔h7 48 ♖h8+! ♔xh8 49 ♘xf7+ ♔h7 50 ♘xg5+ ♔h8 51 ♕c8 mate.

44 ♔h2 ♔h7 45 b7

The passed pawn wins by itself!

45...♖xb7 46 ♖xf8 ♖xb3 47 ♘d2 ♖d3 48 ♘f3 ♖xd5 49 ♘h4 1-0

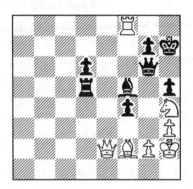

Black resigns in view of 49...♕g5 (or 49...♖e5 50 ♕b2 ♕e6 51 ♕b8 ♔h6 52 ♖xf5 ♖xf5 53 ♕h8+ ♔g5 54 ♕xg7+ ♕g6 55 ♕xg6 mate; 50 ♖h8+ also wins of course) 50 ♘xf5 ♖xf5 51 ♕d3 g6 (51...♔g6 52 ♗h4 wins the queen) 52 h4 ♕g4 53 ♖b8 ♖f7 54 ♕d5 ♕f5 55 ♗d4! and there is no good answer to ♖h8 mate.

Game 7   B58
Kir.Georgiev-Z.Kozul
Sarajevo 2001

1 e4 c5 2 ♘f3 d6 3 d4 cxd4 4 ♘xd4 ♘f6 5 ♘c3 ♘c6 6 ♗e2 e5 7 ♘f3 h6 8 0-0 ♗e7 9 ♖e1 0-0 10 h3 ♗e6 11 ♗f1 ♘b8

This is the approved modern line,

but Black's game is still not easy. The idea seems to be to reposition the knight to d7 (although that doesn't happen here), while avoiding 11...♖c8 12 ♘d5 after which White, snaring one of the black bishops (12...♘xd5 is clearly impossible due to the fork on d5), scores about 65%.

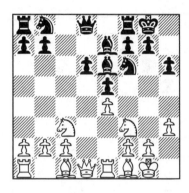

12 b3 a6 13 a4 ♕c7

The consistent 13...♘bd7 will be seen in the next and final game of this chapter.

14 ♗b2 ♘c6

Changing his mind, but that's a couple of tempi just tossed away—no doubt this encouraged White to sac material and go for a quick attack.

15 ♕d2 ♖ac8 16 a5!?

Presumably Black's idea was to prevent this advance! While this sacrifice is evidently quite strong, and I like the psychological aspect of it—prevent a4-a5 - ? Ha! Here it comes!—White can also play more simply with the Geller-style 16 ♘d5. After 16...♗xd5 17 exd5 ♘b8 18 c4 a5 Black can try to blockade the majority, but in the long run I think

White will break through anyway with b3-b4, and the two bishops can cause trouble; e.g. 19 ♗d3 ♞a6 20 ♗f5 ♖a8 21 ♕e3 and White can play across the whole board, while Black has a difficult defensive task.

16...♞xa5 17 ♞d5 ♗xd5

Obviously forced.

18 exd5

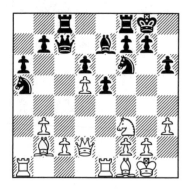

Black has the classic bad knight on the rim, which is simply unable to move. As a quick calculation shows that 18...♕xc2 loses to 19 ♖xa5 ♕xd2 20 ♞xd2 ♖c2 21 ♞c4 b5 22 ♗d3, Black is forced into the following passive defence, and it's obvious White has good compensation for the "insignificant unit"!

18...♗d8 19 ♗d3 b5

Gofshtein on *ChessBase* recommends the counter-sacrifice 19...e4, with the idea 20 ♗xe4 ♞xe4 21 ♖xe4 ♕xc2, but then I like the counter-counter-sacrifice 20 ♖xe4! which Gofshtein doesn't mention. After 20...♞xe4 21 ♗xe4 White's bishops are alarming and the black knight is still a "witness

for the prosecution"—White has more than enough for the exchange.

20 ♖a2

Indirectly defending c2 and preparing to double against the bad knight.

20...e4

Trying for activity—if 20...♖e8 then 21 ♗f5 ♖a8 22 ♖ea1 g6 23 ♗d3 e4 24 ♖xa5 (but not 24 ♕xh6 exd3 25 ♞g5 dxc2 and there is no mate!) 24...exd3 25 cxd3 and White stands better in view of Black's weak pawns at a6 and h6.

21 ♗xf6!

Simple and strong: White recovers his pawn with the better game.

21...♗xf6

If 21...exd3, 22 ♗xd8 wins a piece as the bad knight loses its protector.

22 ♖xe4

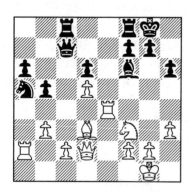

White has his pawn back with a strong opposite bishops attack—as has been pointed out many times, in such positions the defender's bishop can be completely useless, as the attack is coming on squares that bishop can't cover.

22...♗c3 23 ♕f4 ♖fe8 24 b4 ♘c4 25 ♖xa6 ♗xb4

Black restores material equality, but that won't do him much good, as the white pieces are beginning to swarm around his king.

26 ♖c6 ♕b7 27 ♘d4 ♖a8 28 ♘f5

White has a winning attack.

28...♗c3

One pretty variation is 28...♗d2 29 ♖xe8+ ♖xe8 30 ♕d4 ♖e5 31 ♗xc4 ♖xf5 32 ♗d3 ♖e5 33 ♕a7!! winning the queen, which highlights the utter helplessness of Black's bishop against the light square attack.

29 ♗xc4 ♖xe4 30 ♕xe4 bxc4 31 ♘xd6

Now it's the queen and knight attacking machine that finishes things.

31...♕b1+ 32 ♔h2 ♕f1 33 ♕f5 ♖f8 34 ♖c8 ♖xc8 35 ♕xc8+ ♔h7 36 ♕f5+ ♔h8 37 ♘xf7+ ♔g8 38 d6! ♕d1 39 d7 ♗f6 40 ♕xf6! 1-0

White wins a clean piece.

Black's stutter-step (...♘c6-b8-c6) certainly didn't help his cause in the previous game, so now we go to the main line where Black is at least consistent with ...♘c6-b8-d7.

1 e4 c5 2 ♘f3 d6 3 d4 cxd4 4 ♘xd4 ♘f6 5 ♘c3 ♘c6 6 ♗e2 e5 7 ♘f3 h6 8 0-0 ♗e7 9 ♖e1 0-0 10 h3 ♗e6 11 ♗f1 ♘b8 12 b3 a6 13 a4 ♘bd7

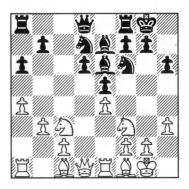

Black has used three moves to bring this knight here—somehow I remain unterrified! White has space and the d5-square to play against, while the best one can say for Black is that he has a solid defensive position.

The French GM Apicella has reached this position six times as White, winning three and drawing three, which seems about right to me. For example, Shirov drew against him—as for what happened to some lesser lights, see the note to move 15.

14 ♗b2 ♖c8

Black got a painful position after

14...♖e8 15 ♘d2 ♘c5 16 a5 ♖c8 17 g3 ♖c7 18 ♗g2 (White puts more pressure on d5, while e5 is indirectly attacked by the e1-rook and b2-bishop) 18...♕c8 19 ♔h2 ♘cd7 20 ♕f3 ♘b8 21 ♖ed1 ♘h7 22 ♕d3 ♘f6 23 ♕f3 ♘h7 24 ♕d3 ♘f6 25 ♖a4 ♘fd7 26 ♕f3 ♘c5 27 ♖aa1 ♘cd7 28 ♘f1 ♘c6 29 ♘e2 ♘b4 30 c4 ♘c5 and now, instead of the extravagant 31 g4 which gave Black chances and White won in messy fashion in P.Negi-S.Vidit, New Delhi 2009, the evident 31 ♕c3 is correct, which gains an important tempo: after 31...♘c6 32 ♘e3 White is much better with his d5 domination.

15 ♘d2

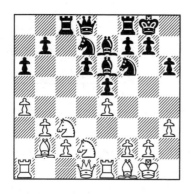

White plans ♘c4-e3. Yes, Black can break with ...d6-d5, but as so often in the Boleslavsky, this is problematic in view of White's pressure against e5.

15...♖e8

The aforementioned Apicella has had this further position twice. In one his opponent tried the critical break 15...d5, but after 16 exd5 ♘xd5 17 ♘xd5 ♗xd5 18 ♘c4 one sees that his "freeing move" has led to a weak e-pawn; when Black shores this up he gets kingside weaknesses: 18...♗e6 19 ♕f3 ♗b4 20 ♖ed1 ♕c7 21 ♕g3 f6 (looks like Geller-Benjamin!) 22 ♗c1 b5 23 axb5 axb5 24 ♘e3 (24 ♗xh6 ♖f7 25 ♘a3 is also good for White) 24...f5 25 ♘d5 ♗xd5 26 ♖xd5 ♘f6 27 ♖xb5 ♗c5 28 ♖xc5 ♕xc5 29 ♗a3 ♕d4 30 ♗xf8 ♖xf8 31 c3 ♕c5 32 b4 and White emerged with an extra pawn that he converted into a full point in M.Apicella-J.L.Chabanon, Versailles 2006.

Apicella also faced continued queen's knight manoeuvres: 15...♘c5 16 a5 ♗d7 17 ♘d5 ♘xd5 18 exd5 ♗f5 19 b4 ♘d7 20 c4 and while Black has spent five moves with his knight to reach a square he could have reached in one, White has set up a classic Gelleresque queenside pawn majority and eventually won in M.Apicella-Ch.Bernard, Bad Wildbad 1990.

16 ♘c4 ♘b6 17 ♘e3

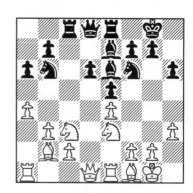

White has d5 locked down and Black has a truly painful position. Generally speaking, White will either win or draw with his permanent positional advantage.

In my opinion, though nothing is dropping off the board—yet—Black should recognize how desperate his position really is and sac the exchange: 17...♖xc3 18 ♗xc3 ♘xe4 when he obtains an extra centre pawn. I don't for a minute think this is objectively sound, as here (unlike in the Dragon where White gets doubled pawns after similar ox sacs) White has a smooth pawn structure. However, from a practical point of view, Black gets some play and avoids the appalling grind to come! While *Fritz* puts White ahead about +0.6 after the sac, there is something to be said for having something to play for—check out the rest of the game and see if you agree!

17...♗f8 18 a5 ♘bd7 19 ♘c4 ♖c6 20 ♕d2 ♘h5 21 ♘d5!

Just four moves after Black's one shot at sacrificial freedom and it's clear he is in dire straits with the Sultans of Swing nowhere to be found.

21...♕g5 22 ♕xg5 hxg5 23 ♖ad1

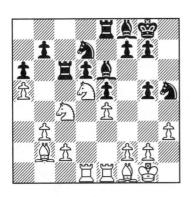

The torture continues.

23...♘f4 24 ♖d2 ♖ec8 25 ♗a3 ♘f6

The knight on d5 was too strong, but now White has two weaknesses to play against.

26 ♘xf6+ gxf6 27 ♘e3 ♗e7 28 ♖ed1 ♗d8 29 ♗b4 ♗c7 30 ♘d5 ♗d8 31 ♘e3 ♗c7 32 g3! ♘g6

Black's one well-placed piece is driven back, as 32...♘xh3+ fails to 33 ♗xh3 ♗xh3 34 g4 ♔g7 35 ♔h2 ♖h8 36 ♔g3 and 37 ♖h1 wins the bishop.

Black is the higher-rated player (2600+) and yet he has been unable to generate any play at all with his Boleslavsky.

33 ♘c4 ♔g7 34 ♘e3 ♖d8 35 ♗c4!

White's pressure is overwhelming, and material will soon fall.

35...b6

If 35...♗xh3 then 36 ♗d5 wins the exchange.

36 axb6 ♗xb6

Black collapses after 36...♖xb6 37 ♗a5 ♖c6 38 ♗xc7 ♖xc7 39 ♗xe6 fxe6 40 ♖xd6, attacking a6 and e6.

37 ♖xd6

A key pawn drops.

37...≌cxd6 38 ≌xd6 ≌b8 39 ≗xe6 ≗xe3 40 fxe3 fxe6 41 ≗a5 g4 42 hxg4 ≌a8 43 ≌xe6 ♘f8 44 ≌e7+ ♔g6 45 c4 ♘h7 46 c5 ≌c8 47 b4 ♘g5 48 ≌a7 ♘xe4 49 ≌xa6 ♔g5 50 c6 ♔xg4 51 ♔g2 ♘xg3 52 c7 ♘e4 53 ≌c6 f5 54 ≌c4 ♔g5

55 ≌xe4!

Pretty and clean: Black gets no counterplay and the pawns walk through.

55...fxe4 56 b5 ♔h4 57 b6 ≌g8+ 58 ♔f2 1-0

Black got a miserable game with the Boleslavsky's "approved main line" and it's not clear how he improves; in general I agree with Dr. Reuben Fine that White has good positional pressure against this system.

I think the chess community is gradually realizing this as well, as few Sicilian players like to reach the passive main line seen in this game—therefore, in practice, after 6 ≗e2 one is far more likely to get the Dragon (6...g6) rather than 6...e5.

Summing up, if you do get the Boleslavsky then it's clear that the objectively best move is the restraining 7 ♘f3, when Black has yet to demonstrate equality. One can have fun with 7 ♘xc6, but I think Black can hold with precise play. Finally, though it pains me to say this, one should not try Karpov's 7 ♘b3, as Black (if he knows the idea) gets too much play with ...a7-a5.

Chapter Two
The Najdorf Variation

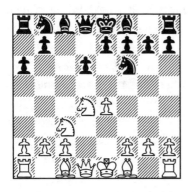

How I miss the Candidates matches and then the final 24-game battle for the World Championship! The player who made it through the Candidates was always a worthy foe for the Champion, and the games of those matches were often classic battles. All that has sadly been lost when what wasn't broke was "fixed" and classic chess was replaced by 8-move draws, blitz chess and "poker strategy"!

Anyway, going back to these classic battles, let's consider two where White was renowned as a foe of the Sicilian and Black was renowned as a master of his *Sicilian Labyrinth*. The first was Karpov-Polugaevsky from 1974, and the second was Tal-Polugaevsky from 1980. Let's take the second one first: Tal went headlong into the labyrinth and, in his crucial first White, attacked Polugaevsky's pet variation with a long prepared sacrificial variation—but Polu's long-prepared defence triumphed! Let's take a look:

M.Tal-L.Polugaevsky
Alma-Ata (2nd matchgame) 1980

1 e4 c5 2 ♘f3 d6 3 d4 cxd4 4 ♘xd4 ♘f6 5 ♘c3 a6 6 ♗g5 e6 7 f4 b5 8 e5 dxe5 9 fxe5 ♕c7 10 ♗xb5+ axb5 11 exf6 ♕e5+ 12 ♕e2 ♕xg5 13 ♘dxb5 ♖a5!! (would you find this over the board?) 14 fxg7 ♗xg7 15 ♘e4 ♕e5 16 ♘bd6+ ♔e7 17 0-0 f5 18 ♖ad1 ♖d5 19 ♕c4 ♖xd1 20 ♖xd1 fxe4 21 ♘xc8+

(see following diagram)

21...♔f7

41

(what's hilarious to me is that we are still in "theory" here; in this more recent game Black had twenty moves memorized, but not twenty-one—and loses in just four: 21...♔f6 22 ♘d6 e3 23 ♖f1+ ♔g6 24 ♕g4+ ♕g5 25 ♕xe6+ 1-0 I.Timmermans-P.Chomet, Paris 1999, as White mates in 11, according to the machine) 22 ♘d6+ ♔g6 23 ♘xe4

23...♘a6 (Black makes a developing move!) 24 ♘f2 ♘c5 25 b4 ♘a4 26 ♘g4 ♕f5 27 ♘e3 ♘b2 28 ♕h4 ♕e5 29 ♕g4+ ♔h6 30 ♖e1 ♗f6 31 b5 ♖f8 32 b6 ♗g5 33 ♕g3 ♕xg3 34 hxg3 ♔g7 35 ♘g4 ♘c4 36 ♖xe6 ♖b8 37 ♖c6 ♘xb6 38 ♖c7+ ♔g8 39 c4 ♘a4 40 ♔f2 ♖b2+ 41

♔f3 ♖xa2 42 ♔e4 ♖e2+ 43 ♔f5 ♗e7 44 ♘f6+ ♗xf6 45 ♔xf6 ♘b6 46 g4 ♖xg2 47 ♔g5 ♖d2 48 c5 ♘d7 49 c6 ♖d5+ 50 ♔h6 ♖d6+ 51 ♔g5 ♘e5 52 ♖c8+ ♔g7 53 ♖c7+ ♘f7+ 54 ♔f5 h6 55 ♔e4 ♔f6 56 ♖c8 ♖d1 57 ♖f8 ♖d6 58 ♖c8 ♘g5+ 59 ♔e3 ♔e7 60 ♔f4 ♘f7 61 ♔g3 ♖d3+ 62 ♔g2 ♖c3 63 ♖c7+ ♔f6 64 ♖c8 ♘e5 65 c7 ♘f7 66 ♖g8 ♖xc7 67 ♔g3 ♖c1 68 ♖a8 ♘e5 69 ♖f8+ ♔g7 70 ♖f5 ♖c3+ 0-1

Tal falls! Yet the great Misha, undaunted, in his next White played the following game in the same variation:

M.Tal-L.Polugaevsky
Alma-Ata (4th matchgame) 1980

1 e4 c5 2 ♘f3 d6 3 d4 cxd4 4 ♘xd4 ♘f6 5 ♘c3 a6 6 ♗g5 e6 7 f4 b5 8 e5 dxe5 9 fxe5 ♕c7 10 exf6 ♕e5+ 11 ♗e2 ♕xg5 12 ♕d3 ♕xf6 13 ♖f1 ♕e5 14 ♖d1 ♖a7 15 ♘f3 ♕c7 16 ♘g5 f5 17 ♕d4 h5 (do you have any idea what's going on here? I don't, but I'm sure someone's 64-apple-core processor is working on it!) 18 ♖xf5 exf5 19 ♘d5

19...♕d7 (still theory of course; in a slightly later game Black somehow wandered off the track: 19...♕a5+ 20 c3 ♗d6 21 ♘f6+ gxf6 22 ♕xf6 ♖e7 23 ♖xd6 ♖g8 24 ♔f1 ♗d7 25 ♗xh5+ ♔d8 26 ♘e6+ ♔c8 27 ♕xe7 ♕xa2 28 ♖xd7 ♘xd7 29 ♕d6 1-0 J.Van der Wiel-H.Grooten, Dutch Championship, Leeuwarden 1981) 20 ♕h4 ♗e7 21 ♔f1 ♗xg5 22 ♗xh5+ ♔f8 23 ♕xg5 ♖xh5 24 ♕xh5 ♕f7 25 ♕h8+ ♕g8 26 ♕h4 ♔f7 27 ♕h5+ g6 28 ♕h4 ♕g7 29 ♕d8 ♗e6 30 ♕xb8 ♖d7 31 c4 bxc4 32 ♘c3 ♖xd1+ 33 ♘xd1 ♕d4 34 ♘c3 ♕d3+ 35 ♔f2 ♕d4+ 36 ♔f1 ♕d3+ ½-½

So Tal made half a point out of his first two Whites and eventually lost the match. I'm sad for Tal, but the followers who imitated Polugaevsky amuse me—memories fail around move twenty and down they go—fast!

But what happened in Karpov-Polugaevsky? Karpov avoided the "maelstrom of forced variations", where Tal and many others have run aground, and played strong positional chess starting with 6 ♗e2, instead of 6 ♗g5. There were no forced variations and thus preparation was not important. What mattered was how the players understood (as opposed to memorized) the position and how they played the middlegame. And the result? Polugaevsky played the Najdorf in all of his four Blacks, and Karpov was true to his 6 ♗e2 in all four of his Whites—and Karpov scored three wins

and just one draw!!

Certainly there is a lesson here—and with computers, the lesson is still more pointed. Avoid your opponent's preparation; play sound, strong chess; above all, just *play*.

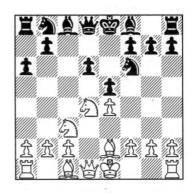

Game 9 B92
A.Karpov-L.Polugaevsky
Moscow
(8th matchgame) 1974

1 e4 c5 2 ♘f3 d6 3 d4 cxd4 4 ♘xd4 ♘f6 5 ♘c3 a6

Unlike 5...♘c6 of the Classical Variation, this move was not played until the 20th century—in the 19th century they still believed in development!

6 ♗e2 e5

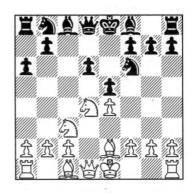

This is Black's most common move; and not far behind it is 6...e6 with a Scheveningen position, for which see Chapter Four. Far back in popularity is the Dragodorf with 6...g6, covered at the end of the next chapter (Games 35-36).

7 ♘b3

Here this is correct, for the situation has varied from the Boleslavsky. Black has lost a tempo (...a7-a6) on the ...a7-a5 push which was good there; while if White played 7 ♘f3 here, Black would not have to spend three moves manoeuvring his queen's knight to d7, but could gain two tempi by moving it to d7 in one!

7...♗e7

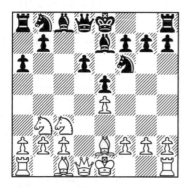

We have now reached our basic Najdorf tabiya. White has no less than five basic positional plans from this position (as opposed to one forced variation!) and I will cover all of them in this chapter.

Here's the list:

1. Karpov's early f2-f4—this works best if Black has played an early ...♗e6 (if White plays f2-f4 too soon, when the black bishop is still on c8, that cleric might fianchetto itself and pressure the white e-pawn which can no longer be defended with f2-f3) and will be covered in Games 9-11.

2. Geller's early ♘d5—just as in the

Boleslavsky, Geller liked to get his knight to d5 as soon as possible and win on the queenside. It's hard to argue with him, as he beat Fischer with it and my friend Sergey Kayumov beat Magnus Carlsen this way (see Games 12-13).

3. Kramnik's 8 ♗g5—White takes d5 under control and maintains the possibility of queenside castling and a kingside attack (see Games 14-15).

4. Kasparov's 8 0-0 0-0 9 ♔h1—White makes a mysterious waiting move that curtails Black's usual counterplay (see Games 16-17).

5. Carlsen's 8 ♗e3—White waits to see if Black will castle (8...0-0?! 9 g4!), and if Black waits to with 8...♗e6, then White can follow with a timely f2-f4, not fearing the weakness of the e-pawn as Black's queen's bishop can't easily get to the long diagonal.

I think you'll be able to get a pretty good sense of White's positional goals in these five variations just by reading through this chapter.

But now, just for a moment, consider the dilemma of those who play the Najdorf with Black! First they have to memorize the reams of theory in the forcing lines after 6 ♗g5, 6 ♗c4 and 6 ♗e3. As we saw in the Tal-Polugaevsky games, people who made memory mistakes around move 20 could lose almost instantly! So our opponent memorizes all this craziness—because if he doesn't, he will lose to someone's home computer! Then, finally, he turns to look at the "quiet" 6 ♗e2. What a relief—no forcing lines, he sighs... But then, worn out by his struggle to remember the 21st move in the Polugaevsky Variation, he falls asleep right after reading that the Najdorf answer to 6 ♗e2 is 6...e5 and zzzzzzzz.

And that's where we come in, my friends, with our solid but varied positional play—and our foes, just like Polugaevsky himself, are unable to compete with us on our home ground.

I was out-rated by four of my five Najdorf opponents but, as I mentioned in the Introduction, I won four games and only gave up one draw—Karpov's "positional push" style seems most unpleasant to the Najdorf player who is dying to show off his new 21st move— but now, on move six, must just *play*!

8 0-0 ♗e6 9 f4

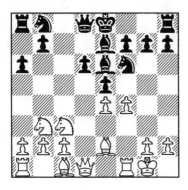

Just as in Game 1 (Karpov-Timman), White immediately answers ...♗e6 with f2-f4. White is then ready to go further and attack the bishop with f4-f5—and also, as I said in the descriptions of White's five ideas, f2-f4 works best

when Black's queen's bishop can't go to the long diagonal to pressure White's slightly weak e-pawn.

For this reason modern Najdorf players prefer a more flexible move order with 8...0-0, which keeps the queen's bishop's options open.

9...♕c7 10 a4 ♘bd7 11 ♔h1 0-0 12 ♗e3

This typical Karpov move, building up while maintaining the pressure, seems stronger than the one often played in Fischer's day: 12 f5, when despite the forced exchange of Black's "good" bishop, Black also gains space and his centre is solid. A modern game failed to revive the line for White: 12...♗c4 13 a5 b5 14 axb6 ♘xb6 15 ♗xc4 ♕xc4 16 ♘a5 ♕c5 17 ♗g5 ♖fc8 and Black's queenside space and open files gave him adequate counterplay in B.Socko-Bu Xiangzhi, Gibraltar 2008.

12...exf4

Black can't wait too long: 12...♖ac8 13 a5 (now ...b7-b5, as in the Bu game above, is not possible and White can secure d5) 13...♗c4 (not 13...b5? 14 axb6 ♘xb6 15 ♗xa6) 14 ♗xc4 ♕xc4 15 ♖a4 ♕c7 16 f5 (White has a bind, as Black can't play either of his natural breaks, ...b7-b6 or ...d6-d5) 16...h6 17 ♕f3 ♕b8 18 ♘d2 ♗d8 19 ♘c4 ♖e8 20 ♖d1 ♖c6 21 b3 ♗e7 22 ♗f2 ♖ec8 23 ♗h4! (getting rid of a knight that can control d5—a common theme in these Boleslavsky-type positions) 23...♗d8 24 ♗xf6 ♘xf6 25 h3 b5 26 axb6 ♗xb6 27 ♘d5 ♗d8 28 ♘xf6+ ♗xf6 29 ♖d5 ♗e7 30 ♕e2 and White has an ideal position with complete light square domination—and the most important light square is d5, from which he cannot be dislodged. Add to that, the far superior minor piece, and it will come as no surprise that White ground out the victory in another twenty moves in G.Cabrilo-J.Fedorowicz, New York Open 1988.

13 ♖xf4

This position essentially cost Polugaevsky the match, as he voluntarily went in for it *four* times, and scored a miserable half point. The most important thing about this position is the nature of the play, rather than the computer evaluation. (By the way, after sitting on this spot for quite a long time, my *Fritz12* says equal but with White holding a tiny +0.09 advantage!)

Here's what I see: both sides have an isolated pawn, which pretty much cancel each other out as far as advantage goes, but White's pawn is slightly more advanced at e4 as opposed to d6. So White might drop a knight in on d5 or f5, while Black has knight outposts

at c5 and e5. Much the same can be said about White's a-pawn, which is also on the fourth (unlike any of Black's pawns) and so slightly cramps Black's queenside.

There are no forcing lines. White's position is comfortable, with a slight advantage in space.

The more creative player should win!

13...♘e5

Some alternatives: 13...♘e8 14 ♘d4 ♗f6 15 ♘xe6 fxe6 16 ♗g4 is obviously much better for White, while after 13...♖fe8 14 ♘d4 ♘e5 15 ♘f5 ♘g6 16 ♖f1 ♗f8 17 ♕d4 White has slightly extended his space advantage—this was Karpov's first White game of the match and Polugaevsky's only success, in that he hung on and made a draw!

14 a5

Most accurate, as the pretty black knight on e5 abandoned the b6-square. In the fourth game Karpov tried 14 ♘d4 ♖ad8 15 ♕g1 ♖d7 16 ♖d1 ♖e8 17 ♘f5 ♗d8 18 ♘d4 ♘g6 19 ♖ff1 ♘e5 20 ♗f4 ♕c5 21 ♘xe6 ♕xg1+ 22 ♖xg1 ♖xe6

23 ♗f3, when Black has reached an equal ending—though Karpov outplayed his foe and won anyway in A.Karpov-L.Polugaevsky, Moscow (4th matchgame) 1974.

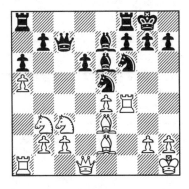

14...♖fe8

In the sixth game Polugaevsky tried 14...♘fd7 15 ♖f1 ♗f6 16 ♘d5 ♗xd5 17 ♕xd5!, but was evidently surprised by this blow—Karpov is not afraid to sac two pawns to activate all his pieces and attack! (we'll see a similar two pawn sac from Anatoly in Game 45)—the game continued 17...♕xc2 18 ♘d4 ♕xb2 19 ♖ab1 ♕c3 20 ♘f5 (note the advanced outpost!) 20...♕c2 21 ♖be1 ♘c5 22 ♘xd6 ♘cd3 23 ♗xd3 ♘xd3 24 ♖d1 ♘b4 25 ♕xb7 ♖ab8 26 ♕a7 ♕c6 27 ♗f4 ♖a8 28 ♕f2 ♖ad8 29 ♕g3 ♕c3 30 ♖f3 ♕c2 31 ♖df1 ♗d4 32 ♗h6 ♘c6 33 ♘f5 ♕b2 34 ♗c1 ♕b5 35 ♘h6+ ♔h8 36 ♘xf7+ ♖xf7 37 ♖xf7 ♗f6 38 ♕f2 ♔g8 39 ♖xf6 gxf6 40 ♕xf6 1-0 A.Karpov-L.Polugaevsky, Moscow (6th matchgame) 1974.

14...♖ac8 is recommended by GM Michael Stean in his book *Sicilian: Na-*jdorf, where he gives the variation 15 ♘d4 ♘fd7 16 ♖f1 ♖fe8 17 ♘f5 ♗f8 and claims equality—but as far as I can see, the position is basically unchanged. White still has his slight space advantage and it's certainly possible to outplay your opponent here, as a check of the database reveals: 18 ♕d2 ♘c4 19 ♗xc4 ♗xc4 20 ♖fd1 ♖e6 21 ♗d4 ♖g6 22 b3 ♗e6 23 ♖a2 ♘e5 24 ♘e2 ♗xf5?! (24...♕c6 was necessary) 25 exf5 ♖h6 26 ♗e3 ♖f6 27 ♘g3 h6 28 c4, when Black suffers from a fixed weakness at d6 and a bad rook—White scored easily in Z.Janko-Z.Repasi, Hungarian Team Championship 2004.

15 ♗b6 ♕d7 16 ♖a4!?

16 ♘d4 is simpler; e.g. 16...♗c4 17 ♗xc4 ♘xc4 18 ♘f5 and White can gradually increase his advantage.

16...♖ac8

If 16...♘c6 then 17 ♘d5 with some advantage (Karpov).

17 ♖d4!?

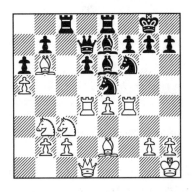

Karpov's creative idea: the rooks exert great pressure despite being exposed to attack by Black's minor pieces.

17...♕c6

The rook can't be attacked right away: 17...♘c6? 18 ♘c5! and the queen goes.

18 ♖d2 ♗xb3 19 cxb3 ♘fd7 20 ♗g1 ♗g5?

Polugaevsky misevaluates the coming position, where it turns out that Karpov's queen and pawn are better than Black's two rooks. 20...♕c7 21 ♘d5 ♕xa5 22 ♘xe7+ ♖xe7 23 ♖xd6 (Safarov-Vladimirov) is correct, when "Black had a comfortable position", according to Karpov—though I'm not so sure, as the white bishops are strong.

21 ♖xd6 ♗xf4

Or 21...♕c7 22 ♖f5 and White is just a pawn up.

22 ♖xc6 ♖xc6 23 b4

Perhaps Polugaevsky thought the extra doubled pawn didn't matter, but now it's clear that White's queenside majority is coming fast, and Black has no time to consolidate.

23...♘f6 24 b5 ♖ce6 25 bxa6 bxa6 26 g3 ♗g5 27 h4 ♗h6 28 ♗b6

Black's Najdorf 5...a6 created a weakness at b6, which White now occupies with great effect!

28...♘ed7 29 ♗c4 ♖e5

If 29...♖c6 30 ♗xa6 ♘xb6, then 31 ♗b5 pins and wins.

30 ♕b3 ♖b8

30...♖f8 31 ♗c7 ♖ee8 32 ♗d6 is no better.

31 ♗xf7+ ♔h8 32 ♕c4 ♗d2 33 ♗c7 ♖c5 34 ♕xc5!

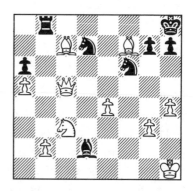

Karpov says the rest is "pure technique".

34...♘xc5 35 ♗xb8 ♗xc3

Another way is 35...♘fxe4 36 ♘xe4 ♘xe4 37 ♗c7 ♗b4 38 ♗c4 ♘c5 39 ♔g2 ♘b7 40 ♗xa6 ♘xa5 41 ♔f3 with a winning ending.

36 bxc3 ♘fxe4 37 c4 ♘d7 38 ♗c7 g6 39 ♗e6 ♘ec5 40 ♗xd7 ♘xd7 41 ♗d6 1-0

After 41...♔g7 42 c5 ♔f7 43 c6 the pawn goes through.

While White got very little out of the opening, he did get *something* (after Black's slightly premature 8...♗e6 which allowed the immediate 9 f4). The resulting position is very tough for

Black to play: he's slightly cramped and, despite a wide range of choices on every move, has few active possibilities. Meanwhile White can enjoy his space advantage and manoeuvre creatively.

Game 10
B92
A.Karpov-E.Bukic
Bugojno 1978

1 e4 c5 2 ♘f3 d6 3 d4 cxd4 4 ♘xd4 ♘f6 5 ♘c3 a6 6 ♗e2 e5 7 ♘b3 ♗e7 8 0-0 0-0 9 a4

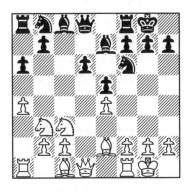

White waits for ...♗e6 before playing f2-f4, but Black's actual next move also encourages this advance, as the c6-knight blocks the long diagonal. In a modern game Black develops the queen's bishop to d7 so as to go either way, but the weakness at b6 and White's potential queenside majority are strong again—see the following note.

9...♘c6

9...♗d7 10 ♗e3 ♗c6 11 f3 (Kasparov-style: since White waited on the

f2-f4 advance, this move is strong) 11...d5 (getting rid of the backward pawn, but now b6 and c5 beckon the white pieces) 12 exd5 ♗xd5 (or 12...♘xd5 13 ♘xd5 ♗xd5 14 a5 with a typical slight positional plus) 13 a5 ♘c6 14 ♗b6 ♕d7 15 ♘c5 ♗xc5+ 16 ♗xc5 ♖fd8 17 ♗b6 ♖e8 18 ♕d2 ♘e7 19 ♖fd1 ♕c6 20 ♗f2 ♗c4 21 ♗xc4 ♕xc4 22 ♖a4 ♕c7 23 ♗b6 ♕c6 24 ♕d6 ♖ac8 25 ♕xc6 ♘xc6 26 ♘d5 ♘xd5 27 ♖xd5 f6 28 c3 (White obtained the superior minor piece and Geller's favourite queenside pawn majority) 28...♔f7 29 ♖a1 ♖e7 30 ♖ad1 h5 31 ♔f2 ♔e6 32 b4 ♘b8 33 ♖d6+ ♔f7 34 ♖1d3 ♖e6 35 ♖d8 ♖e8 36 ♖8d5 ♖e6 37 ♗c5 ♖ec6 38 ♖d8 ♔e6 39 ♖3d6+ ♔f7 40 ♖xc6 ♖xd8 41 ♖c7+ ♖d7 42 ♖c8 ♘c6 43 ♔e3 f5 44 g3 g5 45 c4 ♘d8 46 b5 ♘e6 47 ♗b6 f4+ 48 gxf4 gxf4+ 49 ♔e2 ♔f6 50 bxa6 bxa6 51 ♖a8 e4 52 fxe4 ♔e5 53 ♖xa6 ♔xe4 54 ♖a8 f3+ 55 ♔e1 ♖e7 56 a6 ♘f4 57 a7 ♘d3+ 58 ♔d2 f2 59 ♖f8 ♖d7 60 a8♕+ 1-0 S.Karjakin-I.Nepomniachtchi, Moscow (blitz) 2011.

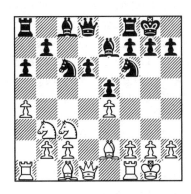

10 ♔h1

Still waiting—if Black fianchettoes to avoid f2-f4, White can switch to Geller's plan: 10...b6 11 ♗e3 ♗b7 12 ♘d5 with an edge, as in Geller-Benjamin (Game 6).

10...♗e6 11 f4

Now!

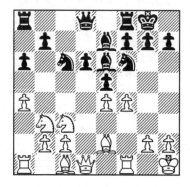

11...♘b4

Instead:

a) 11...♘a5 12 f5 ♗c4 13 ♘xa5 ♗xe2 14 ♕xe2 ♕xa5 15 ♗g5 ♖fc8 16 ♗xf6 ♗xf6 17 ♘d5 is a classic domination position similar to the Cabrilo-Fedorowicz crush given in the notes to the previous game.

b) 11...exf4 12 ♗xf4 d5 (as in Game 1) is evidently best, where Black might make a draw: 13 e5 ♘e4 14 ♗d3 f5 15 exf6 ♗xf6 16 ♘xe4 dxe4 17 ♗xe4 ♕xd1 18 ♖axd1 ♗xb2 19 g3 ♖ae8 20 ♘c5 ♗c4 21 ♖fe1 ♗c3 22 ♗d2 ♗d4 23 ♗e3 ♗c3 24 ♗d2 ♗d4 25 ♗e3 ♗c3 26 ♗d2 ½-½ A.Kovalev-M.Brodsky, Tiumen 2010.

12 f5 ♗d7 13 ♗g5 ♗c6

White always has to watch out for ...♘xe4 in such positions, though it doesn't work here: 13...♘xe4? 14 ♗xe7 ♘xc3 15 bxc3 and White wins a piece as the black knight hangs.

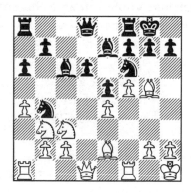

14 ♗f3 ♖c8 15 ♕e2 h6?!

Black has to be super alert to play this kind of position: 15...d5! is necessary, when after 16 ♗xf6 dxe4! (but not 16...♗xf6 17 exd5 ♘xd5 18 ♗xd5 ♗xd5 19 ♖ad1, winning a piece) 17 ♗xe5 (White has to be careful too: 17 ♗xe7 exf3 18 ♗xd8 fxe2 19 ♖fe1 ♖fxd8 20 ♖xe2 f6 favours Black with his stronger centre) 17...exf3 18 gxf3 and Black has compensation for the pawn due to White's somewhat exposed king.

16 ♗h4 b6 17 ♖fd1

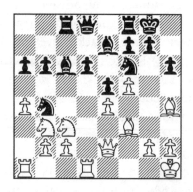

Too late! Now Black must suffer.

17...♕c7 18 ♗g3

As in Chapter One, one way White restrains ...d6-d5 is by pressuring e5; e.g. 18...d5? 19 exd5 ♗b7 20 ♗xe5 and wins.

18...♗b7 19 ♖d2 ♖fd8 20 ♖ad1 ♘e8 21 h4

Karpov tightens his grip square by square—Black is not allowed to activate his bishop on g5.

21...♘f6 22 ♗f2 ♘d7 23 g3

Restraint! g3-g4 will come at the right time.

23...♔f8 24 ♘c1 ♕c4 25 ♕e1 ♕c7 26 ♕g1 ♘c5 27 ♘1e2 ♗c6 28 b3 ♕b7 29 ♕g2 ♕c7 30 ♗e3 ♗f6 31 ♔h2 ♕e7 32 ♕f2 ♗b7 33 ♗g2 ♔g8 34 ♕f3 ♔h7 35 ♕h5 ♕f8 36 ♖f1

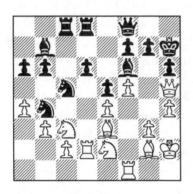

Directed against 36...g6 which now fails to 37 fxg6+ fxg6 38 ♕xh6+!.

36...♘d7 37 ♖c1

37 g4? is still premature due to 37...g6 38 ♕xh6+ ♕xh6 39 ♗xh6 ♔xh6 40 g5+ ♗xg5 and Black comes out a pawn up.

37...♖c6?!

Now White gains a tempo. 37...♖c7 is better, but it's been dreary for a long time and perfect defence is difficult.

38 ♘d5!

White finally occupies the weak square.

38...♘xd5 39 exd5 ♖cc8 40 ♗e4 ♘c5 41 ♗xc5! ♖xc5 42 g4!! 1-0

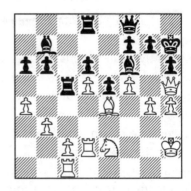

The long-prepared attack (move 42!) is overwhelming as Black can't prevent g4-g5, e.g. 42...♔g8 43 g5 ♗e7 (or 43...hxg5 44 hxg5 ♗e7 45 f6 g6 46 ♗xg6 fxg6 47 ♕xg6+ ♔h8 48 ♖h1 and mates) 44 f6 gxf6 45 gxf6 ♗xf6 46 ♖g1+ ♗g7 47 ♕f5 f6 48 ♘f4 exf4 (or 48...♗c8 49 ♕h7+ ♔f7 50 ♘h5 etc) 49 ♖dg2 ♖c7 50 ♕h7+ ♔f7 51 ♖xg7+ ♔e8 52 ♗g6+ and mates.

I am struck again and again by how difficult Black's defence is in these Karpovian grind positions: from Polugaevsky's destruction in 1974 to Karjakin's squeeze against Nepomniachtchi in 2011 (in the note to move 9), strong GMs are losing these positions due to nothing more than small weaknesses at d6 and b6—it's just not fun to play Black here!

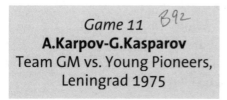

Game 11 *B92*
A.Karpov-G.Kasparov
Team GM vs. Young Pioneers,
Leningrad 1975

1 e4 c5 2 ♘f3 d6 3 d4 cxd4 4 ♘xd4 ♘f6 5 ♘c3 a6 6 ♗e2 e5

Evidently due to this game, Kasparov never played this move again. As I noted in the Introduction, Karpov *never* lost this position. In the Karpov-Kasparov world championship matches to come, Karpov also tried 6 ♗e2 often—but Kasparov invariably answered 6...e6 (see their most famous encounter in Chapter Four, Game 41).

7 ♘b3 ♗e7 8 ♗g5

Instead of castling as in the last two games, Karpov tries a move that would later be popularized by Kasparov's nemesis Kramnik—but whereas Kramnik used this a prelude to queenside castling, Karpov just wants to trick his young opponent into the ...♗e6 met by f2-f4 positions, even with a tempo loss.

8...♗e6 9 f4

Kramnik's idea is 9 ♗xf6 ♗xf6 10 ♕d3 (see Game 14).

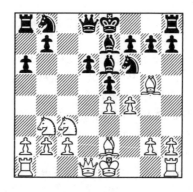

9...exf4

Our typical Boleslavsky bind occurred after 9...♕c7 10 f5 ♗c4 11 0-0 ♘bd7 12 ♔h1 b5 13 a3 ♖b8 14 ♘d2 ♘b6 15 ♘xc4 ♘xc4 16 ♗xc4 ♕xc4 17 ♗xf6 gxf6 18 ♕d5 with positional domination and a White win in Alir.Sanchez-C.Hurtado, Pan American Junior Championship 1998. Note again the key elements of this bind, which we might call the Anti Boleslavsky Delight or ABD: the d5-square is owned by White and the only minor pieces left are a white knight and a bad black bishop. White should always watch for ways to set up this position since, if you can get it, this bind should virtually always win—just not quickly! For the record, Sanchez took 50 moves to score the point, which is about right, even though she was positionally winning after 18. The ABD does demand patience!

10 ♗xf4

White has lost a tempo by this double move of the bishop (recall that in Karpov-Polugaevsky, White was able to capture efficiently on f4 with the rook—not possible here). On the other hand, he has lured a certain young Pioneer into Karpovian territory!

10...♘c6 11 0-0 0-0 12 ♔h1

12...b5

Black can come close to equalizing with 12...d5, again much as in Game 1 (but we already know Karpov likes this position, whether equal or not!). After 13 e5 ♘e4 14 ♗d3 (Karpov played this challenging move against a future world champion, but took a rest day against the namesake of the variation: 14 ♘xe4 dxe4 15 ♘d2 ♗g5 16 ♘xe4 ½-½ A.Karpov-M.Najdorf, Hastings 1971/72) 14...f5 (14...♘c5 may be best, with approximate equality; whereas 14...♘xc3 15 bxc3 is like Game 1) 15 exf6 ♗xf6 16 ♘xe4 dxe4 17 ♗xe4 ♗c4 18 ♗d6 ♗xf1 19 ♕d5+ ♔h8 20 ♕h5 g6 21 ♗xg6 ♗xg2+ 22 ♔xg2 ♕d7 23 ♘c5 ♕g7 24 ♗xf8 ♕xg6+ 25 ♕xg6 hxg6 26

♗d6 ♖e8 27 ♖f1 ♗xb2 28 ♘xb7 ♔g8 29 c4 (after insane complications, White has emerged with an extra pawn, but Anand shows his tiger qualities and claws his way to a draw) 29...♗d4 30 ♔g3 ♗g7 31 ♖b1 ♖e3+ 32 ♔f2 ♗d4 33 ♔f1 ♖f3+ 34 ♔e2 ♖c3 35 c5 ♗e3 36 ♔f1 ♘d4 37 ♖b2 g5 38 ♔g2 ♔f7 39 ♔g3 ♘e6 40 ♘d6+ ♔g6 41 ♖b6 ♗xc5 42 ♖xa6 ♗xd6 43 ♖xd6 ♔f6 44 a4 ♖a3 45 ♖a6 ♔f5 46 a5 ♘f4+ 47 ♔f2 ♔e4 48 ♔e1 ♖a2 49 ♔d1 ♔e3 ½-½ A.Karpov-V.Anand, Sicilian thematic, Buenos Aires 1994. Not many would have drawn this against Karpov!

A worse alternative is 12...♖e8

13 ♕e1 ♘d7 14 ♖d1 ♘de5 15 ♘d5 ♗f8 16 ♕f2, when the lost tempo is forgotten and we see Black's quiet play has led to a Karpovian grind and, simultaneously, terrible suffering and a loss for another GM: 16...♘d7 17 ♗g3 ♘ce5 18 ♗h4 ♕c8 19 c3 b5 20 ♗g5 (note that White has played ♗g5-f4-g3-h4-g5 with positional pressure—now that's Karpov!) 20...♕b7 21 ♘a5 ♕c8 22 ♕d4 ♘c6 23 ♘xc6 ♕xc6 24 c4 ♗xd5 25

cxb5 axb5 26 ♕xd5 ♕xd5 27 ♖xd5 ♖xe4 28 ♗xb5 ♘e5 29 a4 ♖b4 30 ♗c1 ♗e7 31 h3 ♖b8 32 ♖f4 ♖b3 33 ♖f2 ♗h4 34 ♖c2 ♗g3 35 ♗d2 h5 36 ♖c3 (the rooks come off and White grinds his way home) 36...♖xc3 37 ♗xc3 h4 38 ♖xd6 ♘c4 39 ♖d5 ♘d6 40 ♗d3 ♖e8 41 a5 ♘e4 42 ♗xe4 ♖xe4 43 ♔g1 ♖a4 44 ♔f1 f6 45 ♔e2 ♔f7 46 ♖d7+ ♔g6 47 b4 ♗e5 48 ♗d2 ♔f5 49 ♖xg7 1-0 A.Karpov-L.Kavalek, Waddinxveen 1979.

13 ♗f3

As usual, after teasing Black with a fleeting opportunity for ...d6-d5, Karpov shuts down the break.

13...♘e5 14 ♘d4 ♗c4 15 ♖f2

The safe 15 ♖e1 is equal.

15...b4 16 ♘d5 ♘xd5 17 exd5 ♗f6 18 ♖d2 ♕b6 19 ♗e3 ♕c7 20 ♗e4 ♖fe8 21 ♗g1

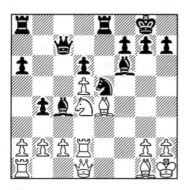

21...g6

The young but already brilliant Kasparov has amazingly outplayed the world champion, and could now take over the game with 21...♗g5! 22 ♕h5 h6! (22...♗xd2? 23 ♕xh7+ ♔f8 24 ♘f5 and mates is no doubt the reason Kas-

parov rejected this line) 23 ♖dd1 ♘d7 24 ♗f3 ♘f6 25 ♕h3 ♗xd5 and Black wins a pawn.

22 a3 a5

Once again 22...♗g5 is correct; e.g. 23 ♖f2 bxa3 24 ♖xa3 ♕b7, forking b2 and d5. Note that in his smooth performance against Bukic that we just saw, Karpov made sure to prevent ...♗g5.

23 axb4 axb4 24 ♖xa8 ♖xa8 25 b3 ♗a6 26 ♘c6 ♘xc6

Kasparov is out of his depth now; rather than give White a passed pawn, he should try to eject the knight with 26...♗b5.

27 dxc6 ♖e8 28 ♗d5 ♗c3 29 ♖f2 ♖e1 30 ♕f3 ♗d4

Kasparov tries to attack when only defence might save him. 30...♖e7 is best, after which Black is worse but holding.

31 ♗xf7+ ♔g7 32 ♗c4

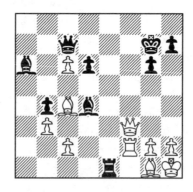

32...♖xg1+

As usual, opposite bishops help White's attack after 32...♗xf2 33 ♕xf2 ♗xc4 34 ♕xe1 ♗d5 35 ♕a1+ ♔g8 36

♕f6 ♕xc6 37 ♗d4, when the long black diagonal is decisive for White, and the long white diagonal is meaningless for Black!

33 ♔xg1 ♗xf2+ 34 ♔xf2 ♗xc4 35 bxc4 ♕a7+ 36 ♔e2 ♕d4 37 ♕d5

Karpov's forte—the pawn-up ending in any form—has been reached, and Kasparov's great talent can't help him here.

37...♕f6 38 ♕e4 b3 39 cxb3 ♕b2+ 40 ♔f1 ♕c1+ 41 ♕e1 ♕f4+ 42 ♔g1 ♕d4+ 43 ♔h1 ♕b6 44 ♕e7+ ♔h6 45 ♕f8+ 1-0

After 45...♔h5 46 ♕xd6 ♕xb3 47 ♕c5+ ♔h6 48 h3 White's safe king and passed c-pawn add up to an easy win—as usual, Karpov's endgame technique is impeccable. That said, the tempo loss with ♗g5-f4 cannot be recommended, except for psychological reasons.

One sees that the early f2-f4 works best when Black voluntarily plays an early ...♗e6, but what if he doesn't? I would say, try any of the following ideas—first let's take a look at Geller's classic ♘d5 plan.

1 e4 c5 2 ♘f3 d6 3 d4 cxd4 4 ♘xd4 ♘f6 5 ♘c3 a6 6 ♗e2 e5 7 ♘b3 ♗e7 8 0-0 0-0 9 ♗e3

9...♕c7

Anand played 9...♗e6 in a recent game where White tried Geller's plan: 10 ♘d5 (alternatively, 10 f4 reaches Games 20-21, where White reverts to a Karpovian early f2-f4 system, as there are two favourable omens: Black has voluntarily played ...♗e6, and White won't lose a tempo with his queen's bishop as 10...exf4 will be answered by 11 ♖xf4; both this and Geller's line are good—in my opinion, White has an embarrassment of riches as far as good lines against the Najdorf are concerned, even within the 6 ♗e2 umbrella) 10...♘bd7 11 ♕d3 ♗xd5 12 exd5 ♘c5 and at this point the former FIDE World Champion decided to move his queen four times in a row to no purpose that I can see, and eventually lost the game: 13 ♕d2 ♘fe4 14 ♕b4 a5 15 ♕b5 ♕c7 16 ♕c4 and 0-1 down the road in R.Ponomariov-V.Anand, Wijk aan Zee 2011. I do not recommend this! 13 ♘xc5 dxc5 14 ♖fd1 is evidently correct, after which best play looks like 14...e4 15 ♕b3 ♗d6 16 g3 ♕c7 17 a4, when White retains a small but lasting advantage due to his bishop pair and passed pawn.

10 a4 ♗e6

If 10...b6, then 11 f3 ♗b7 12 ♕d2 ♘bd7 13 ♖fd1 and White has restrained Black's play and keeps a long-term plus—as, for example, in D.Barua-P.Lakshmi Sahithi, New Delhi 2007.

11 a5 ♘bd7

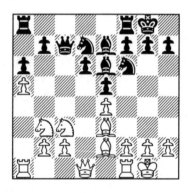

Correct! Up to a certain point, as we will see, Fischer's play was very good. Here he takes advantage of the Najdorf move order (not revealing much "information", which is the modern touchstone) as opposed to the early ...♘c6 seen in the Classical Variation of the previous chapter. Now when White plays ♘d5, Black can take with the king's knight (usually Black has to take with the bishop in the classical Boleslavsky system, as capturing with the knight allows a fork on d5). This means White's advantage will be very slight or maybe not even there—though of course Black has to play well after the opening!

12 ♘d5 ♘xd5

The unforced 12...♗xd5 is a clear mistake; e.g. 13 exd5 b5 14 axb6 ♘xb6 15 c4! a5 (not 15...♘xc4 16 ♕c2 ♖fc8 17 ♖fc1 ♘xe3 18 ♕xc7 ♖xc7 19 ♖xc7 ♘exd5 20 ♖b7 and the ending favours White) 16 ♖xa5 ♖xa5 17 ♘xa5 ♘bxd5 18 ♗d2 ♘f4 19 b4 and the passed b-pawn gave White the edge in A.Bradvarevic-I.Nemet, Bled 1963.

13 exd5

According to the old notes on *Chess-Base*, this position clearly favours White, but I have my doubts.

13...♗f5 14 c4 ♗g6 15 ♖c1

15...♘c5?

This is the problem, which must be described as a positional blunder. White doesn't want his knight on b3 anyway, as his b-pawn needs to advance as part of a general mobilization of the queenside pawn majority.

Correct is 15...♖ac8! (to restrain White and then advance on the kingside; not the impetuous 15...f5?! 16 c5 f4 17 cxd6 ♕xd6 18 ♗c5 ♘xc5 19 ♘xc5 and White is a little better, or 16...dxc5 17 ♘xc5 ♘xc5 18 b4 and White recovers the piece with advantage) 16 f3 (now the immediate 16 c5 is ineffective: 16...dxc5 17 ♘xc5 ♗xc5 18 b4 ♕d6 19 bxc5 ♘xc5 with equality) 16...♕d8 17 ♕d2 f5 18 ♗d3 ♖f7 and the computer can't decide if this unforcing position is equal or slightly better for White. I'll describe it this way: both sides have pawn majorities that are hard to advance—White because his knight is in the way, Black because either of the logical pushes (...f5-f4 or ...e5-e4) actually weakens the pawns—so neither side can undertake anything without preparation. In general there are chances for both sides; the position is far from drawish or symmetrical, and one will have a chance to outplay the opponent.

It's because of this variation that I wouldn't put Geller's plan—so strong against the straight Boleslavsky—at the top of our five anti-Najdorf ♗e2 lines, but it is certainly solid and playable. Young players seem to underestimate it too: the young Fischer falls here and the young Carlsen falls in the next game. So check the age of your opponent, and if he's under 20, drop your knight on d5 and make him play a positional, unforced game!

16 ♘xc5 dxc5 17 b4!

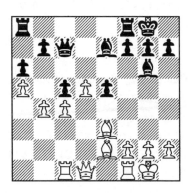

The queenside majority is unleashed and White is clearly better. Now it's obvious that Bobby made a huge mistake by letting White exchange his self-blocking knight.

17...♖ac8

Also good for White are:

a) 17...cxb4 18 ♗b6 ♕d7 19 ♕b3! (not 19 c5 ♗g5 20 ♖c4 b3, when Black has counterplay) 19...♖fc8 20 c5 and the pawns are rolling.

b) 17...f5 18 bxc5 ♗xc5 (18...f4? 19 d6!) 19 ♗xc5 ♕xc5 20 ♕b3 ♖ab8 21 ♕e3 and White breaks the dark square blockade.

18 ♕b3

White enjoys the vacated b3-square!

18...♗d6 19 ♖fd1

White's positional advantage is close to decisive, but that doesn't mean the point is secured.

19...♕e7 20 bxc5 ♗xc5 21 ♗xc5 ♖xc5 22 ♖a1!

The start of a highly creative manoeuvre—up to a point, Geller plays virtually perfectly.

22...♖d8 23 ♖a4 ♗f5 24 ♖b4 ♗c8 25 ♖b6 ♖d6

After 25...♖xa5 26 d6 ♕d7 27 ♗f3 White's bind is too strong,

26 ♕b4 ♕c7 27 ♖xd6 ♕xd6 28 ♖b1 ♕c7 29 ♕a4 ♗d7 30 ♕a3 ♖xa5 31 ♖xb7 ♕xb7

White is better after 31...♖xa3 32 ♖xc7 ♖a1+ 33 ♗f1 ♗f5 34 f3, but Black still has some play left—whereas the game continuation should lead to a clear win for White.

32 ♕xa5 g6

33 h3

So natural, and yet—not best! Chess is amazingly difficult even here, where White has a clearly decisive advantage. 33 ♗f1! should win, as the bishop itself as well as f2 and g2 are protected, which means Black has no random tactics as occur in the actual game. After this sound retreat, play could continue 33...♔g7 34 d6 ♕e4 35 c5 ♗c6 36 ♕xa6 and White wins easily, a pawn up with

connected passers, while Black has nothing to play against.

33...♕b1+ 34 ♔h2

34 ♗f1 is still good enough.

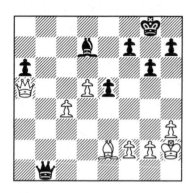

34...♗f5?

Missing his chance! The astonishing 34...♕c2!!, attacking the undefended white bishop and through this the undefended f-pawn (which is crucial to the white king's defence), seems to draw; e.g. 35 ♕d8+ (or 35 ♕e1 a5 with counterplay) 35...♔g7 36 ♕xd7 ♕xe2 37 ♕c7 ♕b2! 38 d6 (38 ♔g3 ♕d4 39 f3 ♕f4+ is a perpetual) 38...♕xf2 and again Black should be able to find a perpetual check and draw.

35 ♕c3

White consolidates and Geller's technique is now faultless.

35...♕e4 36 ♗f3 ♕d4 37 ♕xd4 exd4 38 g4 ♗c8

Nothing works against the connected passers: 38...a5 39 gxf5 a4 40 d6 ♔f8 41 c5 a3 42 c6 a2 43 c7 with an extra piece, or 38...♗c2 39 c5 d3 40 c6 ♗a4 41 d6 and White wins the race.

39 c5 a5 40 c6 ♔f8 41 d6 1-0

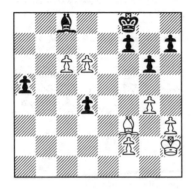

The variations are clear: 41...♚e8 (or 41...a4 42 c7 a3 43 ♗c6 a2 44 d7 ♗xd7 45 ♗xd7 a1♕ 46 c8♕+ with an extra piece) 42 ♗d1 ♗a6 43 g5 ♗b5 (if 43...♚d8 then 44 ♗g4 kills) 44 c7 ♗d7 45 ♗a4 and the death blow comes on another diagonal.

Unlike Geller's similar line against the Boleslavsky, I'm not sure the early ♘d5 here gives White an objective advantage. However, one can certainly play for a win in the unbalanced positional waters that occur—which might not suit sharp young Najdorf players!

In the next game we'll see another junior fall.

> ## Game 13
> ## S.Kayumov-M.Carlsen
> ## Budapest 2003

1 e4 c5 2 ♘f3 d6 3 d4 cxd4 4 ♘xd4 ♘f6 5 ♘c3 a6 6 ♗e2 e5 7 ♘b3 ♗e7 8 0-0 0-0 9 ♖e1

I was also competing in this tour-

nament, and I noticed that Sergey deliberately played in a slow, non-forcing way—forcing the young (13 at the time), but already fearsome Carlsen to play positionally, like it or not.

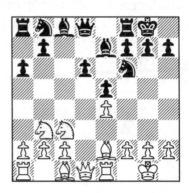

I had unwisely entered the Dragon (as Black) against Magnus, where he first exposed my lack of theoretical knowledge, and then played an accurately calculated attack.

In this game he was unable to use either his memory of variations, or his excellent calculation: he had to assess competing positional ideas—something at which he now excels of course, but back then, he (like Fischer) had trouble with such amorphous positions.

9...♗e6 10 ♗f1

10 ♗f3 is also possible, holding back any future ...d6-d5.

10...♘bd7 11 ♘d5

Geller's idea, in a slightly different position.

11...♖c8

Kayumov nearly scored again in a later game: 11...♘xd5 12 exd5 ♗f5 13 a4 ♖c8 14 c3 e4 15 a5 ♖e8 16 ♖a4 ♗g5? (16...♘e5 is better) 17 f4! and now another higher-rated foe was in big trouble, for if 17...exf3 18 ♖xe8+ ♕xe8 19 ♗xg5 would win a piece. Black tried 17...♗f6, when 18 g4! won material, though Black somehow escaped with a draw in S.Kayumov-E.Ghaem Maghami, Esfahan 2004.

12 c4 ♘b6 13 ♘d2

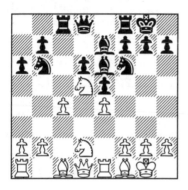

13...♘bxd5

It's time to take, as on quiet moves White builds up in Boleslavsky fashion; e.g. 13...h6 14 b3 ♖e8 15 ♗b2 with a big edge.

14 exd5

Fritz's first pick is 14 cxd5, taking toward the centre, but Sergey is playing for a win by unbalancing the position, Geller-style. Now White has a queenside pawn majority, and Black must act quickly—for the moment Magnus is equal to the task.

14...♗g4 15 ♕b3 b5!

A good sharp pawn sacrifice!

16 cxb5 axb5 17 ♘b1

After 17 ♗xb5 ♖b8 18 a4 ♕a5 Black has excellent Benko-style compensation.

17...♕a5 18 ♗d2 b4 19 ♗xb4 ♕xd5

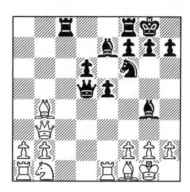

Black has traded two wing pawns for two centre pawns, generally a good deal. But only one of the black centre pawns is passed, whereas White has two running passers.

20 ♘d2 ♕d4?!

A judgment call gone wrong. As it turns out, the white queen is a great help to the passed pawns and should be destroyed: 20...♕xb3 21 ♘xb3 ♗e6, threatening ...♗xb3 devaluing the pawns, looks like the way to go, when I think Black is at least equal.

21 ♗c3 ♕a7 22 ♘e4!

White exchanges the pieces he wants to get rid of, and so limits Black's tactics, while preparing to advance his passers.

22...♗e6 23 ♘xf6+ ♗xf6 24 ♕d1 ♕b8 25 ♕h5 g6 26 ♕e2

White has cleverly repositioned and stands at least equal, restraining Black's centre by pressure on e5—which is, of course, an anti-Boleslavsky idea we already know. Remember, positional themes in similar pawn structures always repeat!

26...♗g7 27 a4 f6 28 a5 d5 29 a6 ♕a7 30 ♗b4 ♖fd8 31 ♖ec1 d4 32 ♗a5 ♖e8 33 b4!

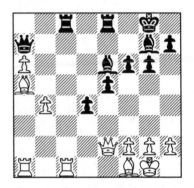

Now it's clear that the white pawns are the more dangerous—there were no combinations in the last thirteen moves, but Carlsen, like Fischer, was strategically outplayed, with the b2-b4 advance playing an important role in both games!

33...f5 34 b5 e4 35 ♕d1 d3 36 ♖xc8 ♖xc8

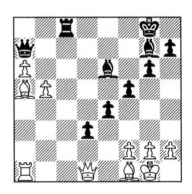

37 ♖c1!

White wants queens on (well known for shepherding passed pawns) rather than rooks (which might be able to hold them up).

37...♖xc1 38 ♕xc1 ♗d4 39 ♕c6!

The queen infiltrates and supports the passed pawns while threatening the e6-bishop; that Black takes a pawn with check is of much less importance.

39...♗xf2+ 40 ♔h1 ♕d7 41 ♕b7 ♔f7

41...♕c8 is necessary to hold up the pawns, though after 42 ♗c7 d2 43 ♗e2 g5 44 ♗d1 it seems White is better anyway with ♗b3 in the air; e.g. 44...e3 (44...♕xb7 45 axb7 ♗a7 46 b6 wins) 45 ♗e5 ♗d7 46 ♕b6 f4 47 ♕f6 ♕f8 48 ♗b3+ and Black's advanced pawns have left his king without defence.

42 b6! ♔e7 43 ♕xd7+ ♔xd7 44 b7 ♗a7 45 ♗b6! d2

Nothing is any better: 45...♗xb6 46 b8♕ or 45...♗b8 46 a7.

46 ♗b5+!

To drive the black king away, for if 46...♔d6 47 ♗a4 e3 48 ♗xa7 e2 49 b8♕+ and mates with all checks.

46...♔e7 47 ♗xa7!!

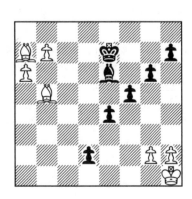

Not many players can say they allowed Carlsen to queen with check—and won the game!! Bravo Sergey!

47...d1♕+

Despite Black's extra queen, nothing can be done about White's deadly passed pawns.

48 ♗g1 e3

Or 48...♕d8 49 a7 and the pawns go through.

49 b8♕ e2 50 ♗xe2 ♕xe2 51 ♕b7+ ♔d6 52 a7 ♗d5 53 ♕xd5+ ♔xd5 54 a8♕+ ♔d6 55 ♕a3+ ♔e6 56 ♕e3+ ♕xe3 57 ♗xe3 ♔e5 58 ♗g5 f4 59 ♔g1 ♔f5 60 h4 1-0

Black resigns, as after 60...♔g4 61 ♔f2 White wins in elementary style as follows:

a) 61...♔f5 62 ♔f3, when one pawn goes and the rest will follow soon.

b) 61...h5 62 ♗h6 ♔xh4 (the pawns drop after 62...f3 63 g3 ♔f5 64 ♔xf3) 63 ♔f3! (Black is in zugzwang) 63...g5 64 ♗g7 g4+ 65 ♔xf4 g3 66 ♗f6 mate.

c) 61...h6 62 ♗xh6 ♔xh4 63 ♔f3 g5 64 ♗f8 ♔h5 65 ♗d6 ♔g6 66 ♗xf4 gxf4 (66...♔f5 67 ♗xg5 ♔xg5 68 ♔g3 is an-

other winning pawn ending) 67 ♔xf4 ♔f6 68 ♔g4 ♔g6 69 g3 and it's all over.

Yes, objectively Black may be able to equalize against the early ♘d5 lines, but White reaches a non-forcing, double-edged positional struggle where he can play for a win.

Now let's look at a more direct line: Kramnik's 8 ♗g5.

Game 14
V.Kramnik-V.Anand
Wijk aan Zee 2004

---

1 e4 c5 2 ♘f3 d6 3 d4 cxd4 4 ♘xd4 ♘f6 5 ♘c3 a6 6 ♗e2 e5 7 ♘b3 ♗e7 8 ♗g5

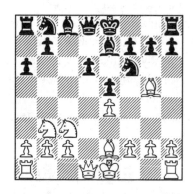

This idea of Karpov's was revived by Kramnik, with the additional points of queenside castling and attack.

8...♗e6

According to Richard Palliser, in his *Starting Out* book on the Najdorf, this is the best move as it prevents the white bishop from reaching c4, and it's certainly a good move—but not the only one. While c4 is indeed a nice spot for the king's bishop, one must also recognize that moving it again loses time, so in my opinion Black can just ignore White's threat with 8...0-0 (for which see the next game).

On the other hand, passive play by Black can allow this strong repositioning: 8...♘bd7?! 9 a4 b6 10 ♗c4 ♗b7 11 ♕e2 0-0 12 0-0 ♕c7 13 ♖fd1 has been played many times, and the verdict is in—White is better as both his bishops are strong, while d5 is even weaker than usual! White scores around 70% from this position.

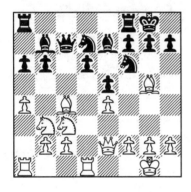

Here are three examples:

a) Ganguly grinds: 13...♖fc8 14 ♘d2 h6 15 ♗xf6 (we've seen all this before: White eliminates the defenders of d5) 15...♘xf6 16 ♗b3 ♗c6 17 ♘f1 ♕b7 18 ♘d5 b5 19 axb5 ♗xb5 20 ♕f3 ♗xf1 21 ♔xf1 a5 22 ♕e2 ♘e8 23 ♖d3 ♗d8 24 ♖f3 a4 25 ♖xa4 ♖xa4 26 ♗xa4 ♕xb2 27 ♕d1 ♘f6 28 ♗b3 ♕d4 29 ♖d3 ♕xe4 30 ♘xf6+ (there goes the other one!) 30...♗xf6 (not 30...gxf6? 31 ♕h5 with a decisive attack) 31 ♖xd6—the dust has

cleared and what do we see? Opposite bishops that favour the attacker, here White; a focus for said attack, f7, that can never be defended by the black bishop; a passed white c-pawn; White owns the d-file and the eternally weak d5-square is a good jumping-off point for all of his pieces. All this means a lot of suffering for Black! Indeed, it took 90 moves, but White finally won in S.Ganguly-H.Nakamura, Khanty-Mansiysk 2005.

b) Kramnik scores twice: 13...h6 14 ♗xf6 ♘xf6 15 ♘d5 ♘xd5 16 ♗xd5 (with just a few quick chops, Kramnik exchanges all the defenders of the d5-square) and now:

b1) 16...♗xd5 17 ♖xd5 (the then World Champion has reached the "ABD—remember the contents of this: there is one minor piece to each side, a knight for White and dark-squared bishop for Black, and White holds the d5-square—the knight normally dominates the bad bishop and White has every chance of winning, as Kramnik does here against the current World

Championship Challenger) 17...b5 18 c3 ♕c4 19 ♕c2 ♖fb8 20 ♘d2 ♕c6 21 a5 ♖c8 22 ♕d3 ♖ab8 23 g3 ♕b7 24 ♘f1 ♖c4 25 b3 ♖c6 26 ♘e3 (the white knight is in range of d5, and any slight counterplay Black may have had is gone; I would call Black positionally busted here, though *Mr. Fritz*, in the absence of direct threats, sees only equality until...) 26...g6 27 h4 h5 28 ♕d2 ♗f8 29 ♘c2 ♖c5 30 ♘b4 ♖bc8 31 ♖d3 ♔h7 32 ♘d5 (the knight actually gets there, when the machine finally spits out clear advantage!) 32...♗h6 33 ♕d1 ♖f8 34 ♘f6+ ♔g7 35 ♕f3 b4? (a blunder under pressure) 36 cxb4 ♕xb4 37 ♘d7 f5 38 ♘xf8 ♔xf8 39 ♖xd6 1-0 V.Kramnik-B.Gelfand, Cap d'Agde (rapid) 2003.

b2) 16...♖ac8

17 c3 ♗xd5 18 ♖xd5 ♕c4 19 ♕xc4 ♖xc4 20 ♘d2 ♖c6 (White can squeeze this ending like a ripe lemon) 21 ♔f1 g6 22 ♔e2 ♔g7 23 ♔d3 ♖fc8 (note that Black's c-file play, so typical of the Sicilian, means absolutely nothing here, as the doubled rooks are stymied by the

well-protected c3-pawn) 24 g3 ♔f6 25 c4 ♗d8 26 b3 ♔e6 27 f4 f5 28 ♖e1 ♗f6 29 ♘f3 fxe4+ 30 ♖xe4 ♖c5 31 fxe5 dxe5 32 ♘d4+ ♔e7 33 ♘e2 ♖xd5+ 34 cxd5 ♔d6 35 ♘c3 h5 36 ♖c4 ♔d7 37 ♘e4 ♗d8 38 ♖xc8 ♔xc8 39 ♘d6+ (the knight utterly dominates the bad bishop) 1-0 V.Kramnik-E.Pähtz, Bonn (simul) 2004. Black resigns in view of 39...♔d7 40 ♘f7 ♗c7 41 ♔e4 ♔e7 42 ♘xe5 and wins.

9 ♗xf6 ♗xf6 10 ♕d3 ♘c6 11 0-0-0

This is the essence of Kramnik's variation: long castling, direct pressure on d6, complete control of d5. All this sounds pretty tremendous, but there was a price: Black has the two bishops, and unlike so many Boleslavsky-type positions, here the dark-squared one can often be activated on g5, or as a support for a ...♘d4 manoeuvre.

11...♗e7

In this tough World Champion vs. World Champion battle, Anand first defends solidly, and only later counter-attacks. However, Topalov later (after Anand switched sides in the position!)

got a short draw with Black with the immediate counter-attack 11...♛b6 which might be best: 12 ♛xd6 (the cautious 12 ♖hf1 0-0 13 ♘d5 doesn't seem to get anywhere after 13...♝xd5 14 ♛xd5 ♖fd8 15 ♚b1 ♘e7, which transposes to Bu Xiangzhi's win as Black given in the note to White's 10th move in the next game) 12...♝e7 13 ♘d5 ♝xd5 14 ♛xd5 0-0 15 ♛d2 (or 15 ♖hf1 ♖ac8 and Black has more than enough for the pawn in view of the open queenside files) 15...♛xf2 (Black has recovered his pawn with equality) 16 ♝c4 ♛h4 17 ♛e2 ♖ac8 18 a3 ♝f6 19 ♚b1 ♘d4 20 ♘xd4 exd4 21 g3 ♛g5 22 ♖hf1 ♛e3 23 ♖f3 ½-½ V.Anand-V.Topalov, Morelia/Linares 2008.

A weaker alternative is 11...♘d4 12 ♘xd4 exd4 13 ♘d5 ♝xd5 14 exd5 as Carlsen demonstrates—with the only minor pieces being opposite-coloured bishops, and only White attacking (even in the endgame), the difference between White's strong bishop and Black's self-blocked one turns out to be significant: 14...0-0 15 ♛f3 ♝e5 16 ♝d3 ♛f6 17 ♛xf6 ♝xf6 18 ♖he1 ♖fe8 19 ♖xe8+ ♖xe8 20 f4 g6 21 b4 ♚f8 22 ♚b2 ♚e7 23 ♚b3 ♖c8 24 g4 ♝h4 25 ♖f1 ♚d7 26 ♖f3 ♖h8 27 ♖h3 ♝f6 28 g5 (Black's bishop is vulnerable and just can't find anything to do) 28...♝g7 29 ♖f3 f5 30 h4 h5 31 ♖f1 ♖e8 32 b5 ♚c7 33 bxa6 bxa6 34 ♚a4 ♖e3 35 ♚a5 ♖h3 36 ♚xa6 ♖xh4 37 ♖e1 ♚d8 38 ♝b5 d3 39 ♚b7 ♝e5 (the poor bishop finally finds a purpose in life—to sacrifice it-

self for its king!—but this only delays the inevitable) 40 fxe5 ♖e4 41 ♖c1 d2 42 ♖d1 ♖xe5 43 ♖xd2 f4 44 a4 1-0 M.Carlsen-S.Karjakin, Nice (blindfold rapid) 2008.

12 ♚b1 0-0 13 ♘d5 ♝g5 14 h4!?

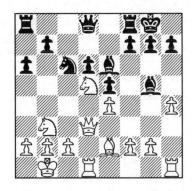

A bold pawn sacrifice to open lines—but while in principle I love such things, here it seems Black has enough defensive resources. In my opinion, the slower 14 g3 a5 15 h4 of S.Ganguly-M.Paragua, Calvia Olympiad 2004, is better, when White was finally able to build up an attack and won in 52 moves. However, this variation doesn't mean too much if Topalov's improvement 11...♛b6 stands up, which I think it does.

14...♝xh4 15 g3 ♝f6 16 ♛f3 ♝g5 17 ♛h5 h6 18 f4 ♝f6 19 ♘d2

Black has made five of his last six moves with his dark-squared bishop, but White still can't find a way to break through—simply because that bishop exists! Even taking it doesn't help: 19 ♘xf6+ ♛xf6 with a strong counter-attack against f4; while after 19 f5

♗xd5 20 ♖xd5 ♖c8 21 ♖hd1 ♕c7 22 c3 (not 22 ♖xd6? ♘d4, when Black interrupts the rooks and wins) 22...♖fd8 Black holds the pawn with advantage, as White can't get g4-g5 in due to the infamous dark square blockade.

In general, the attack is not good enough to win as White has no dark-squared bishop—though one must praise Anand's fine defence, and now... counter-attack!

19...♘d4 20 ♗c4 ♖c8 21 c3 ♘b5 22 f5 ♗xd5 23 ♗xd5

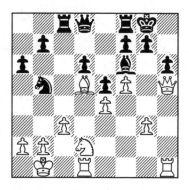

With the bishop on d5 White is threatening ♕g6 and ♖xh6—but Anand has something up his sleeve!

23...♖xc3!!

A rook!

24 ♕g6

It's very dangerous to take the "free gift": 24 bxc3 ♘xc3+ 25 ♔c2 (if the white king goes to a dark square, he must beware the unopposed and suddenly lively dark-squared bishop: 25 ♔b2 ♘xd5 26 exd5 e4+ with a winning attack) 25...♘xd5 26 exd5 ♕a5 and Black's attack is worth the rook.

24...♕b6 25 ♖xh6 ½-½

By threatening mate Kramnik forces Anand to take the draw with 25...♘a3+ 26 ♔a1 ♘c2+ 27 ♔b1 ♘a3+ etc.

A great fighting game between the champions, but I don't think the idea of an opposite side mating attack is really there when Black has counterplay on the dark squares.

Game 15
T.Taylor-D.Pruess
Sean Reader Memorial, Los Angeles 2011

1 e4 c5 2 ♘f3 d6 3 d4 cxd4 4 ♘xd4 ♘f6 5 ♘c3 a6 6 ♗e2 e5 7 ♘b3 ♗e7 8 ♗g5

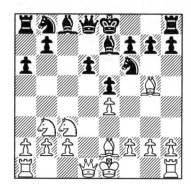

8...0-0

Although Anand held a complicated game after 8...♗e6, the simple text may be best—and statistically Black scores very well with this (White can only make 47% against it!).

A third alternative won't do: 8...♘xe4 fails to 9 ♘xe4 ♗xg5 10 ♘xd6+ ♔e7 11 ♘xc8+ ♕xc8 12 ♕d5!

with a tremendous attack against Black's uncastled king in A.Pomar Salamanca-A.Beni, Lugano 1959.

9 ♗xf6

If the idea of 8...♗e6 is to prevent 9 ♗c4, shouldn't I play it now? Unfortunately, I couldn't find any way to make it work after 9 ♗c4 b5 10 ♗d5 ♘xd5 11 ♕xd5 ♖a7, when Black will drive the white queen back with ...♗e6.

9...♗xf6 10 0-0

Alternatives here seem unpromising:

a) 10 ♘d5 ♗e6 11 ♘xf6+ ♕xf6 12 ♕xd6 ♘c6 and Black had good compensation for the pawn in Vo.Wolf-F.Middendorf, German League 1984.

b) 10 ♕d3 is the most popular move, trying to get back to Kramnik-Anand, but at the board I was put off by the possibility 10...♗e6 11 0-0-0 ♕b6! (instead of 11...♗e7 12 ♔b1 ♘c6 13 ♘d5, which does transpose back to the previous game), when I couldn't find a good answer for White.

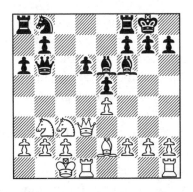

Looking this up later, I was glad I trusted my intuition, as Ganguly—

who, as we have seen, has had much success with this variation—lost from this position! There are two main possibilities:

b1) 12 ♖hf1 ♘c6 13 ♔b1 ♖fd8 14 ♘d5 ♗xd5 15 ♕xd5 ♘e7 (note how Black keeps d5 under control, unlike in our ABD positions where Black has only one minor piece left, the dark-squared bishop) 16 ♕a5 ♕c6 17 ♗f3 b5 18 ♖d3 ♖ac8 19 ♖c3 ♕b7 20 ♖d1? (20 ♖xc8 is better, but Black can play 20...♘xc8 with good prospects and the strong idea of ...♘b6-c4) 20...♘c6! (winning material—the horrible crush that follows is worth looking at as an object lesson!) 21 ♖xc6 ♕xc6 22 ♕d2 b4 23 ♗g4 ♖c7 24 ♕d3 a5 25 ♘xa5 ♕c5 26 ♘b3 ♕xf2 27 ♕e2 ♕a7 28 ♖d5 ♖c6 29 ♕d1 ♖a6 30 ♘c1 ♖a8 31 a3 bxa3 32 b3 a2+ 33 ♔a1 ♕e3 34 ♖d3 ♕xe4 35 ♗f3 ♕b4 36 c3 e4! (the revitalized and unopposed dark-squared bishop supplies the coup de grâce) 0-1 S.Ganguly-Bu Xiangzhi, Internet (blitz) 2006.

b2) 12 ♕xd6 ♕xf2 13 ♘c5 ♗e7! 14 ♕xe7 ♘c6 15 ♕d6 (or 15 ♕xb7 ♕xc5 and Black has compensation for the pawn, with typical Sicilian attacking chances) 15...♖fd8 16 ♕c7 ♕xc5 and Black recovered his piece with a slight advantage, due to his superiority on the dark squares, and finally won in H.Mas-L.Pantsulaia, Dubai 2008.

In short, I already didn't like my position, and I could have been in real trouble if...

10...♗e6 11 ♘d5

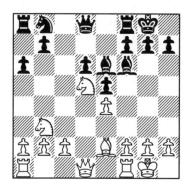

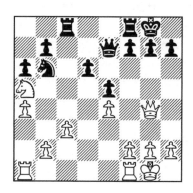

11...♘d7

Black had played 11...♗g5! here, preserving his two bishops. Let's see Gligoric give us a lesson (from 1962!) on how to handle the Black position: 12 ♕d3 ♘c6 13 c3 ♘e7 14 ♘xe7+ ♗xe7 15 ♖fd1 ♕b6 16 ♕c2 ♖ad8 17 ♗f3 ♔h8 18 c4 ♖c8 19 ♘d2 ♕c5 20 b3 ♗d8! (Black has kept one defender of d5 and activates his unopposed bishop) 21 ♕d3 ♗b6 22 ♕e2 ♕a5 23 ♘f1 ♗d4 (that's really activated!) 24 ♖ac1 b5 25 cxb5 axb5 26 ♘e3 ♖c5 27 ♘d5 ♗xd5 28 ♖xc5 dxc5 29 exd5 f5 30 ♕d2 ♕xd2 31 ♖xd2 e4 32 ♗e2 e3 33 ♖c2 exf2+ 34 ♔f1 b4 35 ♗f3 g5 36 h3 ♖f6 37 ♖e2 ♖a6 38 ♗h5 c4! (decisive, as White can't play 39 bxc4 b3!) 39 d6 c3 40 d7 ♖d6 0-1 E.Cobo Arteaga-S.Gligoric, Havana 1962.

12 a4 ♖c8 13 c3 ♘b6

The alternative 13...♗g5 still favours Black—realizing that, I decided not to tempt fate anymore and chopped it off!

14 ♘xf6+ ♕xf6 15 ♘a5 ♕e7 16 ♗g4 ♗xg4 17 ♕xg4

17...d5!?

A risky "freeing" move that also opens the h1-a8 diagonal for White. Simpler is 17...♖c5 18 ♘b3 ♖c7 with solid equality, as Black should always have counterplay with ...♘c4, while the white knight is a long way from d5.

18 ♖fd1! ♖cd8 19 exd5 ♘xd5 20 ♕c4?!

20 ♕e4! with an X-ray attack is best, when Black has a difficult game, though it seems he might equalize with a number of *Fritz* moves: 20...♘f4 (not 20...♘f6 21 ♕xb7 ♕xb7 22 ♘xb7 ♖b8 23 ♘c5 and White stays a pawn up in the endgame) 21 ♕xb7 ♕g5 22 ♕f3 and Black is struggling to show he has enough for the pawn—although he might succeed with the computer's recommendation of 22...♖de8, the burden of proof is still on Black.

20...♘f4 21 g3

21 ♕e4? is too late due to 21...♕c7 22 ♘xb7 f5, winning the knight.

21...♕g5 22 ♘xb7?!

White should run for the draw with 22 ♖xd8 ♖xd8 23 ♘xb7 ♕g4 24 ♕xa6 ♘h3+ 25 ♔g2 ♘f4+ etc.

22...♕g4 23 ♕f1

23...♖b8

Now Black misses his chance! The white king must be forced to g2 to make the X-ray attack on b2 effective: 23...♘h3+ 24 ♔g2 (obviously not 24 ♔h1?? ♕f3+ 25 ♕g2 ♖xd1+ etc) 24...♖b8 and White is in big trouble; e.g. 25 ♘c5 (or 25 f3 ♕c8 26 ♘d6 ♖xb2+ with a strong attack) 25...e4! 26 b4 (26 ♖e1 isn't much better: 26...♖xb2 27 ♖xe4 ♕f5 and Black's attack is too strong) 26...♕f3+ 27 ♔xh3 ♖b6 and White must give up his queen to avoid mate.

24 f3!

The only move, but good enough—the game now devolves to a draw.

24...♕g6

24...♘h3+ 25 ♔h1 ♕c8 26 ♘d6 doesn't work for Black here, as b2 doesn't fall with check.

25 ♖d6 ♕c2 26 gxf4 ♖xb7 27 ♕f2 ♕xf2+ 28 ♔xf2 ♖xb2+ 29 ♔g3 exf4+ 30 ♔xf4 g6 31 ♖xa6 ♖c8 32 a5 ♖xc3 33 ♖b6 ½-½

The draw is clear in view of the

variation 33...♖f2 34 a6 ♖fxf3+ 35 ♔e4 (not 35 ♔g4?? h5+ and Black mates in nine according to the oracle) 35...♖fe3+ 36 ♔d4 ♖ed3+ 37 ♔e4 ♖e3+ and neither side can play for a win.

I would put this Kramnik attack at the bottom of our five ♗e2 Najdorf lines, as Black can essentially ignore it with 8...0-0, when I don't see an effective continuation for White—giving up the dark-squared bishop so early can be traumatic for White if he doesn't get a direct attack, as the old Gligoric game cited in the notes demonstrates.

Game 16
G.Kasparov-N.De Firmian
New York (rapid) 1995

1 e4 c5 2 ♘f3 d6 3 d4 cxd4 4 ♘xd4 ♘f6 5 ♘c3 a6 6 ♗e2 e5 7 ♘b3 ♗e7 8 0-0 0-0 9 ♔h1

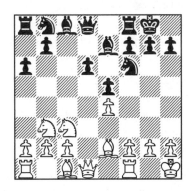

Our fourth try! The main idea of this useful waiting move is to prevent ...b7-b5, as the next note shows. However, it may be too early to lose time with such "sophistication", as Black seems to do well with the quiet 9...b6 (given in the notes) or 9...♘c6 (seen in the next game).

9...♘bd7

Self-blocking and too passive. The seemingly natural 9...b5 is also poor:

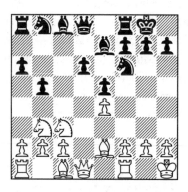

10 a4! b4 11 ♘d5 ♗b7 (11...♘xd5 12 ♕xd5 is obviously good for White; while 11...♘xe4? was drastically punished by 12 ♗f3 f5 13 ♗xe4 fxe4 14 ♘xe7+ ♕xe7 15 ♕d5+ ♕f7 16 ♕xa8— White takes everything that's offered— 16...♗b7 17 ♕a7 e3 18 ♕xe3 ♕g6 19 ♕g3 ♕xc2 20 ♗h6 and Black had nothing for the rook and soon resigned in J.Cuadras Avellana-V.Sara, L'Estartit 2007) 12 ♘xe7+ ♕xe7 13 f3 (White has the two bishops, while Black has ragged pawns and the weakness at d6—but freeing himself also frees the white bishops, as can be seen) 13...d5 14 exd5 ♗xd5 15 ♗g5 ♖d8 16 ♕e1 ♘c6 17 ♕f2 h6 18 ♗e3 ♗xb3 19 cxb3 ♘d4 20 ♗c4 ♘d5 21 ♖ae1 ♘xe3 22 ♖xe3 ♖d6 23 ♖e4 ♘c6 24 f4, when White

opened the game and went on to win in D.Jakovenko-E.Najer, Russian Championship, Krasnoyarsk 2003.

Black does need to cover d5—he can do this with the flexible and good 9...b6, as played by both Anand and his challenger Gelfand (against Anand!): 10 ♗e3 ♗b7 11 f3 b5 (Black did a two-step to get here, but perhaps ♔h1 didn't help White either—the main point is that the d5 weakness is neutralized) 12 a4 b4 13 ♘d5 ♘xd5 14 exd5 (White must take with the pawn, and because he soon has no b-pawn, it's hard to enforce the c4-c5 break) 14...♘d7 15 c4 bxc3 16 bxc3 ♗g5 17 ♗g1 f5 (Gelfand drew easily with 17...♕c7 18 c4 a5 19 ♘d2 f5 20 ♘b1 ♘c5 21 ♘c3 ♖f6 22 ♖b1 ♗a6 23 ♕c2 ½-½ V.Anand-B.Gelfand, Dos Hermanas 1997—as he got nothing with White, the Champion decided to give Black a try!) 18 c4 ♘f6 19 ♖b1 ♘h5 20 g3 f4 (Black uses his kingside pawn majority to create play against the white king and...) 21 g4 ♘f6 22 ♘d2 ♗c8 23 ♗d3 h5 24 h3 ♗h4 25 ♔g2 ♗g3 26 ♗f2 ♗xf2 27 ♖xf2 hxg4 28 hxg4 ♘xg4 (sacrifices a piece!) 29 fxg4 ♕h4 30 ♘f3 ♕g3+ 31 ♔f1 e4 32 ♗xe4 ♗xg4 33 ♕d3 ♗h3+ 34 ♔e2 ♖ae8 35 ♖g1 ♗f5 (plus a queen!) 36 ♖xg3 fxg3 37 ♘d2 gxf2 38 ♔f1 ♗xe4 39 ♘xe4 ♖f4 40 ♘xf2 ♖ef8 41 ♔e1 ♖xf2 42 ♕g6 ♖2f6 43 ♕g4 ♖f1+ 44 ♔e2 ♖1f2+ 45 ♔e1 ♖8f6 46 ♕c8+ ♔h7 47 ♕xa6 ♖a2 48 c5 ♖h6 49 ♕d3+ ♔g8 50 ♕e4 ♖h1+ (and a rook to finish the game!) 51 ♕xh1 ♖a1+ 52 ♔d2

Rxh1 53 c6 ⌖f7 0-1 M.Adams-V.Anand, Bastia (rapid) 2005. A brilliant win against a great player!

10 a4 b6 11 f3 ⌗b7 12 ⌗e3

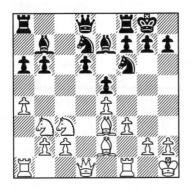

Now White has a stable advantage, where Black has got in neither ...b7-b5 nor ...d6-d5, and Kasparov commences to grind like Karpov!

12...⌗c7

13 ⌗f2

A typical manoeuvre: White doubles on the d-file with the rook in front, so d6 is fixed as a weakness.

13...⌗ad8 14 ⌗f1 ⌗c5 15 ⌗d2 h6

After 15...⌗xb3 16 cxb3 ⌗c8 (or 16...d5 17 exd5 ⌗b4 18 ⌗c1 and Black

doesn't have enough for the pawn) 17 ⌗c1 ⌗d8 18 ⌗c4 White has activated his light-squared bishop while tightening his grip on d5.

16 ⌗xc5 dxc5 17 ⌗c4

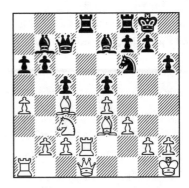

White trades old advantages for new: now it looks like a Rauzer Ruy, with what Fischer used to describe as a "gaping" hole at d5.

17...⌗h5 18 ⌗d5 ⌗xd5 19 ⌗xd5 ⌗g5 20 ⌗g1 ⌗f4 21 ⌗xd8 ⌗xd8 22 ⌗e1 a5 23 ⌗d1 ⌗f8 24 ⌗f2 ⌗d6 25 h4 ⌗e7 26 ⌗xd6 ⌗xd6 27 g3 ⌗e6 28 c3 g5 29 h5

Obviously White has a clear plus, but I don't think the following pawn sac helps Black, as he will always have to watch for a g4-g5 break. Trying to hold on grimly with 29...⌗g7 is better.

29...g4?! 30 fxg4 ⌗g5 31 ⌗g2 ⌗e7 32 ⌗e2 ⌗d2 33 ⌗xd2 ⌗xd2 34 ⌗xe6 ⌗xe6 35 ⌗f3 ⌗d6 36 ⌗e2 ⌗c1 37 ⌗d3 ⌗c6

White wins after 37...⌗xb2 38 ⌗e3 ⌗c6 39 ⌗c4 ⌗d6 40 ⌗b3 ⌗a1 41 ⌗xh6.

38 ⌗e1 ⌗g5 39 ⌗c4 ⌗e3 40 b4 cxb4 41 cxb4 axb4 42 ⌗xb4 ⌗c1 43 ⌗f8 ⌗g5 44 ⌗g7 f6

Black's bishop can only defend pawns on the same colour squares—but with all his pawns on the same colour squares as his bishop, the pawns are indefensible! A lot of players have problems with this paradox!

45 ♗h8 ♔d6 46 ♔b5 ♔c7 47 ♗g7 ♔b7 48 ♗f8 ♔c7 49 ♗e7 ♔d7 50 ♗b4

50...♗e3

Black can only delay the following break: 50...♔c7 51 ♗e1 ♗e3 52 g5! (there it is!) 52...fxg5 (both 52...hxg5 53 h6 and 52...♗xg5 53 ♗f2 win easily for White) 53 g4 ♔d7 54 ♗b4 ♔e8 (or 54...♔e6 55 ♗f8 ♔f7 56 ♗xh6 ♔g8 57 ♔c4 ♔f7 58 ♔d5 ♗f4 59 ♔d6 ♔g8 60 ♔e6 ♔h7 61 ♗f8 and the bishop escapes with an easy win for White) 55 ♗c3 and the pawns begin to drop.

51 g5! fxg5

Again Black has no good choice, as 51...hxg5 52 h6 and 51...♗xg5 52 ♔xb6 both lose quickly.

52 g4 ♔e6 53 ♔c6 ♗d4 54 ♗d6 1-0

A final demonstration that the bishop is unable to defend the pawns on its own colour!

Clearly the self-blocking 9...♘bd7 was a mistake, but 9...b6 (Gelfand/Anand) looks quite reasonable for Black.

In the next game my opponent tries an even simpler move: 9...♘c6.

Game 17
T.Taylor-R.Yankovsky
4th Metropolitan Invitational,
Los Angeles 2011

1 e4 c5 2 ♘f3 d6 3 d4 cxd4 4 ♘xd4 ♘f6 5 ♘c3 a6 6 ♗e2 e5 7 ♘b3 ♗e7 8 0-0 0-0 9 ♔h1 ♘c6

In my view this is Black's simplest move: while White is making profound manoeuvres, Black just develops a piece to a good square! Meanwhile the queen's bishop may still come effectively to either of its regulation spots, e6 or b7. Note that the latter is preferred if White impetuously goes f2-f4, leaving the e-pawn unsupported. I've said this before, but it's worth repeating: generally speaking, f2-f4 is best when the black bishop *is already committed to e6* and thus can't attack e4.

10 ♗e3

What not to play can be seen here, as Black gets good counterplay: 10 f4 (premature, as the black bishop can still go to b7—Carlsen doesn't have his move order worked out yet, but just wait for Game 18!) 10...b5 (correct, of course, to aim the Laufer at e4, which can nevermore be protected by a pawn) 11 ♗e3 ♗b7 12 a4 exf4 13 ♖xf4 ♘e5 14 ♕d4 ♘c6 15 ♕d2 ♘e5 16 ♕d4 ♘c6 17 ♕d2 ♘e5 18 axb5 (Carlsen avoids the short draw but his courage is not rewarded as, objectively, White—if he plays on—is slightly worse in view of the weakness of his e-pawn) 18...axb5 19 ♖e1 (19 ♖xa8 ♕xa8 adds more pressure to the weak e4-pawn) 19...♘g6 20 ♖ff1 b4 21 ♘d5 ♘xe4 22 ♘xe7+ ♕xe7 23 ♕xb4 ♘h4 24 ♗f3 ♘xf3 (Black's central and kingside play is worth more than White's unmoved, if passed, b-pawn) 25 gxf3 ♕d7 26 ♗f4 (not 26 fxe4? ♖a4 and wins) ♖a4 27 ♕b6 ♘f6 28 ♕xd6 ♕g4! (Carlsen is on the wrong side of this mess!) 29 ♘d4 ♖xd4 30 ♕xd4 ♗xf3+ 31 ♖xf3 ♕xf3+ 32 ♔g1 ♕g4+ 33 ♔h1 ♕c8 34 ♕f2 ♕b7+ 35 ♔g1 ♘e4 36 ♕d4 ♖e8 37 ♖e2 h6 38 h3 ♖e6 39 ♔h2 f5 40 b4 ♔h7 41 ♖e3 ♖g6 42 ♖e2 ♕b5 43 ♖e1 ♖c6 44 ♖xe4 fxe4 45 ♕xe4+ ♖g6 46 ♗g3 ♕d7 47 h4 h5 48 c4 ♕d2+ 49 ♔h3 ♕c3 50 ♕f4 ♕xb4 51 ♕f5 ♕xc4 52 ♕xh5+ ♖h6 53 ♕f3 ♕e6+ 54 ♔h2 ♖f6 55 ♕d3+ ♔f5 56 ♕c2 ♕d5 57 ♗f2 ♔h6 58 ♗e3+ ♔g6 59 ♗f2 ♔f6

60 ♗g3 ♖f1 61 ♗f2 ♖d1 62 ♕c3+ ♕e5+ 63 ♕xe5+ ♔xe5 64 h5 ♔f6 65 ♗h4+ ♔f5 66 ♗e7 ♖d7 0-1 M.Carlsen-I.Nepomniachtchi, Wijk aan Zee 2011.

10...♗e6 11 f3

11 f4 is of course playable with the bishop on e6, but the women's world champion uses Timman's method from Game 1 to defuse this: 11...exf4 12 ♗xf4 d5 13 exd5 (or 13 e5 ♘e4 14 ♗d3 ♘c5 with equality—a theme we've seen before) 13...♘xd5 14 ♘xd5 ♕xd5 15 ♗f3 ♕c4 16 ♗e2 ♕d5 17 ♗f3 ♕xd1 18 ♖fxd1 ♖ac8 19 c3 ♖fd8 20 ♗e3 b5 21 ♖xd8+ ♘xd8 22 ♘d4 ♗c5 23 ♘xe6 ♗xe3 24 ♘xd8 ♖xd8 25 ♖d1 ♖xd1+ 26 ♗xd1 ♔f8 27 a4 ♗c1 28 axb5 axb5 29 b3 ♗d2 30 ♗e2 (White wanted a draw and got it) ½-½ A.Entem-Hou Yifan, St Lorrain 2005. The only problem with this line for either side is how drawish it is (see the next note for more practical problems).

11...♘a5

My opponent needed a win to have a chance for the IM norm, so he kept the pieces on—but now White gets a

Geller-style edge. Correct is 11...d5, when Kramnik could find nothing for White. As we have seen, sometimes the ...d6-d5 break is good, sometimes not... all depends on the precise position. Here Black is well placed, while White's f2-f3 and ♔h1 have not accomplished much: 12 exd5 ♘xd5 13 ♘xd5 ♗xd5 14 c3 (White should not try to win a pawn: 14 c4 ♗e6 15 ♘c5 ♗f5 16 ♘xb7 ♕c7 17 ♘c5 ♕a7 is much better for Black due to the pin) 14...♖c8 15 ♕e1 ♘a5 16 ♖d1 ♘xb3 17 axb3 ♕a5 18 ♕g3 ♗e6 19 b4 ♕a2 20 ♗c1 ♗f6 ½-½ V.Kramnik-F.Vallejo Pons, Linares 2004.

12 ♘d5 ♗xd5

Relatively better is 12...♘xd5 13 exd5 ♘xb3 14 axb3 ♗d7 15 ♕d2 f5 16 ♗d3, when White has a slight plus with the plan c2-c4/b3-b4 and c4-c5, whereas Black can't make much of his pawn majority. Nevertheless, the similar position reached in the game should favour White more, due to the two bishops.

13 exd5 ♕c7 14 ♘xa5 ♕xa5 15 c4

I have switched to Geller's plan: the

bishop pair and the sound majority give White a clear advantage.

15...♘d7 16 b4?

Impetuous! There was no need to rush; the advantage wasn't going to vanish! Correct is simply to prepare this advance with 16 a3, when after 16...h6 17 b4 ♕c7 18 ♕d2 White has the kind of position Geller used to win in his sleep!

16...♕xb4 17 ♖b1 ♕a3 18 ♖b3 ♕xa2 19 ♖xb7 ♖fd8 20 ♗d3 ♗f6 21 ♖f2 ♕a3 22 ♖b3 ♕a5 23 ♕b1 ♖db8

After 23...g6 24 ♖a2 ♕c7 25 ♖b7 White has good compensation with Black's pieces tied up—but Yankovsky's actual move just gives back the pawn and equalizes.

24 ♗xh7+ ♔f8 25 ♖a2 ♖xb3 26 ♖xa5 ♖xb1+ 27 ♗xb1 ♗d8 28 ♖a3 ♗b6 29 ♗f5 ♗xe3 30 ♗xd7 ♗c5 31 ♖a2 a5 32 g3

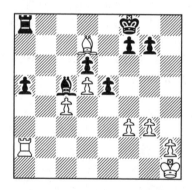

The tactics are over and a dead-equal ending has been reached. Now Black tried to win this unpromising position!

32...♗b4 33 ♔g2 ♔e7 34 ♗c6 ♖h8 35

h4 f5 36 ♖e2 ♔f6 37 ♗d7 ♖a8 38 ♗a4
♖c8 39 ♗c6 ♖c7 40 g4 g6 41 ♔h3 ♖h7
42 ♗b5 ♗c5 43 ♗a4 ♗a3 44 ♖a2 ♗b4
45 ♖e2 ♖c7 46 ♗c6 ♖e7 47 ♔g3 ♔g7 48
♗a4 ♖c7 49 ♗c6 ♖c8 50 ♗b5 ♖f8 51
♗d7 fxg4 52 fxg4 ♖f1 53 ♔g2 ♖f4 54
♖c2 ♔f6 55 ♖f2 ♗e1 56 ♖xf4+ exf4 57
♔f3 ♔e5

57...♗xh4 is the deadest of draws;
e.g. 58 ♔xf4 ♗f2 59 ♔e4 ♔e7 60 ♗b5
♔d8 61 ♔d3 ♔c7 62 ♔c2 ♔b6 63 ♔b3
♔c5 64 ♗a4 ♗e1 and absolutely nothing is happening for either side.

**58 h5 g5 59 h6 ♔f6 60 ♗e8 ♗b4 61
♔e4 ♗c5 62 ♔f3 ♔e7 63 ♗a4 ♗d4 64
♔e4 ♗h8 65 ♗d1 ♔f6 66 ♗b3 ♔g6 67
♗d1 ♗f6**

67...♗xh6 68 ♔f5 ♗d4 69 ♔e6 ♗c5
70 ♔f6 ♗a3 71 ♔f7 ♗b4 72 ♔f6 is another draw.

68 h7!

White sacrifices the outside pawn
to infiltrate with his king. Black must
carefully play for a draw now—
something he doesn't want!

68...♔xh7 69 ♔f5 ♗e7

Black has to go for 69...♗d4! (re-

straining the c4-c5 break), when after
70 ♔xg5 ♔g7 71 ♔xf4 ♗c5 Black
reaches a pawn down but clearly
drawn opposite bishop ending.

70 ♔e6 ♗f8 71 c5!!

Just like that, White is winning, as
the d-pawn will cost Black a piece, and
the bishop on d1 splendidly copes with
both opposing passed pawns. Note that
the anti-Najdorf white king's bishop
won the ending from d1 in Games 12
and 13 as well—must be a magic
square!

**71...dxc5 72 d6 ♗xd6 73 ♔xd6 c4 74
♔c5 c3 75 ♔c4 ♔g7 76 ♔xc3 ♔f6 77
♔d4! ♔e6 78 ♔e4 ♔d6 79 ♔f5 ♔d5 80
♔xg5 ♔e4 81 ♔h4! 1-0**

My opponent took a long time cal-
culating all the variations, then resigned as there is no salvation:

a) 81...♔e5 82 g5 f3 (or 82...♔f5 83
♔h5) 83 ♗xf3 a4 84 ♗d1 a3 85 ♗b3
and Black's only hope is stopped.

b) 81...♔d3 82 g5 ♔d2 83 g6! ♔xd1
84 g7 f3 85 ♔g3 a4 (or 85...♔e2 86 g8♕
f2 87 ♕e6+ ♔f1 88 ♕e3 and mates) 86
♔xf3 a3 87 g8♕ and the a-pawn is
stopped on the sixth rank.

c) 81...♔e3 82 g5 f3 83 ♗xf3! a4 (or
83...♔xf3 84 g6 a4 85 g7 a3 86 g8♕ and
one sees again that White queens on
the perfect square) 84 ♗d5 and the a-
pawn is stopped again.

d) 81...f3 82 ♔g3 f2 83 ♗xf2 ♔f4 84
♔e1! a4 85 ♔d2 and the white king is
in the square of Black's pawn.

What a great bishop on d1!

I think that 9 ♔h1 is just too fancy for practical play: one can get carried away trying not to give your opponent information. Sometimes it's better just to make good moves!

Now let's proceed to the fifth, final, freshest and finest of the ♗e2 anti-Najdorf lines.

Game 18
M.Carlsen-H.Nakamura
Wijk aan Zee 2011

1 e4 c5 2 ♘f3 d6 3 d4 cxd4 4 ♘xd4 ♘f6 5 ♘c3 a6 6 ♗e2 e5 7 ♘b3 ♗e7 8 ♗e3!!

I've tested the other moves, and I've analyzed the other moves, and I've come to the conclusion that this move, 8 ♗e3, and this plan (deferring castling so that 0-0-0 is still possible) is *best* in this position, and indeed critical for the whole 6 ♗e2 line. Black either castles into an attack, or puts his bishop on e6 where it won't be able to pressure e4 from b7 and so allows a Karpovian f2-f4. Whatever Black does, White can

play for an advantage.

First let's see two games where Black makes the natural move and castles here... which is a mistake!

8...0-0

Most likely 8...♗e6 is best, which will be covered in the last two games of this chapter. The advantage White can get there is the typical Karpovian grind—*Fritz* +0.09!—which is fine if you're patient and creative, as we already discussed in Game 9. The weaker alternatives 8...♘c6 and 8...b5 will be covered in the notes to the following game, and they will also score badly on our *Fritz*ometer—but what of the game move? What could be more natural for a 2700 player than just to castle into safety?

9 g4!

Uh oh! Somehow I think Carlsen just defenestrated "safety"! Since White can still go long, he takes the opportunity to launch a savage attack!

9...♗e6

If Black tries to hold up the g4-g5 advance with ...h7-h6, he creates a potential lever so that White can, a bit later, open lines even more forcefully! There are only five games in the database with 9...h6—and White won all five! Here's a drastic example: 10 h4 ♗e6 11 g5 hxg5 12 hxg5 ♘h7 13 ♗xa6! (snapping off the Najdorf a-pawn, sac'ing a piece, and clearing a diagonal for the white queen—one can't ask more from one move!) 12...♘xg5 (if 13...♘xa6 then 14 ♕h5 crushes) 14 ♗xb7 and White was winning in the game E.Rodriguez Guerrero-D.Gomez Anadon, Spanish Junior Championship 2002.

Therefore Black has to allow the following bayonet attack, which gains great space on the kingside, and simply hope to survive.

10 g5

Black only has two choices: here Nakamura tries to activate the knight on b6 via d7, while in the next game we'll see the more defensive 10...♘e8.

10...♘fd7

White must formulate a plan of attack. Black, following Steinitz, has not moved any of his three king-protecting pawns, so there are no obvious levers. How can White break through? To borrow an old quote: "Who can storm fortresses better than Philip of Macedon? Tal!"

It's important to know middlegame motifs as well as opening strategy. Tal figured out a way, in his own battles against the Sicilian, to break down exactly this kind of formation—by means

of a pawn fork on g6! Black will then be forced either to capture (thus creating a protrusion in the straight line of pawns—at g6—against which White can lever open a file), or do nothing and allow White to take the f- or h-pawn, opening a file anyway!

Here are three Tal games where Black tries all three defences, and is dismantled in three ways!

After the opening moves 1 e4 c5 2 ♘f3 ♘c6 3 d4 cxd4 4 ♘xd4 ♘f6 5 ♘c3 d6 6 ♗g5 e6 7 ♕d2 ♗e7 8 0-0-0 0-0 9 ♘b3 ♕b6 10 f3 a6 11 g4 ♖d8 12 ♗e3 ♕c7 13 h4 b5 14 g5 ♘d7, the critical position is reached, and now: 15 g6!!— Tal's patented blow!

Let's take a look at all three defensive tries, but note that, no matter what, Tal opens lines:

a) 15...hxg6 16 h5! gxh5 17 ♖xh5 ♘f6 18 ♖h1 d5 19 e5 ♘xe5 20 ♗f4 ♗d6 21 ♕h2 ♔f8 22 ♕h8+ ♘g8 23 ♖h7 f5 24 ♗h6 ♖d7 25 ♗xb5!! (what a picture!— Tal has sac'ed both bishops, but the rule is, as he liked to point out, that his opponent could take only one piece at a time!) 25...♖f7 26 ♖g1 ♖a7 27 ♘d4 ♘g4 28 fxg4 ♗e5 29 ♘c6 ♗xc3 30 ♗e3 d4 31 ♖gh1 (the h-file is the attacking highway—if now 31...axb5? then 32 ♕xg8+ and mates) ♖d7 32 ♗g5 axb5 33 ♖1h6 d3 34 bxc3 d2+ 35 ♔d1 ♕xc6 36 ♖f6+! ♖f7 37 ♕xg7+ (White has swept aside all defenders) 1-0 M.Tal-A.Koblencs, Riga 1957.

b) 15...fxg6 16 h5 gxh5 17 ♖xh5 ♘f6 18 ♖g5 ♘e5 19 ♕g2 ♗f8 20 ♗e2 ♘c4 21 ♗xc4 bxc4 22 ♘d4 ♖b8 23 ♖h1 (White has two open files to work with) 23...♖b7 24 ♖h6 ♔f7 25 ♖h4 ♕b6 26 ♘d1 ♕c7 27 f4 h6 28 ♖g6 ♖e8 29 f5 e5 30 ♘c3!! (winning: White threatens ♖xf6+ and ♘d5, so Black avoids that—and is killed by a different knight!) 30...♕d8 31 ♘c6 1-0 M.Tal-D.Mohrlok, Varna Olympiad 1962.

c) 15...♘c5 16 gxf7+ ♔xf7 17 ♗h3 (aware that his weak king position will not hold up in the long run, Black launches a wild attack and soon sacrifices material) 17...♘a4 18 f4 ♘b4 19 f5 e5 20 ♘xa4 ♘xa2+ 21 ♔b1 bxa4 22 ♘a5 ♖b8 23 ♕d5+ ♔f8 24 ♔xa2 ♕xc2 25 ♖d2 ♖xb2+ 26 ♔a1! (but Tal, showing his mastery of all phases of the game, calmly sidesteps the attack and, on his next move, forces the exchange of queens when his material advantage will tell) 26...♕c3 27 ♕d3 1-0 M.Tal-G.Stoltz, telegraph game 1959.

Wonderful games! And it's clear from the course of his present victory that Carlsen was well aware of his Great Predecessor!

11 h4

Another kingside crush went 11 ♕d2 ♘c6 12 ♖g1 ♖e8 13 ♘d5 ♗f8 14 0-0-0 b5 15 ♔b1 ♖b8 16 h4 a5 17 h5 a4 18 ♘c1 ♘a5 19 a3 ♘c4 20 ♗xc4 bxc4 21 ♘a2 f5 22 exf5 ♗xf5 23 ♘ab4 ♕c8 24 g6! (White crashes through with Tal's thematic blow) 24...♘f6 25 ♘xf6+ gxf6 26 ♗h6 c3 27 ♕d5+ ♗e6 28 gxh7+ ♔h8 29 ♕f3 ♗f5 30 ♖g8+ ♔xh7 31 ♖xf8 ♖xf8 32 ♗xf8 ♕e6 33 ♕xc3 ♖xf8 34 ♕c7+ ♖f7 35 ♕xd6 ♕xd6 36 ♖xd6 ♔h6 37 ♘d5 ♔g5 38 ♔c1 ♖h7 39 ♖xf6 ♖xh5 40 ♖f8 ♖h1+ 41 ♔d2 ♖h2 42 ♖g8+ ♔h6 43 ♔e2 ♗xc2 44 ♖h8+ ♗h7 45 ♘f6 ♔g7 46 ♖xh7+ ♖xh7 47 ♘xh7 ♔xh7 48 ♔e3 1-0 A.Kosten-K.Zolnierowicz, Aix-les-Bains 1991.

11...♘b6

My feeling is that Black absolutely *must* mix it up right now with 11...a5, before White castles and sets up to attack. White won the following confusing game, but Black certainly had his chances; in my opinion if Black wishes to continue to "castle into it" on move 8, then this position will be the critical battleground: 12 f4!? (White might do well to switch to positional play with 12 a4, exploiting Black's weak b5-square—I think White has the edge here, and we'll see Timoshenko win a similar position in the notes to the next game) 12...exf4 13 ♗xf4 (it's clear that Black is in the game here, and then in a few moves is outplayed in the complications—I recommend 13...a4! 14 ♘d4 ♘c6 with unclear mayhem: at least with the advanced a-pawn, castling queenside for White will always be risky) 13...♘e5 14 ♘d4 ♘bc6 15 ♘db5 f5 16 ♘d5 fxe4 17 ♘bc7 ♗xd5 18 ♕xd5+ ♔h8 19 ♘e6 ♕b6 20 ♘xf8 ♖xf8 21 ♗xe5 ♕f2+ 22 ♔d1 dxe5 23 ♖f1 ♕b6 24 ♖xf8+ ♗xf8 25 ♕f7 ♕d8+ 26 ♔e1 ♘d4 27 ♔f1 ♕c8 28 ♗g4! (White now controls the tactics and wins) 28...♕c5 29 c3 ♘f3 30 ♗xf3 exf3 31 ♖d1 ♕c8 32 ♕xf3 ♗c5 33 ♔g2 ♗e3 34 ♖d7 h6 35 g6 h5 36 ♖xg7 ♕g4+ 37 ♕xg4 hxg4 38 ♖xb7 1-0 A.Delchev-A.Colovic, Subotica 2003.

12 ♕d2 ♘8d7 13 f4!

Carlsen opens every line in sight! Yes, Black gets a nice knight on e5, but the open f-file will be seen to carry more weight in the ensuing battle.

13...exf4 14 ♗xf4 ♘e5 15 0-0-0 ♖c8

15...♘ec4 gets nowhere after 16 ♕d4.

16 ♔b1 ♕c7 17 h5

White has a tremendous attacking position: both g5-g6 and sometimes h5-h6 are threatened.

17...♖fe8

Or 17...♘ec4 18 ♗xc4 ♘xc4 19 ♕d3 ♘a3+ 20 ♔c1 ♘b5 (White doesn't mind the queen exchange here, as after 20...♕c4 21 ♘d4 ♕xd3 22 ♖xd3 ♘c4 23 ♘f5 he will get the two bishops and has a target at d6—note that White must be flexible: it's fun to win with attack, but a positional grind can result in that same full point!) 21 ♘xb5 axb5 22 h6! (less usual, but correct here; not 22 g6? fxg6 and the f4-bishop is loose) 22...g6 23 ♔b1 and the weaknesses at b5 and d6 tell, not to mention g7!

18 ♔a1 ♗f8 19 ♘d4 ♕c5 20 g6!

Channelling Tal! White sacrifices a pawn, and three kingside files open.

20...♘ec4

If the pawn is accepted, then 20...fxg6 21 hxg6 ♘xg6 22 ♘xe6 ♖xe6 23 ♗e3 ♘c4 24 ♗g4!! (this works because of 18 ♔a1!—the white queen does not go with check, but the black rook does) 24...♖ee8 25 ♕h2!, leaving the e3-bishop en prise with a winning attack—you would swear this was a Tal game.

21 ♗xc4 ♘xc4 22 ♕d3 fxg6 23 hxg6 h6

If 23...hxg6, then 24 ♘xe6 ♖xe6 25 ♕h3 and the black king will not survive.

24 ♕g3 ♕b6 25 ♗c1 ♕a5 26 ♖df1 ♘e5 27 ♘d5!

Meeting the threat of ...♖xc3 and launching the final attack.

27...♗xd5 28 exd5 ♕xd5 29 ♗xh6!! gxh6

29...♕xd4 allows a Yandemirov-style h-file mating attack: 30 ♗e3 ♕c4 31 ♖h8+! ♔xh8 32 ♕h3+ ♔g8 33 ♕h7 mate.

30 g7!

The point of 9 g4!—Black could resign.

30...♗e7

There is no defence: 30...♗xg7 31 ♘f5 ♖c7 32 ♘xh6+ ♔h7 33 ♘g4+ ♔g8 (or 33...♔g6 34 ♘xe5 with a beautiful mate) 34 ♘f6+ wins the queen with check!

31 ♖xh6 ♘f7 32 ♕g6 ♘xh6 33 ♕xh6 ♗f6 34 ♕h8+ ♔f7 35 g8♕+ ♖xg8 36 ♕xf6+ ♔e8 37 ♖e1+ 1-0

After the only move, 37...♕e5, White finishes by 38 ♖xe5+ dxe5 39 ♕e6+ and

Black will wind up with a single rook against White's queen and knight.

A spectacular win by Carlsen! The only serious improvement I can see for Black (after 9 g4!) is 11...a5, which makes some positional concessions in order to obtain very necessary counterplay.

1 e4 c5 2 ♘f3 d6 3 d4 cxd4 4 ♘xd4 ♘f6 5 ♘c3 a6 6 ♗e2 e5 7 ♘b3 ♗e7 8 ♗e3

8...0-0

Just what I hoped for, though I didn't expect to get it a few months after Carlsen's celebrated victory—but my opponent usually plays the French! I think this move is only playable if Black has worked out a serious counter-attacking system—at home—against the Carlsen attack.

Other moves are:

a) 8...♘c6 (doubtful) 9 ♘d5 (Geller-style—and even stronger here, as White targets the Najdorf hole at b6) 9...0-0 (of course 9...♘xe4 loses at once to 10 ♗b6) 10 ♗b6 ♕d7 11 ♕d3 ♘xd5 12 exd5 ♘b8 13 ♘a5 ♕e8 14 ♘c4 ♗d7 and now, instead of the absurd 15 ♘a5 ♗c8 16 ♘c4 with a GM draw in E.Bacrot-I.Nepomniachtchi, Wijk aan Zee 2008, White gets a clear advantage after 15 ♗e3 ♗b5 16 a4 ♗xc4 17 ♕xc4 with Geller's thematic two bishops and queenside majority.

b) 8...b5 was played against me, and while this looks like a normal Najdorf move, I sensed there was something wrong about it—and it didn't take me long at the board to figure out why. I knew the Kasparov variation (recall Game 16) 1 e5 c5 2 ♘f3 d6 3 d4 cxd4 4 ♘xd4 ♘f6 5 ♘c3 a6 6 ♗e2 e5 7 ♘b3 ♗e7 8 0-0 0-0 9 ♔h1, when the natural 9...b5 was bad due to 10 a4!. Now in the game position Black has not castled, and White has made the useful ♗e3—so obviously 9 a4!.

After my win, I checked this out in the *Mega* and found White scores 90% (nine wins out of just ten games). This is why I stress learning all lines of an opening, not just a narrow repertoire—those sidelines might help you out! After this powerful positional blow Black has only two serious replies, and neither solves his problems:

b1) 9...bxa4 (my opponent's choice, but this weakens his pawn structure) 10 ♖xa4 ♘bd7 11 ♘d5 ♗b7 12 ♘xe7 ♕xe7 13 f3 ♘c5 (this leaves Black with seriously weak pawns at a6 and c5, but if Black tries to break out with 13...d5 White has 14 ♘a5! d4 15 ♘xb7 dxe3 16 ♘d6+ ♔f8 17 ♘f5 ♕c5 18 ♕c1 g6 19 ♘xe3 ♔g7 20 0-0 ♕b6 21 ♔h1 ♖hb8 22 ♘c4 and consolidates his extra pawn; while 14...♘f8 is met by 15 c3! dxe4 16 ♗c5! with a winning attack, or 15...♖d8 16 ♘xb7 ♕xb7 17 ♖b4 ♕a8 18 ♕a4+ ♘8d7 19 0-0, when White has a decisive positional advantage and will soon take material) 14 ♘xc5 dxc5 15 ♕a1 ♕d6 (if 15...0-0 then 16 0-0! ♘h5 17 g3 ♖ac8 18 b3 and one of Black's weak pawns will fall, similar to the game; but not the premature 16 ♗xa6?! which can lead to trouble: 16...♘xe4! 17 ♗xb7 ♕xb7 18 fxe4 ♖xa4 19 ♕xa4 ♖a8 and it's Black who wins!) 16 0-0 0-0 17 ♖d1 ♕c6 18 b3 ♘d7 19 ♕c3! (emphasizing Black's helplessness—White has the two bishops, targets at a6, c5, e6 and a hole at d5—the finish was simple and instructive...) 19...♖fc8 20 ♕d2 ♘b6 21 ♖a5 c4 22 ♖xe5 cxb3 23 cxb3 h6 24 ♕d4 ♕f6 25 ♖f5! (there are other ways, but this wins more material without complications) 25...♕xd4 26 ♗xd4 ♖c6 27 ♗xb6 ♖xb6 28 ♗c4 ♖f8 29 ♖d7 ♗c8 30 ♖dxf7! ♗xf5 (the best Black can do is 30...♖xf7 31 ♗xf7+ ♔h7 32 ♖e5, but then White is up two good pawns) 31 ♖xf5+ 1-0 T.Taylor-P.Holzer, La Palma 2011.

b2) 9...b4 (this has also been played without success) 10 ♘d5 ♘c6 (relatively better is 10...♘bd7 just giving up a pawn, but after 11 ♘xb4 ♘xe4? 12 ♕d5 or 11...♗b7 12 f3 a5 13 ♘d5 ♘xd5 14 exd5 ♗g5 15 ♗xg5 ♕xg5 16 0-0 ♕e3+ 17 ♔h1 0-0 18 ♗b5 ♘f6 19 ♖e1 ♕b6 20 c4 Black has no compensation) 11 ♗b6 ♕d7 12 ♘c7+ and White won quickly in G.Keschitz-J.Gruz, Budapest 2003.

c) 8...♗e6 seems not only best but necessary, and will be seen in the last two games of this chapter.

9 g4! ♗e6 10 g5

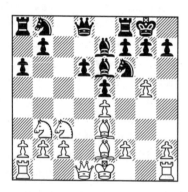

10...♘e8

As we recall, Naka tried 10...♘fd7 without success. I also faced this move in a later game (yes, I was very fortu-nate to get 8...0-0?! twice, when I didn't expect to get it once, and certainly not from a WGM and an IM!), which continued 11 ♕d2 b5 12 ♘d5 ♗xd5 13 exd5 (White already has a clear advantage: the two bishops, square c6, Black can't develop normally—*and* White has the attack—I finally broke through on the kingside and won with a nice rook sacrifice) 13...♘b6 14 ♘a5 ♕c7 15 0-0-0 ♖c8 16 ♗g4 ♖e8 17 ♔b1 ♘c4 18 ♘xc4 bxc4 19 ♕c3 a5 20 h4 ♘d7 21 ♗xd7 ♕xd7 22 ♕xc4 ♖ec8 23 ♕d3 ♖ab8 24 h5 f5 25 f4 e4 26 ♕d2 ♖b5 27 b3 ♗d8 28 ♗d4 a4 29 ♗b2 ♗a5 30 ♕e3 ♕b7 31 h6 ♖xd5 32 ♖xd5 ♕xd5 33 hxg7 axb3 34 axb3 ♕f7 35 ♖xh7! (the white rook destroys the last cover of the black king) 35...♕c7 36 ♖h8+ ♔f7 37 g8♕+! and the black queen goes, so 1-0 T.Taylor-A.Matikozian, Los Angeles 2011.

11 ♕d2 ♘d7

What if Black tries an early ...a6-a5 here? Black attempted this in the following game: 11...♘c7 12 0-0-0 ♘d7 13 h4 a5 14 a4! (White's position is so strong that he takes time out to snuff Black's counterplay...) 14...f5 15 exf5 ♗xf5 16 f4 (and now has the advantage across the board) 16...♔h8 17 ♔b1 ♘a6 18 fxe5 dxe5 19 ♖hf1 ♗h3 20 ♖xf8+ ♗xf8 21 ♗b5 ♘ab8 22 ♕d5 ♘c6 23 ♗c4 (the mate threat is a nice touch—White now takes material and finishes the game professionally) 23...♘e7 24 ♕xb7 ♕c8 25 ♕xc8 ♖xc8 26 ♗b5 ♘b8 27 ♘xa5 ♘f5 28 ♗f2 ♗g2 29 ♘c4 e4 30

♘b6 1-0 G.Timoshenko-E.Valeanu, Galati 2006.

12 0-0-0

The "no waiting" option is also good: 12 f4 g6 13 0-0-0 ♘g7 14 h4 ♖c8 15 ♔b1 f5 16 h5 gxh5 17 ♗xh5 fxe4 18 ♕h2 (White is too fast and...) 18...♖xc3 19 bxc3 ♗f5 20 ♗g4! (too sharp!—much as in Carlsen-Nakamura, White can sac pieces with abandon as all kingside files open to his benefit) 20...♗xg4 21 ♕xh7+ ♔f7 22 ♖df1 ♗f3 23 ♖h6 ♖g8 24 fxe5 ♘xe5 25 ♕xe4 ♔e8 26 ♖xf3 ♘xf3 27 ♕xf3 ♗xg5 28 ♕d5 (devastating!) 1-0 S.Dolmatov-A.Zakharov, Linares Open 2000.

12...b5

After 12...a5 13 a4 only White has play, à la Timoshenko—the more I look at these positions, the more I think Black's natural 8...0-0 must be considered a serious mistake.

13 h4

Another stylish crush occurred after 13 ♔b1 ♕c7 14 h4 ♖c8 15 h5 b4 16 ♘d5 ♗xd5 17 exd5 a5 18 ♗b5 ♖d8 19 g6! (the thematic Tal break) 19...♘df6

20 ♖dg1 ♖b8 21 ♗c6 ♗d8 22 ♗h6!! (and here's the Carlsen sac again, this time on an empty square!) 22...♕e7 (or 22...gxh6 23 ♕xh6 fxg6 24 hxg6 ♘g7 25 ♘c5! dxc5 26 d6! and wins) 23 ♗xe8 ♘xe8 24 ♗xg7 ♘xg7 25 ♕h6 fxg6 26 hxg6 hxg6 27 ♖xg6 ♕f6 (the queen is lost in any case) 28 ♖xf6 ♗xf6 29 ♘xa5 ♖b5 30 ♘c4 ♖xd5 31 ♘e3 ♖d4 32 ♘f5 1-0 A.Glukhov-Ro.Ivanov, Tolyatti 2011.

13...♘b6 14 ♘a5

White can also opt for the Carlsen-style 14 f4 exf4 15 ♗xf4 ♘c4 16 ♗xc4 bxc4 17 ♘d4 ♕d7 18 h5 with a typical attack.

14...♖c8

15 ♔b1

15 a3 is simpler, when Black has no counterplay, but the more complicated pawn sacrifice played here is equally good—if followed up correctly that is!

15...b4 16 ♘d5 ♘xd5 17 exd5 ♕xa5 18 dxe6 fxe6 19 h5?!

The wrong move order! 19 ♗g4, forcing 19...♘c7 20 h5 which transposes to the game, is correct.

19...♘c7?!

Back-to-back errors! I could have been punished for my faux pas by 19...d5! 20 ♗g4 (White doesn't really get through after 20 g6 h6 21 ♗xh6 ♕c5) 20...♖c6 and Black has a more solid defence than in the game, though White still has compensation.

20 ♗g4

Now all's right with the world!

20...♖fe8

Or 20...d5 21 g6 h6 22 f3 d4 23 ♗xh6, as we all know by now.

21 g6!

Let's give Tal credit one more time!

21...♗f8

Again, 21...h6 22 ♗xh6 with a winning attack is White's main idea.

22 gxh7+ ♔h8 23 h6 ♘b5

Black can't keep lines closed: 23...g6 24 ♕d3 ♔xh7 25 ♕e4! (this kills—whereas the impetuous 25 ♗h5 allows a temporary defence with 25...e4) 25...♘d5 26 ♗h5 ♘e7 27 ♗xg6+ ♘xg6 28 ♖dg1 and mates.

24 hxg7+ ♗xg7 25 ♗h6 ♖c7

Black doesn't get a draw after 25...♗f6 26 ♗g5 ♗g7 27 ♗e2! (unwise

is 27 ♖dg1 ♘c3+! with counterplay—this counter-sacrifice is Black's main hope) 27...♘c3+ (White crashes through after 27...♘d4 28 ♗h6 ♗f6 29 ♕d3 ♘xe2 30 ♕g6 ♕d8 31 ♖xd6! and wins by diverting the black queen) 28 bxc3 bxc3 29 ♕xd6 ♖c6 30 ♗d8! and White keeps the extra piece.

26 ♗xe6!?

Sac'ing a piece to lure Black's rooks forward to weaken the back rank, but the cold-blooded 26 ♗e2 ♘c3+ 27 bxc3 bxc3 28 ♗xg7+ ♖xg7 29 ♕c1 ♖b7+ 30 ♔a1 ♖b2 31 ♗c4 seems to win in silicon fashion.

26...♖xe6 27 ♕g5 ♖xh6

Black gives some material back in view of 27...♗xh6 28 ♕g8 mate.

I saw my opponent looking at her aforementioned resource: 27...♘c3+ 28 bxc3 bxc3 and then... 29 ♕xg7+!!—this was the hidden point of my sacrifice: my opponent's face was a picture when she noticed this! White wins after 29...♖xg7 30 ♗xg7+ ♔xg7 31 h8♕+ and mates in four.

28 ♖xh6 ♖f7

28...♖c8!, defending the back rank is necessary, but my opponent, in time trouble, missed my next move. After that correct defence, 29 ♖g6 ♕c7 is close to equal. Nonetheless (as so often) my bold human sacrifice, 26 ♗xe6, led to a quick win, despite mechanical disapproval!

29 ♖e6!

The hits keep coming! Black has no real defence to ♖e8+; e.g. 29...♘c7 30 ♖e7 ♖xe7 31 ♕xe7 ♕b5 32 ♖g1 ♘e8 33 ♕f7 forces mate.

29...♔xh7 30 ♕g6+ ♔g8 31 ♖e8+ ♖f8 32 ♖e7 1-0

Mate is forced.

The play after 8...0-0 9 g4 is great fun for White, horrendously difficult for Black—but what happens if Black does not castle?

Game 20
C.Lutz-M.Womacka
German League 1998

1 e4 c5 2 ♘f3 d6 3 d4 cxd4 4 ♘xd4 ♘f6 5 ♘c3 a6 6 ♗e2 e5 7 ♘b3 ♗e7 8 0-0

The Carlsen move order that I recommend is 8 ♗e3 with the idea 8...0-0 9 g4!. Black's best answer, as I said already, is 8...♗e6! waiting in turn, without prematurely showing White where his king lives. The question arises: can White play 9 g4 here? Unfortunately, Black has an easy Steinitzian counter: 9...d5! 10 g5 (or 10 exd5 ♘xd5 11 ♘xd5 ♕xd5 and Black equalizes easily) 10...♘xe4 11 ♘xe4 dxe4 12 ♕xd8+ ♗xd8 13 0-0-0 ♘d7 14 ♘d2 ♗f5 and White was struggling to justify his pawn sacrifice in G.Andruet-V.Inkiov, France-Bulgaria match 1985.

So after 8 ♗e3 ♗e6 I recommend simply 9 0-0, most likely transposing to the main game—though there is one sideline worth mentioning: 9...d5?!, which can quickly be seen as (paging Nimzowitsch) a *false freeing move*: 10 exd5 ♘xd5 11 ♘xd5 ♗xd5 12 c4 ♗e6 13 ♕xd8+ ♗xd8 14 ♘c5, when White had a big advantage and soon won in J.Mladenovic-A.Benderac, Yugoslav Women's Championship, Budva 2002.

8...0-0 9 ♗e3 ♗e6 10 f4

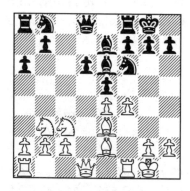

And this is the Karpovian idea we have been tracking: although the move order 8 ♗e3 ♗e6 9 0-0 0-0 (which we've reached here) avoids the direct attack, Black does not get off scot free. As we know, with the bishop on e6, Black has no serious counter against e4, and so f2-f4 is strong. Furthermore White doesn't have to lose a tempo moving his dark-squared bishop again (as in Game 11) but can take back with the rook—shades of Karpov's great wins over Polugaevsky!

10...exf4

10...b5 is weak: 11 f5 ♗d7 12 ♘d5 ♘xd5 (not 12...♘xe4 13 ♗b6 ♕e8 14 ♗f3 ♗xf5, as 15 ♕e2 wins at least a piece) 13 exd5 and White will establish a knight on e4, after which he can attack on both sides of the board; e.g. 13...a5 14 ♔h1 (the immediate 14 ♘d2 is more accurate, when 14...♕c8 is met by 15 ♗d3) 14...♘a6 15 ♘d2 ♖c8 (15...♕c8! is better) 16 ♘e4 and White had a dominating position and went on to win in P.Almagro Llanas-

I.Avendano Mateos, Madrid 2007.

11 ♖xf4

The rook is active on the fourth rank. 11 ♗xf4 seems illogical to me, and will probably soon transpose to Karpov-Kasparov (Game 11), where White's opening advantage was purely psychological.

11...♘c6

11...b5 is no better here, as the white knights spring into action: 12 ♘d4 ♕c7 13 ♘f5 ♘e8 14 ♘d5 ♗xd5 15 ♕xd5 and White's advantage was already decisive in H.Cieslik-H.Biszof, Rowy 2004.

12 ♘d5

White has our familiar, comfortable, if small Karpovian edge. There are no forcing lines and many alternatives. The text is fine—as is *Fritz*'s number one, 12 ♕d2. Even 12 ♔h1 is possible, when 12...♕c7 13 a4 ♘e5 would transpose directly to Karpov-Polugaevsky.

In general, one can play this all night and try to win! While it's not quite as much fun as the Carlsen attack, this is still an excellent way to both put long-term pressure on Black and also avoid all memorized variations!

12...♘e5

12...♗xd5 will be seen in the next game.

13 ♘xe7+

I like 13 c4!? here, when after 13...♘g6 14 ♖f1 ♘xe4 15 ♕d4 ♘f6 16 ♘xe7+ ♘xe7 17 ♗g5 White has strong compensation for the pawn with his two bishops and attacking chances.

13...♕xe7 14 ♗d4 g5

Going for a pawn. One recalls Timman eschewed a similar temptation in Game 1—here Black "boldly" snatches the button, but must suffer due to his weak dark squares and breezy king.

15 ♖f1 ♘xe4 16 ♘d2 ♘xd2

After 16...f5!? 17 c4! ♘xd2 18 ♕xd2 ♘xc4 19 ♗xc4 ♗xc4 20 ♖fe1 White's opposite bishop attack outweighs Black's two pawn advantage.

17 ♕xd2 f6 18 b3!

White is in no hurry—the compensation won't go away.

18...♖ad8 19 ♖ae1 ♗f7 20 a4 ♗g6

Or 20...d5 21 a5 and the eternal Najdorf weakness at b6 is part of White's dark square compensation.

21 c4 h6 22 ♕c3

White methodically lines up and...

22...♗e4 23 ♗h5 ♕h7 24 c5!

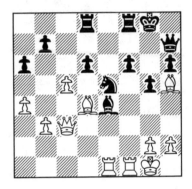

Breaks!

24...d5

Or 24...♖c8 25 ♕h3 and White gets in anyway.

25 ♗xe5 fxe5 26 ♕xe5 ♕g7 27 ♕e6+ ♔h7 28 ♗f7

White has recovered his pawn with advantage, and should probably just consolidate with 28 h3 or (perhaps best) 28 b4. His actual move may be asking too much of the position.

28...a5

28...♖c8 is best, with counterchances against White's queen which right now is tied to his bishop.

29 ♖f2 ♕d4 30 ♕e7 ♔h8 31 ♖ef1 ♖c8 32 ♔h1 ♕xc5?

Greed kills—but we already saw that Black was overeager to snatch pawns! 32...♕g7 is necessary, when it's not clear that White can win.

33 ♕f6+ ♔h7 34 ♖f5!

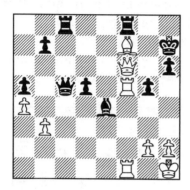

12...♗xd5

A beautiful interference move that seals the opponent's fate—Black has no real defenders of his king and must lose the game, though he does have an extra pawn!

We saw 12...♘e5 previously, when White took the dark-squared bishop. Here also White gets the two bishops, but Black shields his problem pawn at d6.

34...♕c6 35 ♗g6+ ♔g8 36 ♗f7+ ♔h7 37 ♗g6+ ♔g8 38 ♕e7! ♖xf5 39 ♕h7+ ♔f8 40 ♖xf5+ 1-0

13 exd5 ♘e5 14 ♖b4

Mate is forced.

This type of game should be very familiar by now: White has a slight edge in space in a non-forcing position, and can outplay his opponent.

Game 21
J.Hammer-T.R.Hansen
Norwegian Team
Championship 2008

A nice rook!

14...♕c7 15 ♗b6

1 e4 c5 2 ♘f3 d6 3 d4 cxd4 4 ♘xd4 ♘f6 5 ♘c3 a6 6 ♗e2 e5 7 ♘b3 ♗e7 8 0-0

8 ♗e3 ♗e6 9 0-0 0-0 is the game by the Carlsen move order.

8...0-0 9 ♗e3 ♗e6 10 f4 exf4 11 ♖xf4 ♘c6 12 ♘d5

A fun move to make, but unfortunately inaccurate. Correct is 15 a4!, trying to nail down the weakness at b6. We have now moved into Geller territory, and White gets a typical edge after 15...♖fe8 (or 15...a5 16 ♖b5—the adventurous rook doesn't fear the light squares as Black has no light-squared bishop!) 16 a5 with a plus-equals grind-all-night position!

15...♕c8 16 ♗e3

White rejects his own last move, but Black doesn't repeat!

16...♖e8 17 ♖c1 a5!

Black avoids a bind and obtains counterplay.

18 ♖a4 ♕d7 19 ♖xa5 ♖xa5 20 ♘xa5 ♘fg4 21 ♗f4 ♗d8 22 ♘c4 ♘xc4

An excellent alternative is 22...b5 23 ♗xe5 (not 23 ♘xe5?? ♕a7+ with the famous smothered mate to follow) 23...♖xe5 24 ♗xg4 ♕a7+ 25 ♔h1 bxc4 26 a3 c3 27 bxc3 ♕xa3 and White's extra pawn is meaningless.

23 ♗xg4 f5?!

Black misses his opponent's next move: the attacked piece doesn't have to move! Correct is 23...♕e7 with active counterplay on the e-file and against b2, when Black is fine.

24 ♕d3!

An unexpected double attack that gives White the advantage, and completely confuses Black.

24...♘e5

Better is 24...fxg4 25 ♕xc4, when Black is a pawn down, but not as badly off as in the game.

25 ♕xf5 ♘xg4?

Having lost his bearings, Black now loses his queen—though even on other moves Black has no compensation for the two missing pawns.

26 ♕xd7 ♗b6+ 27 ♔f1 1-0

This ends our coverage of the Najdorf. As many have pointed out, this variation, continually tested at the World Championship level, is completely sound. White has no way to knock it out, and I certainly don't claim as much. However, by playing a combination of Carlsen attack and Karpovian cunning, White can get "his" (or our!) position, and Black must really know his stuff to get an acceptable game—but even that acceptable game is, in my view, very very slightly worse. In any case, White can play for a win with 6 ♗e2, and you don't have to memorize 20 moves of theory!

Now let's slay the Dragon!

Chapter Three
The Dragon Variation

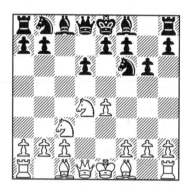

The Dragon Variation is so booked up that entire books are written not just on the variation itself, but on particular variations *within* the Dragon! I have a book (from my Dragon days as Black) that only covers the Yugoslav Attack with 9 ♗c4; that is 1 e4 c5 2 ♘f3 d6 3 d4 cxd4 4 ♘xd4 ♘f6 5 ♘c3 g6 6 ♗e3 ♗g7 7 f3 0-0 8 ♕d2 ♘c6 9 ♗c4. In other words, the book *starts* on move 9 (!) and not even all ninth moves at that. If White plays the equally popular 9 0-0-0 you're out of luck (or you have to buy another book!).

Obviously we are not going into

that memorization morass, not to mention the absurdity of buying a separate book for each variation within a variation!

I offer two systems: one that Karpov played often and with great success, based on kingside castling and developing the queen's bishop to g5. White puts the black position under positional pressure and, when he's ready, can attack the black king using the f4-f5 lever. Karpov's system will be seen in Games 22-26. I will also show that this system is perfectly playable against the Accelerated Dragon move order with 2...♘c6 3 d4 cxd4 4 ♘xd4 g6.

The second system is the Alekhine Attack—and here I have to give you a specific variation (but don't worry, I won't start my analysis at the end of this!): 1 e4 c5 2 ♘f3 d6 3 d4 cxd4 4 ♘xd4 ♘f6 5 ♘c3 g6 6 ♗e2 ♗g7 7 ♗e3 ♘c6 8 ♘b3 0-0 9 f4 ♗e6 10 g4!—the idea is obvious: White plans to castle long, throw all his kingside pawns forward and mate the black king! The

Alekhine Attack will be covered in Games 27-34. Often Black tries to avoid this deadly attack, so I've covered the "escape hatches" where he can bail out before move 10, usually by throwing in an early ...a7-a5. White then often has to castle kingside, as the direct attack is no longer advisable—but positional play always works, while a Karpov-style f4-f5 can come in later.

Finally, I cover the Dragon/Najdorf hybrid, the Dragodorf, in the last two games of the chapter (35-36). This very slow system shouldn't give White any trouble, as we can continue with our basic repertoire with ♗e2.

Game 22
A.Karpov-A.Martin Gonzalez
Las Palmas 1977

1 e4 c5 2 ♘f3 d6 3 d4 cxd4 4 ♘xd4 ♘f6 5 ♘c3 g6

The fundamental position of the Dragon Variation: Black fianchettoes and hopes to show off his improvement in the Yugoslav Attack on move 30!

6 ♗e2

No such luck, says Anatoly—you're going to have to think with your own head!

6...♗g7 7 0-0

If one wants the Alekhine Attack, then 7 ♗e3 is correct, when White can still castle long.

7...0-0 8 ♗g5

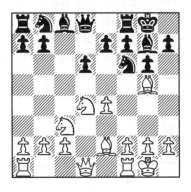

Karpov's patent: White puts positional pressure on e7 and builds up his position. I have found this kind of play is extremely unpleasant to Dragon players—first of all, memorization doesn't help them; and second, the things Dragon players love—the complications and opposite-wing attacks—have been taken off the menu!

8...♘c6 9 ♘b3

Karpov keeps the pieces on the board, especially considering that the knight lacks the normal support of the bishop on e3.

9...♗e6

This might already be a mistake: as we have seen in previous chapters, once the bishop goes to e6, Black can't pressure e4 with this piece—and so White can quickly play f2-f4, with f4-f5 on the agenda at some point.

For the more flexible 9...a6, keeping the option of ...b7-b5 and ....♗b7, see Games 24-25.

10 ♔h1

This and White's next are a typical Karpov manoeuvre. It's always a question whether ♔h1 is a useful waiting move or a loss of time. Here Karpov judges that the black forces, aimed at the queenside, can't threaten anything, so he has time to put his house in order and build up slowly for the attack.

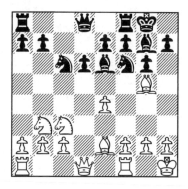

10...a6

Black has a couple of alternatives, one much better than the other:

a) 10...d5? 11 ♗xf6 (one sees the white queen's bishop also prevents this freeing break) 11...♗xf6 12 exd5 ♗xc3 13 dxc6 ♗xb2 14 cxb7 and White's passed pawn is decisive; e.g. 14...♖b8 15 ♖b1 ♗g7 16 ♕xd8 ♖fxd8 17 ♗f3 ♗d5 18 ♖fd1 and the b-pawn costs Black material.

b) 10...♖c8 11 f4 ♘a5 12 f5 (this and the next move launch an attack and consolidate White's centre; weaker is 12 e5 which led to premature exchanges: 12...♘xb3 13 axb3 dxe5 14 ♕xd8 ♖fxd8 15 fxe5 ♘d5 16 ♖xa7 h6 17 ♗c1 ♘xc3 18 bxc3 ♖xc3 and an eventual draw in T.Taylor-J.C.Banawa, 7th Metropolitan IM, Los Angeles 2011) 12...♗c4 13 ♗d3 b5 14 ♕d2 b4 15 ♘e2

♗xd3 16 cxd3 ♘c6 17 ♘f4 a5 18 a4 ♘e5 19 ♕e2 ♘ed7 20 fxg6 hxg6 21 d4 (White is better) 21...♘h7 22 ♗h4 ♘df6 (no forks allowed: 22...g5? 23 ♘h5 gxh4 24 ♕g4 mates) 23 ♗xf6 ♘xf6 24 ♖ae1 ♕d7 25 e5 dxe5 26 dxe5 ♘d5 27 e6! (Black's king position is smashed) ♕d6 28 exf7+ ♖xf7 29 ♘e6 ♖xf1+ 30 ♖xf1 ♕e5 31 ♕a6 ♖c2 32 ♘bd4 (White has a winning attack, so Black tries desperation!) 32...♖xg2!?, when White was bluffed and didn't take the rook in M.Brooks-R.Robson, Saint Louis 2011, with an eventual draw—but it was correct just to take it! White wins after 33 ♔xg2 ♘e3+ 34 ♔h1 ♘xf1 35 ♕c8+ ♔h7 36 ♘f3! with a decisive attack; e.g. 36...♕f5 37 ♘eg5+ ♔h6 38 ♕g8 ♔h5 39 ♕xg7 etc.

11 f4

This is our typical repertoire reaction to a black bishop on e6.

11...b5 12 ♗f3 ♖c8 13 ♘d5 ♘d7 14 c3 ♘b6 15 ♕e2 ♘c4 16 ♖ad1

Karpov sets up a completely harmonious position. There are no weaknesses in the white structure (note that the "dreaded dragon" has been simply neutralized by the pawn at c3), but Karpov's game is not passive—he's pressuring e7 quite a bit already, and will soon launch his main attack.

16...♛d7 17 ♖fe1 ♛a7 18 ♗h4

White could already play 18 f5 ♗xd5 19 exd5 ♘6e5 20 ♗e4 and White is "better"—but Karpov is in no hurry: when he's ready, White's attack will come with "decisive" attached to it, rather than just "better"!

18...♖fe8 19 ♘c1!

The knight is needed to attack the black king.

19...♛b8 20 ♘d3 a5 21 ♘f2 ♗d7 22 ♗g4! ♗xg4 23 ♘xg4 a4

23...h5, despite the obvious weakening of the kingside, is absolutely necessary, as we will soon see. Of course after 24 ♘ge3 ♘xe3 25 ♛xe3 ♛b7 26 ♖f1 White would retain an advantage.

24 a3!

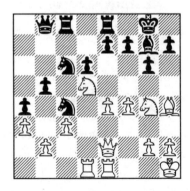

Karpovian—Black must not be allowed even to dream of counter-attack.

24...♛b7 25 ♖f1

White has quietly brought every

single piece into an attacking position.

25...♘d8 26 f5!

Now I'm ready, says Anatoly. It's clear that Black could lose this position almost instantly; e.g. 26...♛d7 27 ♗xe7! ♖xe7 28 ♘gf6+ and the queen goes, or 26...h5 (too late!) 27 fxg6! fxg6 28 e5 hxg4 29 exd6 ♘xd6 30 ♘xe7+ ♖xe7 31 ♗xe7 with a decisive attack.

26...f6

So Black tries a "solid" answer.

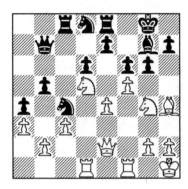

27 ♗xf6!!

When Karpov said he was ready, he was *ready*. Black's kingside disintegrates after this fantastic blow.

27...exf6 28 ♘gxf6+ ♗xf6 29 ♘xf6+ ♔f8 30 fxg6!

Disdaining the rook.

30...hxg6

Also losing is 30...♖e6 31 gxh7 ♘f7 (or 31...♔g7 32 ♛g4+ and mates) 32 ♛g4 ♘ce5 33 h8♛+ ♘xh8 34 ♘d7+ ♔e7 35 ♘xe5 ♖xe5 36 ♛g7+ and White wins the queen, a thematic element throughout the coming tactics.

31 ♛g4

There is no defence, given Black's

wide open king and disconnected rooks.

31...♘f7

Or 31...♘e5 32 ♘d7+ ♔g7 33 ♘xe5 ♖xe5 34 ♖xd6 with a decisive attack, as 34...♘f7 35 ♖xg6+ ♔f8 36 ♖g8+ ♔e7 37 ♖xf7+ ♔xf7 38 ♖g7+ is our theme again.

32 ♕xg6 ♘ce5 33 ♘h7+ ♔e7 1-0

Evidently at this point Black noticed Karpov eyeing the g5-square and resigned rather than suffer the beautiful variations after 34 ♘g5!!.

Black can lose in various ways had he wished to continue:

a) 34...♖f8 35 ♕e6+ ♔d8 36 ♘xf7+ ♖xf7 (36...♘xf7 37 ♖xd6+ mates or wins the queen) 37 ♕xd6+ ♔e8 38 ♕xe5+ ♕e7 39 ♕xb5+ ♔f8 40 ♕xa4 and my feeling is that Karpov could win with five extra pawns.

b) 34...♕c6 35 ♖xf7+ ♘xf7 36 ♕xf7+ ♔d8 37 ♘e6+ ♖xe6 38 ♕xe6 ♔c7 39 ♕e7+ ♕d7 40 ♕xd7+ ♔xd7 41 e5 ♖e8 42 ♖xd6+ ♔e7 43 ♔g1 and four extra pawns will have to be enough.

c) 34...♔f8 35 ♕h6+ ♔e7 (the same

theme follows 35...♔g8 36 ♕h7+ ♔f8 37 ♘xf7 ♘xf7 38 ♕h8+ ♔e7 39 ♖xf7+ etc) 36 ♘xf7 ♘xf7 37 ♖xf7+ ♔xf7 38 ♕h7+ and the thematic queen win occurs.

d) 34...♘xg5 35 ♕xd6 mate is short and sweet.

And for the record, what happens if Black takes the queen?

e) 34...♘xg6 35 ♖xf7+ ♔d8 36 ♖xd6+ ♕d7 37 ♖dxd7 mate is convincing.

I think this is one of Karpov's best games, albeit little known. White's attack was awesomely well prepared—and then completely unstoppable once Anatoly crossed the meridian with 26 f5!. And note that before that break, Black could not generate any middlegame play whatsoever!

Game 23
A.Karpov-G.Sosonko
Bad Lauterberg 1977

1 e4 c5 2 ♘f3 d6 3 d4 cxd4 4 ♘xd4 ♘f6 5 ♘c3 g6 6 ♗e2 ♗g7 7 0-0 ♘c6 8 ♘b3 0-0 9 ♗g5 ♗e6 10 ♔h1 a5

In the previous game this pawn only travelled to a6. The double advance, though well known in Accelerated Dragon lines, has a dark side as well: both b5 and b6 are seriously weakened. Karpov, never one to miss a weakness, occupies both of those squares in the course of the game.

11 a4 ♘d7 12 f4 ♘b6 13 f5

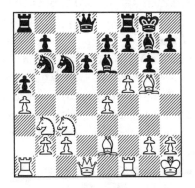

Inducing the following exchange which gives White an important tempo, as b2 isn't really hanging.

13...♗c4 14 ♗xc4 ♘xc4 15 ♕e2! ♘b6

The b2-pawn is poisoned: 15...♘xb2 16 ♘d5 ♖e8 (or 16...h6 17 f6 hxg5 18 fxg7 ♔xg7 19 c4 and the divagating knight drops) 17 c3 and once again the wayward steed is captured. Also if 15...♘4e5 then 16 ♘d5 with evident pressure on e7, which ties Black up.

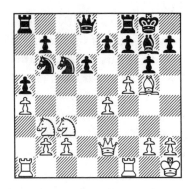

16 ♕b5

Occupying the first weak square! Note that, in Karpov's system, White has to be as ready to play on the queenside (unusual in a Dragon) as on the kingside.

16...♘d4 17 ♘xd4 ♗xd4

No check (due to Karpov's careful 10 ♔h1), so White just gains another tempo and increases the pressure.

18 ♖ad1 ♗g7

On 18...♗xc3 19 bxc3 ♕c7 20 ♖b1 ♖a6 21 ♕b3 Black can't satisfactorily meet the b- and f-file threats.

19 ♗e3

This well-motivated retreat gains control of d5. Karpov makes glacial but inexorable progress, as he restricts his luckless opponent one square at a time.

19...♘d7 20 ♘d5

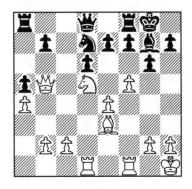

20...♖e8

The knight is painful, but chasing it is worse: if 20...e6 then 21 f6! and Black has no good answer:

a) 21...♗xf6 22 ♘xf6+ ♘xf6 23 ♗g5 wins a piece.

b) 21...♘xf6 22 ♗b6! wins a piece in a different way—note how White uses the second weakness at b6, but we already took advantage of this hole in the Najdorf chapter!

c) 21...exd5 22 fxg7 ♔xg7 23 ♕xb7 with a decisive positional advantage.

21 c3

Once again we see the Dragon player—here the Dragon-advocate Sosonko—reduced to complete passivity with nothing to attack, while Karpov inexorably moves forward at his own pace.

21...♗e5 22 ♗b6!

The second weakness is occupied! One sees in the coming play that the "fearsome" Dragon bishop is helpless against the white knight.

22...♘xb6 23 ♘xb6 ♖a6 24 ♘c4 ♕b8

Or 24...♗g7 25 fxg6 hxg6 26 e5 and Black can't hold all his weaknesses.

25 ♘xa5

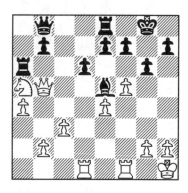

White has won a pawn without losing a drop of his positional advantage.

25...♖c8 26 ♘c4 ♗xh2

Starting tactics from an inferior position hardly ever works, but otherwise Black is only a spectator to Karpov's technique.

27 ♘b6!

27 ♔xh2 ♖xc4! 28 ♕xc4 d5+ is the

trick, which Karpov brushes aside with the text move.

27...♖xb6

Also losing is 27...♖c6 28 ♘d5 ♗e5 29 ♘xe7+ or 27...♖c5 28 ♕b3 ♗e5 29 fxg6, breaking through to f7. Note how Karpov's full-board play combines queenside pressure with the more standard f-file attack.

28 ♕xb6 ♗e5 29 a5 ♖c6 30 ♕e3 ♕c7 31 ♖d5 ♖a6 32 ♕d3

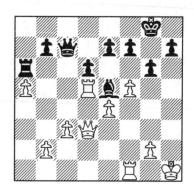

32...♔g7

Now Black has exactly nothing for the exchange, but if he tries to take a pawn with 32...♖xa5 then after 33 ♖xa5 ♕xa5 34 fxg6 hxg6 35 ♕d5! (note how the f-file threats help White's game—here the exchange of queens is forced) 35...♕xd5 36 exd5 White wins the ending by going for the b-pawn with his rook.

33 ♖b5 g5 34 ♕d5 ♖a7 35 g4 ♕c8 36 ♔g2 ♕d7 37 c4 ♕e8 38 b3 ♕d8 39 ♕d2 f6 40 ♖h1 ♗f4 41 ♕c3 ♕h8 42 ♕h3 h5

Black can't wait: if 42...♗d2 then 43 ♕h6+ ♔f7 44 a6 bxa6 45 ♕h5+ ♔g7 46 ♖b8! forces mate.

43 ♕xh5 ♕xh5 44 ♖xh5 ♗d2 45 b4 1-0

What we just saw was Karpov walking right over a strong grandmaster!

> *Game 24*
> **T.Taylor-Z.Amanov**
> Sean Reader Memorial,
> Los Angeles 2011

1 e4 c5 2 ♘f3 ♘c6 3 d4

I knew my opponent had never played the Sveshnikov, so I didn't stick exactly to our repertoire, which is 3 ♘c3 (see Chapter Six).

3...cxd4 4 ♘xd4 ♘f6 5 ♘c3 d6 6 ♗e2

Most of the time, when I offered the Boleslavsky like this, my opponents preferred the Dragon—which was fine by me!

6...g6 7 0-0 ♗g7 8 ♘b3 0-0 9 ♗g5 a6

This is the choice of the 2600/2700 player these days (and well-prepared IMs like my opponent!), as the conventional development 9...♗e6, seen in the previous two games, does not stop White from setting up a Karpovian ma-

chine. Nonetheless Black does not have an easy game after this either!

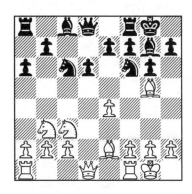

10 f4

My opponent had previously faced 10 a4 ♗e6 11 f4 ♘a5 12 ♔h1 and fell under an attack after he lost a tempo with 12...♕b6 (it's clear that, having repeated the line, he was prepared with the evident improvement 12...♘xb3 13 cxb3 ♕b6) 13 ♘xa5 ♕xa5 14 f5 ♗d7 15 ♗c4 ♖ae8 16 ♗b3 ♗c6 17 ♕e1 ♕e5 18 ♗f4 ♕c5 19 ♖d1 ♕b4 20 ♗d2 ♕b6 21 ♗e3 ♕c7 22 ♕h4 b5 23 axb5 axb5 24 ♗g5 b4 25 ♘d5 ♗xd5 26 exd5 ♖b8 27 ♖f3 h5 28 h3 ♖b5 29 ♖g3 ♔h7 30 ♗c4 ♖c5 31 ♗d3 1-0 G.Kuzmin-Z.Amanov, Elista 2008.

Another, more Karpovian alternative (actually played by Mickey Adams) is 10 ♖e1—for which see the next game.

10...b5 11 ♗f3 ♗b7

Absolutely critical is 11...b4 12 ♘d5 (Black had no trouble after 12 ♘e2 ♘g4 13 e5 ♕b6+ 14 ♘ed4 ♘e3 15 ♕d3 ♘xd4 16 ♕xd4 ♖b8 17 ♗xe7 ♘xf1 18 ♗xf8 ♔xf8 19 ♔xf1 dxe5 20 fxe5 ♕xd4

21 ♘xd4 ♗xe5 22 ♘c6 ♖b5 23 ♘xe5 ♖xe5 24 a3 ½-½ N.Mamedov-A.Motylev, Moscow 2011) 12...♘xd5 13 exd5 ♘a5 and a difficult position is reached where White has space and attacking chances, but Black can pick off at least the b-pawn and pressure c2 and possibly d5 as well.

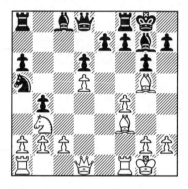

Here are some examples:

a) 14 ♖e1 ♘c4 15 ♖e4 ♕b6+ 16 ♔h1 ♘xb2 17 ♕e1 ♗c3 18 ♕e2 ♗f5 19 ♖xe7 ♖a7 20 ♖xa7 ♕xa7 21 ♗h6 ♖c8 22 ♘a5 ♕d7 23 ♕xa6 ♗xc2 24 h3 ♗d3 25 ♕b7 and now Black mistakenly stayed in the middlegame with 25...♖c7? and eventually fell to White's attack in M.Leon Hoyos-G.Urosevic, Cento 2011—but objectively Black is much better here if he goes for the ending with 25...♕xb7 26 ♘xb7 ♖a8.

b) 14 ♘xa5 ♕xa5 15 ♖b1 ♗f5 16 ♕e2 ♕c5+ 17 ♔h1 ♕xc2 18 ♕xc2 ♗xc2 19 ♖bc1 ♖fc8 20 ♖f2 ♗e4 21 ♖e1 ♗xf3 22 ♖xf3 ♖a7 23 g4 ♗xb2 24 ♗xe7 ♗c3 25 ♖e2 and White has no real compensation for the pawn, though she made the draw with gritty and opportunistic

defence in Ruan Lufei-Hou Yifan, Women's World Championship (1st rapid game), Antakya 2010.

c) 14 ♕e2—Ljubojevic keeps the queens on and goes for attack, and brilliantly defeats our friend Sosonko who falls again to this variation! First let's take a look at this game, then at the *Fritz* solution:

c1) 14...♘xb3?! (this can only be regarded as a mistake after White's following "anti-positional" move, taking away from the centre—one soon sees that the addition of the c-file is a great help to his attack) 15 cxb3! ♕b6+ 16 ♔h1 ♖e8 17 ♖fe1 h6 18 ♗h4 ♕d4 19 ♖ac1 (the open lines give White a persistent initiative, which he carries through with great mastery) 19...♕xf4 20 ♗xe7 ♗f5 21 ♖c4 ♕e5 22 ♕d1 ♕xb2 23 ♖e2 ♕b1 24 ♖c1 ♕d3 25 ♗xd6 ♗c3 26 ♗e7 ♖a7 27 d6 ♕b5 28 ♕g1 ♕b8 29 ♖d1 ♗g7 30 ♕c5 ♖c8 31 ♕e3 ♖c3 32 ♕f4 ♕b5 33 ♖d5 ♕d7 34 h4 a5 35 h5 ♔h7 36 ♗e4 ♗xe4 37 ♖xe4 ♕e8 38 ♖e1 ♔g8 39 hxg6 fxg6 40 ♕g4 ♖d7 41 ♕e6+ ♔h7 42 ♖xa5 ♖c2 43 ♖f1 ♖d2 44 ♖f7 ♖2xd6 45 ♖xg7+!! (a fabulous combination, that allows an almost equally stunning resource from Black—and then refutes it) 45...♔xg7 46 ♕e5+ ♔f7 47 ♗xd6 ♖xd6! (this looks like a brilliant save, since 48 ♕xd6 ♕e1+ forces a perpetual—but White refuses the rook and demonstrates a winning attack!) 48 ♖a7+ ♖d7 49 ♕d5+ ♔e7 50 ♕e4+ ♔f7 51 ♕c4+ ♔f6 52 ♕f4+ 1-0 L.Ljubojevic-G.Sosonko, Tilburg 1984.

Black resigns in view of 52...♔g7 53 ♕d4+ winning a rook, or 52...♔e7 53 ♖a6 and, due to his wide open king, Black can't prevent major loss of material or mate.

This was certainly a beautiful game, but the Oracle likes Black after the cold-blooded...

c2) 14...♖e8!

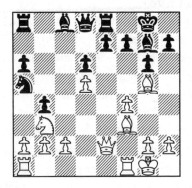

(this has been tried in only two games according to the *MegaBase*, both of which were won by Black) 15 ♖ab1 ♗f5 16 ♗e4 (16 g4?! is too weakening: 16...♘xb3 17 axb3 ♕b6+ 18 ♔h1 ♗d7 19 ♖fe1 ♖ac8 20 ♕g2 ♗f6 21 ♖e4 ♕c5 22 ♖c4 ♕a5 23 ♖xc8 ♖xc8 24 ♖e1 ♕a2!—White's first and second ranks are weak—25 ♗xf6 exf6 26 ♖e7 ♕xb2! 27 ♖xd7 ♖xc2 28 ♕g1 ♖c1 29 ♖xd6 ♖xg1+ 30 ♔xg1 ♕xb3 0-1 S.Frübing-K.Müller, German League 2009) 16...♕b6+ 17 ♔h1 e6 18 ♕d3 ♘xb3 19 axb3 ♕d4 (White has no attack and should just exchange queens and hope to draw, like Miss Ruan above—in the game he is eventually forced to exchange under much worse circum-

stances) 20 ♗xf5 exf5 21 ♕c4 ♖ac8 22 ♕xa6 h6 23 ♖fd1 ♕f2 24 ♖f1 ♕e2 25 ♕xe2 ♖xe2 26 ♗h4 ♖cxc2 (the blind pigs rule) 27 ♖fc1 ♖xb2 28 ♖xb2 ♖xb2 29 h3 ♖xb3 30 ♖c8+ ♔h7 31 ♖c7 ♖b1+ 32 ♔h2 b3 33 ♖xf7 ♔g8 34 ♖e7 b2 35 ♖e8+ ♔f7 36 ♖e7+ ♔f8 37 ♖b7 ♖d1 38 ♖b8+ ♔f7 39 ♖b7+ ♔g8 0-1 A.Bokros-Po.Carlsson, World Junior Championship, Oropesa del Mar 1999.

I think there are possible improvements for White in the complex position after 11...b4, but I will leave them for the reader to discover.

When I found I was playing Amanov again with White a few weeks later, I didn't want to engage in a "whose computer is better?" debate, so I simply changed lines rather than test his preparation. Karpov's openings, being inherently sound, often allow this—as opposed to "knife-edged theoretical battles" where a single improvement can torpedo a whole variation.

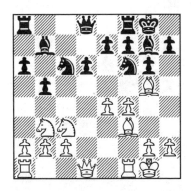

12 ♔h1

12 e5 is premature due to 12...♕b6+ 13 ♔h1 dxe5 with a clear plus to Black.

12...♘d7

If 12...♖e8, 13 e5 is now strong (no check on b6!) and Ljubojevic scores again: 13...b4 14 ♘a4 dxe5 15 fxe5 ♘d7 16 ♘bc5 ♘xc5 17 ♘xc5 ♕c7 18 ♘xb7 ♕xb7 19 ♕d5! (White gets all the mileage he can out of the pin on the long diagonal and then, Karpov-style, suddenly switches to an f-file attack) ♖ac8 20 ♕xf7+!! (surprise!) ♔h8 (20...♔xf7 21 ♗d5 mate seems to come out of nowhere!) 21 ♗f6 ♖g8 22 ♗xg7+ ♖xg7 23 ♕e6 h5 24 ♗e4 ♕c7 25 ♗xc6 1-0 L.Ljubojevic-M.Dougherty, Quebec 1984, as 25...♕xc6 26 ♖f8+ wins a rook.

13 ♕e2 b4

Too late! Chess is all timing, and two moves ago, or even one, this would have been good. Now it just encourages White to take over the centre.

My opponent said he was expecting 14 ♘a4, but I did write a book called *Pawn Sacrifice!*. This one is a fairly direct sac for attack.

14 ♘d5!

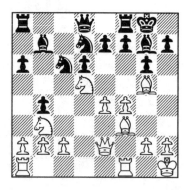

White has won the opening battle, as I have achieved a Karpovian position

with a safe king, pressure on e7, and a potential attack with f4-f5. Black had to fight back earlier (with ...b5-b4) to prevent this set-up.

14...f6

After 14...♗xb2 15 ♖ad1 then e4-e5 will come with great effect and all lines open for White.

15 ♗h4 e6 16 ♘e3 g5 17 ♗g3 gxf4 18 ♗xf4 ♘de5

Black has driven back the attacking white pieces, and gained the e5-square—but he has seriously weakened his king position, which I think is ultimately more important.

19 ♖ad1 ♕c7

Or 19...♘xf3 20 gxf3 ♘e5 21 ♘c5 ♗c8 22 ♕d2 and White wins a pawn, which shows another problem with the pawn advances of moves 14-16— Black's pawn mass looks nice, but it's floating with no real support.

20 ♗h5

My idea was to take the e8-square from the black rooks, and so weaken the e6-pawn. Another possibility is 20 ♗g4 ♘d8 (not 20...♘xg4? 21 ♗xd6) 21 ♘d2, planning to bring a knight to c4 with positional pressure.

20...a5 21 ♖f2 a4 22 ♘c1 ♖ad8

22...a3 23 b3 ♖a5 24 ♕e1 ♖c5 25 ♖fd2 ♖d8 26 ♕g3 is also good for White.

23 ♕e1 ♕b6 24 ♖fd2

White clears the way for the queen to reach the kingside, while stepping up the pressure on the "floating" d6-pawn. This typical Karpovian strategy of pinning Black down to two weaknesses makes things very difficult for the opponent.

24...♕c5 25 ♕g3 ♔h8

Natural, but not best. The hard to see 25...♘e7 is correct, as Black must prepare to block the g-file: 26 ♕h3 (26 ♗h6 ♘7g6 is Black's idea) 26...♗c8 and White has great pressure on the floating pawns and against the black king, but no knockout is apparent.

26 ♕h3 ♗c8 27 ♘d3!

Now the weak king position tells, as White has a combination in mind...

27...♕b6

Black must be wary: 27...♘xd3 28 ♗g6! (no recapture!) 28...h6 (or 28...h5 29 ♖xd3 and Black falls apart) 29 ♗xh6! and White forces mate. Note there is no longer any pawn cover for the black king and no pieces can defend now that the dragon will be slain.

Black is also in a bad way after 27...♕b5 28 ♘xe5 ♘xe5 29 b3 (even stronger than 29 ♖xd6) 29...axb3 30 axb3 and White has so many threats—on both sides of the board—that Black

can hardly hold the position; e.g. 30...♕b7 31 ♖d4 ♕b5 32 ♗g3 ♕b8 33 ♗e1 ♘c6 34 ♗g6 h6 35 ♖c4 ♕b5 36 ♗d2 and Black will have to pitch b4 before h6 falls!

28 ♘xe5 ♘xe5 29 ♘c4!!

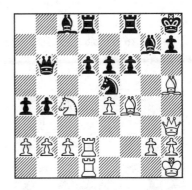

The same idea in a more spectacular setting: Black's king position is just too weak.

29...♕c7

Black can't accept the sacrificed knight: 29...♘xc4 30 ♗g6 h6 (or 30...♗h6 31 ♕xh6 ♕b7 32 ♗xd6 ♘xd2 33 ♗xf8 ♔g8 34 ♗xb4 hxg6 35 ♖xd2 ♖xd2 36 ♕f8+ ♔h7 37 ♗xd2 and the opposite-coloured bishop attack wins once again) 31 ♗xh6 and mates as before—not even 31...e5 helps because of 32 ♗xg7+ (double check!) 32...♔xg7 33 ♕h7 mate.

30 ♘xd6 ♖xd6

Necessary, as 30...a3 31 ♘f7+ ♖xf7 32 ♖xd8+ ♖f8 33 ♗g6 wins immediately.

31 ♖xd6

But now White is up a pawn, an exchange, and still has a powerful attack!

31...♕xc2 32 ♗xe5

The manoeuvre initiated by this move guards my e-pawn with tempo and allows my rooks to penetrate on the d-file—Black has no recourse.

32...fxe5 33 ♗g6 h6 34 ♖d8 ♕c7

The queen must scurry back, since 34...♕xb2 35 ♕f3 forces mate.

35 ♕d3 ♔g8 36 h3 ♗b7 37 ♖d7 ♕c6 38 ♕g3 ♔h8 39 ♖xg7! 1-0

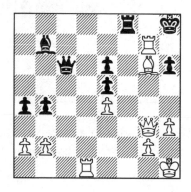

The queen falls after 39...♔xg7 40 ♗e8+.

Once I got the Karpovian position with ♘d5 and ♗g5 (after move 14) my attack just rolled along—but the sharp advance 11...b4 is critical for this variation, when White needs to find an improvement in the ensuing complications.

Game 25
T.Taylor-Z.Amanov
7th Metropolitan IM,
Los Angeles 2011

---

1 e4 c5 2 ♘f3 d6 3 d4 cxd4 4 ♘xd4 ♘f6 5 ♘c3 g6 6 ♗e2 ♗g7 7 0-0 0-0 8 ♗g5 ♘c6 9 ♘b3 a6

As mentioned previously, I was again paired with the same opponent, with the same colour, not long after the previous victory. Amanov made these first nine moves with lightning speed, clearly having an improvement in mind (most likely 11...b4), but I didn't feel like seeing it!

10 ♖e1

As played by Adams, and reminiscent of Kayumov's positional line against Carlsen (Game 13). As in that game, White plans an early ♘d5.

10...b5

Black's play slowed down to a crawl!

11 ♗f1

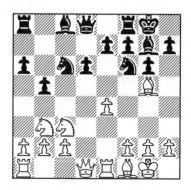

White doesn't commit his f-pawn, but defends e4 and prepares ♘d5, thus neutralizing (quite in Karpov's style) Black's ...b7-b5 thrust.

11...♗b7

Adams faced 11...h6 12 ♗h4 e6 13 ♕d2 ♕c7 14 ♖ad1 ♖d8 15 f4 ♗b7 16 a3 ♖ac8 and now played the premature 17 f5 with an eventual draw in

M.Adams-A.Miles, Tilburg 1993. The patient 17 h3 is better, which improves White's position (♖e3-d3 is in the air) and so maintains a small plus.

11...b4 is a weaker alternative: unlike the previous game, Black has no threat against White's solid play, and the b-pawn itself is exposed to lever action. After 12 ♘d5 ♘d7 13 ♕c1 ♖e8 14 a3! bxa3 15 ♖xa3 White had the advantage across the board in V.Orlov-E.Krassilnikov, St Petersburg 2000.

12 ♘d5 ♘d7

If 12...♘xd5 13 exd5 ♘e5, then 14 a4! (White plays on the queenside, where the black queen's bishop is at least temporarily inactive—weaker is 14 f4 ♕b6+ 15 ♔h1 ♘c4 16 ♗xe7 ♘xb2 17 ♕f3 ♖fc8 18 f5 ♖xc2 19 f6 ♗f2 20 ♕g3 ♗xf6 which turns in Black's favour) 14...h6 15 ♗c1 ♘c4 16 c3 (the typical Karpov block) 16...♖e8 17 ♘d4 ♕b6 (after 17...♗xd5 18 axb5 axb5 19 ♖xa8 ♕xa8 20 ♘xb5 Black has freed his bishop but faces other problems: in view of the threatened fork on c7, he has nothing better than 20...♕c6 21 ♘c7 ♕xc7 22 ♕xd5, when White has an edge with the two bishops and a passed pawn) 18 axb5 axb5 19 ♖xa8 ♖xa8 (or 19...♗xa8 20 b3 and Black has problems with the b5-pawn) 20 ♖xe7 ♗xd4 21 cxd4 ♗xd5 22 ♗xh6 ♖a7 23 ♖e8+ ♔h7 24 ♕g4 ♖a8 25 ♕h4 ♖xe8 26 ♗g5+ (Black, with no dragon bishop, is unable to defend against White's mating attack) 1-0 Mi.Sandu-A.R.Uta, Rumanian Women's Championship, Sarata Monteoru 2011.

13 c3

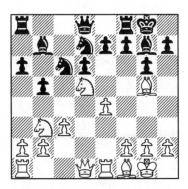

Once again, typical Karpov: I shut off Black's dark-squared bishop, then carry on with the kingside attack. Having their vital piece neutralized like this seems to be most unpleasant for Dragon players!

13...h6 14 ♗h4 g5 15 ♗g3 e6 16 ♘e3 ♘de5 17 ♕h5

Black did not drive off the opposing dark-squared bishop for free: now the h5-square is available for the white queen—which is rather menacing for the black king!

17...♘e7?!

17...♕e7 is better, but after 18 ♖ad1 White has a long-term pull.

18 ♗xe5!

An unprejudiced exchange that leaves Black with a dead dragon and lamed pawns—White's advantage is close to decisive and it's only move 18! Most Yugoslav Dragon lines are booked far past that!

Unfortunately, winning the "won game" turned out not to be so easy!

18...dxe5

Not 18...♗xe5? 19 ♘g4 and White wins a pawn with attack.

19 ♘c5 ♗c8 20 ♖ad1 ♕c7 21 b4

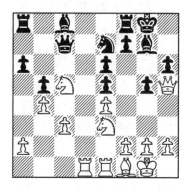

White dominates across the board—I knew then, and *Fritz* concurs now, that White has a decisive advantage.

From an opening point of view, White has won the battle big time—so I will just give light notes on the rest of this long game to show where the cleanest wins can be found, before the most unwelcome draw.

21...♔h7 22 ♖d2 ♘g6 23 ♖ed1 ♖a7 24 g3 ♖h8 25 ♘g4 ♕e7 26 ♖d6 ♘f8 27 c4! bxc4 28 ♗xc4 a5 29 a3 axb4 30 axb4

The unopposed passed pawn adds to White's advantage; also note how his powerful knights dominate both of Black's bishops.

30...♖c7 31 ♗b3 ♗b7 32 ♘e3

Win One: 32 ♗a4 is a nice clean win, since Black must allow the decisive advance of the passed pawn or face a mating attack: 32...♖g8 (32...♗c8 33 ♗c6 ♖a7 34 b5 is easy) 33 ♗b5 ♖h8

34 ♘d7 ♘xd7 35 ♖xd7 ♖xd7 36 ♖xd7 ♕xb4 37 ♘f6+ and mates.

32...♗c6 33 ♕e2 ♗e8 34 ♕d2 ♗c6 35 ♕d3 ♗e8 36 ♗c2 ♘f6 37 ♕a6 ♖a7 38 ♕b6 ♖a3 39 ♘d5 exd5 40 ♖xf6 ♔g7 41 ♖d6 d4 42 ♗d3 ♘g6 43 ♖c1 h5 44 ♗f1 ♔h7 45 ♘d3 ♖a7 46 ♘c5 g4 47 b5 ♖a2 48 ♘e6!

White is back on the right track, simultaneously working to advance the pawn and attack the king. Here taking the knight fails, as 48...fxe6 49 ♖c7 wins the queen.

48...♖a7 49 ♖c7 ♖xc7 50 ♘xc7 ♕g5 51 ♕a7 ♕e7 52 ♕c5 h4 53 b6!

White's pawn is only two squares from queening and Black's kingside demonstration shouldn't come to much. *Fritz* is up to +4 now, if that means anything—but I'll tell you it didn't mean much to me at the board, with about five minutes left in sudden death, surviving on the increment!

53...hxg3 54 hxg3 ♗a4 55 ♘d5 ♕g5

56 b7

Win Two: 56 ♕c7 is a very clear win, the point being to tie Black down to f7 (or break through there with a mating attack) and then queen the b-pawn. Even in time pressure this should have been seen. All Black defences fail miserably:

a) 56...♗d1 57 ♕xf7+ ♔h6 58 ♘e7 and mates.

b) 56...♗e8 57 b7 ♔g7 58 b8♕ ♕h6 59 ♖xg6+ ♔xg6 (59...♔xg6 60 ♕d6+ removes Black's queen, while White has one in reserve) 60 ♕xe5+ f6 61 ♕xf6+ ♕xf6 62 ♘xf6 ♔xf6 63 ♕f4+ and the rest would be absurdly simple.

c) 56...♖f8 (in general, whenever the rook is forced off the h-file White wins easily with the passed pawn, as Black has no counterplay) 57 b7 and queens.

d) 56...♔g7 57 ♖f6 ♖f8 (or 57...♕h5 58 ♕xf7+ ♔h6 59 ♘e7 and mates) 58 b7 and once again the passed pawn decides.

56...♔g7 57 ♘c7

Win Three: 57 ♕c7 ♕h6 58 ♖xg6+ ♔xg6 59 ♘e7+ ♔h7 60 ♕xe5 ♖e8 61 ♕f5+ ♔g7 62 ♕xg4+ ♔h8 63 ♘c8, which is pretty but hard to see.

57...♕h6

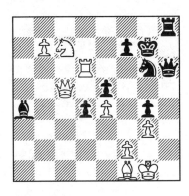

58 ♗g2?

Win Four: 58 ♘e6+ fxe6 (after 58...♔f6 White has a mating attack with all checks: 59 ♘xd4+ ♔g5 60 f4+ gxf3 61 ♘xf3+ ♔g4 62 ♘xe5+ ♔xg3 63 ♕f2 mate) 59 ♕c7+ ♔f6 60 ♖xe6+ ♔xe6 (or 60...♔g5 61 f4+ gxf3 62 ♕c1+ ♔h5 63 g4+ ♔xg4 64 ♕xh6 ♖xh6 65 b8♕ and Black ends up with a single piece for the queen) 61 ♗c4+ ♔f6 62 ♕f7+ ♔g5 63 ♕f5 mate. This win is clean and completely forced, and furthermore the main lines are all checks! This should absolutely have been seen—and worse yet, this was the *last* win. One must always analyze the checks, especially in an attacking position like this.

58...♕d2

Now Black has sufficient counterplay and the game devolves to a draw.

59 ♖xg6+ ♔xg6 60 ♕d6+ f6 61 ♘d5 ♕e1+ 62 ♗f1 ♖h1+ 63 ♔xh1 ♕xf1+ 64 ♔h2 ♕xf2+ 65 ♔h1 ♕f1+ 66 ♔h2 ♕h3+ 67 ♔g1 ♕xg3+ 68 ♔h1 ♕e1+ 69 ♔h2

69...♕f2+

Black can still lose if he plays for a

win; e.g. 69...♕d2+ 70 ♔g1 ♕c1+ 71 ♔g2 ♕b2+ 72 ♔g1 ♕xb7 73 ♕xf6+ ♔h7 74 ♕h4+ ♔g8? 75 ♘f6+ nets the queen—my opponent wisely forces the draw.

70 ♔h1 ½-½

An extremely painful result, but one must praise my opponent for staying focused in such a difficult position. I may be lacking self-criticism (as Botvinnik would say) but I only reproach myself for missing wins one, two and four, but not three! In any case, from an opening standpoint, Adams' modest ♖e1/♗f1 system has more than a drop of Karpovian poison in it, and Black's defence is quite difficult.

Game 26
A.Karpov-R.Hernandez Onna
Las Palmas 1977

1 e4 c5 2 ♘f3 ♘c6

Black indicates that he wants to play the Accelerated Dragon.

3 d4 cxd4 4 ♘xd4 g6 5 ♘c3 ♗g7 6 ♘b3

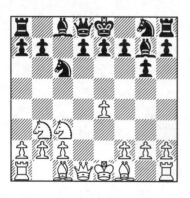

Karpov is certainly not afraid that Black will give up his vital dark-squared bishop!

6...♘f6

This is the normal move (which transposes back into main lines) and White scores a normal 55% against it. Strangely enough, 6...♗xc3+ is often recommended in Accelerated Dragon books but rarely played—in fact, it's played less than 10% as often as 6...♘f6. When Black does venture this exchange, White scores an overwhelming 67% against it, which is easy to understand: Black gives up his fundamental piece, the Dragon bishop, and must suffer due to weak dark squares for the rest of the game! Yes, if he ever reaches an endgame, White's doubled pawns might be weak, but that's a rather unlikely hope. Two following games show two typical White wins: 6...♗xc3+ 7 bxc3 ♘f6

8 ♗d3 (8 ♗c4!? with the idea 8...♘xe4 9 ♗xf7+ ♔xf7 10 ♕d5+ ♔g7 11 ♕xe4 is certainly possible) 8...d5— Black opens lines for White's two bish-

ops; I remember David Levy recommending this years ago in his Accelerated Dragon book, but I didn't believe in it then, and when I saw Andrew Greet recommend it in *Starting Out: Accelerated Dragon*, I still don't believe in it now! What must the average player think of such moves? Mostly, they say, "I'm not going to play that!"— 9 exd5 ♕xd5 10 0-0 and then:

a) 10...♗f5 11 c4 ♕d7 12 ♘c5 ♕c7 13 ♗xf5 gxf5 14 ♗b2 (here Greet has played his own recommendation, but turns out to be another statistic in White's big score: while *Fritz* says White is only slightly better, in practice the long diagonal is very difficult to overcome) 14...♘g4 15 g3 ♖g8 16 ♖e1 ♖d8 17 ♕f3 ♘ce5 18 ♗xe5 ♘xe5 19 ♕xf5 ♖g5 20 ♕xh7 (Black eliminated the white bishop, but at the cost of two pawns) 20...♘f3+ 21 ♔h1 ♕xc5 22 ♕h8+ ♔d7 23 ♖ed1+ ♔e6 24 ♕xd8 ♕xf2 25 ♕c8+ ♔f6 26 ♕h8+ ♔e6 27 ♖f1 ♕e2 28 ♕h6+ f6 29 ♕h3+ ♔f7 30 ♕g2 (White consolidates the extra material and scores the full point)

30...♕xg2+ 31 ♔xg2 ♘d2 32 ♖f4 ♖c5 33 ♖d1 ♘xc4 34 ♖d7 ♘e5 35 ♖f2 ♖b5 36 ♖d4 b6 37 h4 ♖a5 38 ♖e4 ♔g6 39 a4 ♖c5 40 g4 ♖c3 41 g5 ♘c6 42 gxf6 exf6 43 ♖g4+ ♔f7 44 ♖gf4 ♔g7 45 ♖xf6 ♘e5 46 ♖6f5 ♘g4 47 ♖g5+ ♔h6 48 ♖xg4 1-0 M.Leon Hoyos-A.Greet, World Mindsports Games, Beijing (blitz) 2008.

b) 10...0-0 11 c4 ♕d6

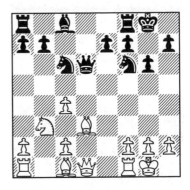

12 c5 ♕c7 13 ♖e1 ♖d8 14 ♕e2 ♗e6 15 ♗b2 (White has the powerful unopposed bishop on the long dark diagonal the black dragon abdicated—I would never voluntarily go in for this with Black!) 15...♖d5 16 h3 ♖h5 17 ♕f3 ♗d5 18 ♕e3 ♖c8 19 ♗e2 ♖h4 20 ♕g5 ♖f4 21 ♗d3 ♖d8 22 ♖ad1 ♗e4 23 ♕g3 ♘h5 24 ♕h2 ♗xd3 25 cxd3 f5 (if 25...♕b8, to put the queen on a protected square, then White wins nonetheless by 26 g4 ♘f6 27 ♗e5!—a typical "dark square" combination—27...♘xe5 28 ♕xf4 with a decisive material advantage) 26 ♗c1 (Black, helpless on the dark squares, loses material) 26...e5 27 ♗xf4 ♘xf4 28 ♕g3 a5 29 a4 ♘d4 30 ♘xd4 ♖xd4 31 ♕e3 ♖d5 32 d4 e4 33 f3 exf3 1-0

A.Rodriguez Vila-R.Quintiliano Pinto, Santos 2010. Black resigned without waiting for 34 ♕e8+ ♔g7 35 ♖e7+ which wins the queen—on a dark square!

7 ♗e2 0-0 8 0-0 a5

8...d6 9 ♗g5 transposes to the previous four games. The text is the "Accelerated Dragon" move, but really doesn't change the game much. Karpov faced down a similar, if later thrust vs. Sosonko (Game 23) and doesn't run into any more trouble here.

9 a4

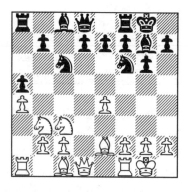

9...d6

Black could try 9...♘b4 intending ...d7-d5. White continues 10 ♗g5 (even 10 ♗f3, as we'll see in a similar position in Game 33, can be played to prevent the break directly) 10...d5 (here Black gets it in, but once again this is a "false freeing move"—lines open for White's pieces, and the b-file weaknesses that come with ...a7-a5 hurt Black) 11 exd5 ♘fxd5 12 ♘xd5 ♘xd5 13 ♗f3 ♘f6 14 ♖e1 ♕c7 15 ♕e2 ♖e8 16 ♕b5!, when White dominated the position and

went on to win in V.Kupreichik-W.Pohl, Schwäbisch Gmünd 1995.

10 ♗g5 ♗e6

One of my Dragon encounters continued with the rare move 10...h6, which slightly weakens Black's kingside—but it took more than that to lead to a White victory in 20 moves: 11 ♗h4 ♗e6 12 f4 ♗xb3 (as usual the "freeing" 12...d5 is indirectly prevented: White has 13 f5 gxf5 14 exf5 ♗c8 15 ♗b5 with great pressure on Black's compromised position—note that the black king is even more exposed now) 13 cxb3 (although White's pawn structure is compromised, the two bishops and c-file provide more than enough compensation; for a further discussion of this structure, and a nice Tiviakov win, see the note to move 12 in Game 32) 13...♕b6+?! 14 ♗f2 ♕b4? (this is the move that transforms "some advantage to White" into decisive!—Black doesn't realize the danger; necessary is 14...♕d8 15 ♗e3 with an obvious plus but nothing immediate) 15 ♗c4! (the black queen is trapped!) 15...d5 (the only way out, but giving up a centre pawn for nothing hardly changes the evaluation) 16 exd5 (weaker is 16 ♘a2 ♕d6 17 e5 ♘xe5, when Black at least gets some centre pawns for the piece, although 18 fxe5 ♕xe5 19 ♗d4 ♕d6 20 ♗xf6 ♗xf6 21 ♕xd5 should nevertheless win for White) 16...♖ad8 17 ♕e2 ♘b8 18 ♖ad1 ♘bd7 (18...♕d6 19 ♘b5 ♕xf4 20 ♗c5 also wins quickly) 19 d6! exd6 20 ♘a2 and as the queen can't be saved (20...♖fe8 21 ♕c2) Black resigned, 1-0 T.Taylor-B.Lazarus, La Palma 2011.

11 ♔h1

11...♖c8

11...♘d7 12 f4 transposes back to Karpov-Sosonko, while the Ladies World Champion (as she was known in those days) also scored from this position with a different plan: 12 ♖b1 ♗xb3 13 cxb3 ♘c5 14 f3 ♘e6 15 ♗h4 ♘ed4 16 ♗c4 ♔h8 17 ♘d5 ♖c8 18 ♕d2 f5 19 ♖be1 ♖e8 20 ♗g5 ♘e5 21 exf5 ♘xf5 22 ♗b5 and White's bishop pair gave her a crushing advantage in N.Gaprindashvili-W.Schinzel, Sandomierz 1976.

12 f4 ♘b4

12...d5 fails: 13 ♗xf6 ♗xf6 14 exd5.

13 ♘d4 ♗c4

13...d5 is still faulty: 14 f5 ♗d7 15 e5 ♘e4 16 ♘xe4 dxe4 17 c3 ♘a6 as 18 f6 buries the Dragon.

14 ♘db5 ♕b6

14...d5 is still false: 15 ♗xc4 ♖xc4 16 ♗xf6 ♗xf6 17 exd5 ♖c5 18 ♕e2 ♗xc3 19 ♘xc3 ♘xd5 20 ♘e4 ♖c6 21 ♖ad1 with a huge positional advantage.

15 ♗h4 ♕c5 16 ♗d3 ♖fd8 17 ♗f2 ♕h5 18 ♗b6

The early ...a7-a5, beloved of the Accelerated Dragon, once again shows up as a weakness.

18...♕xd1 19 ♖fxd1 ♖f8 20 ♘a7!

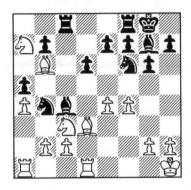

Just 20 moves and the game is decided—without doing anything, or seeming to do anything, Karpov has won material: the pawn at a5, the rook at c8, and the bishop at c4 are all under attack and something's gotta give!

20...♗xd3 21 ♘xc8 ♗xc2

Or 21...♖xc8 22 cxd3 and Karpov will win technically with his extra exchange. Hernandez instead invites complications:

22 ♘xe7+ ♔h8 23 ♗xa5 ♗xd1 24 ♖xd1 ♘g4 25 ♗xb4 ♘f2+ 26 ♔g1 ♘xd1 27 ♘xd1 ♖e8 28 ♗xd6 ♗f6 29 ♘d5 ♗d4+ 30 ♔f1 ♖xe4 31 a5 ♔g7 32 ♗b4 f6 33 ♗c3 ♗xc3 34 ♘1xc3

Winding up with a rook vs. two knights and pawn, an advantage which Karpov mercilessly translates to victory.

34...♖e8 35 ♘c7 ♖e7 36 ♘3d5 ♖e4 37 b4

The two knights shepherd the queenside pawn majority through, and there's nothing Black can do about it.

37...♔f7 38 b5 ♖a4 39 a6 bxa6 40 bxa6 ♖a2 41 ♘c3 1-0

After 41...♖a1+ 42 ♔e2 ♖a3 43 ♘3b5 the rook will be lost in a few more moves.

The great thing about Karpov's line is that it can equally be played against the regular and Accelerated Dragon—Black is struggling to equalize either way.

Now let's move on to something different: if you're facing the Dragon and are not in the mood for Karpovian grinding, I offer something more savage: the Alekhine Attack!

Game 27
A.Alekhine-M.Botvinnik
Nottingham 1936

---

1 e4 c5 2 ♘f3 d6 3 d4 cxd4 4 ♘xd4 ♘f6 5 ♘c3 g6

Once upon a time, back in my high school days, my school was matched against another whose reputation as Dragon fiends had preceded them. It was said that no one dared to play 1 e4 against them, for they had the Dragon memorized out 20 moves! (This was considered very far along in those days—it's nothing now of course.) Anyway, even then I didn't think much of memorization, and even though I normally was a queen's pawn or Bird player, I nonetheless decided to open with 1 e4. At this point I played the Levenfish Attack, 6 f4, and my opponent continued mechanically with 6...♗g7 (6...♘c6 is correct—if you know your Dragon as opposed to only memorizing one line—and after this error the game concluded as follows...) 7 e5 dxe5 8 fxe5 ♘g4 9 ♗b5+ ♗d7 10 ♕xg4 1-0 T.Taylor-Dragon Fiend, school match 1970. My opponent ruefully admitted afterwards that he had not memorized *that* line—and what was the name of it anyway?

I've had much the same experience with the Alekhine Attack—people don't even know the name of it, let alone what to play against it!

6 ♗e2 ♗g7 7 ♗e3 ♘c6 8 ♘b3

White keeps pieces on and restrains ...d6-d5.

8...♗e6

8...0-0 9 f4 a5 is the correct move order according to modern theory, but Black is not out of the woods yet, as Game 32, Taylor-Amanov (again!) will show. However, the game will most likely take more than 30 moves in this variation!

9 f4 0-0 10 g4!

The Alekhine Attack! I have scored six tournament wins in 31 moves or less with this (two of them in only 21 moves!)—two of these wins are seen in Games 29 and 30, with the other four featuring in the notes.

White can also play 10 0-0—but it's not part of my recommended repertoire. In general, White doesn't want to castle short in the Alekhine Attack unless one can get the ...a7-a5 concession, after which b5 and b6 are permanently weakened.

10...d5

This Steinitzian counter in the centre seems the natural response to White's kingside attack—but Fischer convincingly demonstrated that it's a serious mistake, as we'll see in the next game. The one after that features the also frequently played 10...公a5, which also fails to equalize. In my opinion, the only way Black can hope to obtain a

playable game from here is 10...a5!, which leads to a wild slugfest where both sides have chances (see Game 31).

11 f5 இc8 12 exd5 公b4 13 d6

Brilliant but flawed: 13 இf3 is Fischer's improvement, when White is clearly better. Fischer's game will come up next—but first, Botvinnik has to solve Alekhine's wildly imaginative pawn thrust! He did hold a draw with a sparkling resource, but he could have played for more.

13...豐xd6

13...exd6! is stronger. Alekhine thought this was impossible because of "g4-g5 followed by f5-f6 etc", as he wrote in his notes in the famous *Nottingham 1936* tournament book. Superficially this looks correct but, as Vukovic pointed out in his *Art of Attack*, the note is *incorrect* as Black can clearly sac a piece; e.g. 14 g5 இxf5! 15 gxf6 公xc2+ 16 當d2 豐xf6 and Black has a winning attack. Instead, 14 a3 罩e8 15 இg5 is relatively best (15 இf4 公c6 16 g5 公e4 again gives Black a decisive attack), but now there is no g4-g5/f5-f6 advance, so after 15...♘c6 Black is better in view of White's overextended position.

14 ♗c5 ♕f4!

14...♕xd1+ 15 ♖xd1 ♘c6 (15...♘xc2+ 16 ♔d2 traps the knight) 16 g5 ♘d7 17 f6! was Alekhine's great idea, when Black's position cracks at the e7-square.

15 ♖f1 ♕xh2!! 16 ♗xb4 ♘xg4

The second piece sacrifice forces the draw.

17 ♗xg4

17 ♗c5 ♕h4+ 18 ♗f2 ♘xf2 19 ♖xf2 ♗xf5 is way too dangerous for White—Black has three pawns for the piece and a raging attack.

17...♕g3+ 18 ♖f2

Alekhine points out that 18 ♔d2? ♗h6+ wins for Black.

18...♕g1+ 19 ♖f1

Necessary—as after 19 ♔e2? ♕xg4+ 20 ♔e1 ♕xb4 both loose bishops drop, with a win for Black.

19...♕g3+ 20 ♖f2 ♕g1+ ½-½

Short, sharp, brilliant but flawed—now that's a human World Champion vs. World Champion game!

Alekhine's terrific idea lay dormant for many years, until Bobby Fischer saw the possibilities—and blasted his old rival Reshevsky right off the board!

Game 28
R.J.Fischer-S.Reshevsky
Los Angeles
(2nd matchgame) 1961

1 e4 c5 2 ♘f3 ♘c6 3 d4 cxd4 4 ♘xd4 g6 5 ♘c3 ♗g7 6 ♗e3 ♘f6 7 ♗e2 0-0 8 f4 d6 9 ♘b3

9...♗e6

"The old and second rate move" – Fischer. However, I don't think it's that bad if Black follows 10 g4 with 10...a5, as I've already mentioned.

The very passive set-up which I faced in one game is much weaker: 9...♗d7 10 g4 ♘e8 11 h4 a5 12 a4 ♗e6 13 f5 ♗xb3 14 cxb3 gxf5?! (from bad to worse) 15 gxf5 ♔h8 16 ♕d2 ♘f6 17 0-0-0 ♖c8 18 ♔b1 ♖g8 19 h5 ♘d7 20 h6 and White had a decisive advantage in T.Taylor-A.Kretchetov, 3rd Metropolitan

Invitational, Los Angeles 2011.

10 g4 d5

This move is definitely "old and second rate"! We'll see the better 10...♘a5 and probably best 10...a5 in Games 29 and 31 respectively.

11 f5 ♗c8 12 exd5 ♘b4 13 ♗f3!!

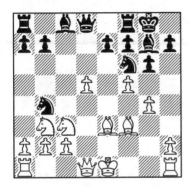

As far as I can see, this refutes the entire variation with 10...d5. "White maintains his centre pawn and sacs two pawns on the kingside where Black must expose his king to get them" – Fischer.

13...gxf5 14 a3!

The black knight is driven to a bad square.

14...fxg4 15 ♗g2 ♘a6 16 ♕d3!

The final link in the chain begun with 13 ♗f3—the c8-bishop is deprived of the f5-square, and so can't defend the kingside.

16...e6

Fischer calls this "the best choice in a difficult position". Black has two main alternatives:

a) 16...♘d7 17 0-0-0 ♘e5 18 ♕e2 "and Black's game is lifeless: White has

h2-h3 and ♗d4 in the offing," says Fischer. I agree—in general, Black's problem is that, due to the target g-pawn, he can't keep lines closed on the kingside.

b) 16...♘c7, repositioning the knight, was tried by my eternal Dragon opponent, Amanov—but this is too slow and White soon had a won game: 17 0-0-0 ♘ce8 18 h3 g3 (lines opened to devastating effect after 18...♘d6 19 hxg4 ♗xg4 20 ♖df1 ♖e8 21 ♗h3 ♗h5 22 ♖fg1 ♗g6 23 ♖xg6!—the first of three powerful sacrifices that leave the black king helpless—23...hxg6 24 ♘d4 ♘d7 25 ♗e6! ♘e5 26 ♕f1 ♘dc4 27 ♗xf7+!!—third and totally decisive: Black may be up material but White has a mating attack—27...♘xf7 28 ♘e6 ♘xe3 29 ♕g1 ♕b6 30 ♕xg6 ♘f5 31 ♕h7 mate, C.D'Amore-P.Passerotti, Rome 1986). Returning to my game, after 18...g3, there is a further split—what I actually played, and what I should have played!

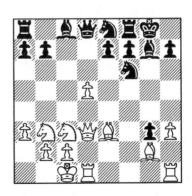

b1) 19 ♘e2 (this is too slow, and Black now gets some chances to hold,

though of course White is still better)
19...♘d6 20 ♘xg3 ♕c7 21 ♖hg1 ♗d7 22
♘d4 ♖ac8 23 ♗e4 ♔h8 24 ♗f4 ♕b6 25
♗f3 ♘c4 26 b3 ♘xa3 27 ♘gf5 ♗xf5 28
♕xf5 ♘xc2 29 ♘xc2 ♕xb3 30 ♖xg7
♔xg7 31 ♖g1+ ♔h8 32 ♗h6 ♖g8 33
♗g7+ (White wins a piece but is running out of pawns) 33...♖xg7 34 ♕xc8+
♘g8 35 ♖xg7 ♔xg7 36 ♕g4+ ♔f8 37
♕f4 ♕c3 38 d6 exd6 39 ♕xd6+ ♔g7 40
♗xb7 ♕xh3 41 ♕d4+ ♘f6 42 ♘e3 ♕d7
43 ♕xa7 ♕c7+ 44 ♔b1 ♕e5 45 ♕b6
(now I accepted a draw offer as I have
no pawns left to win with!) ½-½
T.Taylor-Z.Amanov, 1st Metropolitan
IM, Los Angeles 2010.

b2) 19 ♗d2 is evidently correct, as
White will win the g-pawn and open
the g-file against Black's king; ultimately Black can't stop this plan, so
basically White wins his pawn back
with a huge attack—for the record, *Mr.
Fritz* also goes to "decisive advantage"
after this move: e.g. 19...♕d6 (Black
fails to hold the vital g-pawn after
19...♘h5 20 ♗f3 ♘ef6 21 ♗xh5 ♘xh5
22 ♕f3 ♘f6 23 ♖dg1 and it's all over)
20 ♕f3 ♗d7 21 ♗f4 ♕b6 22 ♗xg3 ♘d6
23 ♗f2 ♕c7 24 ♖hg1 and White's advantage is overwhelming.

I can still hardly believe that
Amanov escaped from those two lost
positions (above and Game 25)—if I
had succeeded in "winning the won
game" in those two cases our "Dragon
match" would not have been 2-2 (two
wins for me, two draws for him) but
rather 4-0!

17 0-0-0 ♘xd5

After 17...exd5 Fischer gives 18 h3
g3 19 ♗d4 with a big White advantage
for all the typical reasons—the g-file is
opening and the black king is decidedly
unsafe; e.g. 19...♘h5 20 ♗xg7 ♕g5+ 21
♔b1 ♕xg7 22 ♘xd5 ♔h8 23 ♗f3 and
ultimately the g3-pawn will fall (as in
the note to Taylor-Amanov above).

18 h3 g3 19 ♖hg1 ♕d6 20 ♗xd5 exd5

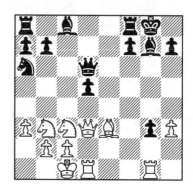

21 ♘xd5

Good but not best. "Nowadays I
would have played 21 ♗d4 without
giving it a second thought," writes
Fischer—and he's right! Black can
hardly hold after this; e.g. 21...♗xd4 (a
check doesn't help: 21...♕f4+ 22 ♔b1
♗xd4 23 ♘xd4 ♘c5 24 ♕b5 b6 25
♘de2 and Black can't hold his numerous weaknesses—one sees that both g3
and d5 are falling to begin with, while
the black king is on the endangered
list) 22 ♕xd4 f5 (if 22...♗e6 then 23 ♕f6
♖fd8 24 ♘e4 wins quickly) 23 ♖xg3+
♕xg3 24 ♖g1 ♕xg1+ 25 ♕xg1+ ♔f7 26
♘xd5 and the queen will beat the disconnected rooks without difficulty.

21...♔h8 22 ♗f4 ♕g6 23 ♕d2

Vukovic likes 23 ♕f3 here—but, as Fischer says, Black at least temporarily holds with 23...♗f5 24 ♖xg3 ♕c6.

23...♗xh3 24 ♖xg3 ♗g4 25 ♖h1 ♖fe8 26 ♘e3 ♕e4?

Losing! After the correct 26...f5 Black, as Fischer says again, holds for now—though I think White still stands better after 27 ♕g2 due to Black's exposed king.

27 ♕h2!

The f4-bishop is immune, while 27...f5 fails to 28 ♕xh7 mate!

27...♗e6 28 ♖xg7

Of course 28 ♘d2 wins the queen—but Fischer's move, destroying the g7-bishop, is also decisive, as Black (as so often in Dragon positions) can't defend his king without this vital piece.

28...♔xg7 29 ♕h6+ ♔g8

Losing the queen but nonetheless forced, as 29...♔h8 allows 30 ♗e5+! and mates.

30 ♖g1+ ♕g6 31 ♖xg6+ fxg6 32 ♘d4 ♖ad8 33 ♗e5 ♖d7 34 ♘xe6 ♖xe6 35 ♘g4 ♖f7 36 ♕g5 ♖f1+ 37 ♔d2 h5 38

♕d8+ 1-0

After this check Black can either get mated—38...♔f7 39 ♘h6 mate or 38...♔h7 39 ♕h8 mate—or "fight on" with 38...♖f8 39 ♘h6+ ♔h7 40 ♕xf8 ♖xe5 41 ♕g8+ ♔xh6 42 ♕h8+ ♔g5 43 ♕xe5+, when White is practically a whole queen up.

The Alekhine Attack is not a forced win even after the faulty 10...d5—note that Amanov held out for a half point and even Fischer faltered and gave Reshevsky chances to hold with 26...f5, but all in all, Black is pretty much desperately fighting for a draw in the position after 16 ♕d3, and I don't see any serious improvements.

If you face a knowledgeable opponent, he will avoid Fischer's line—but the alternatives you face might not be any better! Therefore, in the next two games we will look at various "not quite best" alternatives that I have personally encountered, before covering Black's strongest defences in the final two games of the chapter.

Game 29
T.Taylor-M.Bodek
1st Metropolitan International,
Los Angeles 2011

**1 e4 c5 2 ♘f3 d6 3 d4 cxd4 4 ♘xd4 ♘f6
5 ♘c3 g6 6 ♗e2 ♗g7 7 ♗e3 0-0 8 ♘b3
♘c6 9 f4 ♗e6 10 g4 ♘a5**

I have faced this decentralizing move twice, and it's been played about 200 times in the database—but White scores about 70% against it providing he knows the following two moves. White should take advantage of the knight relinquishing control of the d4-square to play g4-g5 and then ♗d4 to try to remove the dragon. Black doesn't seem to have any satisfactory counter to this.

11 g5 ♘d7 12 ♗d4

The fundamental idea: White simply threatens to slay the dragon and then follow with some combination of moves similar to the main game: h4-h5, 0-0-0, and transferring the queen to the h-file.

12...♗xb3

I faced 12...♗xd4 in my other game in this line: 13 ♘xd4 (I tried to keep it in the middlegame, but perhaps the GM preference 13 ♕xd4 is better, when White successfully played against Black's pawn weaknesses in the endgame: 13...♕b6 14 ♕xb6 axb6 15 ♘d4 ♗c4 16 ♗g4 e5 17 ♘db5 f5 18 ♗h3 ♗xb5 19 ♘xb5 ♘c4 20 0-0 ♘c5 21 exf5 gxf5 22 ♘c7 ♘e3 23 ♘xa8 ♘xf1 24 ♖xf1 ♖xa8 25 fxe5 dxe5 26 ♗xf5 ♖a4 27 ♖e1 e4 28 a3 ♖d4 29 b4 ♘a4 30 ♖xe4 ♖d2 31 ♖e7 1-0 K.Asrian-A.Nikanorov, St Petersburg 1999) 13...♗c4 14 h4 ♖c8 15 h5 (very straightforward but hard to stop!) 15...e5 16 ♘f3 ♗xe2 (going for the queen exchange doesn't necessarily help Black, nor should White necessarily avoid it—this seems to be the lesson of these notes; e.g. 16...♕b6 17 hxg6 hxg6 18 ♗xc4 ♖xc4 19 ♖b1 ♕e3+ 20 ♕e2 exf4 21 ♕xe3 fxe3 22 ♔e2 with advantage to White as the h-file is still a factor in the ending) 17 ♕xe2

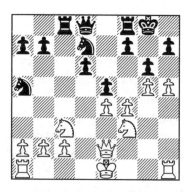

17...♖xc3?! (Dragon players like this, but it's not necessarily good against the Alekhine Attack—see also Games 30 and 32; instead 17...♕b6 is better, when it seems Black has adequate counterplay—this variation is an argument for 13 ♕xd4) 18 bxc3 (White can't rush, as 18 ♕h2? ♖e3+ 19 ♔f2 ♕b6 20 hxg6 ♖c3+ 21 ♔g3 exf4+ 22 ♔g4 ♘e5+ 23 ♘xe5 ♖g3+ wins for Black) 18...♕c7 19 ♕d3 ♖c8 20 hxg6 hxg6 21 ♖d1 ♘c4 22 ♘xe5! ♘cxe5 23 fxe5 ♘xe5 24 ♕h3 (the standard manoeuvre: White gets to the h-file, and Black has nothing better here than to exchange queens with 24...♕xc3+ 25 ♕xc3 ♖xc3 26 ♖xd6 and hope to hold this worse ending—but my opponent stays in the middlegame and loses quickly, as Dragon positions just don't hold without the actual dragon!) 24...♔f8? 25 ♕h8+ ♔e7 26 ♕f6+ ♔e8 27 ♖h8+ ♔d7 28 ♕xe5! (everything is defended and White is a rook up) 28...♖xh8 29 ♕xh8 1-0 T.Taylor-W.Kim, Los Angeles (rapid) 2010.

12...f6 has also been played, which is ugly but does avoid the bishop exchange for the moment: 13 h4 ♘xb3 14 axb3 fxg5 (this seems illogical, but on other moves White continues the attack with h4-h5) 15 ♗xg7 ♔xg7 16 ♕d4+ ♔g8 17 fxg5 ♕b6 18 ♕xb6 ♘xb6 19 h5 (once again there is no safety for Black even after the queen exchange, as the h-file is still a dangerous attacking line) 19...gxh5 20 ♖xh5 a6 21 ♖h6 ♗f7 22 e5! ♗g6 23 exd6 ♖f5 24 0-0-0 ♖xg5 25 ♗f3 ♖d8 26 dxe7 ♖xd1+ 27 ♔xd1 ♔f7 28 ♗xb7 a5 29 ♗e4 ♔xe7 30

♗xg6 hxg6 31 ♖h7+ (the rook breaks through on the file and delivers the decisive blow) 31...♔e6 32 ♖a7 ♖e5 33 ♖a6 1-0 D.Kononenko-A.Sysoenko, Simferopol 2004.

13 ♗xg7!

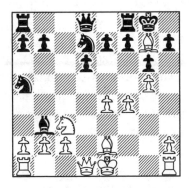

I was stunned to discover that this natural pawn sacrifice for attack (I eliminate my opponent's dragon bishop for Tal's "insignificant unit"), which I came up with at the board, was actually a novelty! It seems to be quite sound, as White's attacking chances are at least equal to the missing material. However, if one is still under the influence of Karpov (rather than Alekhine or Fischer!), it's perfectly possible to simply take toward the centre: 13 axb3 was played in all six games in the database; e.g. 13...e5 (this was clearly Black's idea, which I was willing to sac a pawn to avoid—he saves his dragon here, albeit at the cost of weakening the d5-square) 14 ♗e3 exf4 15 ♗xf4 ♘e5 16 ♕d2 ♘ac6 17 ♘d5 (White has a solid Karpovian edge, but there won't be any Fischeresque "fracturing"

in the middlegame!) 17...罝c8 18 奧e3 罝e8 19 罝f1 ⓝd7 20 0-0-0 ♛a5 21 ♛xa5 ⓝxa5 22 奧g4 罝cd8 23 奧xd7 罝xd7 24 奧d4 罝c8 25 奧f6 ♚h8 26 罝d3, when White exploited Black's weaknesses on both sides of the board and won in a Karpovian 64 moves in J.Ramon Perez-D.Moreno Gracia, Aragon 2008.

13...奧xc2

Clearly 13...♚xg7 14 axb3 gives White an enormous positional advantage, so Black must go for the pawn—but now White is ready to go long.

14 ♛xc2 ♚xg7 15 h4!

Signalling the attack, and preparing to meet 15...e5 with 16 f5.

15...ⓝc6

Bringing the knight back to the centre, but White's next not only stops ...ⓝd4, it furthers the attack. A better try is 15...罝c8 16 0-0-0 ♛b6 17 ♚b1 ♛e3 18 f5, even though this also gives White a big attack.

16 0-0-0 ♛a5 17 ♚b1

White has time for this, as Black's king position can't be shored up in one move.

17...ⓝc5 18 h5!

Now! It's hard to see how Black can defend with no kingside pieces—and especially no dragon—a theme that repeats over and over in this variation. Of course the extra pawn is meaningless here.

18...e5?!

18...ⓝb4 19 ♛d2 ⓝxe4 may have been what Black was hoping for, but this fails to 20 ♛d4+. I believe my opponent noticed this and tried to make it work by playing the text move, but this is a fatal mistake. Instead, the computer tries to hold with 18...ⓝe6, but White's attack is still too strong after 19 罝d5 ♛b6 20 f5! ⓝb4 21 ♛d1.

19 hxg6 fxg6

19...hxg6 20 f5 is decisive.

20 奧c4!!

The winning blow: Black has no significant defence to the threat of a sac on h7; e.g. 20...b5 21 罝xh7+! ♚xh7 22 ♛h2+ ♚g7 23 ♛h6 mate.

20...h5 21 gxh6+ ♚h7 22 f5

It looks like Frank is on the job: "clearing small obstacles off the track"!

22...♘e7 23 ♘d5!

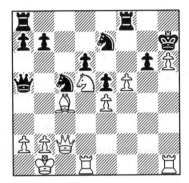

Winning by force, as the defender of g6 is eliminated.

23...♖ae8 24 ♘xe7 ♖xe7 25 fxg6+

White finishes with all checks.

25...♔xg6 26 ♖dg1+ ♔h7 27 ♖g7+ ♖xg7 28 hxg7+ ♔xg7 29 ♕g2+ 1-0

Black resigns in view of 29...♔f6 30 ♖f1+ ♔e7 31 ♕g7+ ♔d8 32 ♖xf8 mate.

Black doesn't equalize in this line (10...♘a5) but he has some chances (better than in Fischer-Reshevsky) of staying slightly worse after the immediate 12...♗xd4, when he can try to draw an inferior endgame.

> ## Game 30
> ## T.Taylor-M.Casella
> SCCF Championship,
> Los Angeles 2010

1 f4

I have often reached the Alekhine Attack by way of Bird's Opening, with devastating results. The effects go more or less like this: 1. The opponent is surprised by the Bird; 2. He seeks safety in the Sicilian; 3. He is stunned by the appearance of Alekhine's ghost; 4. He is lost in twenty moves. I have incorporated some of these short wins in the notes.

1...c5 2 ♘f3 ♘c6 3 e4

In my book on Bird's Opening, I said that I didn't think White had a real chance of getting an opening advantage with any other move—and I still agree with that statement, but I've changed how I play after that. In the book I recommend a version of the Grand Prix Attack—if I ever do an update, I will now recommend the coming transposition to the Open Sicilian and specifically, the Alekhine Attack!

3...g6 4 d4 cxd4 5 ♘xd4 ♗g7 6 ♘b3 d6 7 ♘c3 ♘f6 8 ♗e2 0-0

A pair of short Bird/Sicilian/Alekhine wins occurred after 8...♗d7 9 ♗e3 a6 10 g4 0-0 11 g5 ♘e8 12 h4 and then we have:

a) 12...b5 13 h5 b4 14 ♘d5 a5 15 hxg6 fxg6 16 ♘b6 ♗xb2 17 ♘xd7 ♕xd7

18 ♘c5 ♗c3+ 19 ♔f2 ♕c8 20 ♗c4+ e6 (or 20...♔g7 21 ♖xh7+!!—this combination occurs again and again in the Alekhine Attack, so always keep an eye out for it! Black is mated after 21...♔xh7 22 ♕h1+ ♔g7 23 ♕h6) 21 ♗xe6+ 1-0 T.Taylor-R.Akopian, Los Angeles (rapid) 2010—the extra queen is enough.

b) 12...♖c8 13 h5 e6 14 ♕d2 b5 15 ♗d3 ♘b4 16 ♕h2 (with simple direct moves White gets to the h-file, and the game is virtually decided) 16...♘xd3+ 17 cxd3 b4 18 ♘d1 ♗b5 19 hxg6 fxg6 20 ♕xh7+ ♔f7 21 ♖h6 ♗xd3 22 ♕xg6+ ♔g8 23 ♕xe6+ ♖f7 24 g6 1-0 T.Taylor-T.Kukavica, Los Angeles (rapid) 2010. Here White emerges only one rook up!

9 ♗e3

9...♗e6

Another 21-move win came about after 9...a6 10 g4 b5 11 g5 ♘d7 12 h4 ♘b6 13 h5 ♘a4 14 hxg6 hxg6 15 ♘xa4 bxa4 16 ♘d4 ♘xd4 17 ♗xd4 e5 18 ♗c3 ♕c7 19 ♕d3 d5 20 f5! (the second lever also shields the white queen—the game is already decided) 20...dxe4 21

♕h3 1-0 T.Taylor-M.Miralaie, La Palma 2010.

10 g4

We have now reached Alekhine-Botvinnik by transposition, when I think 10...a5 (see the next game) is best. But here, although my opponent is a strong master, he was clearly surprised in many ways and succeeded only in dragging the game out just past move 30!

10...♖c8

This move has no immediate threat and so is much too quiet for such a sharp position.

11 f5 ♗d7 12 g5 ♘e8 13 fxg6 hxg6 14 h4

There are a couple of interesting things about this position: first of all, Black is on the ropes after only 14 moves in one of the most popular lines of the Sicilian. Try getting that in your booked-up Yugoslav Attack! And the second thing is, speaking of booked up, the game you are looking at is the one and only game in the database with this position! That's almost unbelievable—yet true—and shows both how unpopular, and how strong the Alekhine Attack is. And to think all this came from Bird's Opening!

14...♘a5

Mr. Fritz is so desperate he throws out the radical 14...♝xc3+ as the number one defence, then finds a sparkling refutation of same—which is not at all surprising, for as we have seen over and over again, Black can hardly hold his king position without his pet dragon. The main line runs as follows: 15 bxc3 ♘g7 16 h5 gxh5 17 ♝xh5 ♛c7 18 ♛e2 (preparing to Yandemirov to the h-file) 18...♘e5 19 ♝d4 ♘e6 20 ♝xf7+!! ♖xf7 21 ♛h5 ♖g7 22 ♛h8+ ♚f7 23 ♖f1+ ♚g6 24 ♛h6 mate.

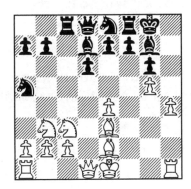

15 h5!

The second lever opens the key file against the king.

15...e6 16 hxg6 fxg6 17 ♛d2

The black king is wide open, and the white queen is getting ready to slide to the h-file, while 0-0-0 is on the agenda to add a second rook to the attack. *Fritz* is at clear +1—no advice can be given

to Black, except study the opening! Move 17 is already too late.

17...♖xc3

A typical dragon sac for counterplay, but as I've mentioned before, this rarely has any effect against the Alekhine Attack. Even worse is 17...♘c4 18 ♝xc4 ♖xc4 19 ♛h2, when White reaches the h-file by express, and the black king will soon perish due to the open h- and f-files.

18 bxc3 ♛c7 19 ♝d4

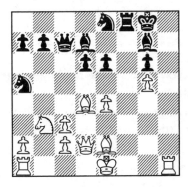

I threaten to destroy the dragon, after which White has a positional and material advantage. Black's answering block creates new problems on the a2-g8 diagonal, much as in the previous game—one sees how many Alekhine Attack ideas repeat, which makes it an easy opening for an attacking player to play.

19...e5 20 ♘xa5 d5

Necessary, since 20...♛xa5 21 ♝c4+ (or the similar 20...exd4 21 ♝c4+) wins another exchange at least.

21 ♝e3

A safe and clear win—the computer

prefers the complicated 21 ♗xa7, which I think is completely unnecessary. After the simple text, Black has to go in for an extremely unfavourable queen exchange.

21...♕xa5 22 ♕xd5+ ♕xd5 23 exd5 b6 24 d6!

White attacks on both the d- and h-files. The latter file is often still a big factor even after the queens are exchanged in this variation.

24...♘xd6 25 ♖d1 ♗c6

Forced, but now...

26 ♖h6!

And Black has no defence to the multitude of threats.

26...♘f7

Or 26...♗xh6 27 ♖xd6 and White comes out a piece up.

27 ♖xg6 ♗e4 28 ♖e6 ♗xc2 29 ♖d2

With a winning position in hand, there was no reason to risk the complications after 29 ♖d7 ♗f5 30 ♗c4, which the Oracle claims is an alternate win.

29...♗f5 30 ♖c6 ♗e4 31 ♖c7 1-0

White's material plus is decisive.

Coming at the Alekhine Attack by way of Bird's Opening is startling to say the least, and is an excellent way to confuse your opponents and score some quick wins! Note that even when the main line was reached, Black reacted too slowly and was in trouble by move 14 (in a virgin database position!) and dead lost by move 20.

> ## Game 31
> ### T.Taylor-G.Carreto Nieto
> 3rd Metropolitan Invitational,
> Los Angeles 2011

1 e4 c5 2 ♘f3 ♘c6 3 ♘c3 g6

No one played the "principled" 3...e5 against me—analysis of this move will be found in Chapter Six.

4 d4 cxd4 5 ♘xd4 ♗g7 6 ♗e3

Remember 6 ♘b3 (not fearing 6...♗xc3+) is necessary if you want to play Karpov's line with a later ♗g5.

6...♘f6 7 ♗e2 0-0 8 ♘b3 d6 9 f4 ♗e6

Fischer's recommendation for Black, 9...a5, will be discussed in the next game.

10 g4 a5!

I run up against a well-prepared opponent! This razor sharp and critical move is, in my opinion, Black's best choice at this stage.

11 f5!

I was surprised by my opponent's quickly played move, but I did find the best answer over the board—it's my next move that started my downfall! White is facing a difficult strategic problem: Black is threatening ...a5-a4-a3, softening the long diagonal, and making queenside castling very dangerous. However, stopping the pawn in its tracks with a2-a4 allows the black knight a good square at b4, and castling long is still really risky as the a4-pawn is a target. One must also watch out for Black's ...d6-d5 counterstroke—and furthermore (during the game I overlooked this possibility until my opponent made his 13th move) if the white king stays in the centre, there are piece sacrifice possibilities for Black to take advantage of White's extended pawns and unsafe king.

So is White just worse? Absolutely not! White has trumps as well, starting with the move I played, which drives the black bishop off its support for ...d6-d5, while White has a big space advantage on the kingside. One has to let go of the 0-0-0 dream, though, and play realistically, as we will see, with a somewhat Birdish position.

First, let's see what happens if White does not play my 11 f5:

a) 11 a4 is not correct as, unlike in Fischer-Reshevsky, the black knight that will come to b4 cannot be kicked by a2-a3—yes, pawns can't move backwards! 11...d5 12 f5 ♗c8 13 exd5 ♘b4 and Black has a good game, as there is no easy way (no a2-a3) to get rid of the interloper.

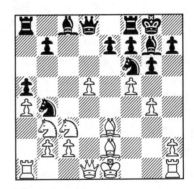

White can try:

a1) 14 d6?! (this just opens lines for Black) 14...exd6 15 ♘d4 ♖e8 16 ♗g5 ♕b6 17 ♘cb5 ♘xg4 18 c3 ♘c6 19 fxg6 hxg6 20 ♘xd6 ♘xd4 21 ♘xe8 ♘f3+ 0-1 G.Popilsky-I.Porat, Givataim 2007.

a2) 14 ♗f3 gxf5 15 gxf5 ♗xf5 with good counterplay against c2—note again the strong knight on b4.

a3) 14 ♕d2

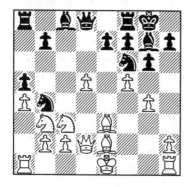

14...♘fxd5 15 ♘xd5 ♕xd5 16 0-0-0 ♕c6! (gaining time by attacking the weak a4-pawn, which sticks out from White's long castling position like the proverbial sore thumb) 17 ♗b5 ♕e4 and White's king appears less safe than Black's; e.g. 18 h3 (or 18 ♖de1 ♕xg4 and it's hard to see any compensation for the pawn) 18...♘xc2! and a king-protecting pawn goes. So that's it for 11 a4.

b) 11 g5 doesn't do much better: 11...♘d7 12 h4 a4 13 ♘d4 a3 14 ♔f2 (or 14 b3 ♕b6 and White is under great pressure) 14...axb2 15 ♖b1 ♕a5 (having faced Ovsejevitsch's technical mastery myself, I knew this game wouldn't last long when I saw who was Black!) 16 ♘cb5 ♗xa2 17 ♖xb2 ♘c5 18 ♗f3 e5 19 ♘xc6 bxc6 20 ♕xd6 ♘b7 21 ♕xc6 exf4 (splendid: the rook and bishop are under attack) 22 ♗c1 ♖ac8 23 ♕xb7 ♗xb2 24 ♗xf4 ♖xc2+ 25 ♔g3 ♗c4 26 ♗d1 ♗xb5 27 ♗xc2 ♕c3+ 28 ♔g4 ♗e2 mate, A.Fadin-S.Ovsejevitsch, Ukrainian

Championship, Donetsk 1993.

c) 11 a3 doesn't help either: 11...a4 12 ♘d2 (after 12 ♘d4 ♗xg4 13 ♗xg4 ♘xg4 Black wins a pawn) 12...d5 and Black is much better with this central break.

So almost by elimination, one sees the played and active 11 f5 is not only best but practically the only move.

11...♗d7

12 a4

Had I known there was a piece sac hidden in the position, I wouldn't have played either this or my next move. In fact, even if I play 12 g5 right now, Black can still sac the piece with 12...♘xe4!! (12...♘e8 is possible too) 13 ♘xe4 gxf5 (now White has to dodge a thicket of pitfalls just to... draw!) 14 ♘g3 (after 14 ♘c3 a4 15 ♘d4 a3 16 b3 f4 17 ♗f2 ♕a5 18 ♕d2 ♘xd4 19 ♗xd4 e5 20 ♗f2 e4 21 ♗d4 e3 22 ♕d1 ♕xg5 Black has a winning attack, while 14 ♘f2 a4 15 ♘d4 f4 also wins for Black) 14...a4 15 ♘d2 (not 15 ♘d4? f4) 15...a3 16 b3, when my analysis runs 16...♗xa1 17 ♕xa1 e5 18 ♘h5 ♘b4 19 ♘f6+ ♕xf6

20 gxf6 ♘xc2+ 21 ♔f2 ♘xa1 22 ♖g1+ ♔h8 23 ♗h6 ♘c2 24 ♗g7+ ♔g8 25 ♗h6+ ♔h8 with a draw! Not exactly what we wanted—and what a struggle that was just to get to the half point! No, there *must* be something better, and there is!

12 ♘d2! is best. This modest move draws the sting from ...a4-a3, protects the centre, and in general leaves White with a good Bird-type position: 12...a4 (the central break doesn't work here: 12...d5 13 exd5 ♘b4 14 ♘c4 gxf5 15 a3! ♘a6 16 gxf5 ♗xf5 17 ♗b6 ♕d7 18 ♖g1 with a powerful attack—note the importance of 15 a3 in this line) 13 a3 (vital) 13...♘e5 14 g5 ♘e8 15 0-0 and let's take a look: White seems to have castled on the wrong side of the board but, on second thought, the king's rook supports the f5-pawn in a simple way and White has a potential Bird attack coming with ♕e1 and ♕g3 or ♕h4. I'd call it a slight edge for White, with a concurrent vote from *Mr. Fritz*.

But needless to say, one must be thoroughly prepared when playing such sharp lines—I was not at the time of this game, and paid the price!

12...♘b4 13 g5

Walking into the main line of my opponent's preparation, but 13 ♕d2 is not much better: 13...♗c6 14 ♗f3 d5 15 exd5 (or 15 e5 ♘e4 and the white pawns are overextended) 15...♘fxd5 16 ♘xd5 ♘xd5 17 0-0-0 ♘xe3 18 ♕xe3 ♕c7 19 ♗xc6 ♕xc6 20 fxg6 hxg6, and once again White's a2-a4 is completely

out of place and, worse yet, Black's dragon is breathing fire down the long diagonal.

13...♘xe4!!

Instantly!

Now I understood my opponent's play—too late! This square should have been overprotected with 12 ♘d2, but now e4 falls and both black bishops come to life.

White can only hope for a draw after this powerful blow.

14 ♘xe4 ♗xf5

Black has only two pawns for the piece, but the raging bishops plus White's unsafe king tip the scales in

Black's favour. This is my kind of position—except I was on the wrong side of it!

15 ♗d3 ♖c8 16 0-0 d5 17 ♘f6+

Or 17 ♘g3 ♗xd3 18 cxd3 ♘c2 19 ♕d2 ♘xa1 20 ♖xa1 b6 and Black's rook and two pawns are better than White's two inactive knights.

17...exf6 18 ♗xf5 gxf5 19 c3 ♖e8 20 gxf6

Better is 20 ♗d4 ♘c6 21 gxf6 ♗xf6 22 ♖xf5 which keeps the damage to a minimum, but White is still a pawn down for nothing.

20...♖xe3 21 fxg7 ♕g5+ 22 ♔h1 ♘d3

Black's attack is too strong—my opponent didn't let me suffer long.

23 ♘d4 ♖ce8 24 ♕b3 ♘f4 25 ♖g1 ♖e1 26 ♕c2

Or 26 ♖axe1 ♖xe1 27 ♖xe1 ♕g2 mate.

26...♕xg1 mate

The sharp move 10...a5 is definitely a game changer, if not a game winner. After this there are no more smooth kingside attacks as in Game 30. White

must adapt to circumstances: overprotect his centre after the sequence 11 f5 ♗d7 12 ♘d2! and then castle short with a slight edge in a Bird-type position.

One must recognize that it's not always possible just to knock your opponent out—especially when he's well prepared!

Game 32
T.Taylor-Z.Amanov
Landon Brownell Memorial, Los Angeles 2011

1 e4 c5 2 ♘f3 d6 3 d4 cxd4 4 ♘xd4 ♘f6 5 ♘c3 g6 6 ♗e2 ♗g7 7 ♗e3 ♘c6 8 ♘b3 ♗e6

This changed move order doesn't seem to have any independent value: 8...0-0 9 f4 a5 10 a4 ♗e6 transposes to the game using Fischer's recommended route.

9 f4 a5

Generally approved by opening books: Black discourages White from castling long.

10 a4 0-0 11 0-0

As we saw in the notes to the previous game, White can hardly castle long with the a-pawn sticking out on a4. However, since White has not committed himself to g2-g4 (as Black rushed forward with ...a7-a5), he can simply castle short as here and play in Karpovian style against the dark side of Black's pawn thrust: that is, the weaknesses at b5 and b6.

11...♖c8 12 ♔h1

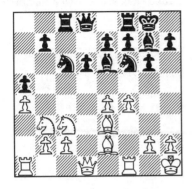

12...♘b4

By far the most popular move, but two alternatives should be mentioned.

a) The early 12...d5 is, as so often, a false freeing move: 13 f5 gxf5 (not 13...♗d7 14 fxg6 dxe4 as 15 gxf7+ ♖xf7 16 ♘xe4! wins, while after 14...hxg6 15 exd5 ♘b4 16 ♗f3 White is a big pawn up) 14 exf5 ♗d7 15 ♕d2 and Black's kingside and d-pawn are weak.

b) 12...♗xb3 seemingly devalues White's pawns, but it also weakens Black's light squares (particularly the already weak b5) and leaves White with the two bishops. Tiviakov gives a Grandmaster class in exploiting these advantages (though he does make one early bobble): 13 cxb3 ♘d7 14 ♗c4 (actually White should simply occupy the file Black gave him with 14 ♖c1—we'll see Shirov use a similar strategy in Game 46—when he has the better game with no problems; as played, Black gets one chance for good counterplay by chopping off White's prema-

turely exposed bishop; that said, the rest of the game is too instructive to omit) 14...♘b4 15 ♕e2 ♘b6 16 ♘d5 ♘4xd5 17 exd5 ♘d7? (Black misses his chance! 17...♘xc4 18 bxc4 ♕d7 both eliminates the bishop pair and gives Black good counterplay—he will suffer dearly for this mistake!) 18 ♖ae1 ♘c5 19 f5!

(White now has a permanent bind on the kingside, and potential attacking chances—Tiviakov takes his time and makes the most of his position) 19...♘d7 20 ♗b5 ♘f6 21 ♗c4 ♘d7 22 h3 ♘c5 23 ♖f3 ♖c7 24 ♗d2 ♕a8 25 ♗g5 ♗f6 26 ♗h6 ♖fc8 27 ♕f2 ♘d7 (Black would trap himself if he tries the trick 27...♘xa4, as White breaks through on the kingside with 28 fxg6 fxg6 29 ♖xf6 exf6 30 bxa4 ♖xc4 31 ♕xf6 ♖4c7 32 ♖e7 and mates, while 28...hxg6? 29 ♖xf6 exf6 30 ♕xf6 mates even more quickly) 28 fxg6 hxg6 29 ♖e4 ♖f8 (since every white piece is attacking, Black decides to eliminate one at the cost of the exchange—there's nothing better anyway; e.g. 29...♘c5 fails to 30 ♖e2 ♘d7 31 ♗b5 ♔h7 32 ♖xe7! ♗xe7 33 ♖xf7+ ♔xh6 34 ♖xe7 and mates) 30 ♗b5 ♕d8 31 ♗xd7 ♖xd7 32 ♗xf8 ♕xf8 33 ♕e1 ♗xb2 34 ♕xa5 ♗e5 (the dragon bishop is not good enough to save the exchange down ending against Tiviakov's excellent technique) 35 ♕b5 ♖c7 36 ♖c4 ♖xc4 37 ♕xc4 ♕h6 38 ♕e2 f6 39 ♕e1 ♕f8 40 a5 ♕c8 41 b4 g5 42 b5 ♕c4 43 ♕f1 ♕xd5 44 a6 bxa6 45 bxa6 ♕a5 46 ♖b3 ♔g7 47 ♖b7 (White combines the advance of the passed pawn with threats to the black king) 47...g4 48 ♖xe7+ ♔f8 49 ♖h7 gxh3 50 ♖xh3 ♕a4 51 ♖h7 ♔g8 52 ♕b1 f5 53 ♖h5 ♕xa6 54 ♖xf5 ♕a1 55 ♕xa1 ♗xa1 56 ♔h2 ♔g7 57 ♔h3 ♔g6 58 ♔g4 ♗e5 59 ♖f8 ♔g7 60 ♖e8 ♔f6 61 ♖a8 ♔f7 62 ♔h5 d5 63 g4 d4 64 ♖a3 ♔e7 65 g5 ♔e6 66 ♔g4 ♔d5 67 ♔f5 ♗d6 68 ♖a5+ ♔c4 69 g6 ♗f8 70 ♔e4 ♗g7 71 ♖d5 ♔c3 72 ♖d7 (the black pawn is stopped, while White's goes through) 1-0 S.Tiviakov-A.Colovic, Benidorm 2009. White's kingside play starting with 19 f5! could not be more instructive.

13 ♘d4 ♗c4

If 13...d5?!, then 14 ♘xe6 fxe6 15 e5 slams the door on the "dreaded dragon" which is now caged.

14 ♗xc4 ♖xc4 15 ♕e2

White has harmonious development with a space advantage and latent kingside attacking chances: not a huge advantage, but a solid plusequals, whereas Black has little counterplay. One important thing is that White can easily improve his position (♖ad1 followed by some kind of central pawn advance), while Black has little to do.

15...♕c8 16 ♖ad1

One of the great things about analyzing with a human being, as opposed to a soulless silicon monster, is that your analytical partner is apt to suggest a (gasp!) human move! My friend Joe and I were looking at this position, preparing for Amanov (and we got exactly the position we wanted, which either indicates our perspicacity or perhaps my opponent's stubbornness), when Joe said, "What if Black sacs the exchange here?" This was not a top pick of the computer, but I realized it was a very human attempt at "getting back to the old Dragon", so we looked at the move for a while, and concluded that Black had no serious compensation for the exchange.

Lo and behold, I'm playing the game, and Amanov... sacs the exchange! Instead of being beset by "sacrificial shock" I simply remembered our joint analysis, which I had then checked with the computer, and easily obtained the advantage!

16...⌶xc3

16...⌶d8 is probably better, but then White moves forward with 17 f5, when Black has a grey and difficult position—take a look at some continuations:

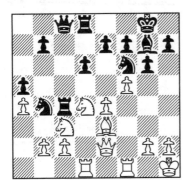

a) 17...♘d7 is passive, and 18 ♘db5 ♘e5 19 ♗d4 gives White has a clear advantage in the centre and incidentally threatens to trap Black's rook with b3.

b) 17...d5 tries for activity, but after 18 e5 Black just loses more space and soon comes under attack: 18...♘e4 19 ♘xe4 dxe4 20 fxg6 hxg6 (if 20...fxg6 then 21 ♘f5 ⌶c7 22 ⌶xd8+ ♕xd8 23 ♘h6+ ♗xh6 24 ♗xh6 creates decisive threats) 21 e6! and White is much better; e.g. 21...f6 (after 21...f5 22 ♘xf5 or 21...♗xd4 22 exf7+ ♔g7 23 ♗xd4+!, White wins immediately) 22 ♕g4 with a powerful attack.

c) 17...⌶e8, waiting, might be best, though obviously White has all the play. The funny thing is how "natural" moves in the "main line" give Black such a difficult game.

From Black's point of view, I prefer Carreto's ...a7-a5 *after* White has played g3-g4, when the committal nature of both sides' play means that Black has chances as well as White.

17 bxc3 ♕xc3

Joe's first thought was 17...♘a2, but we killed that off with 18 ♗d2, when White keeps his centre pawn and the one pawn black gets for the ox is not enough, given his queenside weaknesses. Note how ...a7-a5, whatever its immediate benefits, often hurts Black down the road (them durn pawns don't got no back-up lights!).

18 ♗g1

18...⌶c8

Best, according to *Fritz*, though it seems neither this nor anything else can save Black—let's take a look at the alternatives:

a) 18...e5 (during the game I thought this was absolutely necessary to prevent White playing e5-e5 on the next move, opening lines for the rooks—but this move has its own problems) 19 ♘b5 (White gets a lot of mileage out of this square which was weakened back on move nine) 19...♕xc2 20 ♕xc2 ♘xc2 21 ♘xd6 and Black is struggling to draw an inferior endgame.

b) 18...♘c6 19 e5 ♘e8 20 ♘b5 ♕b4 21 ♖b1 ♕xa4 22 ♘c3 ♕a3 23 ♖b3 traps the queen, which could escape if only the a-pawn was still on a7!

c) 18...♘d7 19 ♕b5 (there's that weak square!) 19...♘c5 (or 19...♕c7 20 c3! ♘c6 21 ♖b1 and the b-file tells) 20 ♖f3 ♕b2 21 c3 wins material.

19 e5!

Without a second's hesitation: White pries open files for the rooks and launches an attack—Black has no compensation for the exchange.

19...dxe5 20 fxe5 ♘fd5 21 e6! f5

Black has to try to keep the position closed. After 21...fxe6 22 ♕xe6+ ♔h8 23 ♕f7, then ♘e6 is coming, while Black can't evict the queen: 23...♖f8 24 ♕xf8+ ♗xf8 25 ♖xf8+ ♔g7 26 ♘e6+ ♔h6 27 ♖f3 and White emerges with an extra rook.

22 ♕b5

Once more with feeling!

22...♕c7

Or 22...b6 23 ♕d7 ♖f8 24 ♘c6! and wins.

23 ♕d7! ♘f6

If 23...♕xd7 24 exd7 ♖d8 25 c4 ♘f6 (or 25...♗xd4 26 ♗xd4 and the bishop dominates), then 26 g4! opens Black up

like a can of sardines; e.g. 26...♔f7 (Black loses after either 26...♘xg4 27 ♘e6 or 26...fxg4 27 ♖xf6! ♗xf6 28 ♘e6 ♘c6 29 ♘xd8 ♘xd8 30 ♗b6 e5 31 ♗xd8 ♗xd8 32 ♖e1 ♗c7 33 ♖xe5!) 27 gxf5 ♖d7 28 fxg6+ hxg6 29 ♘b3 and the rest is just simple technique.

24 ♕xc7

I thought for a moment about sac'ing my queen here, but dismissed it without any real analysis, as I saw a simple clear way to advantage. Meanwhile, Joe, spectating, was furiously analyzing the queen sac! After the game, he said he thought it was sound—though I still dismissed it, saying that *Fritz* would surely find a hole, and my way was simple and clear. So we fired up the evil one, and lo and behold—the queen sac is approved! Great excitement! But then one sees that Black can take the knight instead of the queen, and the queen sac just turns out to be a fancy way of reaching the game continuation!

But for those who love beauty for its own sake, here's the sac in all its glory:

24 ♘xf5!! ♘xd7 (24...gxf5 is relatively best, when 25 ♕xc7 ♖xc7 26 ♖d8+ transposes to the game) 25 ♘xe7+ ♔h8 26 ♘xc8 (although Black has a queen and knight vs. two rooks, White's passed pawn is too strong) 26...♘f6 (or 26...♕xc8 27 exd7 ♕d8 28 ♗b6 and the queen proves once again to be a bad blockader) 27 e7 ♘c6 28 ♗b6 ♕xc8 29 ♖d8+ ♘xd8 30 exd8♕+ ♕xd8 31 ♗xd8 with no technical problems in the ox-up ending.

24...♖xc7 25 ♘xf5!

Black can't hold now that both white rooks have open files.

25...gxf5 26 ♖d8+ ♗f8 27 ♖xf5

White has two big threats: the obvious one is 28 ♖g5+ followed by mate; the slightly hidden one shows up if Black prevents the check: 27...h6 28 ♗b6! (to move the black rook off the seventh rank) 28...♖c6 29 ♖xf6! exf6 30 e7 and queens.

27...♔g7

Relatively best, though still losing.

28 ♖g5+ ♔h6 29 ♖g3

29 ♖xa5! is quicker: 29...♘bd5 (no

forks allowed!—29...♘c6 30 ♗e3+ ♔g6 31 ♖g5+ ♔h6 32 ♖xf8 and wins; while 29...♔g7 30 ♗e3+ ♔g6 31 ♖g5+ ♔h6 32 ♖d4 mates) 30 ♖xf8 b6 (not 30...♖xc2 31 ♖d8 ♘b4 32 ♗e3+ and wins) 31 ♖b5 and White's technical task is much easier than in the game.

29...♘bd5

Not 29...♔g7 30 ♗e3+ ♔h5 31 ♖g5+ ♔h6 (or 31...♔h4 32 ♖d4+) 32 ♖d4 with the now familiar mating net.

30 ♖xf8 ♖xc2 31 h3

The position has clarified: White is a clean exchange up, even if there are still some technical difficulties—which I manage to surmount in mutual time pressure. Note that the pawns are even here; in the above note to move 29, White ended up two pawns ahead, as well as enjoying his extra exchange!

Nevertheless the position is won either way—I just had to work a bit harder!

31...♖e2 32 ♗d4 ♖xe6 33 ♗b2 ♘f4 34 ♖f3 ♘g6 35 ♖a8 ♖e1+ 36 ♔h2 ♘h4 37 ♖f4 ♘g6 38 ♖c4 b6 39 ♖c6 ♘d5 40 ♖g8 ♖e2 41 ♗c1+! 1-0

Black resigns in view of 41...♔h5 (41...♘e3 42 ♖e6 is no better) 42 ♖cxg6! hxg6 43 ♖h8 mate.

Again, let's point out that this "approved main line" with an early ...a7-a5 is not easy for Black if White knows to castle kingside and build up, Karpov-style, while exploiting the queenside weaknesses. Black doesn't have enough active play to justify something like an exchange sac, as he usually can in a "normal" Dragon.

All in all, the Alekhine Attack lives—Black's best chance is to allow the attack with g2-g4, and then strike back with ...a7-a5 (Game 31), when White must really know his stuff (♘d2!) to try to prove an advantage. Meanwhile, less exact play, as in the "Bird" games shown in Game 30, usually leads to quick disaster for Black.

This concludes our coverage of the main line Alekhine Attack. However, it's important to devote two more games to examining how Black can completely avoid it by using an Accelerated

Dragon move order—of course, as one might expect, while one problem is solved, others are not!

Game 33
D.Bronstein-T.V.Petrosian
USSR Championship,
Riga 1958

1 e4 c5 2 ♘f3 ♘c6 3 d4 cxd4 4 ♘xd4 g6 5 ♘c3 ♗g7 6 ♗e3 ♘f6 7 ♗e2 0-0

What every Accelerated Dragon player hopes for since time immemorial (or at least since 1898!) is for White to carelessly play 8 0-0 here, when Black gets in a real freeing move for, well, free—and equalizes easily; e.g. 8...d5! 9 exd5 ♘xd5 10 ♘xd5 ♕xd5 11 ♗f3 ♕c4 12 ♘xc6 bxc6 13 c3 ♗e6 and Black had no problems, despite his famous opponent, and went on to draw in S.Tarrasch-P.Lipke, Vienna 1898.

8 ♘b3

White prevents ...d7-d5, while after 8...d6 9 f4 ♗e6 10 g4 we are right back in the main line of the Alekhine Attack.

However, Black can prevent this.

8...a5

This is the typical Accelerated Dragon move which, as we have seen, basically rules out long castling for White—and so the Alekhine Attack must be put aside, in favour of positional exploitation of Black's new weaknesses.

Strangely enough, 8...d5 is played surprisingly often—even though, from a chess point of view, White's last move prevented this break! Perhaps the Black players were on automatic pilot, expecting the weak 8 0-0 - ? In any case, White should just take the free pawn: 9 exd5 ♞b4 10 ♗f3 ♗g4 (Black failed to get through after 10...♗f5 11 ♖c1 ♞fxd5 12 ♞xd5 ♗xb2 13 ♞xb4 ♗xc1 14 ♕xc1 ♖c8 15 0-0 a5 16 ♖d1 ♕c7 17 ♞d5 ♕d6 18 ♞d4 ♖c4 19 ♞xf5 gxf5 20 ♞b6 ♕b4 21 ♞xc4—White wins by taking everything!—21...♕xc4 22 ♗h6 ♕e6 23 ♗xf8 ♕xf8 24 ♕g5 1-0 T.Upton-F.Gibson, Dubai Olympiad 1986) 11 ♗xg4 ♞xg4 12 ♕xg4 ♞xc2+ 13 ♔e2 ♞xa1 14 ♖xa1 ♗xc3 15 bxc3 ♕xd5 16 ♖d1 ♕b5+ 17 c4 ♕a4 (material is roughly equal, but the two pieces are stronger than the rook in the middlegame, and Black is missing a dragon!—needless to say, as we have seen so many times before, this invites a White attack) 18 ♞c5! ♕xa2+ 19 ♖d2 ♕b1 20 ♕d4 ♕b6 21 ♖b2 ♖fd8 22 ♕e5 ♕c6 23 ♖xb7 ♕xg2 24 ♖xe7 ♕g4+ 25 f3 ♕xc4+ 26 ♔f2 ♕h4+ 27 ♔g2 ♕e1 28 ♞e4! (White's king is safe from all but a few

spite checks, whereas Black's dragonless kingside is ripe for destruction!) 28...♕e2+ 29 ♔g3 ♕e1+ 30 ♗f2 ♕d1 31 ♞f6+ ♔f8 (and the great theorist Suba shows he can do tactics too, as he finds an all checks mating finish) 32 ♖e8+! ♖xe8 33 ♗c5+ ♔g7 34 ♞h5+ 1-0 M.Suba-F.Ruiz Jimenez, Dos Hermanas 2000, in view of mate in two.

9 a4 ♞b4

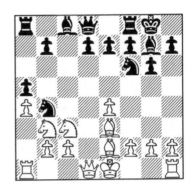

In *Starting Out: Accelerated Dragon*, Andrew Greet optimistically writes that "he [Black] will be able to play ...d7-d5 after all!" Of course this is not the case, as Bronstein could have told him.

10 ♗f3

Not mentioned by Greet, who gives 10 0-0?! (which indeed allows 10...d5) as the main line. Bronstein's obvious move prevents ...d7-d5.

10...d6

One stubborn player tried 10...d5 anyway: 11 exd5 ♗f5 12 ♖c1 ♖c8 13 0-0 ♖xc3 (as Black has nothing for the pawn, he pitches an exchange as well) 14 bxc3 ♞a2 15 c4 (simplest) 15...♞xc1 16 ♕xc1 ♕d7 17 ♕a3 ♖c8 18 ♞xa5

♗e4—White is two pawns up for absolutely nothing and after 19 ♗xe4 ♘xe4 20 ♖b1 Black could already resign. Instead, in X.Montheard-C.Adrian, Clichy 1998, White played the second-best 19 ♗b6 and gradually squandered his huge advantage and finally drew! Nonetheless, this is not an advertisement for 10...d5.

11 0-0 ♗e6 12 ♘d4 ♗d7

For 12...♗c4 see the next game.

13 ♘d5!

White solidifies his advantage with this knight attack; against anyone but Petrosian I would be confident of victory!

13...♘fxd5 14 exd5 ♖c8 15 c3

The dragon is blunted and the black knight sent back into the wilderness—we've seen both these themes before.

15...♘a6 16 ♖a3

Bronstein's sinister plan runs into Petrosian's deep and solid defence. I would prefer the Karpovian 16 ♗g5, or else 16 ♖e1, targeting e7, with a clear advantage to White.

16...♘c5 17 b4 ♘a6 18 ♕d2 ♕c7 19

♗e2 ♖fe8 20 ♘b5 ♕d8 21 ♘a7 ♖b8 22 ♖d1 ♕c7 23 h3 ♖a8 24 ♘b5 ♕d8

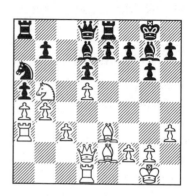

I agree with the computer assessment of clear advantage to White after 25 ♖e1. Let's put this advantage in human terms: the black knight's only safe square is b8; Black can't break out with ...e7-e6 due to the concomitant weakness of the d6-pawn; Black can't get rid of the white knight which has embedded itself on the weak b5-square—that eternal souvenir of the Accelerated Dragon—without giving White a Tiviakov two-bishop edge; White can put more pressure on e7 with a Karpovian ♗g5; and finally, White can consider a kingside attack with h4-h5 while Black is stuck in passivity.

Again, anyone but Petrosian...

25 ♗g5 ♕b8 26 ♗e3 ½-½

So Bronstein took a rest day against the great defender. Nevertheless, the opening battle was won by White, and the ...d7-d5 advance remained a mere chimera.

Game 34
Milo.Vujovic-F.Beeckmans
Imperia 1996

1 e4 c5 2 ♘f3 g6 3 d4 cxd4 4 ♘xd4 ♗g7 5 ♘c3 ♘c6 6 ♗e3 ♘f6 7 ♗e2 0-0 8 ♘b3 a5 9 a4 ♘b4 10 ♗f3

It's forty years later, but no—you still can't play ...d7-d5!

10...d6 11 0-0 ♗e6 12 ♘d4 ♗c4

One recalls that Petrosian retreated the bishop to d7 and grimly defended; here Black plays more actively, determined to get the pawn to d5 as promised!

13 ♖e1 ♖c8

If 13...d5, then 14 e5 ♘d7 15 ♗f4 and Black suffers due to the weakness of d5 and b5, while his light-squared bishop is misplaced and can be driven into the desert with b2-b3 soon.

14 ♕d2 d5

Still too soon! Black's best chance is to throw both centre pawns forward; i.e. 14...e5 15 ♘db5 d5 16 exd5 ♘fxd5 17 ♗xd5 ♘xd5 18 ♖ad1 and now:

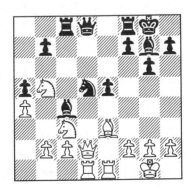

a) 18...♘xc3 19 ♕xc3 ♕h4 20 ♘d6 ♖c6 21 ♘xb7 and White wins a pawn.

b) 18...♗xb5 19 ♘xd5 ♗xa4 20 b3 ♗c6 21 ♗c5 and Black still can't equalize; e.g. 21...♖e8 (21...♕xd5, reaching an exchange down ending, is relatively best) 22 ♘e7+ ♔h8 23 ♕c3 ♕c7 24 ♗d6 wins for White.

c) 18...♘xe3 (the best chance) 19 ♕xe3 ♕e7 20 ♘d6 ♖c6 21 ♘xc4 ♖xc4 22 b3 ♖c6 23 ♘d5 and with the dominant knight on d5 (where no black pawn can annoy it) White maintains a positional advantage, but probably only of plus-equals dimensions.

15 e5 ♘e4

Black consistently throws his pieces forward. 15...♘d7 16 ♗f4 gives White the typical positional advantage we have already noted.

16 ♘xe4 dxe4 17 ♗xe4 ♗xe5

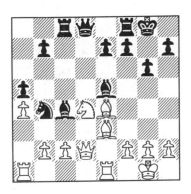

18 ♗xb7

White wants the pawn, but also strong is the attacking option 18 c3 ♘c6 (worse is 18...♘d5 19 ♗h6 ♖e8 20 ♗f5! and White's attack is virtually winning) 19 ♗xc6 bxc6 20 ♗h6 ♗g7 21

Ξad1 with attacking chances against Black's weakened kingside—and after the dragon is exchanged, one can see the knight is stronger than Black's remaining bishop. As a side benefit, White has the superior pawn structure as well.

But an extra pawn is nice too!

18...Ξc7 19 $\triangle$e4 Ξd7 20 c3 $\triangle$xd4 21 cxb4!

This seems anti-positional, but Black doesn't have a good discovery, and White is making a passed a-pawn—a speedy pawn whose queening square is controlled by the light-squared bishop.

21...$\triangle$xe3

21...$\triangle$e5 is met by 22 $\blacksquare$c2 and this tempo gain ensures that Black gets nothing for the pawn.

22 $\blacksquare$xe3 axb4 23 $\blacksquare$c5 Ξd4 24 $\blacksquare$xb4

White has an extra pawn (and connected passers!); Black's compensation is his control of the central file—but it's not enough.

24...e5 25 $\blacksquare$b7 f5 26 $\triangle$c6 Ξd2 27 b3 $\triangle$e2 28 a5!

Nothing else matters: this pawn will decide the game.

28...e4 29 $\blacksquare$b6 $\blacksquare$g5

After 29...$\blacksquare$xb6 30 axb6 White will win with b6-b7 and Ξa8.

30 $\blacksquare$e3!

Forcing the queens off, after which Black has no recourse against the queenside pawns—the game reminds me of Kayumov-Carlsen (Game 13).

30...$\blacksquare$xe3 31 fxe3 Ξb8

The pawns can't be blockaded by 31...$\triangle$a6 because of 32 b4 Ξb2 (32...Ξb3 33 b5! $\triangle$xb5 34 Ξeb1 also wins) 33 Ξab1 and White enforces b4-b5.

32 Ξxe2!

10 $\triangle$f3 shut off the Accelerated Dragon's dream of ...d7-d5, and now this same painful bishop—much stronger than a rook in this position—decides the game.

32...Ξxe2 33 a6 Ξb2 34 a7 Ξ2xb3 35 $\triangle$d5+ 1-0

Now that's a good bishop: it checks the king, forks backward to the black rook on b3, and still holds the queening square!

Black is clearly under positional pressure in this line; defending à la Petrosian is possible but not inviting! This concludes my recommendations against the 'regular" Dragons—but the chapter isn't finished yet! There is one more breed of dragon seen sometimes: the infamous Dragodorf, where Black tries to graft a Dragon onto a Najdorf! This will be the subject of the last two games of this chapter.

Game 35
R.Kholmov-A.Bannik
Minsk 1962

1 e4 c5 2 ♘f3 d6 3 d4 cxd4 4 ♘xd4 ♘f6 5 ♘c3 a6 6 ♗e2

So far a regular Najdorf, where one might expect 6...e5 as in Chapter Two, but no—a new animal enters the scene!

6...g6!?

This shouldn't be particularly terrifying for White, who can pursue his usual development, while it's not clear that ...a7-a6 really fits in a Dragon system; sometimes it might transpose, which is no problem for our repertoire—other times ...a7-a6 might be a waste of a tempo.

7 0-0 ♗g7

Since Black's mixture of systems is slow and non-threatening, White can choose between various set-ups. In the main game and the Fischer crush given in the next note, White opts for f2-f4 and ♗e3. In the next game White plays

a more Karpovian ♗g5. Either way White should get at least a small edge.

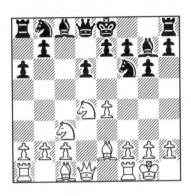

8 f4

Direct! The young Fischer waited a bit on this move—he chose to build up solidly, in no hurry to crush his opponent—but crush him he did... eventually: 8 ♗e3 0-0 9 ♘b3 ♗e6 10 f4 ♕c8 11 ♘d5 ♘xd5 12 exd5 ♗f5 13 c3 ♘d7 14 ♗d4 (let's get rid of the dragon!—*Fritz* recommends that Black just admit his error and play 14...♘f6, but it's hard for a human being to swallow his pride like that!) 14...♗xd4+ 15 ♕xd4 ♗c2 16 ♔h1 ♗xb3 17 axb3 ♕c5 18 ♕d2 a5 19 ♖a4 b5 20 ♖d4 ♘f6 21 f5!

(the typical signal for the attack—recall the Tiviakov game given in the notes to Game 32: White goes for the poorly defended black king) 21...b4 22 ♗c4 ♔h8 23 ♕e2 ♕c7 24 cxb4 axb4 25 h3 g5 26 ♖d3 ♖a7 27 ♖e3 ♖b8 28 ♖e1 ♖bb7 29 ♕d2 ♕c8 30 ♖g3 ♕xf5 (30...h6 was the last hope; now White uses the open lines to finish off the enemy king) 31 ♖xg5 ♕d7 32 ♕d4 ♖a8 33 ♖g3 ♕f5 34 ♖ge3 ♖aa7 35 ♖f1 ♕g5 36 ♖fe1 ♕g7 37 ♕h4 ♘g8 38 ♖g3 ♕f6 39 ♕g4 ♖b8 40 ♖f1 ♕xb2 41 ♖xf7 ♕a1+ 42 ♔h2 e6 1-0 R.J.Fischer-S.Schweber, Stockholm Interzonal 1962. Black resigned without waiting for the crushing 43 dxe6 ♘h6 44 ♕h5! ♘xf7 45 exf7 ♖aa8 46 ♕g4 ♕e5 47 ♗d5!, which forces mate.

8...♘bd7 9 ♔h1 0-0

9...♕b6 is relatively best, to push White's knight back, but after 10 ♘f3 ♕c5 (to prevent e4-e5) 11 ♕d3 0-0 12 ♗e3 ♕c7 13 ♗d4, it's replaced by a bishop and White's centralized pieces give him the edge.

10 ♗e3 ♕c7 11 a4 b6 12 ♘d5!

Geller-style! One sees that the common ideas of our repertoire are often effective against different defences.

12...♘xd5 13 exd5 ♗b7 14 c4

Black has no play at all.

14...a5 15 ♘b5 ♕c8 16 ♕d2 ♘c5 17 ♖a3 ♗a6 18 ♘d4 ♖e8 19 f5!

Without any special fuss, White has denied Black counterplay and then set his own attack in motion.

19...♘e4 20 ♕c2 ♘f6 21 ♖c3 ♘d7 22 fxg6 hxg6 23 ♗g4 ♗f6 24 ♗e6!!

Suddenly it's all over: the dragon bishop may be a good defender, but here there are too many attackers!

24...♔g7

If 24...fxe6, then 25 ♕xg6+ ♔h8 26 ♗g5 ♗xg5 27 ♖h3+ and mates.

25 ♗h6+!!

White crashes through with an orgy of sacrifices.

25...♔xh6 26 ♘f5+! gxf5

After 26...♔h7 White will force mate by giving up practically all his pieces: 27 ♖h3+ ♔g8 28 ♘xe7+!! ♖xe7 29 ♕xg6+ ♔f8 30 ♖h8+! ♗xh8 31 ♖xf7+ ♔e8 32 ♖f8+! ♔xf8 33 ♕g8 mate.

27 ♕d2+

There is no defence.

27...♗g5 28 ♖h3+ ♔g6 29 ♗xf5+ 1-0

Black resigns in view of the following mates: 29...♔f6 30 ♗e4+ ♔e5 (or 30...♔g7 31 ♕xg5+ ♔f8 32 ♖h8 mate) 31 ♖f5+ ♔xe4 32 ♕d3 mate.

The main game above and the Fischer grind given in the notes show the Dragodorf faltering against a sound, solid build-up. While that's good enough, the following error-filled sharp encounter is quite amusing!

Game 36
V.Tseshkovsky-V.Savon
Krasnodar 1996

1 e4 c5 2 ♘f3 d6 3 d4 cxd4 4 ♘xd4 ♘f6 5 ♘c3 a6 6 ♗e2 g6 7 0-0 ♗g7 8 ♗g5

Karpov-style!

8...♘c6 9 ♘b3 b5 10 ♖e1 b4

Now 10...0-0 11 ♗f1 ♗b7 12 ♘d5 would transpose to Game 25. Instead of this, Black uses his quickly advanced

b-pawn to snatch a button—but this is extremely risky.

11 ♘d5 ♘xe4 12 ♗h4 g5

If 12...0-0, then 13 ♗f3 and e7 is cracking.

13 ♗f3 gxh4 14 ♗xe4

Black is up an insignificant unit, but has a discombobulated position.

14...♖a7

The greedy 14...♗xb2 is more than the position can stand; e.g. 15 ♖b1 ♗e5 16 ♘f6+ ♗xf6 17 ♗xc6+ ♗d7 18 ♕xd6! ♗xc6 19 ♕xf6! wins a piece; while 14...0-0 is also poor due to 15 ♕h5 with dual threats of mate and ♘xe7+.

15 ♕h5 e6 16 ♘e3 ♘e7 17 ♖ad1 ♖c7

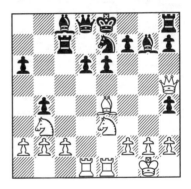

Black is putting up a great defence, but is unable to solve all the problems of his position with his king stuck in the centre.

18 f4 ♖f8 19 ♕xh7 ♗xb2 20 f5??

Wait a minute! These players are both Grandmasters! Correct is 20 ♕xh4, when White has recovered his pawn with some advantage, but there is no evident knockout.

20...exf5??

Sometimes GMs err just like the rest of us—sometimes even two of them! Of course 20...♖h8 wins the queen and the game.

21 ♗xf5 ♖g8?

21...♖h8 still wins, but obviously Black does not see the effect of the distant bishop on b2, defending backwards.

22 ♘d4!

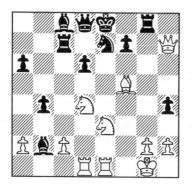

That's enough of that nonsense! White cuts off the bishop and wins quickly.

22...♖c3 23 ♗xc8 ♕xc8 24 ♕h6 ♕c5 1-0

Black resigns in view of 25 ♘ef5 with a decisive attack.

Providing one doesn't overlook one's queen (!) the Dragodorf is rather innocuous: White can choose between various recommended systems, where Black's best is to transpose to previously covered lines, as early aggression on Black's part should backfire due to a lack of development.

Thus we end coverage of the whole Dragon complex: as mentioned in the introduction, I faced the old fire-breather more often than any other Sicilian variation, and scored extremely well. From my experience, I would say the "fearsome" Dragon is not very fearsome at all against either Karpov or Alekhine. The only real danger is that you could be out-computered in the Yugoslav Attack—but we're not going near that morass!

Chapter Four
The Scheveningen Variation

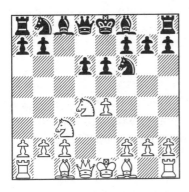

In the first two chapters, we fought Black's Boleslavsky Wall, where the opponent put his centre pawns on d6 and e5. In the previous chapter we slew the Dragon, where Black only advanced the d-pawn one square and fianchettoed his king's bishop. Now we face our fourth Sicilian pawn structure: in the Scheveningen Black creates a "little centre" (as Nimzowitsch called it) with pawns at e6 and d6. Obviously this limits both of Black's bishops, which must take a defensive role for a while. However, the hedgehog-like central pawns make it difficult for White to advance

in the middle—while also keeping him guessing, as either of Black's centre pawns might move forward at a later moment.

The most common move order (but by no means the only one) to reach the Scheveningen today is 1 e4 c5 2 ©f3 d6 3 d4 cxd4 4 ©xd4 ©f6 5 ©c3 a6 6 &e2 e6, when Black avoids the Boleslavsky hole at d5 and prevents, for the moment, any white pawn or piece advance to e5 or d5.

The problem for Black is that the small centre threatens nothing, so White can use his freedom to build up an attack. Black must find the right moment to counter-punch, but does he give up too much ground in the opening?

The Scheveningen is extremely popular at the highest levels and was regularly tested in the world championship matches between Karpov and Kasparov (one such crucial matchgame will be seen in this book: Game 41). For my part, I recommend that White follow Karpov by setting up a big centre with pawns on e4 and f4, and be ever watchful for chances to use this extra space to attack the black king.

1 e4 c5 2 ♘f3 e6 3 d4 cxd4 4 ♘xd4 ♘f6 5 ♘c3 d6

Black's second move might have indicated a Taimanov Sicilian (the subject of the next chapter), but by a simple transposition Spassky creates his small centre and transposes to the Scheveningen.

6 ♗e2 ♗e7 7 0-0 0-0 8 f4

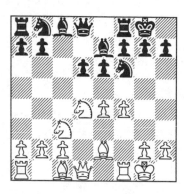

This is White's basic set-up, which should be played against any Scheveningen move order. Karpov used this variation 24 times against the Scheveningen, fighting world champions like Spassky and Kasparov, and top GMs like Ljubojevic and Hübner—and

he scored 10 wins, 12 draws and only two losses, for a powerful 67% against very tough opposition.

The excellent score is no surprise, for in this line White has space and good central control, which might at any moment translate to a kingside attack.

8...♘c6

This is the most popular move at this juncture, but I believe that 8...a6—transposing to the Najdorf Scheveningen—is objectively stronger, as one can see by comparing the present game to the up-to-the-minute ...a7-a6 lines in Game 44.

The modern ...a7-a6 variations will be studied in the remaining games in this chapter, though one must know the old lines as well, of course.

9 ♗e3 ♗d7

Another possible move is 9...e5, but after 10 ♘b3 exf4 11 ♖xf4 we see the Karpovian grind position of Games 9, 20 and 21 (except that here the White grinder is Tal!):

11...♗e6 12 ♕e1 ♘d7 13 ♖f1 ♘de5

14 ♘d5 ♗g5 15 ♕d2 ♗xe3+ 16 ♘xe3 ♕h4 17 ♘f5 ♗xf5 18 exf5 ♕f6 19 ♖ad1 ♖ad8 20 c4 ♖fe8 21 ♖f2 h6 22 ♕f4 ♕g5 23 g3 f6 24 h4 (Tal goes into the ending where he soon wins a pawn) 24...♕xf4 25 gxf4 ♘f7 26 ♗f3 ♖e3 27 ♔g2 ♔f8 28 ♖fd2 ♖de8 29 ♔f2 h5 30 c5 d5 31 ♖xd5 (the pawn falls: as Borat might say, "I'm so excite!") 31...♘e7 32 ♔xe3 ♘xd5+ 33 ♔f2 ♘xf4 34 ♖d4 ♘h3+ 35 ♔g2 ♖e3 36 ♗xb7 ♘h6 37 c6 1-0 M.Tal-L.Vogt, Tallinn 1981.

10 ♘b3

Karpov keeps pieces on, which is fine. On the other hand I don't believe the exchange of knights really benefits Black.

From a repertoire point of view 10 a3 (which transposes to a recent high-level White victory—Ivanchuk defeating Radjabov—and is a useful little move, directed against an eventual ...b7-b5-b4) might be best; e.g. 10...♘xd4 (10...a6 11 ♕e1 ♖c8 12 ♖d1 ♘xd4 13 ♗xd4 ♗c6 14 ♕g3 is V.Ivanchuk-T.Radjabov, Bilbao 2008; this is very similar to the main

Scheveningen lines we'll see later in this chapter, and will be discussed in the notes to Karpov-Ljubojevic, Game 42) 11 ♕xd4 (this looks stronger than the bishop recapture, as the queen defends e4 in advance, so Black's counterplay is limited) 11...♗c6 12 ♗f3 ♕c7 and White has won both games in the database from this Karpovian position. White doesn't worry about memorizing main lines but simply puts his pieces in the centre and plays.

Here's a quick look at those games:

a) 13 ♔h1 e5 14 ♕c4 exf4 15 ♗xf4 ♖ac8 16 ♖ad1 ♘d7 17 ♕d4 ♘e5 18 ♗xe5 dxe5 19 ♕xa7, when White pirated a pawn and went on to win in Zhang Zhong-Li Ruofan, Manila 2007.

b) 13 ♕c4 ♖fd8 14 ♘d5! exd5 15 exd5 ♖ac8 16 dxc6 bxc6 17 ♕a4 c5 18 c4 and White's two bishops and superior pawns gave him the edge in L.Tapaszto-J.Aldrete, Tel Aviv Olympiad 1964.

10...a5

10...a6 is still main line. After the text, as we saw in the Dragon chapter,

White can stop Black's a-pawn and then, while b5 and b6 are permanently weak, White's b4 (see move 26) is only *temporarily* weak!

11 a4 ♘b4

That knight on b4 sure looks pretty—until it gets kicked back!

12 ♗f3

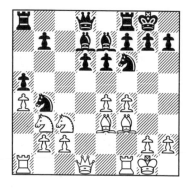

12...♗c6

This was Spassky's improvement on a famous game of the time where 12...e5 was played. As mentioned above, White has to be ready for either of Black's central pawns to advance; here Geller is able to use that advance to open the f- and d-files in his favour: 13 ♔h1 ♗c6 14 fxe5 dxe5 15 ♕e2 ♕c7 16 ♕f2 ♘d7 (since b6 is weak, Black can't occupy the d-file) 17 ♖ad1 ♔h8 18 ♗g4 ♘f6 19 ♗f3 ♘d7 20 ♗g4 ♘f6 21 ♗f5! g6 22 ♗b6! (always look to see if you can use this hole in Black's position—here Geller drives the opposing queen out of play) 22...♕b8 23 ♗h3 ♘xe4 24 ♘xe4 ♗xe4 25 ♖d7 (White has given up a pawn to get a rook to the seventh) 25...♕e8 26 ♗c5 ♗xc5 27 ♕f6+ ♔g8 28 ♘xc5 ♘d5 (not 28...♗c6? as 29 ♘e6! wins) 29 ♕d6 (Black has to give up material to save his tangled minor pieces) 29...♖a6 30 ♘xa6 bxa6 31 ♖fxf7 ♖xf7 32 ♗e6 ♗xg2+ 33 ♔g1 1-0 E.Geller-L.Polugaevsky, Portoroz 1973—a typically powerful Geller victory.

13 ♘d4 g6

Black doesn't want to give the white knight the f5-square after ...e6-e5.

14 ♖f2

But the advance itself is not dangerous for White—who simply accepts it and occupies the soon to be opened f-file.

14...e5 15 ♘xc6 bxc6 16 fxe5 dxe5 17 ♕f1 ♕c8 18 h3

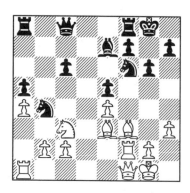

Timman, in his book *The Art of Chess Analysis*, calls this a "typical Karpov move" and goes on to say there was no threat of ...♘g4 (because White takes it off and plays ♕c4 with positional advantage), yet Karpov takes away the possibility anyway, just to restrict Black's pieces! Note that later on the white king gets the important h2 sanctuary square as well, so the move was far from purposeless.

18...♘d7

18...♔g7 is recommended by Timman as Black's best chance, with the long-winded idea of ...h7-h5/...♘h7/...♗g5, although White can simply play 19 ♖d1, seizing the d-file with advantage.

19 ♗g4!

White prevents a favourable exchange (...♗c5) and gets his queen to c4 on his own terms.

19...h5 20 ♗xd7 ♕xd7 21 ♕c4 ♗h4 22 ♖d2 ♕e7 23 ♖f1 ♖fd8 24 ♘b1!!

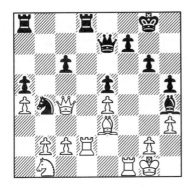

Perhaps a hard move to find, but completely logical: as we have already seen, in such positions the b4-knight is strong only up to a point—now it will be driven back to a terrible square, while the white knight will head to the kingside to attack. In typical Karpov fashion, White has a obtained a big advantage (against a World Champion!) and it's hard to see where Black made his mistake—do we have to go all the way back to 10...a5 - ?

24...♕b7 25 ♔h2

Karpov, typically in no hurry, evades future checks; Black can't stop c2-c3 anyway.

25...♔g7 26 c3

So much for the pretty knight!

26...♘a6 27 ♖e2!

Black has another piece on the fifth rank—now Karpov makes room for the knight to drive that one back too!

27...♖f8 28 ♘d2 ♗d8

Or 28...♗e7 29 ♖ef2 f6 30 ♘b3 and Black has weaknesses on both sides of the board.

29 ♘f3 f6

Black's game looks like someone ran the film in reverse: everything has been driven back, and White has a d-file highway for attack—while the f-file is not completely blocked either.

30 ♖d2 ♗e7 31 ♕e6 ♖ad8 32 ♖xd8 ♗xd8

Not 32...♖xd8 33 ♘xe5! as the f-file is still a big factor.

33 ♖d1!

Now the d-file again!

33...♘b8

Is the film still running backwards? Black's once proud knight has succeeded in returning to its original square!

34 ♗c5 ♖h8 35 ♖xd8! 1-0

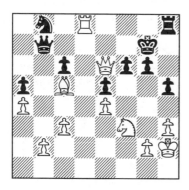

This shattering blow abruptly terminates the game. There is no defence, as can be seen: 35...♖xd8 36 ♗e7 and now Black must surrender material with 36...♖f8 (36...♖d1 is *not* check, so White can force mate: 37 ♕xf6+ ♔g8 38 ♕f8+ ♔h7 39 ♘g5 mate) 37 ♗xf8+ ♔xf8 38 ♕xf6+ and the house falls.

Evidently the Accelerated Dragon idea of ...a7-a5 does not work well in the Scheveningen (it often doesn't work that well in the Dragon either!), so now let's take on the critical ...a7-a6 lines.

> ## Game 38
> ### V.Smyslov-C.Kottnauer
> Groningen 1946

1 e4 c5 2 ♘f3 d6 3 d4 cxd4 4 ♘xd4 ♘f6

5 ♘c3 a6 6 ♗e2 e6

Popular for over 50 years: Black reaches a Scheveningen by way of the Najdorf.

7 0-0 b5

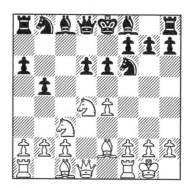

7...♗e7, preparing castling before embarking on queenside operations, is the normal move.

About 7...b5, Smyslov writes: "This move—a typical one in the Sicilian Defence—is premature at this stage. Black is starting an attack on the queenside before completing his development. Such tactics can only bring success if White plays passively."

Exactly so! And yet, I used to have a friend who played 7...b5 regularly, and with success (at the 2000 rating level). One day I asked him why, given that Smyslov had basically refuted the line. His answer was simple: he said he didn't like to waste time, so by playing this move he would find out right away if he was going to win or lose the game. If White played Smyslov's 8 ♗f3 (which very rarely happened) he would save energy by playing quickly and usually lose in time for a long rest before the next game (we are talking American tournaments of two or three games a day!). On the other hand, if White played "passively" as Smyslov said, with 8 a3 or 8 f3, then he would be invigorated, expect to win, and usually would!

Working on this book, I remembered this conversation from about forty years ago, and I wondered what the statistics could tell us—and my friend was absolutely right! If White plays the good 8 ♗f3, he scores a handsome Clintish 57%; but if he plays the bad 8 a3, he gets dropped in the graveyard with a measly 28%, and with the ugly 8 f3 he barely improves to 33%! So those of you who want an early decision are free to take your chances!

8 ♗f3!

Good! White defends the e4-pawn with a slightly veiled attack on the a8-rook. But don't play passively!

a) 8 a3 ♗b7 9 ♗d3 ♗e7 10 ♗e3 ♘bd7 11 f4 0-0 12 ♕f3 ♖c8 13 ♔h1 ♖xc3! 14 bxc3 ♘c5, when the e-pawn falls, so Black has more than enough for the exchange and went on to win in M.Adamowicz-R.Wojtaszek, Warsaw (rapid) 2008.

b) 8 f3 ♗e7 9 a4 b4 10 ♘a2 0-0 11 ♗e3 (not 11 ♘xb4? e5 12 ♘b3 ♕b6+, winning a piece) 11...e5 12 ♘f5 ♗xf5 13 exf5 d5 and Black was clearly better in D.Rovner-M.Yudovich, Kiev 1938.

8...♖a7

The usual move. One of my opponents played 8...e5 here, which is obviously bad after 9 ♘f5. Indeed, the lovely Maria Manakova created a picture almost as pretty as herself in just six more moves: 9...♗e6 10 ♗g5 h6 11 ♗xf6 gxf6 12 a4 b4 13 ♘d5 a5 14 ♗e2 ♘d7 15 ♗b5 and this beautiful bind, with three white pieces already on the fifth rank, soon led to a win in M.Manakova-O.Alexandrova, Antalya (blitz) 2002.

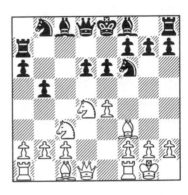

9 ♕e2!

Most accurate, reserving d1 for the rook, and preventing ...♖d7.

The obvious 9 ♗e3 is not bad—and White won quickly in the following game—but as Smyslov pointed out in his notes, Black has an improvement: 9...♖c7 (Smyslov recommends 9...♖d7, when Black can follow with ...♗b7 and keep defensive chances) 10 ♖e1 ♘bd7 11 a4 bxa4 12 ♖xa4 ♗b7 13 ♘b3 ♗e7 14 ♘a5 ♗a8 15 ♘c4 ♘c5 16 ♗xc5 ♖xc5 17 e5 ♗xf3 (not 17...dxe5? 18 ♕xd8+ ♗xd8 19 ♗xa8) 18 ♕xf3 dxe5 19 ♘xe5 0-0 20 ♘c6 ♕c7 21 ♘xe7+ ♕xe7 22 ♖xa6 and my First Saturday comrade,

Sergey Kayumov, won a pawn for nothing, and soon took the full point in S.Kayumov-V.Arbakov, Alushta 2002.

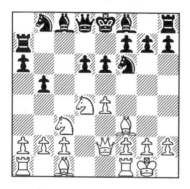

9...罝c7

Smyslov's last move was intended to force this. 9...罝d7 doesn't work here in view of 10 e5! dxe5 11 ♘c6 ♕c7 12 ♘xb8 ♕xb8 13 ♗c6, winning the exchange.

10 罝d1

White's quick and harmonious development has put great pressure on Black, who can't find time to castle.

10...♘bd7 11 a4!

"Black's opening idea has suffered a reversal" – Smyslov.

11...bxa4

11...b4 12 ♘a2 a5 13 ♘b5 wins for White—one now appreciates (Smyslov saw it much earlier!) the unfortunate position of the rook on c7.

12 ♘xa4 ♗b7 13 e5 ♘xe5?!

Relatively best is 13...dxe5 14 ♗xb7 罝xb7 (after 14...exd4 15 ♗xa6 White has a clear advantage as Black has no good way to hold d4) 15 ♘c6 ♕c8 16 ♘xe5 ♘xe5 17 ♕xe5 ♗e7 (not 17...♕xc2 18 ♗g5 with a decisive attack) 18 ♘c3 0-0 19 ♕e2, when Black survives for the moment but is stuck with a chronic weakness at a6.

14 ♗xb7 罝xb7 15 ♕xa6 ♕b8 16 ♘c6 ♘xc6 17 ♕xc6+ ♘d7

Material is even and Black is still hoping to make those two necessary moves: ...♗e7 and ...0-0—but he won't be able to accomplish either one!

18 ♘c5!! dxc5

Black can't decline: 18...罝c7 19 ♘xd7 罝xd7 20 罝a8 wins the queen.

19 ♗f4!

Smyslov finishes precisely; whereas 19 罝xd7? would be overhasty:

19...♖xd7 20 ♖a8 ♕xa8 21 ♕xa8+ ♔e7 22 ♕f3 f6 with equality.

19...♗d6

On 19...♕xf4 Smyslov gives 20 ♕c8+ ♔e7 21 ♕xb7 ♔f6 22 ♖xd7 ♔g6 23 g3 ♕f5 24 ♖a7 and the heavy pieces invade.

20 ♗xd6 ♖b6 21 ♕xd7+! 1-0

White emerges with an extra piece.

For the White repertoire player, 8 ♗f3 is a move you just have to *know*. I have faced 7...b5 only once in my career—and it *is* a rare guest—but at club level it can be powerful indeed if you are not prepared. In general, by playing the open Sicilian, you are committed to a rather aggressive outlook—so don't go passive on move 8!

Game 39
T.Taylor-A.Matikozian
4th Metropolitan Invitational,
Los Angeles 2011

---

1 e4 c5 2 ♘f3 d6 3 d4 cxd4 4 ♘xd4 ♘f6 5 ♘c3 a6 6 ♗e2 e6

In Games 18-19, we saw that 6...e5 7 ♘b3 ♗e7 8 ♗e3 was a strong move order for White, in order to meet 8...0-0 with 9 g4.

7 0-0

But here, the fact that White has not "wasted" a tempo on ♘b3 makes the same plan less effective. After 7 ♗e3 ♗e7 Black still hasn't castled, and White doesn't have a useful waiting move. On 8 g4 immediately Black can

keep his options open with 8...♘c6 (8...d5, counter-attacking immediately in the centre, is also possible) 9 g5 ♘d7, when he has a good retreat square for his knight and is not committed to kingside castling.

7...♘bd7

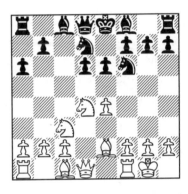

Again, 7...♗e7 is most popular and was always chosen by Kasparov, notably in his World Championship matches (against both Karpov and Anand). 7...♕c7 is often played as well, and usually transposes to the Kasparov line. Here's a typical game where both those moves come in: 7...♗e7 8 a4 ♘c6 9 ♗e3 0-0 10 f4 ♕c7 11 ♔h1 ♖e8 12 ♗d3 ♘b4 13 a5 ♗d7 14 ♘f3 ♖ac8 15 ♗b6 ♕b8 16 e5 dxe5 17 fxe5 ♘fd5 18 ♘xd5 exd5 19 ♖e1 h6 20 c3 ♘xd3 21 ♕xd3 ♗c5 22 ♕xd5 ♗e6 23 ♕d2 ♗xb6 24 axb6 ♖c6 25 ♖a4 ♖xb6 ½-½ V.Anand-G.Kasparov, World Championship (7th matchgame), New York 1995. I will cover this popular development in Games 41-44.

On the other hand, the text, 7...♘bd7, is both significantly less popular and seems objectively weaker too. There are three main objections to this knight move:

1. If White restrains Black's queenside play with a2-a4, Black can't profit with ...♘b4.

2. On d7 the knight fails to pressure White's strong knight on d4.

3. If White embarks on a caveman attack with g2-g4 (as we'll see in this game), the f6-knight wants to retreat to d7 following g4-g5—but here does not have that square!

8 a4

As mentioned above, with the black knight committed to d7 White does not fear the slight weakness of b4.

8...b6

Black prevents a4-a5; for 8...♘c5 see the next game.

9 f4 ♗b7 10 ♗f3 ♕c7 11 ♕e2

11...♖c8

Natural, but is it best? My chess guru Joe Cepiel thinks not—unless ...♕c4 works, which it doesn't seem to (see the note to move 12)—which means that the rook move can be seen

as a loss of tempo.

Smyslov caught another black king in the centre after 11...e5 12 ♘d5 ♘xd5 13 exd5 g6 14 ♘c6 ♗g7 15 fxe5 ♘xe5 16 ♘xe5 ♗xe5 17 ♗h6! (preventing ...0-0, and one doubts Black wants to go long here) 17...f6 18 c4 ♔f7 19 ♗g4 ♗c8 20 ♗xc8 ♖axc8 21 ♖xf6+!! (the late opera singer hits a high note!) 21...♔xf6 22 ♕g4 ♕c5+ (or 22...♖he8 23 ♖f1+ ♔e7 24 ♗g5+ and mates) 23 ♔h1 ♔e7 24 ♗g5+ 1-0 V.Smyslov-K.Grigorian, USSR Championship, Moscow 1976— Bravo!

Another try is to get back to Kasparov territory with 11...♗e7, but since Black remains uncastled, White can hit hard with 12 e5 when the complications seems to be in his favour: 12...dxe5 13 fxe5 ♗c5 (or 13...♘d5 14 ♘xd5 exd5 15 e6! and Black won't get out of the opening alive) 14 ♖d1 ♘xe5 15 ♗xb7 ♖d8 16 ♗e3 ♘fg4 17 ♗xa6 ♘xe3 18 ♘cb5 ♕b8 19 ♕xe3 ♘g4 20 ♕g3 ♕xg3 21 hxg3 e5 22 c3 exd4 23 cxd4 (White emerges from the mêlée with an extra pawn) 23...♗b4 24 ♘a7 ♗d6 (24...♖a8 25 ♗b5 is no better) 25 ♘c6 ♖d7 26 ♗c8 ♖c7 27 ♖e1+ ♔f8 28 ♗xg4 ♖xc6 29 ♗d7! 1-0 R.Teschner-Ra.Hess, Lugano 1984.

What all these variations show is that Black is running grave risks by developing his queenside first when White has quick development and a strong centre, which can combine for a speedy attack on Black's uncastled king.

12 ♗e3 ♗e7

My opponent's improvement on an earlier game of his, which seems to indicate that the ...♕c4 idea is dubious—but if so, why 11...♖c8 - ?

Matikozian had previously played 12...♕c4 13 ♕e1 h5 (this early attack will be rebuffed, but if 13...♘c5 then 14 ♘d5! exd5 15 ♗e2 ♘d3—forced—16 ♗xd3 ♕c7 17 exd5 ♘xd5 18 ♘f5 and White has a huge attack) 14 h3 e5 15 ♘b3 ♗e7 16 ♖d1 g6 17 ♕f2 ♕c7 18 ♘c1 exf4 19 ♗xf4 ♘e5 20 ♘d3 ♘fd7 21 ♗e2 0-0 22 ♘b4 (there is no attack for Black left, whereas we can see White is ready to go into the weak d5-square) 22...♕c5 (or 22...♘c5 23 ♘bd5 with a big plus for White) 23 ♘cd5 ♕xf2+ 24 ♖xf2 ♗h4 25 g3 ♗d8 26 ♗xa6 (White snaps off a pawn and wins with GM technique) 26...♗xa6 27 ♘xa6 ♖a8 28 ♘ac7 ♖xa4 29 ♗h6 ♖xe4 30 ♗xf8 ♔xf8 31 ♘e6+ ♔e8 32 ♘xd8 ♔xd8 33 ♘c3 ♖e3 34 ♔g2 g5 35 ♖d4 g4 36 hxg4 hxg4 37 ♘b5 ♘c5 38 ♘xd6 ♔c7 39 ♘c4 ♘xc4 40 ♖xc4 1-0 K.Asrian-A.Matikozian, Armenian Championship, Yerevan 1999.

13 g4!

Caveman! I threaten with g4-g5 to push the knight back to g8, since d7 is not available.

13...♘c5

Black makes a retreat square for the f6-knight—but neither horse is very secure. If instead 13...0-0, then 14 g5 ♘e8 15 f5 and White's attack is well under way, while Black still has no counterplay.

14 ♗d2!

My opponent had previously lost to the following wild attack: 14 ♕g2 0-0 15 g5 ♘fd7 16 ♘de2 ♘b8 17 f5 ♖fe8 18 f6 ♗f8 19 ♗h5 g6 20 ♗xg6!? fxg6 (however, *Mr. Fritz* favours Black after 20...hxg6) 21 f7+ ♕xf7 22 ♖xf7 ♔xf7 23 ♖f1+ ♔g8 24 ♕f3 ♖e7 25 ♗xc5 bxc5 26 ♘f4 ♖f7 27 ♕d3 ♖e8 28 ♕c4 ♗c8 29 ♘fe2 ♖xf1+ 30 ♔xf1 ♘c6 31 ♘d5 ♔h8 32 ♘f6 ♖e7 33 ♕d3 ♖f7 34 ♘f4 ♘e5 35 ♕b3 ♘g4 36 ♘xg6+ hxg6 37 ♕h3+ ♘h6 38 ♔e2 ♗g7 39 ♘e8 ♗f8 40 ♘f6 ♗g7 41 e5 1-0 J.Peters-A.Matikozian, Burbank 2007.

I looked at this in my preparation, and saw no reason to test the silicon evaluation of the piece sac—and so I planned to play the text: a simple and strong move that overprotects the e4-square and in many variations threatens b2-b4, when again the black knights are tangled.

14...g6

Black's position is already extremely difficult. After 14...0-0 15 g5 ♘e8 16 b4 ♘d7 17 ♗g4 White has a tremendous attack, and Black can't even counter with 17...♕c4 due to 18 ♕xc4 ♖xc4 19 ♘xe6! and wins. 14...e5 has been tried, but after 15 ♘f5 0-0 16 g5 ♘e8 17 ♘d5 ♗xd5 18 exd5 g6 19 ♘h6+ ♔g7 White has 20 fxe5! (in K.Gorbatenko-D.Shmeliov, Kharkov 2004, White started down the wrong path with the less forceful 20 ♘g4 and even managed to lose) 20...dxe5 21 ♗g4 ♖d8 22 b4 ♘d7 23 ♖ae1 with an overwhelming board-wide advantage.

15 g5 ♘fd7 16 b4

The black position is so cramped and tangled that this thrust almost wins a piece; Black manages to hold material, but at the high cost of opening the e-file for White to attack his uncastled king.

16...e5 17 ♘d5!

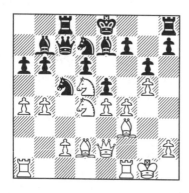

This powerful knight must evidently be taken, but now the white queen smiles on the black king.

17...♗xd5 18 exd5 exd4 19 ♖ae1! ♕d8

Or 19...0-0 20 bxc5 ♖fe8 21 c6 ♘c5 22 ♕c4 and White's protected passed pawn on the sixth is too strong.

20 bxc5 ♘xc5 21 f5!

My typical Bird attack: Black's problems are already insurmountable.

21...gxf5 22 ♗h5 ♖g8

Black manages to castle after 22...♖c7 23 ♖xf5 0-0, but then 24 ♖ef1 wins easily; e.g. 24...f6 25 g6! and Black's king position collapses.

23 ♖xf5 ♖g7 24 ♖xf7!

Finishing off the uncastled king.

24...♖xf7 25 ♖f1 1-0

Black resigns in view of 25...♕d7 (or 25...♔d7 26 ♖xf7 ♕e8 27 ♖xh7 ♕f8 28 g6 ♖c7 29 g7 ♕g8 30 ♖h8 ♕xg7+ 31 ♗g4+ ♕xg4+ 32 ♕xg4+ ♘e6 33 ♕xe6 mate, while 28...♖d8 29 ♗g5 is simple enough) 26 ♖xf7 ♔d8 27 ♖xh7 ♘xa4 28 g6 (the Excelsior theme seems to be the fastest way to win) 28...♘c3 29 ♗xc3 dxc3 30 g7 ♔c7 31 ♖h8 ♗f6 32 ♖xc8+ ♕xc8 33 ♕c4+ ♔b7 34 ♕xc8+ ♔xc8 35 g8♕+ and the extra queen is enough.

Kasparov was right to prefer 7...♗e7 with quick castling! By developing the queenside first—with 7...b5 of the previous game, or 7...♘bd7 here—it's clear that Black runs grave risks, as will be seen once again in the next game.

Game 40
V.Anand-I.Sokolov
Brussels (rapid) 1992

1 e4 c5 2 ♘f3 e6 3 d4 cxd4 4 ♘xd4 a6 5 ♘c3 d6

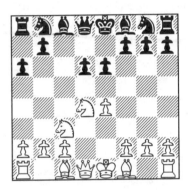

An ever more popular transposition from the Kan to the Scheveningen.

6 a4

Not to knock the World Champion, but I would prefer to wait on this move until I saw where Black's queen's knight was going—after ...♘bd7 this is a good move; whereas it is not so good, in my opinion, if Black develops to the knight to c6, observing b4. Therefore 6 ♗e2 ♘f6 7 0-0 ♘bd7 8 a4 would be my preferred move order.

6...♘f6 7 ♗e2 ♘bd7

Black should play ...♗e7/...0-0/...♕c7/ ...♘c6 with a reasonable game, à la Kasparov.

8 0-0 ♘c5

Instead of Matikozian's 8...b6, Black buys time to castle with this attack on the e4-pawn—but this problem knight is still not well placed, and Sokolov succeeds only in lengthening the game by one move!

9 ♗f3 ♗e7

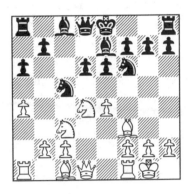

10 g3

Other GMs have exploited the b6-square and won slowly, but the World Champion doesn't want to wait that long!

K.Asrian-H.Odeev, Dubai 2001, saw 10 ♗e3 0-0 11 a5 (the b6-square is weak and White goes to work: Asrian's positional style is well suited to this kind of grind—recall the note to move 12 in the previous game, when he ground down Matikozian—and once again he makes slow but steady progress) 11...♕c7 12 ♖e1 ♖b8 13 ♘b3 e5 14 ♘c1 b5 15 axb6 ♖xb6 16 ♘d3 (White's pressure through to b6 leads to the creation of two isolated black pawns) 16...♖b8 17 ♘xc5 dxc5 18 ♕c1 ♖b4 19 ♗e2 c4 20 ♖a2 h6 21 f3 ♗c5 22 ♘d1 ♖d8 23 ♗xc5 ♕xc5+ 24 ♕e3 ♕c7 25 ♘c3 ♕b8 26 ♖d1 ♗e6 27 ♖xd8+ ♕xd8 28 ♔f2 ♕b6 29 ♘d1 ♕b7 30 ♕c3 ♘d7 31 ♘e3 a5 32 ♗xc4 (one of which now falls, which is the end of the game when playing Asrian) 32...♗xc4 33 ♘xc4 a4 34 ♘e3 ♘f6 35 ♕xe5 ♕b6 36 ♔e2 ♕a6+ 37 ♔d2 ♕b6 38 ♖a3 ♖xb2 39 ♖xa4 ♔h7 40 ♕d4 ♕b8 41 e5 1-0.

Also possible is 10 a5 with an immediate queenside bind, and after 10...0-0 11 b4 ♘cd7 12 ♘a4 ♘e5 13 ♘b6 White just took over the square and ground to victory in M.Panchanathan-V.Belov, Mumbai 2009.

10...0-0 11 ♗g2 ♕c7 12 ♗e3 ♖b8 13 f4!

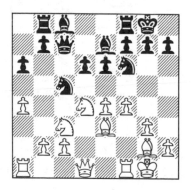

Anand zeroes in on Black's central weak point: the e5-square that the early ...♘c5 neglected; while if Black retreats with 13...♘cd7, he gets another cramped undeveloped position that invites g3-g4-g5.

13...♖e8?!

Underestimating the following attack. As noted above, 13...♘cd7 is weak due to 14 g4, which means that 13...e5 is relatively best. This pawn block stops the immediate attack and will so prolong the game, though Black's positional problems remain after the evident 14 ♘f5.

14 e5!

The e-pawn will be indirectly protected by a potential skewer, so Black's last move can now be seen as a mistake: the f-file opens and f7 is weak.

14...dxe5

Virtually forced, as after 14...♘fd7 15 exd6 ♕xd6 (15...♗xd6 16 ♘db5 axb5 17 ♘xb5 ♕b6 18 ♕xd6 is another easy winner) 16 b4 a tangled knight drops—as we see, this is a common theme in the ...♘bd7 variation.

15 fxe5 ♘fd7

Not 15...♕xe5? 16 ♗f4 skewering.

16 ♖xf7!!

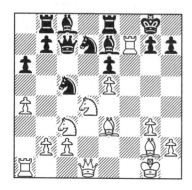

16 b4 can be answered by 16...♘b3 and Black survives for the moment—but I bet he didn't see this blow coming!

16...♔xf7 17 ♕h5+

Black's king has no defenders, the miserable rook on e8 prevents the safe retreat to g8, and the white reserves are coming up—in short, the World Champion shows us how it's done: White has a winning attack against a GM after only 17 moves.

17...♔f8 18 ♖f1+ ♘f6 19 exf6 ♗xf6 20 ♘db5!!

An exchange down at this point, Anand sacs a piece just to gain one tempo!

20...axb5 21 ♘xb5 ♕d7

Not 21...♕e7? 22 ♗xc5, winning the queen.

22 ♕xh7!

Now a full rook down, Anand ignores the black knight that is hanging with check—and snaps off a pawn!

22...♕e7

22...♖e7 23 ♗xc5 b6 24 ♖xf6+ gxf6 25 ♗f3 bxc5 26 ♕h8+ ♔f7 27 ♗h5 is one of many pretty mates hiding in the position.

23 ♖xf6+!

When you're one rook down already, it's easy to give another.

23...♕xf6

The suicidal line is 23...gxf6 24 ♗h6+ ♕g7 25 ♕xg7 mate.

24 ♗xc5+ ♖e7

If 24...♔f7 then 25 ♘d6+ ♔e7 26 ♘e4+ picks off the queen.

25 ♕h8+ ♔f7 26 ♘d6+ 1-0

Black resigns in view of one more pretty mate: 26 ♘d6+ ♔g6 27 ♗e4+ ♔g5 28 ♕h4 mate.

While one would hardly say that the early ...♘d7 loses for Black, it's obvious White gets a positional advantage by combining an a2-a4 clamp with an f2-f4 attack! As White, always watch to see if the black knights (which on f6 and d7 occupy each other's flight squares) may become tangled—you might be able to pick one of them off! Finally, just take a moment to appreciate the World Champion's fabulous attack and multiple sacrifices!

But now things are not going to be so easy: Mr. Kasparov is in the house!

Game 41
A.Karpov-G.Kasparov
World Championship (24th matchgame), Moscow 1985

1 e4 c5 2 ♘f3 d6 3 d4 cxd4 4 ♘xd4 ♘f6 5 ♘c3 a6 6 ♗e2 e6

This move order is the most popular way to reach the Scheveningen now—there are over 10,000 games in the database! After Game 11, Kasparov was not about to play 6...e5 again and enter Karpov's positional realm.

7 0-0 ♗e7!

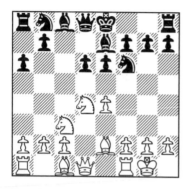

Kasparov's regular move: Black prepares to castle on the next move, for otherwise, as we have seen, he might not get another chance.

8 f4

Karpov in turn plays his patented attack.

8...0-0 9 ♔h1

We've seen throughout this book that Karpov likes to put his king here whenever he plays f2-f4, so avoiding annoying checks that might come at the wrong time. On the other hand, I have seen many strong players just get on with it by playing 9 ♗e3 ♘c6 10 ♕e1, heading to g3 (we do know where Black's king lives!) with attack. We'll see that basic idea in the final two games of this chapter.

9...♕c7 10 a4

In my opinion this is not best here (though it's very strong vs. ...♘d7), when the black knight can still go to c6. Essentially, this means ...♘b4 is possible, while Black has not had to pay (as in Karpov-Spassky, Game 37) with the weakening ...a7-(a6)-a5. Karpov himself evidently came to this conclusion, and in the next game he played 10 ♕e1; subsequently he allowed ...b7-b5 and then stopped the pawn with the modest but effective a2-a3, so keeping the black knight out of his position.

10...♘c6 11 ♗e3 ♖e8 12 ♗f3 ♖b8 13 ♕d2 ♗d7 14 ♘b3 b6 15 g4!?

Do or die! Karpov was undoubtedly influenced by a previous game in this match where he tried his typical manoeuvring and got absolutely nothing: 15 ♗f2 ♗c8 16 ♗g3 ♘d7 17 ♖ae1 ♗b7 18 e5 ♖bd8 19 ♕f2 ♖f8 20 ♗e4 dxe5 21 fxe5 ♘c5 22 ♘xc5 bxc5 23 ♗f4 ½-½ A.Karpov-G.Kasparov, World Championship (18th matchgame), Moscow 1985.

The match situation was also critical: this was the final game of the match and Karpov was a point behind, so he absolutely had to win to retain his title.

However, I believe Black has sufficient defensive resources, one of which is ...♞b4!. In my opinion, in the present position, White has at least two pieces misplaced: the queen should be on g3, and the king's bishop should be on d3, aiming for the king. So it's hard to believe White has an objective advantage—or that he can win by direct attack here.

But Karpov does go for it! And after a couple of slight errors by Kasparov, he reaches a near-winning position.

15...♝c8 16 g5 ♞d7

It's crucial that Black's knight has this safe retreat square; note that the black knights do not trip over each other.

17 ♕f2 ♝f8 18 ♝g2 ♝b7 19 ♖ad1 g6 20 ♝c1!

A good move, clearing the third rank for the rook. Kasparov doesn't notice the danger until it's almost too late!

20...♖bc8?!

20...♞c5! (Kasparov) is correct, which forestalls the rook manoeuvre, and if 21 ♞xc5 bxc5 then Black gets the b-file and d4-square for counterplay. *Mr. Fritz* has it as dead even after this knight move, which shows that White's attack has (until now, anyway) made no impression on Black's solid game.

21 ♖d3 ♞b4

Black does get this knight tempo in, without weakening the b5-square with ...a6-a5.

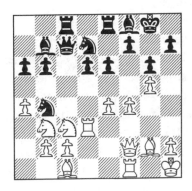

22 ♖h3 ♝g7?!

Careless, as Kasparov himself says. It's time to hit back with 22...f5 23 gxf6 ♞xf6, which appears to lose a piece to 24 ♕d4, forking, but doesn't, due to the following fantastic resource: 24...e5! 25 ♕xb4 d5!, when both small centre pawns move forward with tempo and White has nothing better than to return the piece with 26 ♞b5 axb5, after which Black is slightly better.

Instead, White should not go for the piece, but rather play for attack with 24 f5 exf5 25 exf5 ♝g7, reaching "a complicated and unclear" position – Kasparov.

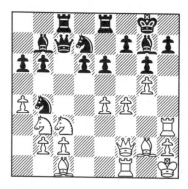

23 ♗e3?

White could have taken advantage of Black's two inaccuracies with the resolute 23 f5!, when things are bad for Black: f5-f6 is threatened, the counterattack ...f7-f5 is prevented and, in general, White has every chance of winning the game—note that *Mr. Fritz* sits at a big +1.2 after the f-pawn advance.

Had Karpov won this game and retained his title, who knows what would have happened to the Kasparov express?

But all this is "analysis"—this was Kasparov's year, and while Karpov missed his big chance, Kasparov did not miss his!

23...♖e7

White should probably still play 24 f5 now, though it is nowhere near as strong as before. When he hesitates again, Black prevents the advance.

24 ♔g1 ♖ce8!

An original conception: by doubling rooks on the closed e-file, Black pre-

vents f4-f5, which would now be met decisively by ...e6xf5, opening the e-file for the rooks to attack the e3-bishop.

25 ♖d1 f5!

Given his chance, Black is the one to play the critical f5; at this moment one can see the World Championship shifting owners.

As an aside, when I think of all the colossal drama of the 24-game World Championship matches such as this one, Spassky-Fischer, Petrosian-Spassky, Tal-Botvinnik—and the phenomenal Candidates matches that led up to these (I already mentioned this in the book, but once again: can anyone who lived through those times forget Fischer's 6-0 crush of Mark Taimanov?), I have to say, the system wasn't broke—why has it been fixed?

Bringing back the system as it existed in 1972: interzonal, candidate matches, 24-game world championship match would do so much to restore excitement and credibility to chess—every change since has made things worse!

Now back to the game, as Kasparov, with the initiative in hand and favoured this day by fortune, romps home like Zenyatta at Santa Anita.

26 gxf6 ♘xf6!

"Black, of course, sacrifices the pawn" – Kasparov. That kind of note is rarely seen today!

27 ♖g3 ♖f7 28 ♗xb6 ♕b8 29 ♗e3

29 ♖d4 ♘c6 30 ♖c4 ♘h5 shows White's weaknesses across the board.

29...♘h5 30 ♖g4 ♘f6 31 ♖h4

Given the match situation, 31 ♖g3 ♘h5 with a draw was no good for Karpov.

31...g5!

Kasparov isn't counting pawns, but rather counting on the initiative!

32 fxg5 ♘g4 33 ♕d2 ♘xe3 34 ♕xe3 ♘xc2

The black knight, that long ago got the b4-square, suddenly strikes a fierce blow deep in White's territory.

35 ♕b6 ♗a8 36 ♖xd6?

Blundering under pressure. Correct is 36 ♕xb8 ♖xb8 37 ♗h3! with the idea of obtaining rook and pawn vs. two

pieces in the endgame and good chances of drawing—but a draw still lost the match.

36...♖b7

A simple skewer; but in the final moves of the final game of a world championship match, anything is possible. The champion and challenger are human after all.

37 ♕xa6 ♖xb3 38 ♖xe6 ♖xb2 39 ♕c4 ♔h8 40 e5 ♕a7+ 41 ♔h1 ♗xg2+ 42 ♔xg2 ♘d4+ 0-1

Black comes out a full rook and bishop up, and Kasparov became the new World Chess Champion!

Two things must be noted: White got nothing out of the opening (I mainly blame 10 a4)—but even so, White got a close to winning attack after only two slight inaccuracies by Black, which shows how precise the Scheveningen player must be, given that he concedes the first four ranks. Both White and Black must be resolute without blinking. Kasparov's nerves held up better, and he was willing to give up two pawns to get his play going!

We will now look at White's best opening lines against Kasparov's development system.

Game 42
A.Karpov-L.Ljubojevic
Sicilian thematic,
Buenos Aires 1994

1 e4 c5 2 ♘f3

If White plays 2 ♘c3 here, one might think he is heading for the Closed Sicilian—instead, in the following game, a real modern transposition-fest occurs as it careens across openings finally to reach a Scheveningen! This is the great Ivanchuk win I referenced in Game 37, and well worth studying: 2...e6 3 ♘f3 ♘c6 4 d4 cxd4 5 ♘xd4 (maybe this is a Taimanov?) 5...♘f6 6 a3 d6 (no, Scheveningen!) 7 ♗e2 ♗e7 8 ♗e3 ♗d7 9 f4 0-0 10 0-0 a6 11 ♕e1 ♖c8 12 ♖d1 ♘xd4 13 ♗xd4 ♗c6 14 ♕g3 ♕c7 15 ♔h1 ♖fd8 16 ♗d3 b5 17 ♖de1 ♕b7 18 b4 ♖c7 19 ♖e3 g6 20 ♕h3 ♖dc8 21 ♘d1 ♘h5 22 c3

(I will reference this position in the note to move 21 in the main game) 22...♗d7 23 e5 ♗c6 24 f5 (the same break Karpov uses to win!) 24...dxe5 25 ♗xe5 exf5 26 ♗xf5 ♗g5 27 ♗xc8 ♖xc8 28 ♖ee1 ♖d8 29 ♕g4 ♗h6 30 ♗d4 ♗g7 31 ♘e3 ♗d7 32 ♕h4 ♖c8 33 ♗xg7 ♘xg7 34 ♕e7 f5 35 ♘g4 ♗c6 36 ♘h6+ ♔h8 37 ♘f7+ ♔g8 38 ♕xb7 ♗xb7 39 ♘d6 ♖c7 40 ♘xb7 ♖xb7 41 ♖f3 ♔f7 42 ♖d1 ♘e6 43 ♖e3 ♘g5 44 ♖d6 ♖a7 45 ♖ed3 ♔e7 46 ♔g1 ♘e4 47 ♖c6 a5 48 h3 axb4 49 cxb4 1-0 V.Ivanchuk-T.Radjabov, Bilbao 2008.

2...d6 3 d4 cxd4 4 ♘xd4 ♘f6 5 ♘c3 a6 6 ♗e2 e6 7 0-0 ♗e7 8 f4 ♕c7 9 ♔h1

Karpov sticks to his guns here, but...
9...0-0 10 ♕e1

Varies now! One recalls that he played 10 a4 against Kasparov, whereas here he allows ...b7-b5—but does *not* weaken the b4-square which so often invites a black knight.
10...♘c6

If 10...b5, then we stick with our basic repertoire and play 11 a3, after which the play becomes similar to

Game 56 (ideas repeat!) where the opening was a Kan system! Here's an example from this particular move order: 11...♗b7 12 ♘f3 ♘c6 13 ♗e3 ♖ad8 14 ♖d1 ♘xd4 15 ♗xd4 ♗c6 16 ♕g3 ♕b7 17 ♖fe1 g6 18 f5 gave White had a nice attack, who went on to win in J.Reyes Larena-A.Villavicencio Martinez, Las Palmas 1993.

11 ♗e3 ♗d7

A recent great attacking game from this position went as follows: 11...♘xd4 12 ♗xd4 b5 13 a3 (White's typical setup: restraint on the queenside, attack on the kingside) 13...♗b7 14 ♕g3 (the veiled threat of mate on g7 indirectly defends e4) ♖ad8 15 ♖ae1 ♖d7 16 ♗d3 ♖e8 17 ♖f3 ♕d8 18 ♕h3 g6 19 ♖ef1 d5 20 f5!!

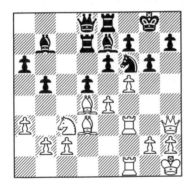

The young Italian American GM senses his moment and crashes through on the f-file. As White must always watch out for ...e6-e5 or ...d6-d5 from Black, so Black must always reckon with e4-e5 or f4-f5 from White—both of which are all the more disturbing for invading Black's terri-

tory. Here we see GM Sasikiran got his ...d6-d5 break in—but is demolished by the more significant attack against his king: 20...dxe4 21 fxg6 fxg6 (21...exf3 22 ♕xh7+!! ♘xh7 23 gxh7+ ♔f8 24 h8♕ mate is White's incredible point!) 22 ♖xf6 ♖xd4 23 ♖f7 ♗h4 24 ♗e2 ♗c6 25 g3 e3+ 26 ♔g1 a5 27 gxh4 (White takes a piece, accurately defends for a while...) 27...b4 28 axb4 axb4 29 ♘d1 ♕d5 30 ♘xe3 ♕c5 31 ♗d3 b3 32 ♕g3 bxc2 33 ♗xc2 ♖d2 34 ♖7f2 ♖ed8 35 ♖xd2 ♖xd2 36 ♖f2 ♖d4 37 ♗xg6 (and then suddenly goes back on the attack!—by sacrificing back his extra piece, he destroys Black's king position) 37...hxg6 38 ♕xg6+ ♔h8 39 ♕h6+ ♔g8 40 ♕xe6+ ♔h8 41 ♕h6+ ♔g8 42 ♕e6+ ♔h8 43 ♕c8+ ♔g7 44 ♖g2+ 1-0 F.Caruana-K.Sasikiran, Wijk aan Zee 2009. Black resigns, as after 44...♔f6 45 ♕h8+ ♔e6 46 ♕g8+ ♔d7 47 ♖g7+ White mates or wins the queen.

12 ♕g3

The ideal place for the white queen in this variation, as played by Caruana, Ivanchuk, Karpov, etc. Her Majesty directs her laser stare directly at the black king, while also monitoring e5 and d6.

12...♚h8

Note that 12...♘b4 is possible but meaningless here, as White (with the a-pawn still at home) can just kick it back with 13 a3.

Ljubojevic's actual move is an echo of Karpov's ♚h1, avoiding checks as could occur in the following variation: let's say White carelessly played the "combination" 13 e5 dxe5 14 fxe5 ♕xe5 15 ♘xc6 ♕xg3, thinking he had a winning 16 ♘xe7—but would then notice to his horror that the last move is not check!—and so would have to back out with 16 hxg3, losing a big pawn.

13 ♗f3 ♖ac8 14 ♖ad1 b5 15 a3

This is White's typical set-up, and if you understand this position, you can play against the Scheveningen with confidence. One recalls (from the note to move two) that Ivanchuk reached the same kind of position. White prepares a rook lift to attack the king and is also ready to advance either the e- or

f-pawn, while restraining Black on the queenside. In particular, unlike the previous game where Kasparov had the easy ...♘b4 manoeuvre into White's territory (and even deeper into c2!), here Black has a hard time finding something useful for that knight, as b4 is not available, and spending two moves to get to c4 might not be advisable in such a sharp position. Therefore, Ljubo just exchanges it, but this brings the white bishop to a better square, bearing down on the black king.

15...♘xd4

The aforementioned 15...♘a5 has been tried without success: 16 e5 (White takes advantage of the knight on the rim, which no longer monitors the centre: note the strength of the white queen here) 16...♘g8 17 ♗e2 ♘c4 18 ♗xc4 ♕xc4 19 ♖f2 dxe5 20 fxe5, when White is better with space and kingside attacking chances. Black tries to break out with 20...♗xa3?, but after 21 ♘de2! he suddenly lost a piece and the game, E.Pupo-B.Pineda, Cuba 1997.

16 ♗xd4 ♗c6 17 ♖d3

The rook to the third rank manoeuvre is also typical of the Schev; Black's defence is very difficult.

17...♕b7 18 b4!

Karpov shuts off Black's queenside play before turning his attention to the king.

18...♖g8 19 e5 ♘e4 20 ♘xe4 ♗xe4 21 c3!

Take another look at Ivanchuk-Radjabov after White's 22nd move, which was also c2-c3!—White secures his dark-squared bishop and so limits the opponent's queenside counterplay, while he enjoys permanent pressure against the king. Note how Karpov's ideas are completely relevant many years after his games were played.

21...♗xf3 22 ♖dxf3 ♕e4

Relatively best, especially as one looks at the alternatives below. Note that White's superficially "bad" bishop actually makes his position invulnerable, while any shift in pawn structure might make this a very good bishop, aiming at Black's king position.

Some other tries for Black are:

a) 22...f6 23 ♕g6!! with a decisive attack as the queen is immune.

b) 22...dxe5 23 fxe5 and f7 is weak.

c) 22...d5 23 f5 and Black has a bad French.

23 ♖e3 ♕d5 24 ♕h3

Karpov-style: he continues to probe the weaknesses, while Black has no counterplay available, as his only break

weakens his structure; e.g. 24...f6 25 exf6 ♗xf6 26 ♕xe6 and a pawn drops.

24...♖c4 25 f5!

Both White's attack in general and his bishop in particular are now threatening to increase their powers. Amusingly enough, Ivanchuk played c2-c3 one move later, on move 22, but hit Radjabov with the f4-f5 break one move earlier!

25...♗g5 26 ♖g3 ♗h6 27 fxe6 fxe6 28 exd6 ♕xd6 29 ♕h5

29 ♕xh6 is met by 29...♕xd4, but Karpov is patient: he prevents ...e6-e5 and ties Black down to his weaknesses.

29...♖xd4

If 29...♕d5, White infiltrates with 30 ♕f7, when Black can hardly plug all the holes; e.g. 30...♕d6 31 ♖h3 e5 32 ♗c5 ♕g6 33 ♕xg8+! ♔xg8 34 ♖f8 mate.

30 cxd4 ♕xd4

Black's desperation sacrifice has eliminated the attacking bishop and given him an extra pawn—but his own inactive bishop and the open files all over the board make it clear that White is winning regardless.

31 ♖gf3 ♕d6 32 ♖f7 ♗e3 33 ♕f3 ♗d4 34 ♖f8 ♗f6 35 ♖xg8+ ♔xg8 36 ♖d1! ♕b6 37 ♕a8+ ♔f7 38 ♖d7+ ♔g6

38...♗e7 39 ♕a7 is clean and clear. **39 ♕e4+ ♔h6 40 ♖d3 ♕f2 41 ♖h3+ ♔g5 42 ♖g3+ ♔h6 43 ♖h3+ ♔g5 44 ♖f3 ♕d2 45 h4+ ♔h6 46 ♕xe6! 1-0**

Even stronger than 46 ♕f4+ which should also win. Karpov simply takes a pawn and the queen exchange cannot be long avoided, after which there will be no technical problems—and so Black resigns.

The above game, along with the Caruana and Ivanchuk wins in the notes, constitute model play for White in this variation. The basic idea is simple: White restrains Black on the queenside with minimal force (a2-a3), then manoeuvres his queen to g3 and sets up an attack. Memorizing moves is less important than understanding the ideas of this set-up, after which creative play is paramount. However, it must be said there are forcing lines known to theory, some of them inaccurately analyzed—two of these will be examined in the final two games of this chapter.

Game 43
V.Kupreichik-K.Langeweg
Dortmund 1975

1 e4 c5 2 ♘f3 e6 3 d4 cxd4 4 ♘xd4 ♘c6 5 ♘c3 a6

Let's take a moment to enjoy a famous Tal brilliancy—from a Candidates match of course! 5...d6 6 ♗e3 ♘f6 7 f4 ♗e7 8 ♕f3 0-0 9 0-0-0 ♕c7 10 ♘db5 ♕b8 11 g4 a6 12 ♘d4 ♘xd4 13 ♗xd4 b5 14 g5 ♘d7 15 ♗d3 b4 16 ♘d5!!

(Tal said that if Larsen didn't take it now, he was going to give it up even closer, on f6!) 16...exd5 17 exd5 (for the piece, Tal has opened a terrific attacking diagonal for his light-squared bishop—Larsen is only able to plug it at the cost of other problems; remember this sac when we get to move 17 in the main game) 17...f5 18 ♖de1 ♖f7 19 h4 ♗b7 20 ♗xf5 ♖xf5 21 ♖xe7 ♘e5 22 ♕e4 ♕f8 23 fxe5 ♖f4 24 ♕e3 ♖f3 25 ♕e2 ♕xe7 26 ♕xf3 dxe5 27 ♖e1 ♖d8 28 ♖xe5 ♕d6 29 ♕f4 ♖f8 30 ♕e4 b3 31 axb3 ♖f1+ 32 ♔d2 ♕b4+ 33 c3 ♕d6 34 ♗c5! (Tal sacs another piece, and this time there is no possible defence) 34...♕xc5 35 ♖e8+ ♖f8 36 ♕e6+ ♔h8 37 ♕f7! 1-0 M.Tal-B.Larsen, Bled (10th matchgame) 1965.

6 ♗e2 d6 7 0-0 ♘f6

The typical Taimanov to Scheveningen route that we have seen a few times now.

8 ♗e3 ♗e7 9 f4 0-0 10 ♕e1 ♘xd4 11 ♗xd4 b5 12 a3

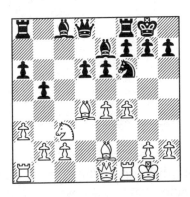

Note that White waits for ...b7-b5, then plays the least committal defen-

sive move possible, namely the text a2-a3.

12...♗b7 13 ♕g3

Here we see an accelerated attack. Unlike Karpov, Kupreichik plays neither ♔h1 nor ♗f3, but gets his queen in attacking position as quickly as possible. Of course the e-pawn is indirectly defended by the mate at g7.

A more Karpovian treatment is 13 ♗f3 ♕c7 14 ♔h1 e5 15 ♗e3 exf4 16 ♗xf4 ♘d7 17 ♖d1 ♘e5 18 ♗e2 ♖fe8 19 ♕g3 ♗f8 and indeed White is slightly better here. Karpov would no doubt have won this, whereas in the cited game M.Apicella-H.Olafsson, France-Iceland match 1993, Black struggled and finally made a draw.

13...♗c6

For the safer 13...g6, which prevents future sacs on h7, see the next and final game of this chapter.

14 ♖ae1 ♕d7

Black's last two moves prepared ...a6-a5, but while this queenside counterplay has its place, White is meanwhile lining up on the black king! I don't trust Black's set-up—even if it seems, by the current state of analysis, that White might only reach "the better of a draw" once the fireworks start—in such razor sharp positions improvements can always be found. In any case, this human's assessment is that Black is courting danger by failing to take precautions against the mob of white pieces outside his king's castle. This is why I view 13...g6 as the best line for Black at this moment in time, and also the hardest nut for White to crack.

Here White can channel Tal and throw in a Bird assist!

15 ♗d3 a5 16 ♖f3 b4 17 ♘d5!!

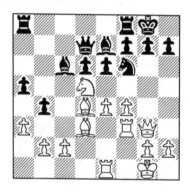

Tal! Yes, ideas repeat!

17...exd5 18 exd5

White's main point, just as in Tal-Larsen, is to open the diagonal for the d3-bishop.

18...♗xd5 19 ♗xh7+!

I've made this type of sacrifice on h7 many times myself, and it still surprises people!

19...♔xh7!

Best! John Emms, in *Play the Najdorf, Scheveningen Style*, says that 19...♔h8 leads to a forced draw, but with my Bird lens on I see it as a forced win for White! After 20 ♗e4! (Emms mentions this move but misses the Bird f-pawn advance two moves later) 20...♗xe4 21 ♖xe4 ♔g8 (John gives this an exclam but it doesn't hold; similar is 21...bxa3 22 f5!!—Bird!—22...axb2 23 ♖h4+ ♔g8 24 ♕xg7+ ♔xg7 25 ♖g3 mate) 22 f5!! (Taylor) seems to win for White (John only gives 22 ♕g5, which is not correct as now the rook on e4 can't play on the kingside). As in many Bird attacks, White has a double rook lift here plus a bishop on the long diagonal; I don't see how Black can hold, and my fearless *Fritz12* agrees, stating "clear advantage to White" in all variations. After 22 f5, neither my computer nor I can find any defence:

a) 22...bxa3 23 ♕xg7+!! ♔xg7 24 ♖g4+ showcases White's basic idea of swinging both rooks over against the king, while the vital dark-squared bishop pins the only defender, and mate follows: 24...♔h6 25 ♖h3+ ♘h5 26 ♗g7+ ♔h7 27 ♖xh5+ ♔g8 28 ♖h8 mate.

b) 22...♖fe8 23 ♖h4 ♗d8 24 ♕h3 ♖e1+ 25 ♖f1 ♖xf1+ 26 ♔xf1 ♕b5+ 27 ♔e1 (Black is out of checks, and must now perish) 27...♘f8 28 ♗xf6 gxf6 (or 28...♗xf6 29 ♖h8+ ♔e7 30 ♖xa8 with a decisive material advantage) 29 ♖e4 ♔g7 (or 29...♕e5 30 ♖xe5 and White wins technically) 30 ♕g3+ ♔f8 31 ♕xd6+ ♔g7 32 ♖g4+ ♔h7 (or 32...♔h6 33 ♕f4+ ♔h7 34 ♖h4+ ♔g8 35 ♕h6 and mates) 33 ♕f8 ♕e5+ 34 ♔d1 ♕d5+ 35 ♔c1 and White mates.

c) 22...♖fc8 23 ♕g5 ♖c4 (or 23...bxa3 24 ♖h3 a2 25 ♕xg7+ ♔xg7 26 ♖g4+ ♔f8 27 ♖h8+ ♘g8 28 ♖hxg8 mate) 24 ♖g3 ♔f8 (24...♘e8 25 ♖xe7 wins easily) 25 ♕xg7+ ♔e8 26 ♕g8+ ♘xg8 27 ♖xg8 mate.

In any case it's clear that 22 f5! gives White a tremendous attack that even a computer can't defend against, let alone a human being! So we conclude that taking the bishop on h7 is forced.

20 ♕h4+ ♔g8

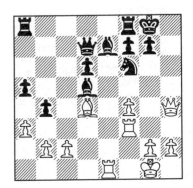

21 ♖xe7

White now recovers his material with—maybe—a very slight edge. 21 ♖h3? is weaker, as after ♕xh3 22 ♕xh3 ♖fe8 Black has too much for the queen. Otherwise White can settle for a draw with 21 ♖g3 ♗e6 22 ♖xg7+ ♔xg7 23 ♕g5+ and perpetual check, ½-½ Z.Lanka-L.Sandler, Latvian Championship, Riga 1980.

21...♕g4

Not 21...♕xe7? as then 22 ♖h3 wins.

22 ♕xg4 ♘xg4 23 ♖g3

White recovers the second piece and keeps the initiative into the ending, though best play may result in a draw after all.

23...♗e6

Not 23...♘h6? 24 ♖xg7+ ♔h8 25 ♖gxf7+ ♔g8 26 ♖g7+ ♔h8 27 ♖h7+ ♔g8 28 ♖h8 mate.

24 h3 ♖fc8 25 hxg4 ♖xc2 26 f5 ♗d5 27 g5 ♖c1+ 28 ♔h2 ♖f1

28...♖c2 may improve, with a likely draw.

29 f6

Another possibility is 29 g6 ♖xf5 30 gxf7+ ♖xf7 31 ♖xg7+ ♖xg7 32 ♖xg7+

♔f8 33 axb4 axb4 34 ♖d7 ♖a6 ½-½ J.Bielczyk-Wl.Schmidt, Polish Championship, Krakow 1978—though White's passed pawn is superior and he could try 35 g4 and play out this slightly better position.

29...♖f4 30 ♗b6

Stronger is 30 ♖d3! ♖g4 31 ♖d2 gxf6 32 ♗xf6 ♗c6 33 ♖xd6 ♗xg2 34 a4!, when White still attacks in the endgame; e.g. 34...♗e4 35 g6! ♗xg6 (both 35...fxg6? 36 ♖dd7 and 35...♖xg6? 36 ♖xe4 lose for Black) 36 ♖a7! ♖e8 (not 36...♖xa7? 37 ♖d8+ ♔h7 38 ♖h8 mate) 37 ♖xa5, again with a slight advantage in the ending due to the superior passed pawn.

30...gxf6 31 ♗c7 bxa3 32 gxf6+ ♔h7 33 ♖xa3 ♖xf6

34 ♗xa5!?

White takes a chance. 34 ♖d3 would secure a draw. I imagine both sides were in time pressure after all these complications!

34...♖f2 35 ♖h3+ ♔g6 36 ♖g3+ ♔f6 37 ♗e1 ♖xg2+ 38 ♖xg2 ♗xg2??

The simple 38...♔xe7 would be slightly better for Black.

39 ♗h4+! 1-0

Clearly completely unexpected: White wins a piece.

A hair-raising struggle—it seems this wildly risky line is playable for Black, but in a practical game all my money is on White, whose torrent of sacrifices demand incredibly exact defence by Black all the way into the endgame!

> ### Game 44
> ### J.R.Koch-E.Relange
> French Team
> Championship 2002

1 e4 c5 2 ♘f3 d6 3 d4 cxd4 4 ♘xd4 ♘f6 5 ♘c3 ♘c6 6 ♗e2 e6 7 ♗e3 ♗e7 8 0-0 0-0 9 f4 a6 10 ♕e1 ♘xd4 11 ♗xd4 b5 12 a3 ♗b7 13 ♕g3 g6

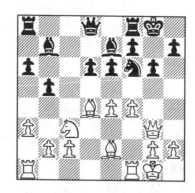

This is the "latest word" in theory—see the very high-level game (in the next note) between US Champion Kamsky and Azeri strongman Mamedyarov, which was won by the latter. Black does not allow any classic bishop sacs on h7! All the same, White still has attacking chances, and the position is not well explored; a possible novelty is available on move 14 as I point out, and even in the game's main line White is able (with a slight assist from Black) to set up an attacking position.

14 ♗d3

Alternatively:

a) 14 ♕e3 has never been played according to the database, but I'd like to give it a try: the queen defends e4, while keeping an attacking eye on the h6-square that Black just weakened with his "safe" ...g7-g6.

b) 14 ♗f3 (although played by the mighty Kamsky, this looks inaccurate to me: I would prefer to aim the bishop at the king, as in the main game) 14...a5! 15 b4 (15 ♘xb5 ♘xe4 is obviously Black's point) 15...♖c8 (Black has immediate queenside counterplay, whereas I can't see any attacking chances for White) 16 ♖ad1 axb4 17 axb4 ♖c4 18 ♔h1 ♘d7 19 ♗e2 ♖xb4 20 ♘xb5 ♗xe4 21 ♗g7 ♗xc2! (cleverly finding a better way to sac the exchange; White was evidently playing for 21...♔xg7 22 ♕c3+) 22 ♗xf8 ♕xf8 (Black has two central pawns for the exchange and goes on to win stylishly) 23 ♖d4 d5 24 ♖xb4 ♗xb4 25 ♖c1 ♗e4 26 ♖c7 ♕d8 27 ♕e3 ♕h4 28 ♕g3 ♕f6 29 ♕e3 ♕a1+ 30 ♕c1 ♕a2 31 ♖c8+ ♔g7 32 ♕d1 ♘f6 33 h3 ♗d2 34 ♕f1 ♗xf4! (decisive—Black's bishop pair is

stronger than White's rook and minor piece) 35 ♘c7 ♕d2 36 ♘e8+ ♘xe8 37 ♖xe8 ♕e3 38 ♗f3 ♗xf3 39 gxf3 ♕d2 40 ♕g1 ♕e2 0-1 G.Kamsky-S.Mamedyarov, Moscow 2008.

14...a5 15 ♖ae1 b4 16 axb4 axb4 17 ♘d1 d5?!

This may be the ultimate cause of Black's downfall, as White can lock in his space advantage. I think 17...♖a5 is Black's best, when the rook is active in both directions—White will have a hard time getting across the fifth rank.

18 e5

Now this wedge gives White eternal kingside attacking chances.

18...♘e4 19 ♕e3 ♕c7 20 ♘f2!

White removes Black's best piece.

20...♘xf2 21 ♖xf2 ♗a6 22 ♖ef1 ♗xd3 23 cxd3

As in Karpov-Ljubojevic, White's "bad" bishop is actually good, since the pawn structure is more fluid than it looks and f4-f5 will come, after which the bishop will turn out to be a strong attacking piece.

23...h5?

A fatal weakening, but even after 23...♖fc8 24 f5! gxf5 25 g4!, White's attack is worth more than a pawn.

24 f5!

Black's weakened kingside can hardly be defended after this blow.

24...exf5

Or 24...gxf5 25 ♕h6 with a powerful attack.

25 ♕h6

Intending e5-e6 which activates the vital dark-squared bishop; e.g. 25...♖a6 26 e6 and mates.

25...g5 26 ♖xf5 ♕d8 27 e6

Once the bishop enters the attack, there is no hope for Black.

27...f6 28 ♖xg5+! 1-0

Crunch!

This game concludes our coverage of the Scheveningen. The specific position after 13...g6 is one of those critical main line variations where no one really knows what's going on. My advice is to think with your own head—for example, try the never played 14 ♕e3—and always watch for your chance to attack Black's king! In general I like White's position, with his space advantage arising from the e4/f4 duo.

Overall, the Scheveningen can't be refuted of course—as we've seen, it can be played at the World Championship level! However, I think that White's game is much the easier: just set up as in Games 42-44 and *play*—and remember, fortune favours the attacker!

Chapter Five
The Taimanov/Kan Complex

The Taimanov/Kan Complex, as opposed to the Baader-Meinhof Complex, is less violent but more ideologically flexible. The common thread throughout this chapter is that Black plays ...e7-e6 early, usually on the second move, though sometimes on the third or fourth.

The pure Taimanov occurs after 1 e4 c5 2 ♘f3 e6 3 d4 cxd4 4 ♘xd4 ♘c6 5 ♘c3 a6 and this will be covered in Games 45-48. As usual I will recommend a solid Karpovian system based on 6 ♗e2.

Sharper variations occur if Black in-

sists on playing ...♗b4 early: the lines 1 e4 c5 2 ♘f3 e6 3 d4 cxd4 4 ♘xd4 ♘f6 5 ♘c3 ♗b4 (the Pin Variation, where White gets the advantage with the forcing 6 e5), and the somewhat more respectable pawn snatching line—as above until Black's fifth move and then 5...♘c6 6 ♗e2 ♗b4, when I say sacrifice with 7 0-0!—will be covered in Games 49-51.

The pure Kan comes about after 1 e4 c5 2 ♘f3 e6 3 d4 cxd4 4 ♘xd4 a6 and presents quite a strange appearance. After 5 ♘c3 (our repertoire move) White has two minor pieces out and Black has only two pawns on his third rank! And in the true Kan (here 5...♘c6 transposes back into the Taimanov) Black will play either 5...b5 or 5...♕c7—in neither case will he develop a single minor piece! Against such original play I recommend 5...b5 6 ♗d3 (a necessary repertoire exception, as will be explained), while against 5...♕c7 we can stick happily to 6 ♗e2. The Kan will be covered in Games 52-56.

Even then we're not done with this complex! In Game 57 we'll deal with the zany Gå På (1 e4 c5 2 ♘f3 e6 3 d4 cxd4 4 ♘xd4 ♘f6 5 ♘c3 ♕b6?!), when I propose that we punish Black immediately with 6 e5.

Finally, there is a line Morphy seemed to knock out in 1857, though some are still trying to revive it: 1 e4 c5 2 ♘f3 e6 3 d4 cxd4 4 ♘xd4 ♗c5, and now I follow the first American World Champion with 5 ♘b3, after which Black has problems with his dark squares, notably d6.

That's lots of variations to bash! Let's get to it.

Game 45
A.Karpov-M.Taimanov
USSR Spartakiad,
Moscow 1983

1 e4 c5 2 ♘f3 ♘c6 3 d4

3 ♘c3 e6 4 d4 cxd4 5 ♘xd4 reaches the game by our repertoire move order.

3...cxd4 4 ♘xd4 e6 5 ♘c3 a6

The basic position of the Taimanov: a typical modern "information" system where Black waits to see what White does, without committing himself very much. I am not a great supporter of such systems, however—White can just set up a nice position with attacking chances without any hindrance from Black.

6 ♗e2

This is the sensible development I

advocate against the Taimanov System, and against some Kan lines as well. In general, as in the Boleslavsky, Najdorf, Dragon and Scheveningen, White puts his bishop on e2 and follows quite often with f2-f4. This means that transpositions are easy to deal with as the ideas overlap and the repertoire positions, even from different variations, often give quite similar play.

6...♘ge7

Black plans the exchange ...♘xd4 followed by bringing the other knight to c6, but it's not clear that removing the last knight from kingside defence helps Black.

7 0-0

Shirov's sharper 7 f4 will be seen in the next game.

7...♘xd4 8 ♕xd4 ♘c6 9 ♕d3 ♘b4 10 ♕d2

10 ♕d1 ♕c7 11 a3 ♘c6 12 ♗e3 is good enough for a solid opening plus, but Karpov has an interesting idea in mind.

10...♗e7 11 b3

The point of ♕d2: White fianchettoes the queen's bishop, aiming at the black king if he castles kingside, while the c4-square—a typical Sicilian outpost— is taken away from Black.

11...0-0 12 ♗b2 ♕c7 13 ♖ad1 ♖d8 14 a3 ♘c6 15 f4

Our usual pawn structure for White has arisen. Without doing anything special, Karpov has obtained a solid plus-equals (space/centre/better development) with latent attacking chances.

15...b5 16 ♔h1

No points for guessing this move! By this time we know that, as soon as he plays f2-f4, Karpov puts his king in the corner to dodge a future check.

16...♗b7 17 ♕e3 b4 18 ♘b1

18 axb4 ♘xb4 19 ♕g3 f6 (not 19...♘xc2?, since 20 ♘d5 wins the queen) 20 ♖d2 is a simpler way to a solid plus; e.g. 20...d5 21 ♗g4 with an attack.

18...bxa3 19 ♘xa3 d5 20 ♕g3 ♗f8 21 e5

As usual, this wedge guarantees long-term attacking possibilities; 21

exd5 exd5 is weaker, as in the open position that has arisen, the white knight is out of play.

21...♘e7 22 ♗d3 ♖ac8 23 ♕h3 ♘f5 24 ♘b1

But here White has time to reposition as the centre is mostly closed.

24...g6 25 ♘d2 ♕b6

26 ♗xf5!!

An extraordinary conception, even for Karpov: White begins a manoeuvre that requires the sacrifice of two pawns—for a positional advantage!

Anyone could play 26 ♘f3 just bringing the knight over, as White gets a slight edge after 26...d4 (26...♘e3? is illusory: 27 ♗d4 ♗c5 28 ♗xe3! ♗xe3 29 ♕h6 and there is no real defence to ♘g5; e.g. 29...♖c7 30 ♘g5 f5 31 exf6 and wins) 27 ♗xf5 ♗xf3 (not 27...exf5 28 ♗xd4) 28 ♕xf3 exf5 29 ♕f2 ♗c5 30 ♖d3 etc.

But much as in Game 22, Karpov is not interested in the "slight edge in hand"—when the complete destruction of his opponent's king position is possible!

26...exf5 27 ♘f3!

The positional basis of Karpov's combination is that he prevents ...d5-d4, activating Black's pieces, especially his b7-bishop. Of course this requires the first pawn sacrifice.

27...♖xc2 28 ♗d4

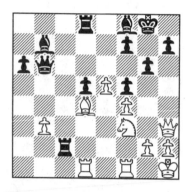

White stifles Black's play with tempo.

28...♕c6

Not 28...♕xb3 29 ♖b1 ♕c4 30 ♕h4! (30 ♖xb7?? is impatient and "slightly" flawed, due to 30...♕xf1+ and Black wins) 30...♖d7 (after 30...♖e8 31 e6 fxe6 32 ♕f6 or 31...♖xe6 32 ♘g5 h6 33 ♘xe6 fxe6 34 ♕f6, it's all over) 31 e6 fxe6 32 ♕f6 with a decisive attack—the common theme is the battery that White wants to set up on the long black diagonal.

29 ♕h4

A Kotovian creep which gains a further tempo on the rook at d8.

29...♖e8 30 e6! fxe6

I think Black would have done better to give up the exchange with 30...♖xe6 31 ♘g5 h6 32 ♘xe6 ♕xe6 33

♖fe1 ♖e2, when he still has some drawing chances.

31 ♘e5

Two pawns down! I'd love to have this position!

31...♕c7 32 ♘xg6!

There's one back right away, for if 32...hxg6 33 ♕h8+ ♔f7 34 ♕h7+ and Guéridon's mate comes next.

32...♗g7 33 ♘e5 ♕e7

33...♗xe5 34 ♗xe5 ♕f7 35 ♖f3 is decisive—the attack with pure opposite-coloured bishops is obviously winning, as the b7-bishop is not playing at all.

34 ♕g3 ♖ec8 35 ♖fe1 ♖8c7 36 ♘f3 ♔h8 37 ♗xg7+ ♕xg7 38 ♘d4

In true Karpov fashion, our hero recovers his second pawn to reach a... superior ending! Note the enormous difference between White's good knight and Black's bad bishop; and now one can appreciate why Karpov was ready to sac (at least temporarily) two pawns to keep that bishop blocked by its own pawn at d5.

38...♕xg3 39 hxg3 ♖2c3 40 ♘xe6 ♖c8 41 ♔h2 ♖xb3 42 ♘d4 ♖b6 43 ♘xf5

Black's badly-placed king will soon face mating threats.

43...♖f8 44 ♘d4 ♖g8 45 ♖e7 ♖g7 46 ♖de1 ♖h6+ 47 ♔g1 ♖hg6 48 f5!

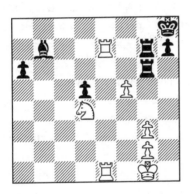

Passed pawns must be pushed. Not only is there a simple queening threat in a few moves, the aforementioned mating threats become more real once this pawn reaches f6, taking the black king's flight square.

48...♖b6

Or 48...♖xg3 49 f6 ♖xg2+ 50 ♔h1 ♖g8 (50...♖7g6 51 ♖e8+ ♖g8 52 f7 is too strong) 51 f7 and White wins at least a rook.

49 ♖7e6 ♖xe6

49...♖b4 50 f6 ♖g8 51 f7 ♖f8 52 ♖e8 ♔g7 53 ♘e6+ is another way to lose a rook.

50 fxe6 ♖g8

50...♖e7 allows the knight to run rings around Black's unstable pieces: 51 ♘f5 ♖e8 52 ♘d6 ♖e7 53 ♘xb7 ♖xb7 54 e7 etc.

51 e7 ♖e8 52 ♘f5 ♗c6 53 ♘d6 ♖g8 54 e8♕ ♗xe8

The hapless bishop finally perishes.

55 ♘xe8 ♖xg3 56 ♘f6 1-0

Black resigns in view of 56...♖g6 (56...d4 57 ♖e7 ♖g7 58 ♖e8+ ♖g8 59 ♖xg8 mate is even faster) 57 ♘xd5, when one wouldn't insult Karpov by checking his technique in this simple position.

Karpov played a truly fabulous game here, and not everyone can play on that level. Nevertheless, the positional ideas can be clearly seen: there is the e4/f4 centre, the e5-wedge, and the attacking chances on the kingside.

A nice brew: just add your own double pawn sacrifice!

1 e4 c5 2 ♘f3 ♘c6 3 ♘c3 e6 4 d4 cxd4 5 ♘xd4 a6 6 ♗e2 ♘ge7 7 f4

One recalls that Karpov played 7 0-0 here, and didn't throw out f2-f4 until move 15. Both methods are strong; it's a stylistic difference. While I admire Karpov's play to the max, I might in this position follow Shirov, as Black must already face problems or go down to a quick attack.

7...♘xd4 8 ♕xd4 b5

8...♘c6 will probably transpose to the game: White answers 9 ♕f2 and demonstrates one reason for the early f-pawn move—freeing a kingside launching post for his queen.

9 0-0 ♕c7 10 ♕f2 ♘c6 11 ♗e3 ♗e7 12 a4!

White plays across the board: first he softens Black's queenside, then he mates the king!

12...b4 13 ♘b1 ♖b8 14 ♘d2

White has obtained the c4-square and deadened Black's play.

14...0-0 15 ♗d3

Smiling at the black king. Just like Karpov, Shirov has obtained a solid plus with non-spectacular moves. However, again like Karpov, the spectacular moves are coming! And here White will not just be sac'ing pawns...

15...d6 16 ♖ad1 b3!?

Black tries to open lines for counterplay as 16...♗f6 17 b3 is the kind of passive position that he was evidently trying to avoid—but that might have been the better choice, as the "active" text leads to c-file problems (see move 35!).

17 cxb3 ♗f6 18 ♖c1!

Shirov is not interested in keeping the pawn; he gives it back to activate all his pieces, while Black loses time recovering the small unit.

18...♗xb2 19 ♖c2 ♗a3

An awkward square for the bishop, but this holds c1. On the natural 19...♗f6, 20 ♖fc1 ♗b7 21 ♗xa6! wins a pawn.

20 e5 d5

After 20...dxe5 21 ♘c4 White wins with combinative play: 21...♗d6 22 ♘xd6 ♕xd6 23 ♗xh7+ ♔xh7 24 ♗c5 ♕d8 25 ♗xf8 ♘d4 26 fxe5 ♘xc2 27 ♕xc2+ ♔g8 28 ♗d6 ♕b6+ 29 ♖f2 and White is a good pawn up with a strong attacking position.

21 ♘f3

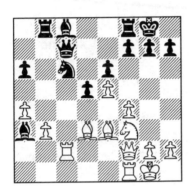

Note how ideas and structures repeat: though he used a different move order and piece set-up, Shirov has nonetheless created the same kingside pawn structure with that attacking wedge on e5 as used by Karpov in the previous game. White is much better already, despite facing a strong GM.

21...♕d7 22 ♗xh7+

According to GM Jon Tisdall, spectating, "Shirov bashed this out without a second's hesitation!".

This is the typical "Greek gift" sacrifice. Black's undeveloped queenside (even at move 22 Black hasn't found time to move his c8-bishop!) and divagating dark-squared bishop show that White's sac must prevail.

22...♔xh7 23 ♕h4+ ♔g8 24 ♘g5 ♖e8 25 ♖f3

White calmly brings up the reserves: the fire won't go out!

25...♘e7 26 ♕h7+ ♔f8 27 ♕h8+ ♘g8 28 f5!!

Shirovian! White clears the seventh rank of pawns, anticipating his 35th move.

28...exf5 29 e6 fxe6 30 ♖g3 g6

Black has no time for counterplay, since 30...d4 31 ♘h7+ ♔e7 32 ♖xg7+ wins the queen.

31 ♘h7+ ♔f7 32 ♗h6! ♔e7

Not 32...♘xh6 33 ♕f6+ ♔g8 34 ♖xg6+ and mates.

33 ♗g5+ ♔f7

He can't run either! If 33...♔d6, then 34 ♗f4+ e5 35 ♖xg6+ ♖e6 36 ♕xe5+ ♔e7 37 ♕g7+ ♔d8 38 ♗c7+! mates.

34 ♗f6

The threat of mate in one always gets the opponent's attention. Black parries this, but it's a trick or treat situation—this move is the trick, and the next is the treat—and only a treat for White, I'm afraid.

34...♖f8 35 ♖c7!!

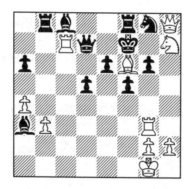

The stunning point of Shirov's pawn-clearance breaks: White wins the queen, as he now owns the seventh rank.

35...♘xf6

Or 35...♕xc7 36 ♕g7+ ♔e8 37 ♕xc7 and both black rooks are hanging.

36 ♕xf6+ ♔e8 37 ♕xg6+ ♔d8 38 ♖xd7+ ♗xd7 39 ♘xf8 ♗xf8 40 ♕f6+ ♗e7 41 ♖g8+ ♔c7 42 ♕c3+ ♔b7 43 ♖xb8+ ♔xb8 44 h4! 1-0

Stylish! The passed pawn goes through, as 44...♗xh4 loses at once to 45 ♕h8+.

Shirov scores with another beautiful

"fire on board" game. Again we see Black unable to solve the problems of defending his kingside after weakening it himself by transferring the king's knight to c6.

The next two games will show the more sensible development of the knight to f6.

Game 47
M.Tal-M.Taimanov
USSR Championship, Yerevan 1962

1 e4 c5 2 ♘f3 ♘c6 3 d4

3 ♘c3 e6 4 d4 cxd4 5 ♘xd4 a6 6 ♗e2 ♕c7 7 ♗e3, transposing to the game, would be my recommended move order.

3...cxd4 4 ♘xd4 e6 5 ♘c3 a6 6 ♗e3 ♕c7 7 ♗e2 ♘f6

7...♗b4?! is a rather common move order mistake for Black: 8 ♘xc6 (White scores 75% after this) 8...dxc6 9 ♕d4 and White seizes the advantage by forking b4 and g7—Black can't get out without some serious concessions; e.g. after 9...♗xc3+ 10 ♕xc3 ♘f6 11 0-0-0 the 2200 player with the white pieces stood so much better that he was able to defeat the 2500+ GM playing Black as follows: 11...0-0 12 f3 ♖e8 13 ♗c5 b5 14 h4 ♘d7 15 ♗d6 (Black is never able to compensate for his weak dark squares) 15...♕b6 16 h5 h6 17 e5 a5 18 g4 f6 19 exf6 ♘xf6 20 ♗c5 ♕c7 21 ♔b1 ♘d5 22 ♕e1 ♕f4 23 ♕f2 e5 24 ♗d3

♗e6 25 ♗e4 ♖ad8 26 ♕e1 b4 27 ♔a1
♖d7 28 ♗f2 a4 29 ♗g3 ♕f8 30 ♗xe5
(White wins a pawn and shows "GM
technique" to his foe!) 30...b3 31 a3
♘f6 32 ♗xf6 ♕xf6 33 ♖xd7 ♗xd7 34
cxb3 axb3 35 ♕b4 ♗e6 36 ♖c1 ♗f7 37
♖xc6 ♕g5 38 ♕c3 ♕d8 39 ♕c1 ♗d5 40
♗xd5+ ♕xd5 41 ♖c8 ♖f8 42 ♖xf8+
♔xf8 43 f4 ♕f3 44 g5 hxg5 45 fxg5
♕xh5 46 ♕f4+ ♔e7 47 ♕e3+ ♔d6 48
♕xb3 ♕xg5 49 ♕b6+ ♔d7 50 a4 ♕c1+
51 ♔a2 g5 52 ♕d4+ ♔e6 53 ♔b3 ♕e1
54 ♕c4+ ♔f5 55 ♕b5+ ♔f4 56 a5 g4 57
a6 g3 58 ♕a4+ ♔f3 59 a7 1-0
L.Butkiewicz-J.Gdanski, Polish Team
Championship 2008.

8 a3!

This is my repertoire suggestion,
which I found in *Dangerous Weapons:
The Sicilian*—only to discover that Tal
knew of this fifty years ago! I think it's
the perfect move: it stops the main line
of the Taimanov, which is 8 0-0 ♗b4
(and so avoids reams of theory), and
dovetails perfectly with my Scheveningen recommendation, where White
will answer ...b7-b5 with a2-a3.

Essentially White is happy with his
position, having his usual space advantage and attacking chances—and so
simply limits Black's activity, while
avoiding the "maelstrom of forced
variations".

8...♘xd4

Black might switch variations here,
but 8...d6 9 0-0 ♗e7 10 ♔h1 0-0 11 f4
just leads to our Karpovian Scheveningen repertoire. Here's another nice win
from the white side: 11...♖e8 (for
11...♘xd4 12 ♗xd4 b5 13 ♕e1 see the
notes to Game 42) 12 ♗f3 ♘xd4 13
♗xd4 e5 14 ♗e3 b5 (one sees this is
inoffensive with a2-a3 in place) 15 fxe5
dxe5 16 ♘d5 ♘xd5 17 exd5 ♗d6 18
♗e4 (White methodically sets up
against the black kingside) 18...g6 19
♖f6 ♕d8 20 ♕f3 ♖e7 21 ♖f1 (every
move brings another piece to the attack) 21...♕c7 22 ♗h6 ♗b7

23 ♖xg6+!! (the explosion!) 1-0
Ch.Andersson-A.Kopinits, European
Team Championship, Heraklio 2007.
Black resigns in view of the mate,
whether the rook is captured or not.

Another way to reach the Scheveningen is 8...♗e7 9 0-0 0-0 10 f4 d6, when Tal again demolished Black as follows: 11 ♕e1 ♘xd4 12 ♗xd4 e5 13 fxe5 dxe5 14 ♕g3 ♗c5 15 ♗xc5 ♕xc5+ 16 ♔h1 ♕e7 17 ♖f2 (Black's kingside is already under pressure as White will simply double rooks next—but the pawn sacrifice offered does not propitiate Tal!) 17...♗e6 18 ♕xe5 ♖fe8 19 ♕g3 ♖ad8 20 e5 ♘d7 21 ♘e4 ♖f8 22 ♗d3 (we've seen the bishop shift to this square many times: Karpov! Shirov! Tal!—it's no secret the attack is coming) 22...♔h8 23 ♘f6! h6 (not 23...gxf6 as 24 ♕h4 wins the queen or mates) 24 ♖e1 ♘c5 25 ♖f4 ♘xd3 26 cxd3 ♕c5 27 ♖h4 ♖d4 28 ♖h5 ♖c8 29 ♕e3 ♖e4 30 ♖xh6+! (mate is coming) 1-0 M.Tal-F.Perez Perez, Havana 1963.

The natural 8...b5, which is perhaps best, will be seen in the next game.

9 ♕xd4

9...♗d6

An extremely artificial manoeuvre that leads to serious weaknesses on the dark squares—but clearly Taimanov was not ready to leave *his* variation for a Scheveningen system with ...d7-d6.

10 ♕d2 ♗e5 11 ♗d4 ♗xd4

Recent games with the "improvement" 11...♗f4 have not improved Black's chances. Joyless endgames arose quickly after 12 ♕d3 in the following games:

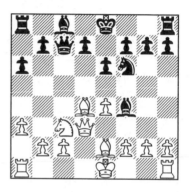

a) 12...d6 13 g3 ♗e5 14 0-0-0 ♗d7 15 f4 (the exchange of dark-squared bishops is forced, which means d6 is weak) 15...♗xd4 16 ♕xd4 ♗c6 17 ♕xd6 ♕xd6 18 ♖xd6 ♗xe4 19 ♘xe4 ♘xe4 20 ♖d4 ♘f6 21 ♗f3 (Black faces a long, painful, and probably futile defence, as White has the Fischeresque "anti-Taimanov" ending of light-squared bishop vs. knight) 21...♖b8 22 ♖hd1 ♔e7 23 ♖c4 ♘e8 24 ♖cd4 ♘f6 25 g4 h6 26 h4 b5 27 g5 hxg5 28 hxg5 ♘e8 29 ♖d7+ ♔f8 30 f5 ♖h2 31 g6 fxg6 32 fxe6 ♖b6 33 e7+ ♔f7 34 ♗d5+ ♔f6 35 ♖f1+ ♔g5 36 ♗f7 (the Fischer bishop triumphs) 36...♖c6 37 c3 1-0 D.Popovic-I.Miladinovic, Serbian Team Championship 2006.

b) 12...b5 13 g3 ♗d6 14 0-0-0 b4 15

♗xf6 gxf6 16 ♕xd6 ♕xd6 17 ♖xd6 bxc3 18 b3 (Black hasn't solved the problem of the weak d6-square that White is enjoying, while various weak black pawns are scattered about the board— White picks them off, one by one) 18...♗b7 19 f3 ♔e7 20 ♖b6 ♖hb8 21 ♖d1 a5 22 ♗b5 ♗c8 23 ♖xb8 ♖xb8 24 ♗c4 ♗b7 25 ♖d3 f5 26 exf5 ♖c8 27 fxe6 fxe6 28 f4 ♖c5 29 ♖e3 a4 30 ♗e2 axb3 31 cxb3 d5 32 ♖e5 ♔d6 33 ♗d3 ♖c7 34 ♖h5 ♖c6 35 b4 ♖b6 36 b5 ♔c5 37 ♔c2 ♔d4 38 a4 ♗c6 39 ♖xh7 ♖b8 40 ♖c7 ♖h8 41 h4 ♗e8 42 ♖xc3 (three pawns up and a better position should be enough!) 42...♖g8 43 ♗e2 ♗g6+ 44 ♔d2 ♖a8 45 ♗d1 (and now the magic d1-bishop convinced Black of the futility of continuing) 1-0 B.Socko-F.Handke, Bermuda 2002.

12 ♕xd4 e5 13 ♕b4 b6 14 0-0-0

White's lock on d6 gives Tal a huge advantage—another way to put it is that Taimanov, playing his own variation, has practically a lost position after only 14 moves!

14...♗b7 15 ♖d6

Positionally the game is over, but watch Tal's spectacular tactical realization of his advantage!

15...♗c6 16 ♖hd1 0-0 17 g4!

Let's get to it!

17...♖fc8 18 g5 ♘e8 19 ♖6d2 b5 20 ♗g4 a5 21 ♕e7

The dark squares must be pretty weak when the enemy queen can come to e7 on move 21!

21...b4

The computer suggests that Black might want to "enjoy" a slow death by entering the following bad ending, much like the two above: 21...d6 22 ♘d5 ♗xd5 23 ♕xc7 ♖xc7 24 ♖xd5 etc.

22 ♖xd7!

Tal! With one piece hanging, Tal offers another, trusting in his famous aphorism that his opponent can "only take one at a time"!

22...♗xd7 23 ♖xd7 ♕c4 24 b3!

With perfect coordination, Tal offers a taboo piece and allows a harmless check—in the end Black's kingside will be indefensible.

24...♕f1+ 25 ♘d1

Holding f2, which means Black must give up a knight, as his queen has no way to defend f7.

25...♘d6 26 ♕xd6 ♕g2 27 ♕d5!

Tal repositions to continue the attack, while leaving more pieces en prise!

27...♔h8

27...♖f8 28 ♖xf7 ♕xg4 29 ♖f4+ is an amusing win.

28 ♕xf7 ♖g8 29 ♕h5

29...♕xe4

29...bxa3 30 g6 h6 31 ♕xh6+! gxh6 32 ♖h7 mate is another fantastic conception from the wizard of Riga!

30 ♗f3 ♕f4+ 31 ♘e3 ♖a6

Now 31...bxa3 32 g6 h6 33 ♖f7 a2 34 ♔b2 ♕g5 35 ♕xg5 hxg5 36 ♗xa8 ♖xa8 37 ♔xa2 turns out to be technical, not spectacular.

32 ♗d5 ♖b8 33 ♖f7 ♕d4 34 ♕f3 ♕a1+ 35 ♔d2 ♕d4+ 36 ♔e2 ♕c5

Not 36...bxa3? 37 ♖f8+ and mates.

37 a4

After tactically preventing ...b4xa3 for many moves, Tal finally takes time to prevent it completely, leaving Tai-

manov without play or hope.

37...♖a7 38 g6 ♖a6 39 ♖xg7!

It's only a rook!

39...♖xg6

If 39...♔xg7 then 40 ♕f7+ ♔h6 41 ♕xh7+ ♔g5 42 h4+ ♔f6 43 ♕f7 mate or 42...♔f4 43 ♕h6 mate.

40 ♖xg6 hxg6 41 ♕f6+ ♔h7 1-0

The game was most likely adjourned here, with Taimanov resigning once he had taken a look at the following clear and winning attacking lines: 42 ♕f7+ ♔h6 (or 42...♔h8 43 ♕xg6 and mates) 43 ♘g4+ ♔g5 44 ♕f6+! ♔h5 (or 44...♔xg4 45 ♕xg6+ ♔h4 46 ♕h6+ ♔g4 47 ♗e6 mate, or 45...♔f4 46 ♕f6+ ♔g4 47 ♗f3+ ♔h3 48 ♕h6 mate) 45 ♗e4! (quiet but deadly) 45...♖g8 (again Black can't take the knight: 45...♔xg4 46 ♕xg6+ ♔f4 47 ♕f5 mate or 46...♔h4 47 ♕h6+ ♔g4 48 h3 mate) 46 h4! and this second quiet move forces mate.

Tal was a force of nature! And yet his opening play (8 a3) was quite calm, though still very difficult for his opponent—even if said opponent had his name on the variation!

Game 48
D.Csiba-R.Cvek
Presov 2010

1 e4 c5 2 ♘f3 e6 3 d4 cxd4 4 ♘xd4 ♘c6 5 ♘c3 ♕c7 6 ♗e3 ♘f6 7 ♗e2 a6 8 a3 b5

Black succeeds in maintaining a Taimanov system and avoiding an immediate severe disadvantage. Nonetheless I prefer White, who appears to get a slight edge after the following exchange.

9 ♘xc6 dxc6

Black must block his potential queenside fianchetto, for if 9...♕xc6? then 10 e5 ♘d5 11 ♘xd5 ♕xd5 12 ♕xd5 exd5 13 0-0-0 ♗b7 14 ♗f3 was already miserable for Black. After 14...d6 15 ♗xd5 ♗xd5 16 ♖xd5 dxe5 17 ♖xe5+ Socko was a pawn up for nothing (recall his pawn-devouring victory given in the notes to the previous game) and scored another easy ending win in B.Socko-F.Berend, Beijing 2008.

10 f4

Our standard set-up appears once again! In Bird's Opening White must struggle to achieve this ideal centre—I must admit it's much easier when facing the Sicilian!

10...♗b7 11 0-0

11...c5

11...♖d8 does not solve Black's opening problems, as the white queen is just driven where it wants to go—on e1 it's ready to attack the black king or even support queenside play from f2: 12 ♕e1 ♗e7 13 e5 ♘d5 (13...♘d7 might be better) 14 ♘xd5 ♖xd5 15 ♕g3 g6 16 c4! bxc4 17 ♗xc4 ♖d7 18 b4 c5 and here White should have used the c-file à la Shirov with 19 ♖ac1 with great pressure on Black's game. Instead, he allowed a passed c-pawn which led to his downfall as follows: 19 b5? axb5 20 ♗xb5 ♗c6 21 a4 ♗xb5 22 axb5 0-0 23 ♕f2 ♖b8 24 ♖fb1 ♖d3 25 h3 c4 26 b6 ♕c6 27 ♔h2 ♗h4 28 ♕xh4 ♖xe3 29 ♖a7 ♖e2 30 ♖g1 ♖f8 31 b7 ♖b2 32 ♕e7 c3 33 ♕a3 ♖b8 34 ♖a8 ♖2xb7 35 ♖xb8+ ♖xb8 36 ♖c1 ♖b2 0-1 B.Green-J.Emms, London League 2006.

12 e5 ♘d7 13 ♗f3 ♗e7

If 13...罝d8 14 營e1 c4 (Black gains space on the queenside, but it's too slow as White is developed and ready) 15 兔xb7 營xb7 16 f5! (a typical Bird attack—made even stronger by White's advanced e-pawn) 16...分xe5 17 兔f4 分c6 18 fxe6 (White regains his pawn while exposing Black's uncastled king) 18...f6 19 堂h1 兔d6 20 兔xd6 罝xd6 21 分e4 罝d4 22 c3 罝d8 23 分c5 營e7 24 分d7 分b8 25 分xb8 罝xb8 26 罝d1 罝b7 27 營e4 0-0 28 營c6 營c7 (or 28...a5 29 罝d6 with an overwhelming positional advantage) 29 營xa6 and White converted the pawn-up heavy piece ending in J.Dworakowska-A.Lutz, Istanbul Olympiad 2000.

14 f5!

The Bird blast bludgeons Black before he can castle.

14...exf5 15 分d5 兔xd5

15...營xe5 16 兔f4 wins for White, and 15...營d8 16 分xe7 兔xf3 17 營xf3 堂xe7 18 營xf5 is also terrible for Black.

16 營xd5 罝a7 17 兔f4?!

A bobble—White should keep coming with 17 e6 fxe6 18 營xe6 with much

more than enough for the pawn, given his dominating bishops and safe king.

17...g5

Black could even get away with 17...0-0 as the f4-bishop is unprotected.

18 兔g3

18 e6 looks like an improvement.

18...f4 19 e6

This should come too late, but...

19...fxe6?!

Correct is 19...fxg3 20 exd7+ 營xd7 and White doesn't have a clear continuation of the attack.

20 營xe6

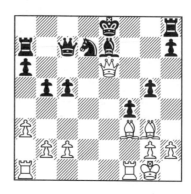

20...營d6

Not 20...fxg3 21 罝ad1 gxh2+ 22 堂h1 with a decisive attack against Black's "centralized" king.

21 營e2 營e5

After 21...fxg3 22 罝ad1 White still has a great attack.

22 兔h5+ 堂d8 23 兔e1 營xe2 24 兔xe2 兔f6 25 兔a5+ 堂c8 26 c3

White has long-term compensation for his pawn despite the queen exchange: Black's structure is ragged on both flanks, and middlegame factors such as Black's weak king position are still in play.

26...♘e5 27 ♖fd1 ♗d8 28 ♖d5 ♗xa5

Black errs under pressure: correct was 28...♖e7 29 ♖e1!, when I think the most likely result is a draw.

29 ♖xe5 h6 30 ♖xc5+ ♖c7 31 ♖e5 ♗b6+ 32 ♔f1 ♗b7 33 a4 bxa4 34 ♖xa4 a5 35 ♗f3+ ♔a7 36 c4 ♖d8 37 ♗d5

White takes over the centre and gradually grinds to victory.

37...♖g7 38 b4 ♗c7 39 ♖e6 h5 40 b5 ♗b6 41 ♖xa5+!

A nice trick that wins a pawn.

41...♗xa5 42 ♖a6+ ♔b8 43 ♖a8+ ♔c7 44 ♖a7+ ♔d6 45 ♖xg7 g4 46 ♖g6+ ♔c5

47 b6 ♖e8 48 b7 ♔d4 49 ♖e6 ♖b8 50 ♖e4+ ♔c5 51 ♖xf4 ♗c7 52 ♖f5 h4 53 ♗e6+ ♔d4 54 ♖d5+ ♔c3 55 ♗c8 ♗xh2 56 c5 ♔c4 57 ♖g5 ♔b5 58 ♖xg4 ♗g3 59 ♖g5 1-0

Black resigns, as after 59...♔c6 60 ♖xg3 hxg3 61 ♔e2 White wins as in a king and pawn ending.

Despite the bobbles from both sides in the early middlegame, the opening play was quite instructive: White's e4/f4 pawn roller was extremely strong—the fact that both these pawns advanced to the fifth rank by move 14 showed that objectively White had a solid advantage out of the opening.

If as may be true, Black's best against the a2-a3 line is to transpose to the Scheveningen, then White will, if nothing else, have discouraged Taimanov players and made them do a lot of extra work to learn another line—but the Scheveningen so reached is no picnic for Black either, while being quite comfortable for White!

We now leave the pure Taimanov—

next up is the Pin, which is not, as we will see, mightier than the Svidler!

Game 49
A.Kovacevic-K.Shirazi
European Championship,
Aix-les-Bains 2011

1 e4 c5 2 ♘f3

In the previous four games, we saw Black's f8-bishop developed at e7 or d6. Indeed, White prevented it from pinning his queen's knight by an opportune a2-a3. However, Black can enforce this pin against our repertoire by accelerating his kingside development—the drawback is that, while Black is doing this, his kingside, particularly some dark squares close to home such as d6 and g7, can become quite weak.

2...e6 3 d4 cxd4 4 ♘xd4 ♘f6 5 ♘c3 ♗b4

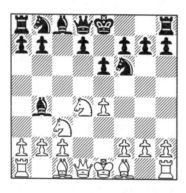

A sharp but doubtful line. Svidler had a great comment when surprised with this Pin Variation: "This did not exactly cheer me up, since I looked at this line when I was a kid and decided that it was pretty bad for Black (and it's probably true) and never had a look at it again." But he remembered enough to demolish his opponent in 25 moves (see the note to move 7).

A slightly delayed pin, 5...♘c6 6 ♗e2 ♗b4, will be the subject of the next two games.

6 e5!

Best: the black knight is attacked, d6 is weakened, and after the knight moves White will have ♕g4 to attack g7.

White has tremendous results with this advance—64% on the database as a whole—and much, much higher than that at the top rating levels. If you check this position against "Elo White" and look at the top twenty games, you'll see that White won 18, and gave up one draw and one loss, for a winning percentage of 92%! Basically Black wants to see if White knows the strong move, 6 e5, and if so, he will try to defend either a dubious position (in this game) or an exchange down technical position of the "maybe I have a remote chance of drawing this" variety.

However, if White is buffaloed and wimps out with the defensive 6 ♗d3, Black suddenly scores over 50%! Even Euwe made this passive move: 6 ♗d3 d5 (6...♘c6 is the modern reply, and in a large rating difference game—White was the lower—the first player was so terrified he succeeded in losing a centre pawn in three more moves: 7 ♘b3 d5 8 0-0 ♗xc3 9 bxc3 dxe4 and Black was just a pawn up and went on to win in V.Kozlov-H.Olbrikh, Moscow 1990) 7 exd5 ♘xd5 8 ♘de2 (the only way to describe what follows is that White plays very quietly and succeeds in drawing the game; Euwe was not yet playing like a world champion!) 8...♘c6 9 0-0 e5 10 ♘xd5 ♕xd5 11 a3 ♗a5 12 b4 ♗c7 13 ♖e1 ♗e6 14 ♘c3 ♕d7 15 ♘e4 ♗g4 16 ♘c5 ♕c8 17 ♕d2 0-0 18 ♗e4 ♗b6 19 ♕c3 ♗xc5 20 ♕xc5 ♗f5 21 ♗xc6 ♕xc6 22 ♕xc6 bxc6 ½-½ M.Euwe-A.Alekhine, Bad Pistyan 1922.

6...♘d5

Things are already a Svidlerian "pretty bad", and the other two tries are no better:

a) 6...♘e4 7 ♕g4 (White trampolines off the knight and gets to g7 with tempo) 7...♘xc3 (7...♗xc3+ 8 bxc3 f5 9 ♕xg7 is even more fun: 9...♖f8 10 ♗a3—catastrophe on the dark squares—10...♘c6 11 ♕xf8 mate, M.Vachier Lagrave-X.Loutre, Pontoise rapid 2006: a most rapid "rapid" game!—while 10...d6 11 ♗b5+ ♗d7 12 ♘xe6 doesn't prolong the game too much) 8 ♕xg7 and now:

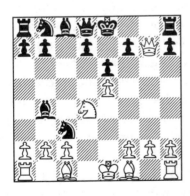

a1) 8...♘e4+ 9 c3 is decisive as Black has too many pieces hanging.

a2) 8...♖f8 9 a3 ♕a5 10 ♗h6 ♘c6 (or 10...♗e7 11 ♗d2 f6 12 ♘b5 fxe5 13 ♕xe5 ♘c6 14 ♕g3 ♖b8 15 ♗xc3 ♕a4 16 ♗e2 and White has both a material and positional advantage) 11 ♘xc6 bxc6 12 ♗d3 ♗e7 13 ♗d2 ♗a6 14 ♗xc3 ♕b6 15 ♗xa6 ♕xa6 16 ♕xh7 0-0-0 17 ♕d3, when White was two pawns up for nothing and won clinically in S.Nikolenko-R.Zargarian, Volodarskij 2007.

a3) 8...d5 9 ♕xh8+ ♔d7 10 ♕xd8+ ♔xd8 11 ♗d2 ♘c6 12 bxc3 and White managed to win with his extra rook in Wang Hao-Mai Dongqi, Wuxi 2005.

b) 6...♕a5 (this loses to a forced sequence—as long as White knows it) 7 exf6 ♗xc3+ 8 bxc3 ♕xc3+ 9 ♕d2 ♕xa1 10 c3!

(all forced to here, and even now Black has no choice as 10...gxf6 11 ♘b3 ♕b1 12 ♗d3 wins the queen) 10...♕b1 (trying to escape, but now White gets a monster passed pawn) 11 ♗d3 ♕b6 12 fxg7 ♖g8 13 ♕g5 (White is winning due to the g-pawn on the seventh) 13...h6 14 ♕f6 ♕d8 15 ♕xd8+ ♔xd8 16 ♗xh6 f5 17 ♘xf5! exf5 (or 17...♘c6 18 ♘e3 ♘e7 19 ♗h7 and wins) 18 ♗c4 ♖e8+ 19 ♔d2 ♘c6 20 ♗f7 d6 21 ♖e1! ♘e5 22 f4! ♔e7 23 g8♕ ♖xg8 24 ♗xg8 ♗d7 25 ♗d5 ♔f6 26 fxe5+ dxe5 27 h4 and White emerged with a good extra piece and won in a few more moves in M.Kozakov-T.Todorov, Valjevo 2000.

7 ♗d2

7...♗xc3

Relatively best. World Cup Champion Svidler faced 7...♘xc3 8 bxc3 ♗e7 9 ♕g4 0-0 (both 9...g6 and 9...♔f8 leave Black with a permanently compromised kingside, so Black usually makes the following dubious exchange sac; many of the top GMs [certainly including Svidler] have an almost computer like-technique these days, so this "unprovoked" sacrifice just doesn't succeed at all—even if you haven't looked at it since you were a kid!) 10 ♗h6 g6 11 ♗xf8 ♗xf8 (a technical position where Black's only compensation for the exchange is White's doubled

pawns; Almasi and Svidler don't break much of a sweat demonstrating White's advantage) 12 ♕g3 ♕a5 and now:

a) 13 f4 d6 14 exd6 ♗xd6 15 ♖d1 e5 16 ♘b5 exf4 17 ♕g5 ♗f8 18 ♗c4 (Svidler has all his pieces in play and begins an attack against f7 which should—but doesn't!—have a rook protecting it) 18...♕b6 (or 18...♘c6 19 ♕f6 intending ♗xf7 mate) 19 ♕xf4 ♗e6 20 ♘c7 ♗xc4 21 ♕xc4 ♕e3+ 22 ♔f1 ♗c5 23 ♖d8+ (with no rook defending the back rank, Black falls into a mating attack) 23...♔g7 24 ♘e8+ ♔f8 25 ♘d6+ 1-0 P.Svidler-A.Rodriguez Cespedes, World Team Championship, Lucerne 1997. For the record, White either mates or wins the queen: e.g. 25...♔e7 26 ♖e8+ gets the queen, while 25...♔g7 26 ♖g8+! mates with all checks in at most five more moves. Note that the GM playing Black has yet to develop his queen's knight and rook, and now never will!

b) 13 ♗c4 (another way) 13...♘c6 14 ♘xc6 bxc6 15 0-0 ♗g7 16 ♖ae1 f6 17 exf6 ♗xf6 18 ♖e3 ♕g5 19 ♖b1 ♕xg3 20 ♖xg3 ♗e5 21 ♖f3 ♗c7 22 ♗e2 ♔g7 23 ♔f1 ♗b6 24 c4 ♗c5 25 ♖fb3 ♗d6 26 c5! (a typical blow to break in with the rooks; I really don't understand Black's opening sacrifice—usually when you give up material you have good development to compensate for your material loss, but here on move 26 Black has still not even moved his queen's rook or bishop!) 26...♗e5 (not 26...♗xc5 27 ♖b8, winning a piece) 27 ♖d3 a5 28 a4 ♔f6 29 ♖f3+ ♔e7 30 ♗d3 ♗d4 31 ♖h3 ♗xc5 32 ♖xh7+ ♔f6 33 h4 ♗f8 34 g4 g5 35 f4 gxf4 36 g5+ ♔e5 37 g6 d5 38 g7 (and there goes a piece, which means White is now a rook up—the 2600 Federov could make absolutely nothing of Black's position) 1-0 Z.Almasi-A.Fedorov, Polanica Zdroj 2000.

8 bxc3 d6 9 ♕g4

9...0-0

Shirazi insists on another exchange sac, but 9...dxe5 10 ♕xg7 ♕f6 11 ♕xf6 ♘xf6 12 ♘b5 ♘a6 as in P.Simacek-Y.Meister, Pardubice 1998, is better—where Black actually made a draw after

13 c4. Then again, had White played the stronger 13 ♗c1, Black would really have had to suffer due to his weak dark squares—even if it must be admitted that, after 13...0-0 14 ♗a3 ♖e8 15 ♖d1, despite White's evident advantage, Black is not yet material down!

10 ♗h6 g6 11 ♗xf8 ♕xf8

12 ♕g3?

Even though Black's opening is suspect—is indeed "pretty bad"—accuracy is still required. Here the correct continuation is 12 exd6 ♕xd6 13 ♕g3 ♕a3 14 ♗c4! ♕xc3+ 15 ♕xc3 ♘xc3 16 ♔d2 ♘e4+ 17 ♔e3, giving back a pawn to reach an exchange up ending that should win for White—whereas now, after a single mistake, Black gets right back into the game and conjures up serious counterplay.

12...dxe5 13 ♕xe5 ♕a3

White has lost two tempi, as his queen belongs on g3 but takes three moves to settle there (12 ♕g3/13 ♕xe5/15 ♕g3—whereas in the previous note the white queen got there in one) and in such sharp positions that's quite a serious loss of time.

White must now go through contortions to avoid Black's threats.

14 ♘b3 ♘c6 15 ♕g3 ♕b2 16 ♗c4 ♕xc2?

The wrong pawn. Correct is 16...♘xc3 17 0-0 e5! which gives Black a pawn and good play for the exchange; for instance, if White tries the Svidler attack against f7, Black not only defends but counter-attacks: 18 ♕f3 ♗f5 19 g4 e4! and Black is at least equal, and his queen's rook is even in play!—what a turnaround that would have been. Instead, Shirazi's actual move allows White to chop the active knight and so reach the same type of technical position he could have had by force earlier.

17 ♗xd5 exd5 18 0-0 ♗f5 19 ♖fd1

White has consolidated and the one pawn for the exchange is insufficient.

19...♖d8 20 h3 ♕b2 21 ♖d2 ♕a3 22 ♖e1 h5 23 ♕c7 ♖d7 24 ♖e8+ ♔g7 25 ♕f4 ♖d6 26 ♖de2 ♗d3 27 ♖2e3 ♗e4 28 f3 ♗f5 29 ♖h8!

Nicely played: now the GM shows

his stuff, attacking on the weak dark squares, no matter how distant. With material in hand plus the initiative, White has a decisive advantage.

29...♖e6 30 ♕h6+ ♔f6 31 g4!

White accurately calculates and forces the win.

31...♕xa2 32 g5+ ♔e7 33 ♕f8+ ♔d7 34 ♕xf7+ ♔d6 35 ♖xe6+ ♗xe6 36 ♕f4+ ♘e5 37 ♕f8+ ♔c7 38 ♕b8+ ♔b6 39 ♕xe5 ♗xh3 40 ♕d6+ ♔b5 1-0

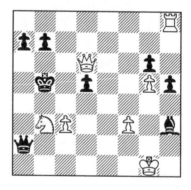

After making this move Black evidently saw the mate in five and didn't wait to be shown: 41 ♕b4+ ♔c6 42 ♕c5+ ♔d7 43 ♖h7+ ♔e6 44 ♘d4+ ♔e5 45 ♕c7 mate.

The Pin is close to being a "refuted" variation, and yet... a 2600 GM, after one inaccuracy, lets an IM out of the bag and would have had to fight for equality after a single mistake (12 ♕g3?). I think that's the reason this "pretty bad" line is still seen. White is forced to play tactically (6 e5 is the only way to get an advantage) and Black hopes his opponent (perhaps unfamiliar with the variation) will make a mistake in the ensuing sharp position. And that's just what happened here—giving hope to many Pin advocates!

So study the ideas as shown in the main game and notes above—particularly the various attacks on the dark squares—as I'm sure you *will* get this variation... ten years from now!

Now we go to a "not so bad" pin variation, where White must again play resolutely to get the advantage.

> ## Game 50
> ## V.Gashimov-V.Belikov
> ### Cappelle la Grande 2006

1 e4 c5 2 ♘c3 e6 3 ♘f3 ♘c6 4 d4 cxd4 5 ♘xd4 ♘f6 6 ♗e2

Of course there are other moves for White here, but I like to stick within our general repertoire with ♗e2 if possible, and in any case I don't believe the ...♗b4 pin is to be feared, but rather welcomed—does Black really want to give up his dark-squared bishop when his dark squares (such as d6) are al-

ready weak, and when his other bishop doesn't even have any legal moves?

6...♗b4

Black takes up the challenge. This is the most popular move—though I'm not convinced it's best. The second most popular move here for Black is 6...d6, transposing back to our Scheveningen repertoire—or one can delay ...d7-d6 but still head in a Scheve direction:

a) 6...♕c7 (6...d6 7 0-0 will probably transpose) 7 0-0 ♗e7 8 ♗e3 a6 9 f4 d6 10 ♕e1 0-0 11 ♕g3 ♗d7 12 ♔h1 b5 13 a3 (our friend Mr. Svidler has got back into our repertoire and went on to win as follows) 13...♖ac8 14 e5 ♘e8 15 ♘f3 f6 16 exf6 ♘xf6 17 ♗d3 ♘a5 18 ♖ae1 ♘c4 19 ♗c1 ♘xa3 (I mentioned in the Scheveningen chapter that White played a2-a3 to create a minimal target; here Black has managed to win this pawn anyway—at the cost of his king of course!) 20 ♘g5 (Svidler has a tremendous attack and soon mates on the back rank) 20...♘c4 21 ♕h3 h6 22 ♘xe6 ♕b7 23 ♕g3 ♗xe6 24 ♖xe6 ♗d8

25 ♕g6 d5 26 ♖fe1 ♔h8 27 ♘xd5 ♕f7 28 ♕xf7 ♖xf7 29 ♖e8+ ♘g8 30 ♗g6 1-0 P.Svidler-S.Mamedyarov, World Blitz Championship, Moscow 2010.

b) 6...a6 is weak (though it has been played by some strong players) as White nails down the d6 weakness with tempo after taking on c6. After 7 ♘xc6 either recapture has serious drawbacks as can be seen:

b1) 7...dxc6 (if you enjoy slow torture, you can try to draw the coming ending—but preferably not against Geller, even if your name is on the complex!) 8 ♕xd8+ ♔xd8 9 e5 ♘d7 10 f4 ♔c7 11 ♗e3 (clear advantage to White: the hole at d6 is painful, and middlegame factors such as Black's unsafe king are still important, despite the exchange of queens) 11...b5 12 ♘e4 ♘b6 13 ♗c5 ♗xc5 14 ♘xc5 ♘d5 15 0-0 ♖d8 16 ♖f3 (the c8-bishop has no useful moves, whereas White is poised to attack on either flank) 16...f5 17 exf6 gxf6 18 a4 ♔b6 19 ♘e4 a5 20 ♖d1 ♗a6 21 axb5 cxb5 22 f5! (Black's only good piece is undermined) 20...♘e7 23 ♖xd8

♖xd8 24 fxe6 ♗b7 25 ♖d3 ♖xd3 26 ♗xd3 ♗xe4 27 ♗xe4 f5 28 ♗d3 (a pawn up, the superior minor piece, Geller—enough said) 28...♔c5 29 ♔f2 b4 30 b3 ♔d5 31 ♔e3 ♔xe6 32 ♔d4 ♔d6 33 g3 h6 34 h3 ♔e6 35 ♔c5 ♔e5 36 ♔b5 ♔d4 37 ♔xa5 ♔c5 38 ♔a4 f4 39 gxf4 ♘d5 40 f5 ♘f6 41 ♔a5 ♘d5 42 ♔a6 ♘f6 43 ♔b7 ♘d5 44 ♗c4 1-0 E.Geller-I.Kan, USSR Championship, Moscow 1955.

b2) 7...bxc6 8 e5 ♘d5 9 ♘e4 (it hurts to even look at Black's d6-square—how did the world-class Ljubojevic wind up in this position after only nine moves?) 9...♕c7 10 ♘d6+! ♗xd6 11 exd6 ♕b6 (Black must allow this white pawn on the sixth, as 11...♕xd6? 12 c4 wins a piece) 12 c4 ♘f6 13 0-0 0-0 14 ♗e3 ♕xb2 (when your position is this bad, you may as well take anything on offer; while 14...♕d8 15 ♗d4 ♖e8 16 f4 might take longer to win, Black is just as dead, given White's total bind on the position) 15 ♗d4 ♕a3 16 ♗xf6 gxf6 17 ♕d4 ♖b8 18 ♖ac1 e5 19 ♕g4+ ♔h8 20 ♕f5 ♔g7 21 ♖cd1 (you don't need to consult your *Fritz* to put down a decisive advantage sign here) 21...e4 22 ♕g4+ ♔h8 23 ♕xe4 (White threatens ♖d3 or ♗d3 or ♕e7, all of which win—Ljubo has had enough punishment!) 1-0 A.Shirov-L.Ljubojevic, Monte Carlo (rapid) 2000.

7 0-0

Of course—now the pin is gone and the only remaining function of the b4-bishop is to give itself to snatch a pawn. Just what I'd want from White's point of view!

7...♗xc3

Other moves give Black a difficult position without even a pawn for consolation:

a) 7...d6 8 ♘xc6 bxc6 9 ♕d3 (White keeps his pawns intact and goes for the bishop pair) 9...0-0 10 a3 ♗c5 (or 10...♗xc3 11 ♕xc3 and White has a stable two bishops advantage) 11 b4 ♗b6 12 ♖d1 with great pressure on Black, whose three bishop moves have not helped his cause, and now he may have to grovel with ...♗c7.

b) 7...0-0 8 ♘xc6 dxc6 9 e5 and then:

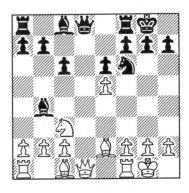

b1) 9...♘d5 10 ♘e4 (Black's king's bishop is adrift and the queen's bishop blocked) 10...♕c7 11 f4 f5 12 exf6 ♘xf6 (Black has freed his position at the cost of a sick e-pawn which...) 13 ♗d3 ♘xe4 14 ♗xe4 ♗c5+ 15 ♔h1 g6 16 ♕e2 ♕f7 17 ♗d3 ♕g7 18 ♗c4 ♔h8 19 ♗e3 ♗e7 20 c3 ♗f6 21 ♖ad1 b6 22 ♗d4 ♗d7 23 ♗xf6 ♖xf6 24 ♕e5 ♖af8 25 ♔g1 c5 26 ♖d6 ♗c8 27 g3 h6 28 ♖c6 ♖6f7 29 ♕xg7+ ♔xg7 30 ♖xc8! ♖xc8 31 ♗xe6 (finally falls and...) 31...♖d8 32 ♗xf7 ♔xf7 (White reaches a winning ending—which, alas, he does not win against his GM foe!) 33 ♔g2 ♖d3 34 ♖f2 b5 35 ♔h3 a5 36 a3 a4 37 ♖e2 b4 38 cxb4 cxb4 39 axb4 ♖b3 40 ♔g4 ♖xb4 41 ♖c2 ♔f6 42 h3 ♔f7 43 ♖c7+ ♔f6 44 ♖c6+ ♔f7 45 ♖a6 ♔g7 46 ♖a5 ♔f6 ½-½ C.Silva Sanchez-J.Granda Zuniga, Santiago 1987.

b2) 9...♗xc3 10 bxc3 ♘d5

11 ♕d3 (Black has a terrible dark square problem, much as in the main game, but no extra pawn—Adams scores easily) 11...♕c7 12 c4 ♘b4 13 ♕e4 c5 14 ♗g5 b6 15 a3 ♘c6 16 ♗d3 f5

17 exf6 gxf6 18 ♗h6 (an unopposed dark-squared bishop and gaping holes on the kingside lead to...) 18...♖f7 19 ♖ae1 ♔h8 20 ♕h4 e5 21 f4 ♗b7 22 fxe5 ♘xe5 23 ♗xh7!!

(this crushing sacrifice!—Black's open king is indefensible) 23...♔xh7 24 ♖e3 ♘g6 25 ♕h5 ♖h8 26 ♖e8!! (splendid!—Black has no reasonable way to save the queen) 26...♖xe8 27 ♗f4+ ♔g7 28 ♕h6+ ♔g8 29 ♗xc7 ♖e2 30 ♖f2 ♖e1+ 31 ♖f1 ♖e2 32 ♖d1 ♖xg2+ 33 ♔f1 ♖g7 34 ♖d8+ ♘f8 35 ♗d6 ♖g1+ 36 ♔e2 ♖7g2+ 37 ♔d3 ♖d1+ 38 ♔c3 1-0 M.Adams-S.Halkias, Gibraltar 2010.

8 bxc3

Now, having made an unprotected hole at d6 (inviting ♘b5 or ♗a3), Black can only justify his previous two moves by taking the e-pawn.

8...♘xe4

Obviously White has compensation for the pawn with his lead in development, two bishops, and Black's weak dark squares. The question is, should White sac another pawn for a further tempo, or stop at just one foot soldier?

Let's look at the "one pawn line" first, then go all in with the double pawn sac in the next game.

9 ♕d3

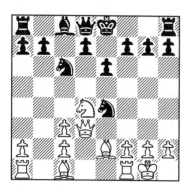

Statistically White scores 62% with this, and "only" 60% with the two-fer 9 ♗d3—both excellent scores of course.

9...d5

Black has tried other moves, but none of them allow a smooth path to castling and king safety. The problem is that Black has no dark-squared bishop, while the a3/f8 diagonal is wide open for White. Sample variations are:

a) 9...f5 10 ♗a3 (the problem manifests itself—castling is not legal!) 10...♔f7 11 ♖ad1 ♕f6 12 ♘b5 a6 13 ♘d6+ ♘xd6 14 ♗xd6 ♖e8 15 ♕h3 ♔g8 16 ♖d3 ♕d8 17 ♖g3 ♕f6 18 ♗f4 ♔h8 19 ♗h5 ♖g8 20 ♗g6 h6 21 ♗xh6 (Black's queen's bishop has yet to make a move—indeed, has no legal moves—but White's fourth move with his own bishop forces mate!) 1-0 M.Paragua-N.Guglielmi, Nichelino 2004.

b) 9...♘c5 10 ♕e3 d6 (not 10...0-0? 11 ♘xc6 bxc6 12 ♕xc5) 11 ♖d1 ♘xd4 (or 11...0-0 12 ♘b5 and White recovers his pawn with advantage) 12 cxd4 ♘d7 13 ♕g3 0-0 14 ♕xd6 (Black still had to pay with a big pawn in order to get castled) 14...♘f6 15 ♕g3 ♗d7 16 ♗h6 ♘e8 17 c4 ♖c8 18 d5 exd5 19 cxd5 ♔h8 20 ♗g5 ♘f6 21 ♕h4 ♕b6 22 ♗d3 h6 23 ♗xh6! (slightly more complicated than the same sac above, but just as effective) 23...gxh6 24 ♕xh6+ ♔g8 25 ♕g5+ ♔h8 26 d6! (interference—of course the pawn cannot be taken) ♘g8 27 ♕e5+ f6 28 ♕h5+ ♔g7 29 ♕h7 mate, J.Arizmendi Martinez-F.Sawatzki, Internet (blitz) 2000.

c) 9...♘f6 (this led to yet another dark square débâcle)

10 ♗a3 a6 11 ♕g3 g6 12 ♘xc6 bxc6 13 ♖fd1 d5 14 c4 ♘e4 15 ♕e3 f6 16 f3 ♘g5 17 ♖ab1 ♘f7 18 cxd5 cxd5 19 c4 (sometimes doubled pawns can be useful!—this second bash at Black's centre leaves him defenceless) 19...e5 20 ♖xd5 ♕c7 21 ♖c5 ♕d7 22 ♖d5 ♕c7 23 ♖b6 f5 24 ♖c5 ♕d7 25 ♖xe5+! (the uncastled black king and rook are forked, the breakthrough occurring of course on

the dark squares) 25...♘xe5 26 ♕xe5+ ♔f7 27 ♕xh8 1-0 A.Ahmed Harjour-J.Rodriguez Garcia, Asturias 1996.

10 ♗a3

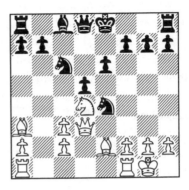

One can categorize this as a "preventive" sacrifice: White has prevented Black from castling at the cheap price of one pawn.

10...♕a5

It's possible to rule out White's next move, but this loses time as well: 10...a6 11 c4 (White plays this move twice—we've seen this theme before—and so opens the game decisively for his bishops) 11...♘e7 12 cxd5 exd5 13 c4 ♘f6 14 cxd5 ♘fxd5 15 ♗f3 (the bishops dominate: Black gives up material but can't find relief) 15...0-0 16 ♗xd5 ♘xd5 17 ♗xf8 ♕xf8 18 ♖fe1 ♘f4 19 ♕e4 ♘e6 20 ♘xe6 fxe6 21 ♖ac1 ♗d7 22 ♕xb7 ♕e8 23 ♖c7 ♖b8 24 ♕a7 ♖d8 25 ♖d1 1-0 L.Aroshidze-D.Fernandez Lago, Seville 2008.

Black can also counter in the centre: 10...e5 11 ♘xc6 bxc6 12 c4 ♗a6 13 ♕e3 f5 14 cxd5 ♗xe2 15 ♕xe2 ♕xd5 (15...cxd5 16 f3 wins, as Black's centre collapses) 16 ♖fd1 ♕e6 and now, instead of 17 ♕a6 (when Black managed to draw in G.Gopal-Y.Vovk, Martuni 2007), the incisive 17 ♕h5+ should lead to a winning attack; e.g. 17...♕g6 (or 17...g6 18 ♕h6 ♔f7 19 ♖ab1 and White infiltrates decisively) 18 ♕h3 and I don't see how Black can organize his position: his king is vulnerable in the centre and he can't castle either way.

11 ♘b5 a6 12 ♘d6+ ♘xd6

Worse is 12...♔f8? 13 ♘c4+, winning the queen, or 12...♔d7 13 ♘c4 ♕c7 14 ♕e3 with a winning attack.

13 ♗xd6

White scores 70% from this position: it's obvious the first player has excellent compensation due to the strength of the dark-squared bishop, while Black is a long way from king safety. *Fritz* claims only plus-equals, but I think the defensive task is far too difficult for mere humans, thus explaining the poor statistics.

13...♕d8 14 ♕g3 ♘e7

If 14...♕f6 then 15 ♖fd1 and Black hasn't improved his position, while

White threatens to blow things open with our thematic c3-c4.

15 ♕xg7

Also strong is 15 ♗d3 ♘g6 (or 15...0-0 16 ♗xh7+! ♔xh7 17 ♕h4+, winning) 16 ♖fe1 ♗d7 17 c4 dxc4 18 ♗e4 ♗c6 19 ♗xc6+ bxc6 20 ♖ad1 ♖a7 21 ♗c5 ♖d7 22 ♖b1 ♕h4 23 ♖b8+ ♖d8 24 ♖d1 (bada bump!) 1-0 L.D.Nisipeanu-Il.Schneider, German League 2010.

15...♖g8 16 ♕e5 ♘f5 17 ♗a3 ♕h4 18 f4?!

It's because of this move, exposing the white king to a check (now Karpov would never have allowed such a thing!), that Black has an equalizing chance later.

Instead, 18 ♗f3 is correct, when Black can hardly hold; e.g. 18...♕c4 (after 18...♘e7 19 ♖fe1 ♕g5 20 ♕c7 White infiltrates on those helpless dark squares, while 18...♗d7 19 ♗xd5 0-0-0 20 ♗f3 sees White recover his pawn with the much safer king) 19 ♖fe1 and the black king will perish in the centre.

18...♗d7 19 ♗f3 0-0-0 20 ♖ab1 f6 21 ♕e2 ♕xf4 22 ♖xb7

With the simple point 22...♔xb7 23 ♗xd5+ exd5 24 ♖xf4 and the queen goes—but Black has a counter-chance!

22...♕e3+?

Which he misses! 22...♘d4! is correct, which is only possible because 18 f4 opened up a checking diagonal: 23 ♕xa6 (not 23 cxd4 ♕xd4+ 24 ♔h1 ♔xb7 and Black is better, as his queen escaped the f-file with tempo) 23...♘xf3+ 24 ♖xf3 ♖xg2+! and Black draws; e.g. 25 ♔xg2 ♕d2+ 26 ♔f1 ♕d1+ 27 ♔g2 ♕d2+ 28 ♔h3 (White can't avoid the draw, for if 28 ♖f2 then 28...♖g8+ 29 ♔f3 ♕xc3+ 30 ♕d3 ♕xd3+ 31 cxd3 ♔xb7 and Black is a good pawn up) 28...♕h6+ with a perpetual.

23 ♕xe3 ♘xe3 24 ♖fb1

White recoordinates his pieces and wins with his dominating rooks and bishops—in both cases these are better than their opposite numbers.

24...♗b5 25 ♖a7 ♘c4 26 ♗e7 ♘d2

Not 26...♖de8 27 ♗h5, which shows the power of White's bishops.

27 ♗xd8 ♘xf3+ 28 ♔h1 ♘d2 29 ♖xb5 axb5 30 ♗xf6 ♖g6 31 ♗d4

The complications are over and White has emerged with his big bishop intact and an extra pawn.

31...h5 32 ♖h7 ♘c4 33 ♖xh5 ♔d7 34 h3 ♔d6 35 g4 e5 36 ♗f2 e4 37 ♔g2 ♖g7 38 ♖h6+ ♔d7 39 ♗d4 ♖f7 40 g5 e3 41 g6 ♖f2+ 42 ♔g3 ♖f1 43 g7 ♔e7 44 ♔g2 ♖f2+ 45 ♔g1

45...♘d2

45...♔f7 also loses immediately to 46 ♖h8.

46 ♗xe3 1-0

The dark-squared bishop strikes the final blow.

It's true that Gashimov let Black out at one point (18 f4?!), but with 18 ♗f3 there he would have had a clear advantage—and earlier still, the 15 ♗d3 line looks great for White.

White gets all this for just one pawn? This is a line I would never play for Black—Steinitz aside, I don't think a pawn is worth *that much* trouble.

Now let's see what happens when White accelerates his attack by pitching two pawns!

1 e4 c5 2 ♘f3 e6 3 ♘c3 ♘c6 4 d4 cxd4 5 ♘xd4 ♘f6 6 ♗e2 ♗b4 7 0-0 ♗xc3 8 bxc3 ♘xe4 9 ♗d3!?

One can argue that the c3-pawn was only in the way of the dark-squared bishop—on the other hand, risk has increased.

9...♘xc3 10 ♕g4

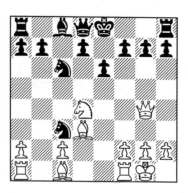

White launches the typical attack against the undefended (dark square) g7-pawn.

10...♕f6

Black can trap himself with 10...♘xd4 expecting 11 ♕xd4 ♕f6, but White crosses him up with 11 ♕xg7! ♘ce2+ 12 ♔h1 ♖f8 13 ♗xe2 ♘xe2 14 ♗a3 d6 15 ♖ad1 and the dark squares collapse, along with Black's position.

I think Black's best is to castle *while he can* (it's interesting that there is no castling prevention when White sacs two pawns, but there is if he just gives

up one) and then defend, unloading pawns as necessary. This is in accordance with modern principles of defence, as opposed to clinging on to material. After 10...0-0 11 ♘xc6 dxc6! (but not 11...bxc6 12 ♗b2 ♕f6 13 ♖ab1!, which wins for White, as John Emms has pointed out) 12 ♗b2 e5! (this dynamic defence is only possible because the black d-pawn moved out of the way of his queen's bishop) 13 ♕g3 ♘d5 14 ♗xe5 f6 15 ♗d6 ♖e8,

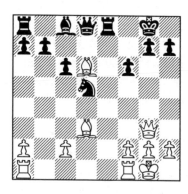

White's two bishops are equal to the missing pawn, but probably no more than that: the main feature is that Black is *castled* and still has a pawn to give back if necessary. As one sees in the following play, Black, using GM defence, finally reaches an endgame with an extra pawn and actually wins it! So there is risk: 16 c4 ♘b6 17 ♖ab1 ♕d7 18 c5 ♘d5 19 ♕h4 g6 20 f4 ♖e3 21 ♗c4 ♕f7 22 ♖fe1 ♖xe1+ 23 ♖xe1 ♗e6 24 ♗xd5 cxd5 25 f5 gxf5 26 ♖e3 ♖e8 27 ♗f4 ♗d7 28 ♖xe8+ ♗xe8 29 ♗e3 ♕e6 30 ♕g3+ ♗g6 31 h4 ♕e5 32 ♗f4 ♕e2 33 ♔h2 ♕g4 34 ♕f2 ♗e8

35 ♗g3 d4 36 ♕e1 ♕e4 37 ♕f2 ♗c6 38
♗f4 d3 39 ♕g3+ ♔f7 40 ♗h6 ♕g4 41
♕f2 ♕e2 42 ♕g3 ♕g4 43 ♕f2 ♔g6 44
♗f4 ♔h5 45 ♗g3 f4 46 ♕xf4 ♕xf4 47
♗xf4 ♔xh4 48 ♔g1 ♔g4 49 ♗d2 f5 50
♔f2 f4 51 a3 h5 52 ♗c3 h4 53 ♗a5 f3
54 gxf3+ ♗xf3 55 ♔e3 h3 56 ♗c7 ♗e4
57 ♗d6 d2 58 ♔xd2 ♔f3 59 ♔c3 ♔g2
60 ♔b4 h2 61 ♗xh2 ♔xh2 62 a4 ♔g3
63 a5 a6 0-1 A.Delchev-
G.Mastrokoukos, World Student Team
Championship, Sofia 1994.

11 ♘xc6 bxc6

11...h5 is an interesting counter-
attack: 12 ♕g3 bxc6 13 ♗d2 h4 14 ♕g4
c5 15 ♕c4 ♘d5 16 ♕xc5 h3 and Black
had good counterplay in Y.Rantanen-
B.Ivanovic, Tallinn 1979.

12 ♗g5 ♕e5 13 ♗f4 ♕d4 14 ♕g3

14...♘e4

No better is 14...♖g8 15 ♖ae1 g6 16
♗e5 ♕c5 17 ♕f4 ♘d5 18 ♕h4 h5 (the
Swiss cheese defence?) 19 ♕g3 ♔e7 20
♖e4 d6 21 ♗d4 ♕a5 22 ♕g5+ ♔e8 23
c4 c5? 24 ♕xd5 ♖b8 25 ♕xd6 1-0
I.Cheparinov-K.Rusev, Bulgarian Team
Championship 2003.

15 ♗xe4 ♕xe4 16 ♕xg7

The dark squares cracking, plus no
castling, equals one point for White.

**16...♕xf4 17 ♕xh8+ ♔e7 18 ♕xh7 ♗a6
19 ♖fe1 ♕f6 20 ♕e4 ♖g8 21 ♖ab1 ♕g5
22 ♖e3 ♕h5 23 ♖a3 ♗e2 24 h3 a6 25
♖e3 ♗b5 26 a4 1-0**

After studying the single and double pawn sacrifices, there is absolutely
no doubt in my mind: the single pawn
sacrifice is objectively stronger. The
main point is that, when White sacs
only one insignificant unit, he gains a
tempo with 9 ♕d3 to enforce ♗a3 and
so prevent castling. When he plays 9
♗d3 as in this game, Black takes on c3
which also attacks the queen, which
gains time for him to castle!

Yes, White still has a terrific attack
for the two pawns, but the risk factors
are also high, as not only castling, but
the ...h7-h5 counterthrust was possible.

Meanwhile in the Gashimov game
and others given in the notes, White
was down a single pawn that was often
quickly recovered, and Black could not

castle. Now that's a risk-free pawn sacrifice, and gives White excellent chances for advantage. So I say, Bash with Gash, and sac only one pawn, but keep that black king in the middle where we like him!

We now wander into another part of this complex, the Kan Variation.

1 e4 c5 2 ♘f3 e6 3 d4 cxd4 4 ♘xd4 a6 5 ♘c3 b5

Even Johan Hellsten, who wrote a book on the Kan, considers this further non-development to be too extravagant. He came by this wisdom the hard way—by playing and, as we see in this game, losing.

Instead, he recommends 5...♕c7, the "normal" Kan move, which still looks pretty extravagant to me: Black makes two little waiting pawn moves, then develops his queen!? I recommend

sticking to our basic repertoire against this with 6 ♗e2—see Games 54-56.

However, we first have to deal with the provocative 5...b5 as seen here and in the following game. There is some method behind Black's madness, much as in the Smyslov-Kottnauer sideline of the Scheveningen (Game 38), which also featured an early ...b7-b5. If White plays passively, and defends with a2-a3 or f2-f3 against the evident threat of ...♗b7 and ...b5-b4, targeting the e4-pawn, then Black gets a good game. So just like Smyslov, one must defend the e-pawn immediately with the king's bishop, in this case with 6 ♗d3 instead of Smyslov's ♗f3. In both cases the bishop looks a bit like a tall pawn, but the greater good is that, as Smyslov showed then and Felgaer shows now, Black's counterplay is immediately snuffed out, and his prematurely advanced b-pawn becomes a target for an a2-a4 lever—yes, ideas repeat throughout the repertoire!

6 ♗d3!

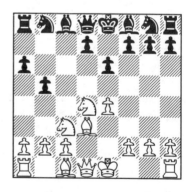

Best. I will never tell you that one

system is a panacea against all variations. There are always exceptions in chess! Here our usual development, 6 ♗e2, is weaker in view of 6...♗b7, threatening 7...b4. This is quite annoying for White and, worst of all, the first player will be unable (as he will in the 5...♕c7 6 ♗e2 variations) to set up his e4/f4 pawn duo.

But now, after playing the accurate 6 ♗d3, White has every chance of an opening advantage.

Hellsten in his book, *Play the Sicilian Kan*, gives a good explanation of Black's problems in this variation, which I will now summarize and relate to our repertoire: Black has a hole at d6, so he would like to play ...d7-d6 to occupy this square and prevent White's e4-e5 advance (Hellsten plays that way in this game). However, White then breaks like Smyslov with a2-a4. If Black takes, his pawn structure is broken, but if he advances to b4, that pawn will be weak, as the f8-bishop's diagonal has been blocked by the d6-pawn. On the other hand, if Black decides to live with the weakness at d6, so as to keep the f8-bishop's diagonal unobstructed, then White (as we will see in the next game) plays e4-e5, taking the d6- and f6-squares under control, with strong central pressure on Black's game.

In short, Hellsten doesn't believe Black's problems can be solved if White plays accurately after 5...b5—and I don't either!

6...♕b6

We'll look at the alternative 6...♗b7 in the next game.

7 ♘f3

Best, as explained above: White must be ready to play e4-e5.

7...♘c6 8 0-0 d6

This leads to the aforementioned problems on the queenside, but White was ready to play e4-e5.

Even worse is 8...♘ge7?, even if played by the US Champion, as d6 is utterly without defence now. (I was just thinking that after 1 e4 c5 2 ♘f3 e6 Black *already* has a permanent hole at d6—what other opening creates such a central weakness so early?) Anyway, returning to the dubious 8...♘ge7, White answers 9 ♗e3 ♕c7?! (9...♕b8 10 a4 is good for White, but not as horrible as the game) 10 ♗xb5! and there are two lines:

a) 10...axb5 11 ♘xb5 ♕b8 (11...♕d8 12 ♘d6 is an amusing smothered mate right in the opening!) 12 ♘d6+ ♔d8 13 ♘xf7+ ♔e8 14 ♘xh8 and wins as the knight can't be caught; e.g. 14...g6 15 ♘g5 h6 16 ♘gf7 and the second knight finds its way to the eternal d6 weakness.

b) In the game Kamsky simply accepted the loss of the pawn with 10...♖b8, but was unable to hold: 11 ♗xc6 ♘xc6 12 b3 ♗b7 13 ♘d5! (White plays sharply, even when material ahead—a sign of a strong player) 13...exd5 14 exd5 ♘d8 15 ♖e1 ♘e6 16 ♕d2 ♗b4 17 ♕xb4 ♗xd5 18 ♕d2 ♗xf3 19 ♗f4 d6 20 gxf3 ♖d8 21 ♖ad1 0-0 22 ♗xd6 ♕c8 23 f4 ♘c5 24 ♕c3 ♖fe8 25 ♖xe8+ ♖xe8 26 f3 ♖d8 27 ♖d5 ♕e6 28 ♕xc5 ♖c8 29 ♕xc8+! ♕xc8 30 ♗e7 1-0 E.Sutovsky-G.Kamsky, Khanty-Mansiysk Olympiad 2010.

9 a4

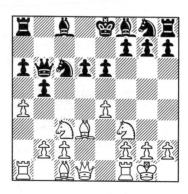

In general (referring to Hellsten's and my comments above) when Black plays ...d7-d6, White should bash him with a2-a4—when the black pawn goes to b4 it will be weak with no bishop to guard it, and may eventually be lost as happens here.

However, one should keep in mind that a2-a4 does not have to be played immediately—see the note to Black's seventh move in the next game, where it's important to delay the break one move.

9...b4

9...bxa4 splits Black's pawns and is tactically weak as well: 10 ♗e3! ♕c7 (not 10...♕xb2? 11 ♘xa4 ♕b7 12 ♘b6 ♖b8 13 ♗xa6, winning) 11 ♖xa4 and White is better across the board, with especially great pressure on a6.

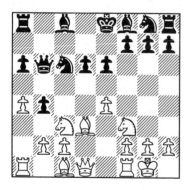

10 a5!

I remember scoring with this nice "blow for blow" against GM Arthur Bisguier in a similar position: White takes advantage of the vulnerable black queen position to gain a tempo to activate his knight, and furthermore, artificially isolate the exposed black b-pawn. That White is a pawn down has no significance—Black's queenside is so weak White will inevitably recover material.

10...♘xa5 11 ♘a4 ♕c7 12 ♗e3

Remember how often Karpov exploited the weak b6-square? Here White threatens to win a piece with 13 ♗b6.

12...罝b8

Stopping one invader but not the other!

13 ②b6! 罝xb6 14 罝xa5 罝b8 15 豐a1

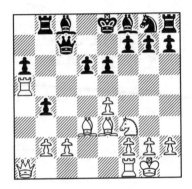

Already the a-pawn can't be held, while Black has yet to develop a kingside piece.

15...②e7

Or 15...②f6 16 奧xa6 奧xa6 17 罝xa6 ②xe4 18 罝e1 ②f6 19 ②d4 奧e7 20 ②c6 (White has a big advantage on the queenside—in this particular variation, White's play is on the queenside, which is rare in the Sicilian) 20...罝c8 (Black can barely hold the eighth rank and has to give up the seventh) 21 ②xe7 豐xe7 22 罝a7 豐d8 23 豐a4+ 含f8 24 豐xb4 含g8 (if 24...罝xc2? then 25 豐b7 wins immediately) 25 c4 and White has an undisputable advantage with the superior minor piece and passed pawn, while Black is hampered in defending against all this as his king's rook is still out of play.

16 奧xa6 ②c6

Black can snatch pawns into an early grave: 16...豐xc2 17 罝c1 豐xe4 18

奧xc8 ②xc8 19 豐a4+ 含e7 20 奧g5+ and mates.

17 奧b5 奧d7 18 奧xc6 奧xc6 19 罝a7 罝b7 20 罝a8+ 罝b8 21 罝a7 罝b7 22 罝a8+ 罝b8 23 罝xb8+

No draw!

23...豐xb8 24 ②d4

24...奧d7

If 24...奧xe4, then 25 豐a4+ 含e7 26 ②c6+ 奧xc6 27 豐xc6 (the threat is 28 罝a1 etc) 27...豐e8 28 豐b7+ 豐d7 29 豐xb4 and Black can't get developed without making concessions; e.g. 29...g6 30 罝d1 奧g7 31 罝xd6! and White should win.

25 豐a6 奧e7 26 ②c6 豐c8 27 豐xc8+ 奧xc8 28 罝a1

Even in the endgame the open a-file is an important attacking avenue.

28...奧f6 29 罝a7 0-0

After 29...奧xb2 30 罝e7+ 含f8 31 罝c7 奧a6 32 罝a7 奧c8 33 罝a8 White wins a piece.

30 b3 e5

And also after 30...奧c3 31 ②e7+ 含h8 32 罝a8.

31 ②xb4

The weak b-pawn, a legacy of Black's extravagant opening (recall that his first five moves were all pawn moves, culminating in 5...b5), finally falls, and the game is decided. Note again that in the ...b7-b5 Kan, White's main play is on the queenside.

31...♗e6 32 ♘d5 h5 33 ♗b6!

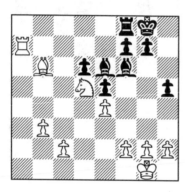

A nice manoeuvre to target the weak d6-square, which thoughtfully has a pawn on it!

33...♗g5 34 ♗c7 f5 35 ♗xd6 ♖d8 36 ♗xe5 ♗xd5 37 exd5 ♖xd5 38 f4 ♗d8 39 ♔f1 1-0

Black resigns in view of the following simple variations:

a) 39...♗b6 40 ♖xg7+ ♔f8 41 ♖b7 with three extra pawns.

b) 39...♖d2 40 ♔e1! ♖xc2 41 ♖a8 winning a piece.

c) 39...♗f6 40 ♗xf6 gxf6 41 ♔e2 and the connected passers win easily in the rook ending.

Black certainly faces difficult problems in this line, but White players need to know the crucial moment comes when Black plays ...d7-d6, after which White should hit hard on the queenside with a2-a4.

1 e4 c5 2 ♘f3 e6 3 ♘c3 a6 4 d4 cxd4 5 ♘xd4 b5 6 ♗d3

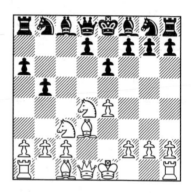

6...♗b7

Tal faced 6...♕c7 (6...♕b6 7 ♘f3 was the previous game) 7 0-0 ♗b7 8 ♖e1 ♗d6 (Black is trying to prevent e4-e5, but of course the bishop is very awkward on this square) 9 h3 ♘c6 10 ♘xc6 dxc6 11 ♕g4 (Tal is pressing, while Black has the usual dark square problems) 11...♘e7 (since 11...♗e5 12 f4 evidently favours White, Black gamely sacrifices against Tal, but...) 12 ♕xg7 ♗e5 13 ♗f4! (...is stunned almost immediately by this counterblow) 13...♗xg7 14 ♗xc7 ♖c8 15 ♗d6 c5 16 e5 and let's see: hole at d6; destroyed dark squares; pawn up; Tal!—the only miracle that occurred in this game is that Black made it to move 50 before resigning in M.Tal-M.J.Franklin, Hastings 1963/64.

In another Hastings tournament, the unlucky Mr. Franklin had Black again against Karpov! Alas, his result did not improve, as we will see in Game 66.

7 0-0 ♘c6

If instead 7...d6, to prevent e4-e5, then White hits on the other side, as we saw in the previous game: 8 ♖e1 (smiling at the black king—see line 'b' for the explanation) 8...♘f6 9 a4! and now:

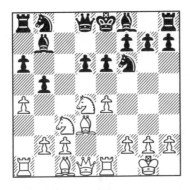

a) 9...bxa4 (already a success for White, as Black is left with a weak a-pawn) 10 ♘xa4 ♘bd7—I reached this position in a tournament game, and remembered Keres got the advantage by getting his knight to a5, but couldn't remember how he did it! I played the over-committal 11 c3 ♗e7 12 b4 0-0 13 ♘b3 ♕c7 14 ♘a5 which is actually not too bad, with White having a slight edge in T.Taylor-A.Inants, 7th Metropolitan IM, Los Angeles 2011. However,

Keres played the more precise, efficient and stronger 11 ♗d2 ♗e7 12 ♘b3 0-0 13 ♘a5 with a big advantage in P.Keres-M.Najdorf, Los Angeles 1963.

b) 9...b4 10 ♘d5! (the reason why White inserted ♖e1 before a2-a4 was to prepare this blow) and then:

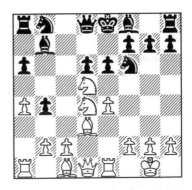

b1) 10...exd5 (taking the piece allows a savage attack) 11 exd5+ ♔d7 12 c4! g6 13 a5! (Black's centralized king can't find a safe square, while White builds up) 13...♗g7 14 ♗f4 ♔c8 15 ♖c1 ♘h5 16 c5!! (offering a second piece, but if accepted the black king will perish in the ensuing crossfire: 16...♘xf4 17 cxd6+ ♔d7 18 ♕g4+ and wins) 16...♕f6 17 cxd6+ ♔d8 18 ♕c2 and the king perished anyway, 1-0 Al.David-E.Lobron, Amsterdam 1996.

b2) 10...♘bd7 11 ♘xb4 (notice how the self-blocking pawn on d6 allows this capture) 11...♘c5 12 ♗g5 ♕b6 13 ♘d5! (once more with feeling!) 13...♘xd5 (or 13...exd5 14 exd5+ ♔d8 15 ♗xf6 gxf6 16 ♕h5 with a winning attack) 14 exd5 ♗xd5 15 c4 ♗b7 16 b4 (White wins with a most entertaining attack after this, though Black had one defensive resource—so, objectively, the simple 16 a5 is probably more accurate, with the idea ♗c2-a4, when Black has few, if any, defensive chances) 16...♕xb4 17 ♖b1 ♕a5 18 ♕h5 g6 19 ♕g4 e5 20 ♗f6 ♘xd3 21 ♗xh8 ♗e7 22 ♖e3 ♘c5 (22...♕d2!) 23 ♗xe5 dxe5 24 ♖xe5 f6 25 ♖xb7! 1-0 A.Zhigalko-V.Meijers, Turin Olympiad 2006—Black resigns, since if either white rook is taken, the other sacrifices itself on e7, with a winning fork in mind.

8 ♘xc6 dxc6

8...♗xc6 can also be met by 9 e5.

9 e5

Simple and strong—can Black get out of the opening alive?

9...♘e7

Black is plagued by the hole at d6 and White's strong e5-pawn.

10 ♕h5 ♕c7 11 ♖e1

It's obvious that Black has no pain-free way to complete his development, or even castle. Going long will allow the line opening a2-a4, but Black can't go kingside without incurring serious weaknesses, as the game shows.

11...♘g6

The alternative 11...g6 looks even worse with the dark square holes: 12 ♕g5 ♗g7 13 ♘e4 ♗xe5 (not 13...♕xe5? 14 ♕xe5 ♗xe5 15 ♘c5, winning a piece) 14 ♘f6+ ♗xf6 15 ♕xf6 with a tremendous attack on the dark squares.

12 ♗xg6 fxg6

Black has to take back this way, but now his split pawns add another weakness to the eternal hole at d6.

13 ♕g4 ♕f7 14 ♘e4 ♕f5 15 ♕h4 c5

15...♕xe5 16 ♗g5 is too much to bear.

16 ♘d6+ ♗xd6 17 exd6

I've always felt that threatening mate in one gets the opponent's attention—besides this minor threat, the opposite-coloured bishops favour White's attacking chances.

17...0-0 18 ♗g5 ♖f7 19 ♖ad1 ♗d5 20 ♖d2 h6 21 ♗e7

Now the passed pawn on the sixth (on d6 of course, weakened by Black's second move!) becomes the crucial factor: one could say White has a decisive advantage already, and John carries it through professionally.

21...♖a7 22 f3 ♖d7 23 ♕f2 c4 24 ♖de2 g5 25 ♕c5 ♗b7 26 ♕xf5 exf5 27 ♖e5 g4 28 f4 g6 29 ♖c5 ♗e4 30 a4!

Any way you slice it, Black's queenside disintegrates or the passed pawn goes through.

30...♖h7

Nothing works: 30...bxa4 31 ♖xc4, or 30...♖b7 31 ♖c7 ♖xc7 32 dxc7 ♗b7 33 ♗d6, or finally 30...♗xc2 31 ♖c7 is an easy win for White in all cases.

31 axb5 axb5 32 ♖xb5 ♔f7 33 ♖c5 ♗xc2 34 ♖c7 ♗a4 35 ♖xc4

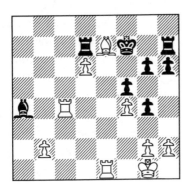

By playing the best defence (giving up a pawn) Black ensures that he will get to look at his terrible position and White's monster d-pawn for another ten moves.

35...♗b5 36 ♖c8 ♖b7 37 ♖f8+ ♔g7 38 ♖c1 ♖h8 39 ♖c7 ♖xc7 40 dxc7 ♗a6 41 ♖d8 ♖g8 42 b4 ♔f7 43 b5! ♗c8 44 b6 ♗a6 45 ♗d6 ♖e8 46 ♗e5 ♔e7 47 ♖b8 1-0

White will win a piece with the

coming b6-b7.

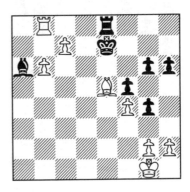

Much more than an editor, this was a sharp and convincing win by GM Emms.

The extra extravagant 5...b5 seems to be under a cloud now—given that Kan-advocate Hellsten can't find anything, Kamsky self-destructed, and Keres demonstrated how to play against this 50 years ago!

If you know the ideas (e4-e5 if Black sits as here, a2-a4 with a queenside attack if he plays ...d7-d6), White should get the edge against this non-developing system.

Now we take on the main line Kan, where at least Black develops *something* on his fifth move!

Game 54
D.Kryakvin-D.Bocharov
Irkutsk 2010

1 e4 c5 2 ♘f3 e6 3 d4 cxd4 4 ♘xd4 a6 5 ♘c3 ♕c7

The main line of the Kan, with only about 17,000 games in the database! What should we do against such a popular system? Simple: stick to our basic repertoire and just play chess.

6 ♗e2

Since Black's last move threatened nothing, typical development is fine.

6...b5 7 a3

Not 7 0-0 ♗b7, when White has no active defence of e4—remember, we want to set up the e4/f4 pawn duo for attacking purposes, and the text move slows Black up just long enough to achieve it.

7...♗b7 8 f4

8...d6

Black transposes into a Scheveningen-type system, which may be psychologically painful for him. But it's hard to find something better, as clearly e4-e5 may otherwise come soon. Three main alternatives have been tried:

a) 8...♘c6 9 ♗e3 ♘xd4 10 ♕xd4 (Black has glaring weaknesses at d6 and b6) 10...♘e7 11 ♖d1 ♖d8 12 0-0 ♘c6 was M.Tal-R.Hübner, Leningrad Interzonal 1973. Here White could continue technically 13 ♕b6 ♕xb6 14 ♗xb6 ♖b8 15 ♗f2 with a solid plus: Black has not solved his opening problems, and the hole at d6 beckons White's knight, which might arrive there after ♗f3/e4-e5/♘e4 etc. However, Tal understandably wants more, and with justification. The game continued 13 ♕d2 ♗e7 14 ♕e1 (14 ♘d5 exd5 15 exd5 is another good attack) 14...d6 15 f5 0-0, and now 16 ♕f2 was correct, gaining a tempo off that b6-square—threat ♗b6, winning the exchange—and prepares a strong attack against the poorly defended black king (just as in Games 45-46, the black knight's manoeuvre to c6 leaves his monarch in danger). Instead of this sound course, Tal sac'ed even more, rushing with the overly impetuous 16 f6 ♗xf6 17 ♖xf6 gxf6 18 ♕h4 ♕e7 19 ♖d3 f5, when Hübner defended and eventually scored the win. Nevertheless, I'd love to have Tal's position after move 15!

b) 8...b4 is another risky attempt to

grab material: 9 axb4 ♗xb4 10 0-0 ♗xc3 11 bxc3 ♗xe4,

when 12 f5 is recommended by Wade, Blackstock and Kotov in *World Championship Interzonals* as giving a strong attack—I agree, though this has never been tried. In practice we see 12 c4 ♘f6 13 ♗a3 d6 14 f5 ♔e7? (14...e5 is better, though after 15 ♘f3 White has good compensation) 15 fxe6 fxe6 16 ♗f3 ♗xf3 17 ♕xf3 ♕xc4 18 ♕b7+! ♘bd7 19 ♘c6+ ♔f7 20 ♕xd7+ (Black is busted, but the GM declines to resign against his lower-rated opponent) 20...♔g6 21 ♘e7+ ♔h6 22 ♕xd6 ♘e4 23 ♕e5 ♖ad8 24 ♗c1+ g5 25 ♗xg5+! ♘xg5 26 ♖f6+ ♔h5 27 ♖f4! (it's either mate or White wins the queen, but Black had to play one more move!) 27...♖d5 28 g4+ 1-0 M.Dambacher-G.Forintos, Haarlem 1994—Black finally resigned as it's mate in two.

c) 8...♘f6 9 ♗f3 d6 returns to the main game, Trying to avoid this with 9...d5 is not good, since the game opens and White gets to the e-file first; e.g. 10 exd5 ♘xd5 11 ♘xd5 ♗xd5 12 ♗xd5 exd5 13 0-0 ♗e7 14 a4 b4 15 ♘f5 and Black must shed material in view of the threatened ♖e1.

9 ♗f3

Castling is natural here and in our next game Tal plays 9 0-0, probably without much thought. It's a good move and White has chances for a reasonable pull.

However, Kryakvin wants to charge like a madman (my kind of guy!) and so makes a non-committal move, waiting for the knight to appear on f6 and give him an enemy to justify a bayonet attack!

9...♘f6

10 g4!?

Possibly not a Karpov move, and not a Tal move either (10 0-0 would transpose to the next game again)—but an Alekhine-type attack, and one shouldn't limit oneself to positional play!

10...e5?!

Black hits back in the centre in the "approved" way—and immediately gets a difficult position.

Instead, the cool 10...♘c6 11 ♗e3 ♗e7 is correct, when the following games show the risky side of White's endeavour:

a) 12 g5 (too impetuous) 12...♘d7 13 ♘xc6 ♗xc6 14 ♕e2 0-0 15 0-0 ♖fe8 16 ♗g2 ♕b7 17 b4 ♘b6 18 ♖ad1 ♘c4 19 ♗c1 ♖ac8 20 ♖d3 ♗d8 21 ♔h1 g6 22 ♘d1 ♗b6 23 ♘f2 ♗xf2 24 ♖xf2 d5 25 e5 d4! 26 ♕g4 ♗xg2+ 27 ♕xg2 ♕a7 28 ♖e2 ♖ed8 29 ♕e4 a5 30 bxa5 ♕xa5 31 h4 ♕a4 32 h5 ♘b6 33 hxg6 fxg6 (Black defends and breaks through on the queenside before White has real king-side threats—recognizing this, White tries something on the queenside, but falls into a cul-de-sac) 34 ♕b7? ♘d5 35 ♖b3 ♖c7 0-1 S.Brenjo-Z.Mijailovic, Serbian Championship, Kragujevac 2000.

b) 12 ♕e2 ♘a5 13 0-0-0 ♖c8 14 g5 ♘d7 15 ♗g4 ♘c5 16 f5 ♘xe4 17 ♘xe4?! (correct is 17 fxe6, with incalculable complications) 17...♗xe4 18 fxe6 ♘b3+ 19 ♔b1 ♘xd4 20 exf7+ ♔f8 21 ♗xd4 ♗xc2+? (Black *has* to get the queens off: 21...♕xc2+ 22 ♕xc2 ♗xc2+ 23 ♔a2 ♖c4 24 ♗e6 ♗xd1 25 ♖xd1 ♗xg5 26

♗xc4 bxc4 27 ♗c3 ♗e7 28 ♖d4 ♔xf7 29 ♖f4+ ♗f6 30 ♖xc4 and White can only hope to draw) 22 ♔a1 ♗xd1 23 ♖xd1 ♖b8 24 ♗e6 (despite being technically material down, White is winning in view of Black's imprisoned rook and defenceless king) 24...♗xg5 25 ♕g4 ♕d8 26 ♕g3 ♕e7 27 ♗a2 ♗f6 28 ♖e1 ♗e5 29 ♖xe5 dxe5 30 ♗xe5 1-0 F.Bindrich-Ax.Heinz, Pulvermühle 2002.

If you like wild and crazy and who knows who is winning, 10 g4 is for you! Otherwise, in the next game we'll see Tal win just like Karpov—nothing wrong with that either.

11 ♘f5 ♘fd7

Surely 11...g6, driving off the knight, is correct, but Black is reeling and retreats unnecessarily.

12 0-0 ♘b6 13 fxe5 dxe5 14 ♔h1

The immediate 14 ♘d5 may be even stronger.

14...♘8d7 15 ♘d5

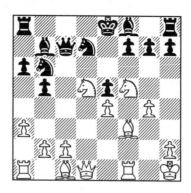

Facing two knights on the fifth already, it's amazing Black holds out as long as he does.

15...♘xd5 16 exd5 ♖c8 17 c3 g6 18 ♘h6

f6 19 ♗g2 ♗e7 20 a4!

A typical blow in these Kan positions. The lever is there, so use it! Meanwhile Black can't legally castle in either direction.

20...b4 21 cxb4 ♗xb4 22 ♗d2 ♕d6 23 ♖c1?!

This gives Black a chance. 23 ♗xb4 ♕xb4 24 ♖a3! is correct, which indirectly defends b2 and attacks across the board—advantage to White.

23...♔e7

Black misses his opportunity in turn: 23...♖xc1 24 ♗xc1 ♘b6 gives him good counterplay as White's pawn at d5 is weak—but White is going to solve that problem.

24 ♗xb4 ♕xb4 25 ♖c6!!

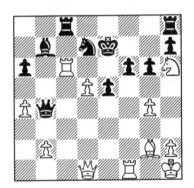

A typical sacrifice against an uncastled king: White extends the range of his attacking pieces (notably bishop and queen) and hits Black hard before he can consolidate. And a further benefit is that the weak d-pawn becomes a strong c-pawn, a passer just two moves from queening!

25...♗xc6 26 dxc6 ♘b8 27 g5!

"A hit, a palpable hit!"

27...♖hf8

If 27...♖hd8 then 28 ♕f3 with a powerful attack.

28 ♘g4 f5

28...fxg5 looks ugly but may be Black's best chance of survival.

29 ♘xe5 ♖fd8 30 ♕f3 ♔f8 31 ♕g3

Black's problem is that he is playing without a knight, due to the strong pawn on c6.

31...♕d6?!

Even for 2600 GMs, it's hard to defend a difficult position for a long time. Here 31...♔g8 is correct, defending h8 (an important square, though that's hard to see right now), when White obviously has excellent compensation for the exchange, but *both* sides are still playing.

32 ♕c3! ♖e8

32...♔g8 is too late in view of 33 ♕b3+ and the queen infiltrates via f7.

33 ♘c4!

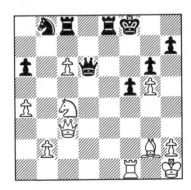

A decisive retreat, clearing the long diagonal for the queen with tempo.

33...♕e6 34 ♕h8+ ♔f7

Or 34...♕g8 35 ♕xg8+ ♚xg8 36 ♘d6 and White wins the exchange back, after which his extra, passed pawn should be quickly decisive.

35 ♕xh7+ ♚f8 36 ♘b6!

Tactically alert—yes, we have a 2600 GM on the white side too, and it's much more fun to play from his side—as now the rook must move off the c-file and so allow the coming fork.

36...♖cd8

Not 36...♖xc6 37 ♗d5, winning the queen.

37 c7 ♕xb6 38 cxd8♕ ♖xd8 39 ♕h8+ ♚f7 40 ♕h7+ ♚f8 41 ♗f3 ♕e6 42 ♕h8+ ♚e7 43 ♕g7+ ♚e8 44 b4

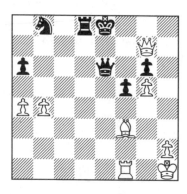

Now that the dust has cleared, one sees that White has regained the exchange he invested, is up a good pawn, has the superior minor piece—and is still attacking Black's wandering king which, after a long journey, has returned to its original square.

44...♘c6 45 ♕c3 ♘e7 46 ♖e1 ♕d6 47 ♕g7 ♖b8 48 ♕f6! 1-0

White wins more material without slowing the attack.

Certainly 10 g4 is equally bold and risky: as the games given in the note to Black's 10th move above show, the result could go either way, but a draw is most unlikely!

I think this would be a terrific surprise weapon—now let's look at Tal's *quieter* play.

Game 55
M.Tal-Z.Vranesic
Amsterdam Interzonal 1964

1 e4 c5 2 ♘f3 e6 3 d4 cxd4 4 ♘xd4 a6 5 ♘c3 ♕c7 6 ♗e2 b5 7 a3 ♗b7 8 f4 d6 9 0-0

Not thinking of 9 ♗f3 ♘f6 10 g4.

9...♘f6 10 ♗f3 ♘bd7 11 ♕e2

The Karpovian 11 ♚h1, followed by the well-known ♕e1-g3 attack, will be seen in the next game.

11...h6

11...e5 12 ♘f5 g6 13 fxe5 dxe5 14 ♘h6 gives White an annoying knight, similar to the previous game.

12 ♚h1

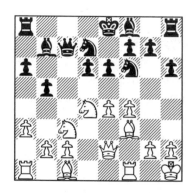

12...e5

This looks like a good place to find an improvement for Black, as Tal will soon get his knights to f5 and d5, again just as in the previous game.

12...♕c4 13 ♕f2 ♘c5 14 ♖e1 0-0-0 would certainly make it interesting, but I am convinced Tal would have found the backward attacking move 15 ♕g1! (threatening 16 ♗e2, winning the queen, as Black does not have 16...♘cxe4 as a saving resource) 15...♘cd7 16 ♗d2 and White's attack (with the Kan lever a2-a4 coming in soon) looks much more substantial than anything Black can dream up.

13 fxe5 dxe5

14 ♘d5!

If 14 ♘f5 then 14...g6 is possible, so Tal finds another way in.

14...♕c4

After 14...♘xd5 15 exd5 ♗c5 16 ♘f5 White threatens g7, while the advance d5-d6 is in the air.

15 ♕xc4

Tal is not averse to a queen exchange, since Black's new c-pawn will

be isolated and weak, while the white knights wreak havoc.

15...bxc4 16 ♘f5

Again this matched pair!

16...♘xd5 17 exd5 g6?!

This chases the knight where it wants to go, attacking the c-pawn. Black's only hope is the counter-attack 17...♘f6, though White still keeps an edge with 18 ♖e1.

18 ♘e3 ♘b6 19 ♗d2

Tal's first goal is to pick up the black c-pawn, but he also keeps his kingside options open.

19...♖c8

19...♗c5 20 ♘g4 ♗d6 21 ♗b4 highlights Black's weaknesses on both sides of the board.

20 ♖ae1 ♗g7 21 ♗a5

Black is lost after only 21 moves—Tal had quiet wizardry too!

21...♘d7 22 ♗e2 0-0 23 ♗xc4 e4 24 d6 ♘e5 25 ♗b3 ♔h7 26 ♗c7

And it's all over: Black drags it out to move 30 for form's sake.

26...f5 27 ♗d5 ♗xd5 28 ♘xd5 ♘d7 29 b4 ♗e5 30 c4 1-0

GMs swear by the Sicilian, but when White gets the centre plus a strong knight on d4, Black has to be very careful—whereas White (even without playing g2-g4 in the opening!) can still win in 30 moves!

Game 56
W.Rosen-A.Jugow
European Seniors Championship, Bad Homburg 2005

1 e4 c5 2 ♘f3 e6 3 d4 cxd4 4 ♘xd4 a6 5 ♘c3 ♕c7 6 ♗e2 b5 7 a3 ♗b7 8 f4 ♘f6 9 ♗f3 d6 10 0-0 ♘bd7

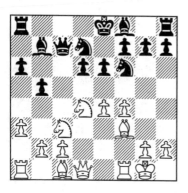

As we've learned, once this knight takes away the retreat square for its fellow, then g2-g4 comes even more strongly into question—even Tal lost to this attack!

11 ♔h1

White follows Karpov, but it's possible to go wild too, and the wildest of wild men was Tal's nemesis, Nezhmetdinov! 11 g4!? ♘c5 12 ♕e2 e5 13 ♘f5 g6 14 fxe5 dxe5 15 ♘h6 (there's our annoying knight on h6, evidently a staple of the g2-g4 anti-Kan lines) 15...♘e6 16 ♗g2 ♗g7 17 ♖xf6! (now there's a Tal sac—no, wait, a Tal-slaying sac!) ♗xf6 18 ♘d5 ♕d8 19 ♕f2 ♘f4 20 ♗xf4 exf4 21 e5 ♗xe5 22 ♖e1 f6 23 ♘xf6+!! (and there's another: White catches the king in the centre and wins) 23...♕xf6 24 ♕d4 ♔f8 25 ♖xe5 ♕d8 26 ♖f5+ gxf5 27 ♕xh8+ ♔e7 28 ♕g7+ ♔e6 29 gxf5+ 1-0 R.Nezhmetdinov-M.Tal, USSR Championship, Baku 1961.

11...♗e7 12 ♕e1 ♖d8 13 ♕g3

Instead of Nezhmetdinov's violent pawn storm, here White uses Karpov's classic anti-Scheveningen piece attack, of which we saw various examples in Chapter Four—and it's still strong in this current transpositional environment.

13...g6?!

I think Black has to castle while he can, even if after 13...0-0 14 f5 e5 15 ♗h6 ♘e8 16 ♘b3 White is better with an excellent ♗e2 Najdorf as in Chapter Two—note again that ideas from various variations are starting to repeat and transpose, reinforcing the strong points of our repertoire.

14 e5!

White strikes before Black can connect his rooks, and takes advantage of the fact that the black queen is now kind of overloaded: it wants to defend against the just played break but must also defend the bishop on b7.

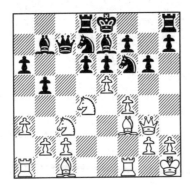

14...♘g8

This can't be good, but it's hard to find any playable move. After the obvious 14...dxe5 15 fxe5 ♘xe5 (or 15...♕xe5 16 ♗xb7 ♕xd4 17 ♗xa6 b4 18 axb4 ♕xb4 19 ♖a4 ♕b6 20 ♗h6 and Black won't get out of the opening alive) 16 ♗f4 wins material against Black's disorganized game as can be seen:

a) 16...♘xf3 is not check! Karpov's ♔h1 scores again, as here White can just take a queen.

b) 16...♘h5 17 ♗xh5 ♖xd4 18 ♗xe5 ♗d6 19 ♗xd6 ♖xd6 (19...♕xd6 loses to 20 ♕f2) 20 ♗f3 and White is a piece up.

c) 16...♖xd4 17 ♗xe5 ♗d6 18 ♗xd6 ♖xd6 19 ♗xb7 and White again nabs a piece.

All that's left is the computer answer 14...♘h5, but I doubt a human would play it—in any case, White maintains his advantage with 15 ♗xh5 gxh5 16 f5 with good attacking chances.

15 exd6 ♗xd6

16 ♘dxb5!

Smackdown! White gets a winning position right out of the opening.

16...axb5 17 ♘xb5 ♕b6

Note again how important it is that this move *is not check*—evidently Karpov was on to something when he always tucked his king away like that, and now many others are profiting.

18 ♘xd6+

White's final point is revealed: due to the overloaded queen, White recovers his piece and emerges with an extra pawn—but even more important are White's two bishops and attacking chances.

18...♕xd6 19 ♗xb7 ♕c7 20 ♗a6 ♕xc2 21 f5!

Rather than cling to material, White sacrifices his extra pawn with my favourite attacking blow—and Black can't find a way to take it.

21...♘gf6

Black gets no joy by restoring the material balance: 21...gxf5 (even worse is 21...exf5 22 ♕d6 with a winning attack against Black's wide open king) 22 ♗d3! (a false trail that could lead to Little Bighorn: 22 ♕g7 ♘gf6 23 ♕xh8+ ♔e7 24 ♕g7 ♖g8 25 ♕h6 ♕xg2 mate!) 22...♕b3 23 ♕g7 ♕xd3 (the previous variation no longer works: 23...♘gf6 24 ♕xh8+ ♔e7 25 ♕g7 ♖g8 26 ♕h6 and

White wins easily, as the black queen has been diverted from its mating posture) 24 ♗g5 and White gains a decisive material advantage.

22 fxe6 fxe6

White is still a pawn ahead, and Black has a permanent weakness at e6. Add the bishop pair, and one sees Black is not long for this world.

23 ♗d3 ♕c5 24 ♗d2 ♕d5 25 ♗xg6+!

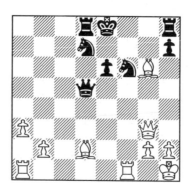

White finishes stylishly.

25...♔e7

25...hxg6 26 ♕xg6+ ♔e7 27 ♗b4+ ♘c5 28 ♗xc5+ ♕xc5 29 ♕xf6+ wins.

26 ♗b4+ ♘c5 27 ♕c7+ 1-0

White mates prettily after 27...♘fd7 (or 27...♖d7 28 ♗xc5+) 28 ♖f7+ ♔e8 29 ♖xh7+ ♔f8 30 ♕xd8 mate.

"No one ever said the Sicilian is an easy defence to play," said Larsen, and these last three games certainly show that. Black is playing a main line—and yet still has to walk a tightrope just to get out of the opening alive.

Meanwhile White can bash with an early g2-g4 like Kryavkin or Nezhmetdinov, or play a nice Karpovian crush as above.

My point is that even though these are "main lines", if you look at the positions objectively (as opposed to saying these lines must be good because currently trendy GMs A, B and C play them) you can see that Black gives up all presence in the centre—recall again Black's first five moves: ...c7-c5/...e7-e6/...c5xd4/...a7-a6/...♛c7—and falls behind in development. So it stands to reason that White, with a strong central control and good development—White's first five are e2-e4/♘f3/d2-d4/♘xd4/♘c3—can use his advantages to launch any number of attacks.

Now let's take a quick look at some non-main lines.

Game 57
G.Milos-J.Bellon Lopez
Oviedo (rapid) 1993

1 e4 c5 2 ♘f3 e6 3 d4 cxd4 4 ♘xd4 ♘f6 5 ♘c3 ♛b6

This the Gå På, a Swedish specialty according to the Sicilian *Dangerous Weapons* books, but I think it's just bad! Nevertheless, since the admired Almira Skripchenko lost to it, and the young Filipino star Wesley So held off a fellow GM with it, I thought I should put in one game.

6 e5

White should go for it, and so put the finger on the Gå's weak paw: no control of e5! This is stronger than the unnecessarily defensive retreat of a surprised GM: 6 ♘b3 (the knight wasn't even threatened!) 6...♗b4 7 ♗d3 ♗xc3+ 8 bxc3 d6 9 ♗a3 ♘bd7 10 0-0 0-0 11 e5 dxe5 12 ♗xf8 ♔xf8 13 ♖e1 ♛c7 14 ♛d2 b6 15 ♖ad1 ♗b7 16 ♗b5 ♘c5 17 ♘xc5 ♛xc5 18 ♛d6+ ♛xd6 19 ♖xd6 ♖c8 and Black, with positional compensation for the exchange, held the ending in R.Felgaer-W.So, Dresden Olympiad 2008.

6...♗c5

Evidently this was Black's idea.

7 ♗e3

So much for that! Now Black has no good move with his king's knight. Obviously not 7...♛xb2? 8 ♘a4 ♗b4+ (White also comes out a piece up after 8...♛a3 9 ♘xc5 ♛c3+ 10 ♔e2 ♛xc5 11 exf6) 9 ♔e2 ♛a3 10 c4! ♘e4 (necessary to save the queen: 10...♘g4 11 ♗c1 wins the Dame) 11 ♘b5 ♘c3+ (forced) 12 ♘axc3 ♛a5 13 ♘e4 and White wins easily with the extra piece—note the ever present hole at d6, where a white knight will soon be ensconced, which is so characteristic of the Taimanov/Kan complex once things start to go wrong.

7...♘d5

Relatively best, but now Black has long-term pawn structure problems.

8 ♘xd5 exd5

9 ♗e2

This is our good repertoire developing move, and scores the best against the Gå På (a mighty 75%). White develops fast and prepares to castle, and so avoids the tactical tricks that are the raison d'être of this subvariation.

Instead of this sound move, Miss Skripchenko thought she could bash the Gå immediately—and fell for the following trick: 9 ♘f5 (looks great, doesn't it? White threatens to invade at the traditional weak d6-point) 9...♕xb2! (suddenly White's position is loose and Black's c5-bishop is indirectly defended) 10 ♗xc5 (10 ♗d4 might give White some hope... of a draw!—what a shock to get such a position when facing such a doubtful opening; don't let this happen to you!) 10...♕c3+ 11 ♔e2 ♕xc5 12 ♘d6+ ♔f8 13 f4 ♘c6 14 ♔f3 f6

15 ♘xc8 fxe5! (the white knight can't be saved, while Black's attack gains momentum with every move) 16 fxe5 ♘xe5+ 17 ♔f4 ♖xc8 (a complete débâcle: all White has developed is her king!) 18 ♔xe5 ♖e8+ 19 ♔f5 ♖e4 20 ♕f3 ♕e7 and White resigns in view of imminent mate, 0-1 A.Skripchenko-P.Cramling, Belgrade 1996.

9...♘c6

Instead of fighting back, Black can just accept that he is worse and hope to draw: 9...0-0 10 0-0 ♘c6 11 c3 d6 12 exd6 ♘xd4 13 ♗xd4 ♕xd6 14 ♗f3 and White has a clear positional advantage against Black's weak and blockaded isolani. After 14...♗e6 15 ♖e1 ♖ad8 16 ♕d2 Black somehow held the draw in A.Kaplivatski-M.Ravia, Israeli Team Championship 2002, but had White played the more accurate 16 ♕d3 b6 17 ♖e2, it's difficult to believe that Black could have held out against the positional pressure.

10 c3

White holds firm in the centre, and offers the e- or b-pawns—but Black's position is already too compromised for a pawn more or less to help.

10...♗xd4

If Black accepts one of the pawns (he can't take two at once!) White gets excellent play, as can be seen:

a) 10...♘xe5 11 b4 ♗xd4 (or 11...♗e7 12 ♘f5 ♕f6 13 ♘xe7 ♕xe7 14 ♕xd5 or 13...♔xe7 14 0-0 with a great attack against the "centralized" black king) 12 ♗xd4 ♕e6 (12...♕c7 is a little better, though White still has a solid plus after 13 0-0 0-0 14 f4, since Black's extra pawn is meaningless, whereas White's two bishops and attacking chances are not!) 13 0-0 f6 14 f4 ♘c6 15 ♗f3 ♔d8 (this is hopeless; the desperate 15...♘xd4 16 ♖e1 ♘xf3+ 17 ♕xf3 0-0 18 ♖xe6 dxe6 was relatively best, but even then White should win as the rook and bishop won't be doing anything for a while and the queen is strong) 16 ♗f2 ♕d6 17 ♗xd5 ♕c7 18 ♕f3 ♘e7 19 ♖ad1 ♘xd5 20 ♖xd5 ♖e8 21 ♖fd1 ♕c6 22 ♕d3 h6 23 ♖d6 ♕c7 24 ♕d5 ♖f8 25 b5 ♔e8 26 ♖e1+ ♔d8 27 c4 (Black doesn't wait for the bulldozer to flatten him) 1-0 E.Szalanczy-F.Wiedermann, Vienna 1991.

b) 10...♕xb2 11 0-0 (this is possible due to the timely ♗e2—and so the black queen is left offside, and White has excellent attacking chances) 11...♘xe5 12 ♘b5 ♗xe3 13 ♘d6+ ♔e7 14 ♘f5+ ♔d8 15 fxe3 g6 16 ♘d6 f6 17 ♗b5 ♖f8 18 ♕xd5 and White's attack is worth far more than the pawn.

11 cxd4 ♕xb2

A deflecting sacrifice: the black queen is out of play, and White dominates in the centre.

12 0-0 d6

Here's a very short story: 12...0-0 (Black has castled, but then...) 13 ♗d3 ♕a3 14 ♗g5 d6 15 ♗f6! (was mangled, and then was...) 15...gxf6 16 exf6 ♖d8 17 ♕d2 ♔f8 18 ♖ae1 ♗e6 19 ♖xe6 fxe6 20 ♕h6+ ♔e8 21 ♕g7 (mated!) 1-0 F.Holzke-B.Svensson, Gothenburg 1993.

13 ♖b1

White offers another pawn.

13...♕a3 14 ♖b3!

I insist!

14...♕xa2 15 exd6 0-0 16 ♗d3

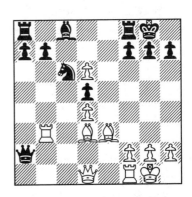

Black does not have a single kingside defender, and must also defend against White's passed pawn on the sixth.

16...♗g4

Against quiet moves White will employ ♗b1 and ♗f4 to clear the third rank, so the rook can come across for a fully fledged kingside attack.

17 f3 ♗e6 18 ♖xb7

Material equality has not lessened White's attacking chances.

18...♖ab8 19 ♖c7 ♖b6 20 ♕c1 ♘b8 21 ♗f4 ♕a4 22 ♗c2 ♕b4 23 ♕e3 ♘c6 24 ♖d1 ♕c4 25 ♖d2 ♕a6 26 ♗h6!

The same type of blow that we saw in the Holzke game above: the sacs come easily when there are no defenders!

26...g6

Or 26...gxh6 27 ♕xh6 ♕a1+ 28 ♔f2 and mate follows soon.

27 ♖xc6!

Why take the exchange when you can sac it? But it's not much of a sac: 27...♖xc6 28 ♕e5 and mates.

27...♖e8 28 ♕e5 f6 29 ♕xf6 1-0

An absolutely crushing victory! Yes, instead of riskily taking a pawn, Black can play the positional disadvantage line with the isolated d-pawn (as after 9...0-0), but joyless defence was probably not on Black's mind when he launched the Gå På.

In my opinion the Gå På is strictly a surprise weapon, dangerous only to the Black player—if White is prepared of course! Remember that, once again, our repertoire ♗e2 (here on move nine) is the key to the position.

Now we'll check one final rare line: the "anti-Lasker" 4...♗c5, by which Black exposes his dark-squared bishop when his dark squares are already weak.

Game 58
P.Morphy-L.Paulsen
New York 1857

---

1 e4 c5 2 d4 cxd4 3 ♘f3

Morphy liked this move order, as he always enjoyed it when players tried to hold the pawn: 3...e5 4 ♗c4 (4 ♘xe5?? ♕a5+ is Black's cheap trap) 4...♗b4+ (or 4...♗e7 5 c3 d6 6 ♕b3—the f7-square is already indefensible!—6...dxc3 7 ♗xf7+ ♔f8 8 ♘xc3 ♘c6 9 ♗g8 ♖xg8 10 0-0 ♕e8 11 ♘g5 ♗xg5 12 ♗xg5 ♗e6 13 ♘d5 h6 14 f4!—no retreat! Black is lost—14...♕d7 15 fxe5+ ♔e8 16 ♘c7+ ♕xc7 17 ♕xe6+ 1-0 P.Morphy-P.Journoud, Paris 1858) 5 c3 dxc3 6 bxc3 ♗c5 7 ♘xe5 (the f7-square is already indefensible, or am I repeating myself?) 7...♕f6 8 ♗xf7+ ♔f8 9 ♘d3 ♗b6 10 ♗b3 ♘c6 11 ♗a3+ d6 12 0-0 ♘h6 13 e5! (a crushing blow that ends the game for evaluation purposes, but Morphy's attacking technique is always worth seeing) 13...♕g6 14 ♘f4 ♕g4 15 ♘e6+!! (a beautiful interference move that allows the white queen to join the attack with tempo) 15...♗xe6 16 ♕xd6+ ♔f7 17 ♕d7+ ♔g6 18 ♗xe6 ♕g5 19 ♗d5 ♘xe5 20 ♗e4+ ♘f5 21 ♕e6+ ♕f6 22 ♗xf5+ ♔h5 23 g4+ ♘xg4 24 ♗xg4+ 1-0 P.Morphy-J.Preti, Paris (simul) 1858.

3...e6 4 ♘xd4

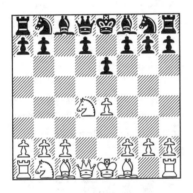

Reaching the basic position of the Taimanov/Kan complex. We've already covered the three very popular alternatives at this stage (4...♘c6; 4...a6; 4...♘f6). The fourth most popular move, 4...♕b6, has been tried by GMs, but it seems to me that White can get the advantage by straightforward play; e.g. 5 ♘c3 ♗c5 (5...♘f6 6 e5 goes back to the Gå På) 6 ♘a4 ♕a5+ 7 c3 ♗xd4 (after 7...♗e7 8 b4 ♕d8 9 ♗d3 d6 10 0-0

♘f6 11 c4 White obtained a good Maróczy Bind position in B.Kantsler-D.Kudischewitsch, Givataim 2007: 11...0-0 12 ♗b2 ♖e8 13 ♘c3 ♘fd7 14 ♗e2 ♘c6 15 a3 a6 16 ♘b3 b6 17 f4 ♗b7 18 ♕d3 ♕c7 19 ♖ac1 ♗f8 20 ♘d5!, and now an attacking position as well, which led to a White victory) 8 ♕xd4 (as much as I admire Nigel Short's creative play, I don't know what he was aiming for here: as far as I can see, White has just been given the two bishops, and the unopposed dark-squared bishop has weaknesses in the enemy camp to exploit—Ivanchuk did just that) 8...♘f6 9 ♘c5 b6 10 ♘b3 ♕h5 11 f3 0-0 12 ♗f4 (note the weakness at d6, the black hole of the Taimanov/Kan, exacerbated here by the early exchange of Black's dark-squared bishop) 12...♘c6 13 ♕e3 e5 14 ♗g5 ♘e8 15 g4 ♕g6 16 0-0-0 ♕e6 17 ♔b1 ♗b7 18 ♕d3 d6 19 h4 ♔h8 20 ♖h2 f6 21 ♗e3 ♘e7 22 c4 ♕f7 23 h5 h6 24 ♘a1 ♘c6 25 ♖hd2 ♖d8 26 ♘c2 (Black has no compensation for his weakness at d6: Ivanchuk has no problems converting) 26...♕e6 27 ♗f2 ♖f7 28 ♘e3 ♕c8 29 ♕a3 ♘d4 30 ♘d5 ♘c6 31 ♘c3 ♕b8 32 ♘b5 ♖fd7 33 c5! (the pawn at d6 falls—White wins) 33...bxc5 34 ♗xc5 ♗c8 35 ♘xd6 ♘xd6 36 ♖xd6 ♖xd6 37 ♖xd6 ♗e6 38 ♖xe6 ♖d1+ 39 ♔c2 ♖xf1 40 ♖xc6 ♕b5 41 ♕a6 1-0 V.Ivanchuk-N.Short, Dortmund 1997.

4...♗c5

This "anti-Lasker" move (bishop before knight!) at least develops a minor piece, though after Morphy's simple answer, it's not clear what is to be done about the d6-square. It's not surprising that this is Black's *fifth* most popular move at this stage, and the last I will cover.

5 ♘b3

5...♗b6

5...♗e7 at least keeps d6 under control, but allows White to set up an easy attacking position reminiscent of Carlsen-Nakamura (game 18): 6 ♘c3 d6 7 ♗d3 ♘c6 8 f4 a6 9 ♗e3 ♘f6 10 ♕f3 ♕c7 11 g4 b5 12 g5 ♘d7 13 0-0-0 0-0 (when I first looked at this game I thought this had to be a mistake—castling into the attack—but it seems going long is no picnic either, given Black's very breezy king: 13...♗b7 14 h4 0-0-0 15 ♔b1 ♘a5?!—a natural-looking move that fails to the following long-winded combination, which is based both on Black's advanced queenside pawns and exposed king—16 ♗xb5! axb5 17 ♘xb5 ♕c4 18 ♘a7+ ♔b8 19 ♘xa5 ♗xe4 20 ♘7c6+ ♔c7 21 ♘xc4 ♗xf3 22 ♘xd8 ♔xd8 23 ♖he1 ♗xd1 24

♖xd1 and after all that work, White won a pawn (!) which he eventually converted in C.Lamoureux-S.Nemirovski, Paris 1992) 14 ♔b1 ♖e8 15 h4 b4 16 ♘e2 a5 17 h5 ♗f8 18 g6! (there's the Tal/Carlsen break) 18...fxg6 19 hxg6 h6 20 ♘bd4 ♘xd4 21 ♗xd4 e5 22 fxe5 ♘xe5 23 ♗xe5 dxe5 24 ♗b5 ♗e6 25 ♖d7 (here 25 ♗xe8 is a simple and easy win, though the more complicated text also works) 25...♕b6 26 ♗a4 ♖e7 27 ♖dd1 ♖c7 28 ♘g3 ♖c3 29 bxc3 bxc3+ 30 ♗b3 a4 31 ♕xc3 axb3 32 cxb3 ♖c8 33 ♕f3 ♗a3 34 ♘f5 ♕c6 35 ♕d3 ♔h8 36 ♘e3 ♗g8 37 ♘c4 ♗b4 38 ♘xe5 ♕f6 39 ♕d4 ♗c3 40 ♘f7+ ♗xf7 41 ♕xf6 ♗xf6 42 gxf7 ♔h7 43 ♖hf1 ♖f8 44 ♖d5 1-0 S.Tiviakov-S.Drazic, Bratto 2008.

6 ♘c3 ♘e7

Since 6...♘f6 7 e5 gives White an obvious plus by nailing down the d6 weakness with tempo, Black must try this unnatural development.

7 ♗f4

This simple move, targeting the weak d6-square, gives White a 61%

score in the database: apparently no one has found a serious improvement for Black's already doubtful position in the last 150 years!

7...0-0

Just as in the Gå På, Black can bail out here by playing 7...d5 with a long-term positional inferiority, as White gets a favourable anti-isolani position: 8 exd5 ♘xd5 9 ♘xd5 exd5 10 ♗d3 ♕f6 11 ♕e2+ ♗e6 12 ♗e5, when White has a large positional advantage and went on to win in M.Himdan-S.Sale, Dubai 2006.

A shorter story was 8...exd5 9 ♗d3 ♘bc6 10 0-0 a6 11 ♕h5 (White is much better already) 11...♘b4 12 ♗g5! ♘xd3 13 ♗xe7! ♕xe7 14 ♘xd5 (the weak pawn drops off, and White wins after a brief tactical flurry) g6 15 ♕h6 ♗xf2+ 16 ♖xf2 ♕e5 17 ♘f6+ ♔e7 18 cxd3 ♗f5 1-0 M.Ulibin-V.Doncea, Predeal 2006.

8 ♗d6

Morphy clamps down on Black's eternal weakness, and makes sure the c8-bishop won't move for a long time.

Black's position looks *terrible* to this human's eyes, and our friend *Mr. Fritz* has White up about one point, which is pretty substantial for move eight.

Nonetheless, a modern GM (undeterred by both Morphy and *Fritz*) will try this line again—see the next game.

8...f5 9 e5

9...a6

I don't think anything can help Black here, but for the record 9...♘bc6 is the modern "improvement" that will be seen in Game 59.

10 ♗e2 ♘bc6 11 0-0 ♖f7

Black unpins his knight, but White prepares for this...

12 ♔h1 f4

After 12...♘g6 13 f4 White maintains the bind. Therefore Black tries to get some space on the kingside himself, but allows the c3-knight to come into the centre.

13 ♘e4 ♘f5 14 ♗h5 g6 15 ♗g4 ♘g7 16 ♕f3 h5 17 ♗h3 ♕h4

Evidently if 17...g5 then 18 ♖ae1! g4 19 ♗xg4 hxg4 20 ♕xg4 and White's piece "sac" is hardly risky, as Black's kingside is demolished and his "extra" piece is that worthless chunk of wood on c8 with no legal moves!

18 ♘f6+ ♔h8 19 ♕e4

Just like that the game is decided—notice White uses the e4-square again. Black's kingside is coming apart no matter what he plays.

19...♕g5 20 g3 f3

A desperate attempt to keep lines closed, as after 20...fxg3 21 fxg3 White's rooks can attack down the f-file, while Black is still light years away from even connecting his own rooks, let alone doing something with them!

21 ♘d2

White picks up a pawn, and the only way Black can get it back is to exchange his king's bishop, his last defender of the dark squares.

21...♗d8

Otherwise White will have both an enormous positional advantage and an extra pawn.

22 ♘xf3 ♕h6 23 ♖g1 ♗xf6 24 exf6 ♘e8

24...♖xf6 25 ♗f4 ♕h7 26 ♖ad1 maintains material equality, but with all Black's pawns on light squares, no

dark-squared bishop and still no queenside development, it's clear that White has a decisive positional advantage.

25 ♗f4 ♘xf6

While Black is strategically busted in the note above, now he loses tactically.

26 ♕xc6! ♕xf4 27 ♕xc8+ ♖xc8 28 gxf4 ♖xc2 29 ♖ac1 ♖xf2 30 ♖c8+ ♘g8 31 ♘e5 ♖g7 32 ♘xg6+ ♔h7 33 ♘f8+ ♔h6 34 ♘xd7 ♖xd7 35 ♖cxg8 ♖xf4 36 ♗xe6 ♖e7 37 ♖8g6+ ♔h7 38 ♗g8+ ♔h8 39 ♖h6+ ♖h7 40 ♖xh7 mate

Decisive, crushing, all that... Has anything changed? Let's see.

Game 59
A.Shchekachev-Ch.Bauer
Metz 2006

1 d4 e6 2 ♘f3 c5 3 e4 cxd4 4 ♘xd4 ♗c5 5 ♘b3 ♗b6 6 ♘c3 ♘e7 7 ♗f4 0-0 8 ♗d6

Following Morphy, and why not? White scores 77% with this move!

8...f5 9 e5 ♘bc6

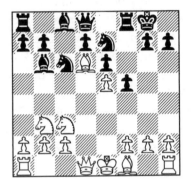

9...a6 was played against Morphy. Does this improvement rehabilitate Black's game?

10 ♗b5

I don't think so, nor does *Mr. Fritz*, and soon GM Bauer has to agree that his situation is desperate!

10...♖f7 11 ♕d2 f4

Just as in the previous game, Black concedes the e4-square, as 11...♘g6 12 f4 is just too painfully cramped.

12 0-0-0 ♘f5 13 ♘e4

Just like Morphy—and Shchekachev soon reaches a position where...

13...♕h4 14 ♔b1

Black's c8-bishop has no legal moves, and White is ready to open lines

on the kingside—sound familiar?

14...f3

And just like Paulsen, Bauer tries this desperate lunge.

15 gxf3 ♘cd4 16 ♘xd4 ♘xd4 17 ♕b4 ♘xf3 18 ♗e2

Black got his pawn back, but the systemic problems relating to the lock on d6 and failed queenside development remain.

18...♗d8 19 ♖d3 a5 20 ♕c3 ♕xe4 21 ♗xf3 ♕h4 22 a3 ♗e7

Or 22...♕xf2 23 ♗e4 and the attack begins. Black then has an extra pawn, while White (given Black's still un-moved queen's bishop and rook) has two extra pieces!

23 ♗xe7 ♕xe7 24 ♗e4 ♖xf2 25 ♖h3 g6 26 ♖g1 ♕f7 27 ♕d3 ♖f5

Black gives up the exchange in view of 27...♖b8 28 ♗xg6 hxg6 29 ♖xg6+ ♔f8 30 ♖h8+ ♔e7 31 ♕d6 mate.

28 ♗xf5 exf5 29 e6!

But now the white rooks blast through.

29...♕e7

Both 29...dxe6 30 ♕d8+ ♕f8 31 ♖d1

and 29...♕xe6 30 ♖e3 lead to easy White wins—who still has that two piece lead!

30 ♕xf5 dxe6 31 ♖xg6+! 1-0

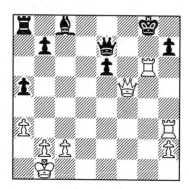

After this blow White mates with all checks: 31...hxg6 (or 31...♔h8 32 ♕e5+ ♕g7 33 ♕xg7 mate) 32 ♕xg6+ ♕g7 33 ♕e8+ ♕f8 34 ♖g3+ ♔h7 35 ♕g6+ ♔h8 36 ♖h3+ ♕h6 37 ♖xh6 mate.

White can follow Morphy with confidence!

This concludes our coverage of the Taimanov/Kan Complex. The hole at d6 is surprisingly critical, and costs Black dearly in many games. In general, despite the large number of variations, I find the Taimanov/Kan much easier to get an advantage against than the Najdorf or the Scheveningen. With that in mind, Black's best chance may be the transposition into the Scheveningen (by playing ...d7-d6 early Black covers the hole that Morphy, for example, occupied with such devastating effect), which we saw was possible in Games 47 and 48—and indeed that transposition is often played today. So go back and reread Chapter Four!

Chapter Six
No Sveshnikov Allowed

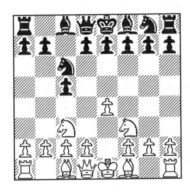

We now move on to deal with those fanatics who want to play the insane Sveshnikov, booked up with thirty illogical moves on both sides! As I mentioned in the Introduction, I have no interest in memorized illogic—instead, let's play chess with my recommended 1 e4 c5 2 ♘f3 ♘c6 3 ♘c3!

Game 60
A.Karpov-M.Chiburdanidze
Bilbao 1987

Of the seven Karpov games that

head the seven chapters in this book, this is the only draw! While he showed no mercy against one fellow World Champion (see Karpov-Spassky, Game 37) in this one, despite obtaining an edge in the opening, he not only fails to convert—but, for a second, offers serious winning chances to his rival, the *female* world champion!

1 e4 c5 2 ♘f3 ♘c6 3 ♘c3

The only "Anti-Sicilian" in the book—although in practice, every time I played this, Black answered 3...g6, and I was delighted to reach another Dragon with 4 d4. Thus I both stayed in the Open Sicilian and increased my already huge plus score against the Dragon.

An interesting transposition is worth noting here: if White plays 3 ♗b5, the Rossolimo Variation, Black has many defences, of which 3...g6 is generally considered the most solid. Instead, 3...♘f6 has always been thought to be much more risky, for after 4 ♘c3 the black knight on f6 is in danger from White's potential and threatened e4-e5. By using my move order, if Black plays 3...♘f6 as here (hoping for 4 d4 cxd4 5 ♘xd4 e5 and a return to the Sveshnikov), then White answers 4 ♗b5, which reaches a Rossolimo where 4...g6 (as seen in the main game) allows White to advance (5 e5) with tempo and some advantage. Of course, in the Rossolimo move order, after 1 e4 c5 2 ♘f3 ♘c6 3 ♗b5 g6 it would make no sense for White to play 4 e5.

A further point is that the insertion of the knight moves for both sides favours White for another reason: the bishop on b5 is protected, which is important the variation 3 ♘c3 ♘f6 4 ♗b5 ♘d4 5 e5!—see the next game.

3...♘f6

After 3...g6 (which I always faced) or 3...d6 or 3...e6, White just answers 4 d4 cxd4 5 ♘xd4 and returns to our open Sicilian repertoire.

3...e5 is the other possible "anti-Sicilian" (recommended by Rogozenko), but I think White gets a positional edge with 4 ♗c4, taking over the weak d5-

square—this line will be covered in Games 63-65.

4 ♗b5

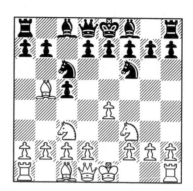

Not so much an "Anti-Sicilian" as an Anti-Sveshnikov: White throws Black out of his opening and into a risky line of the Rossolimo.

4...g6

For a long time the position after Karpov's fourth move, 4 ♗b5, was just considered bad for Black—due to the above-mentioned threat of 5 e5—but it has been rehabilitated to some extent by the recent improvement 4...♕c7, which will be discussed in Game 62.

Besides 4...g6, seen here, I will also look at the above-mentioned counterattack 4...♘d4 in the next game.

Two other moves merit attention, both of which try to deal directly with the e4-e5 threat:

a) 4...d6 tries to control e5 but fails to prevent the attack: 5 e5 (compare this to the Rossolimo line 3 ♗b5 d6 which, along with 3...g6, has a good reputation—in this variation if White plays 4 e5 [the natural 4 0-0 would be much better] he threatens nothing and Black equalizes easily with 4...♗d7— but here White threatens a knight!) 5...♘g4 (obviously 5...dxe5 6 ♘xe5 leads to split pawns for Black) 6 exd6 ♕xd6 (Black has problems with the pin and his misplaced knight on g4 no matter how he takes; e.g. 6...exd6 7 0-0 ♗e7 8 d4 ♗d7 9 ♘d5 0-0 10 ♗f4 and White has a clear advantage with great pressure on Black's game, particularly the weak d6-square—I love those eternal and repeating advantages!—and went on to win in G.Guseinov-N.Umudova, Baku 2006) 7 ♘e4 ♕d5 8 d3 e6 9 c4 ♕d8 10 h3 ♘f6 11 ♘e5 (White exploits the pin to the max) 11...♗d7 12 ♘xf6+ gxf6.

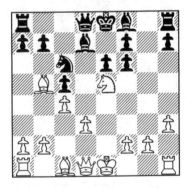

Now instead of 13 ♘xc6 bxc6 14 ♗a4, when Black had some counter-chances due to White's offside bishop in S.Fedorchuk-C.Debray, Avoine 2007—White should play 13 ♗xc6! bxc6 14 ♘xd7 ♕xd7 15 ♕f3, attacking every weak pawn in sight with a big advantage.

b) 4...e5 has been played by former World Champion Kramnik, but it seems incredibly risky to lesser mortals like myself. Yes, if White doesn't take up the challenge (see Morozevich-Kramnik below) then Black equalizes easily. But if White takes the offered pawn, Black faces innumerable difficulties in getting out of the opening alive. I like Glek's line with the early f-pawn advance, where White was clearly better by move 10, even if I suppose Kramnik and his computer have something against this! Over the board, though, this would be a terrifying attack unless you had everything worked out to the nth degree, as can easily be seen: 5 ♗xc6 (not the passive 5 0-0 d6 6 d3 ♗e7 7 h3 0-0 8 ♗c4 h6 9 a3 ♖e8 10 ♘h2 ♗e6 11 ♘d5 ♗f8 12 ♘xf6+ ♕xf6 13 ♘g4 ♕g6 14 ♗xe6 fxe6, when Black was fully equal with his central pawn mass and even went on to win in A.Morozevich-V.Kramnik, Frankfurt rapid 2000) 5...dxc6 6 ♘xe5 (White is up a centre pawn—Black must lose a great deal of time with his queen to get it back) 6...♘xe4 7 ♘xe4 ♕d4 and now:

b1) 8 ♕e2 ♕xe5 9 f4 ♕xf4 10 d4 ♕h4+ 11 g3 ♕e7 12 0-0 f5 13 ♘d6+ ♔d7 (how Black survived this, in a battle of world champions, I cannot explain, but Kramnik did survive!—I can only suspect a ton of computer hours went into making this difficult draw) 14 ♕xe7+ ♗xe7 15 dxc5 ♗xd6 16 ♖d1 ♔e8 17 cxd6 ♗e6 18 ♗g5 ♔d7 19 ♖e1 h6 20 ♗e7 (I would expect to win this with White, with the big passed pawn, but I have never played Kramnik) 20...g5 21 ♖e5 ♖hg8 22 a4 b6 23 b4 (instead of creating a target for his opponent, Anand should build up with 23 ♖ae1 ♖g6 24 ♔f2, when it's hard to see how Black holds the game in the long run—instead, after the text, one sees Kramnik find counterplay and finally end on a high note with the better half of a draw) 23...a6 24 ♖c1 f4 25 c4 fxg3 26 hxg3 a5! 27 c5 axb4 28 cxb6 ♖xa4 29 ♖ce1 ♗d5 30 ♗f6 b3 31 b7 ♖b4 32 ♖e7+ ♔xd6 33 ♖h7 c5 34 ♖xh6 ♖xb7 35 ♗e5+ ♔e7 36 ♖d1 b2 37 ♖b1 ♖a8 38 ♖xb2 ♖xb2 39 ♗xb2 ♖a2 40 ♗f6+ ½-½ V.Anand-V.Kramnik, Monte Carlo (rapid) 2003. Black can go up a pawn in the final position but has no serious winning chances, this being the last pawn on the board.

b2) 8 0-0 ♕xe5 9 d4 (another way is this fierce Carlsen attack—a pawn sac for development) 9...cxd4 (9...♕xd4 10 ♕e2 ♗e6 looks like a chance to survive) 10 ♖e1 ♗e6 11 ♗g5 ♗e7 12 f4! (White has a tremendous attack and Black won't be able to castle after this

move—Carlsen won quickly) 12...♕d5 13 ♗xe7 ♔xe7 14 f5 ♕xf5 15 ♕xd4 ♕d5 16 ♕b4+ c5 17 ♘xc5 a5 18 ♕a3 ♕d4+ 19 ♔h1 ♕b4 20 ♕e3 1-0 M.Carlsen-J.Deepan Chakkravarthy, Dubai 2004.

b3) 8 d3 ♕xe5 9 f4 (I like this line the best: White gets a tremendous attack and doesn't have to sacrifice anything) ♕c7 10 0-0 ♗f5 (or 10...♗e7 11 f5 and there is no good way to stop the further advance of this pawn; e.g. 11...f6 12 ♕h5+ with a decisive attack) 11 ♘g3 ♗d7 12 ♖e1+ ♔d8 13 ♕h5, when White was much better and eventually won in I.Glek-V.Kachar, Saratov 2006.

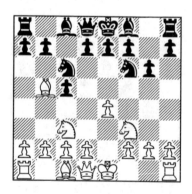

5 e5 ♘g4 6 ♗xc6 dxc6 7 h3 ♘h6 8 g4

Good knight, Miss Chiburdanidze!

8...♗g7 9 ♕e2

A good move, but the current Women's World Champion, Hou Yifan, takes down a 2700 with the perhaps more accurate 9 d3 (with the white queen not yet committed to e2, Black must watch for ♗e3 and ♕d2) 9...f5 (Black rushes for counterplay, as 9...0-0

10 &e3 b6?—10...f6, giving up the c-pawn, is necessary—11 ♕d2 wins a whole piece!) 10 exf6 exf6 11 ♕e2+ ♔f7 (11...♕e7 is relatively best, though after 12 ♕xe7+ ♔xe7 13 &e3 White is somewhat better in the queenless middlegame with active development and weaknesses on both sides to attack) 12 &e3 ♖e8 13 0-0-0 ♔g8 14 d4 (White opens the game to target the still unsettled black king) 14...cxd4 15 ♘xd4 ♕c7 16 ♖he1 ♘f7 17 ♕c4 ♕h2 18 ♘ce2! ♕xh3 19 ♘f4 ♕xg4 20 ♖g1 ♕d7 21 ♘de6 (White's attack is too strong—the powerful knights coordinate with the rook on the open g-file) ♕e7 22 ♘xg7 ♔xg7 23 ♘h5+ ♔h8 24 &c5 ♕e6 25 ♖ge1 ♕xe1 26 ♕xf7 ♕xd1+ 27 ♔xd1 &g4+ 28 ♔d2 ♖ad8+ 29 ♔c3 &xh5 30 &d4 ♖xd4 31 ♕xe8+ 1-0 Hou Yifan-F.Vallejo Pons, Wijk aan Zee 2009.

9...0-0 10 d3 f6

11 &f4?

A surprising tactical oversight from Karpov, which allows the "dim" knight on the rim to strike a powerful blow: 11...♘xg4! (see the next note for the

gory details).

Correct is 11 &e3!, when Black has four responses, of which only the last is critical.

a) 11...♘xg4?! (the combination Karpov allows in the game doesn't work here with the white bishop protected) 12 hxg4 &xg4 13 ♖h4 ♕c8 (13...h5 also loses: 14 ♖xg4 hxg4 15 ♘h4, as the two white knights are much more active than either black rook) 14 e6! and it transpires that Black has no sufficient compensation for the piece, since 14...♕xe6 fails to 15 ♘g5.

b) 11...f5 12 g5 ♘f7 13 &xc5 snaps off a pawn.

c) 11...b6 12 0-0-0 is good for White.

It's easy to see that White is better in all three of the above variations—but what happens if Black just takes a centre pawn? Then White needs to show some real mastery!

d) 11...fxe5 (best) 12 ♘g5! (White has not lost a pawn, but rather given a "pawn-cracker" sacrifice: the black pawns are discombobulated, and White has a wonderful permanent square on e4; thus he risks nothing and may achieve much—the following game is one of the best manoeuvring wins I've seen since the heyday of Petrosian!) 12...♘f7 13 ♘xf7 ♖xf7 14 ♘e4 b6 15 c4 ♗e6 16 0-0-0 ♕d7 17 f3 ♖af8 18 ♖hf1 h6 19 ♕g2 ♕c8 20 ♔b1 a5 21 ♕g3 a4 22 ♕g2 ♕d7 23 ♕e2 (Black has no play and must wait to see where White might break—certainly h4-h5 with an eventual piece sac on g5 is possible, but Guseinov keeps his opponent guessing for a very long time...) 23...♕c8 24 ♖f2 ♖d8 25 ♖ff1 ♖df8 26 ♔c1 ♖d8 27 ♖d2 ♖df8 28 ♔d1 ♕a8 29 ♔c1 ♕c8 30 ♕g2 ♕a6 31 ♖c2 ♕c8 32 ♕e2 ♖d8 33 ♔d1 ♖df8 34 ♔e1 ♕a6 35 ♖f2 ♕c8 36 ♔f1 ♔h7 37 ♔g2 ♗f6 38 ♖c1 ♗h4 39 ♖ff1 ♗f6 40 ♕c2 ♕a6 41 ♕d2 ♗g7 42 ♕e1 ♗f6 43 ♕g3 ♕c8 44 ♕f2 ♕d7 45 ♕d2 ♗g7 46 ♕c2 ♕a7 47 ♖f2 ♕a6 48 ♖cf1 ♕a7 49 ♕d1 ♖d8 50 ♖d2 ♕a6 51 ♕e1 ♗f6 52 ♖h1 ♖df8 53 ♕g3 ♕c8 54 ♖f1 ♕d7 55 a3 ♕c8 56 ♕e1 ♕d7 57 ♕c1 ♗g7 58 ♖dd1 ♕c8 59 ♖f2 ♕d7 60 ♕c2 ♕a7 61 ♖b1 ♖a8 62 b3!! (until this!—White breaks on the queenside!) 62...axb3 63 ♖xb3 ♖ff8 64 ♕b1 b5 (64...♖fb8 65 ♖fb2 doesn't save anything) 65 ♘xc5 ♗g8 66 a4! 1-0 G.Guseinov-A.Secer, Istanbul 2008. White breaks through however Black plays; e.g. 66...bxa4 (or 66...bxc4 67 dxc4 ♗xc4 68 ♖b7 ♕a5 69 ♘d7 ♖f7 70 ♘b6 and White picks up an exchange) 67 ♖b7 ♖ab8 68 ♖xa7 ♖xb1 69 ♖a2 ♖fb8 70 ♖2xa4 and White has not only recovered his long ago sacrificed pawn,

but will soon pick up one of the weakies (c6/e7/e5).

11...♘f7?!

What Karpov—and Chiburdanidze—missed is 11...♘xg4! 12 hxg4 fxe5, which works because of the cluttered white pieces on the f-file.

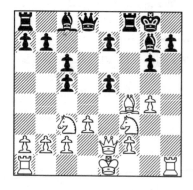

Guseinov fell into this too, but after the blow was struck, somehow found a way to confuse his opponent: 13 ♖xh7 (no time to manoeuvre here; if 13 ♗xe5 ♗xg4 14 ♗xg7 ♗xf3 15 ♕e5 then 15...♖f5 and Black wins—so Guseinov boldly goes for a confusing but unsound sacrifice) 13...exf4 (Black should just take it: 13...♔xh7 14 ♘g5+ ♔g8 and it's hard to see what White has for the exchange; e.g. 15 ♕e4 ♖xf4 16 ♕xg6 ♕d6 wins, or 15 ♗e3 e4 16 ♘gxe4 ♕a5 and Black has activated his position while retaining a material advantage) 14 ♖h4 (somehow Guseinov came out smelling like a rose again, and won as follows...) 14...♗f6 15 ♕e4 ♔g7 16 ♘e5 ♕e8 17 ♖h2 ♗e6 18 0-0-0 ♗d5 19 ♕xf4 ♖h8 20 ♖xh8 ♕xh8 21 ♘xd5 cxd5 22 g5 ♕b8 23 gxf6+ exf6 24

♘xg6 ♚xg6 25 ♕g4+ ♚f7 26 ♕d7+ ♚f8 27 ♖h1 ♕f4+ 1-0 G.Guseinov-G.Gopal, Dubai 2009.

I like a good swindle as much as the next man, but I certainly don't recommend such play—either go with Hou Yifan's 9 d3 or Guseinov's positional sac 11 ♗e3.

12 0-0-0 fxe5 13 ♗g3 ♗e6 14 ♘xe5

No doubt Karpov saw his mistake right after he made his eleventh move, and so decides not to tempt fate and heads for a draw. On another day he might have played on à la Guseinov with 14 ♘d2, having pawn-cracker compensation.

14...♗d5 15 ♘xf7 ♖xf7 16 ♘xd5 cxd5 17 ♗e5 ♗xe5 18 ♕xe5 ½-½

Equality results after 18...♕d6.

The eleventh move oversight is interesting—even a knight on the rim may be bloodthirsty—but the real revelation is Guseinov's pawn sac (11 ♗e3) which gives White long-term chances.

Also note Hou Yifan's interesting move order, which poses quicker and perhaps more difficult problems for Black.

One could go so far as to say that Karpov was dissed by *two* Women's World Champions in this game: one almost beat him and made him head for the draw, and another improved on his play! All of us macho men have to realize: the women are *serious*.

Going back to the opening, 4...g6, allowing that quick e4-e5 for White, clearly does not solve Black's problems: the king's knight wanders about and, except for fortune, rarely has a good chance to get back into the game—and is even a static target on h6, as Hou Yifan showed.

Game 61
M.Tal-E.Mnatsakanian
Yerevan 1986

1 e4 c5 2 ♘f3 ♘f6 3 ♘c3 ♘c6 4 ♗b5 ♘d4

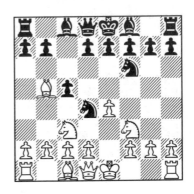

5 e5

Black allows this early attack, to

White's advantage—which is possible, as previously noted, due to the fact that the b5-bishop is protected.

While I'm sure Tal didn't hesitate a second to cross the meridian with attack—and I hope the reader will follow him—it is possible for an out-of-form genius in a blitz game to lose a piece after a couple of passive moves: 5 d3?! (Shirov?) 5...♘xb5 6 ♘xb5 d5 7 ♕e2?? (of course 7 ♘c3 is equal) 7...♕a5+ 8 ♘c3 d4 9 e5 ♘d5 10 ♗d2 dxc3—and yes, that's a whole piece that Shirov dropped, with a quick win for Black in A.Shirov-B.Savchenko, World Blitz Championship, Moscow 2007.

5...♘xb5

Necessary, as otherwise Black has no good place to put his problematic king's knight.

6 ♘xb5 ♘d5 7 ♘g5!

Tal must love to get two knights to the fifth rank (recall Game 55). But there it took him to move 16 to advance the cavalry so far—here both steeds are attacking almost ten moves earlier!

There is a not-so-hidden immediate threat: let's say Black plays 7...b6 (or some other innocuous move) then White wins at once with 8 ♕f3!, which threatens mate and the loose knight at d5. Furthermore, as we will see in the following note, if the g5-knight is "driven back" with 7...h6—it won't go back, but rather forward to sac itself on f7!

7...f6

The most common defence, at least avoiding the ♕f3 double attack and the sac on f7, but not an equalizer. Instead, a number of players have provoked the sac, so let's take a look at that, and then at the seemingly "safe" defence 7...e6.

a) 7...h6 8 ♘xf7! ♔xf7 9 ♕f3+

and now the sane option is 9...♘f6 to give back the material at once, although after 10 exf6 exf6 11 ♕d5+ White was much better as the black king had to run to g6, so eventually 1-0 in V.Jansa-G.Souleidis, Spanish Team Championship 2006.

Alternatively, there is 9...♗e6, trying to hold on to the piece. Black has essayed this monarchial centralization six times in the database—and White has won all six! After 10 c4 Black has tried various defences to no avail:

a1) 10...♘b6 11 d4 d5 12 dxc5 dxc4 (after 12...♘xc4 13 ♘d4+ ♔d7 14 ♕xd5+ ♔e8 15 ♕xc4 White recovered his piece while retaining the attack and won quickly in D.Skorchenko-A.Netrebko, Dombai 2010) 13 ♗e3 ♘d5 14 0-0-0 1-0 I.Nataf-T.Roussel Roozmon, Kapuskasing 2004—Black resigned as there is no defence to 15 ♖xd5.

a2) 10...♘b4 11 a3 ♘c2+ 12 ♔d1 ♘xa1 (now Black can enjoy his extra rook and knight for two more moves—one move for each sacrificed piece!) 13 g4 g6 14 ♕d5 mate!

a3) 10...♘c7 11 g4 g6 12 ♘xc7+ ♔xe5 (or just 12...♕xc7 13 ♕d5 mate, getting it over with) 13 d4+ ♔d6 14 ♗f4+ e5 15 ♗xe5+ ♔e7 16 ♕f6 mate, N.Jactel-J.Masset, Ermont 2009.

b) 7...e6, defending the knight on d5, looks plausible and has been played many times—with terrible results! White answers 8 ♘e4 and it's immedi-

ately apparent that our old friend, the hole at d6, is fatal for Black; e.g. 8...a6 9 ♘bd6+ ♗xd6 10 ♘xd6+ ♔f8 11 0-0 ♕e7 12 d4 cxd4 13 ♕xd4 ♔g8 14 ♗d2 h6 15 ♗a5 ♕g5 16 f4 ♕g4 17 h3 ♕h4 18 ♖ad1 g5 19 ♗e1 ♕h5 20 ♖d3 ♘xf4 21 ♖xf4! (with every black piece on the back rank except for the queen, such attacking sacrifices are easy peasy) 21...gxf4 22 ♕xf4 ♔h7 23 ♘e4 ♕f5 24 ♘f6+ ♔g7 25 ♖g3+ and Black resigned just before mate: 1-0 F.Vallejo Pons-J.Planas, Calvia 2005.

8 ♘e4

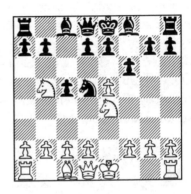

Simple and strong—Tal keeps both attacking knights.

8 ♕f3 is also good but more complicated: 8...fxg5 9 ♕xd5 a6 10 ♘c3 ♕c7 11 e6! (a strong obstructive sac, as opposed to the too quiet 11 0-0 e6 12 ♕e4 d5, when Black freed himself and even won in A.Gonzalez Verges-M.Munoz Pantoja, Barcelona 2011) 11...h6 12 h4 dxe6 13 ♕e4 ♕f4 14 hxg5 ♕xe4+ 15 ♘xe4 (White's advantage persists into the endgame, as Black's pawns obstruct both his bishops) 15...b6 16 d3

♗b7 17 ♗f4 ♔f7 18 ♗c7 b5 19 ♘xc5 ♗xg2 20 g6+ ♔e8 21 ♖h5 ♗f3 22 ♖e5 ♖c8 23 ♗a5 ♖c6 24 a4! bxa4 25 ♖xa4 h5 26 ♖d4 (both rooks come into the centre via the edge files—a very rare sight) ♖c8 27 ♘xe6 (White takes back the obstructive pawn with a mating attack) 1-0 P.Simacek-P.Bazant, Slovakian Team Championship 2001.

8...f5

A tempo loss with the f-pawn, but 8...fxe5 9 ♕h5+ is too strong, while after 8...a6 9 ♘bc3 ♘xc3 10 dxc3 d6 11 exd6 exd6 12 ♗f4 ♗f5 (12...d5 13 ♕h5+! g6 14 ♕xd5! is a crusher) 13 ♘xd6+ ♗xd6 14 ♗xd6 ♕d7 15 ♕e2+ ♔f7 16 ♗xc5 ♕d5 17 ♗e3 ♕xg2 18 ♕c4+ ♗e6 19 ♕c7+ ♔g6 20 0-0-0 White, with an extra pawn and attack, won quickly in S.Bromberger-P.Bensch, Austrian League 2004.

9 c4

Blow for blow! The knight is given no peace. Of course Tal would not fall for 9 ♘xc5 ♕b6, forking.

9...♘c7

Since 9...fxe4 10 cxd5, with central

domination, is obviously bad for Black, Mnatsakanian must move his knight again.

10 ♘xc5 ♘xb5 11 cxb5 ♕b6 12 d4 ♕xb5 13 ♘d3

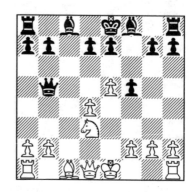

Simple chess: White prepares castling and counts on his central pawn wedge to assure the advantage.

13...e6

Black fared no better after 13...g6 14 0-0 ♗g7 (this bishop may be developed, but it's certainly not contributing!) 15 a4 ♕c4 16 ♗e3 b6 17 ♖c1 ♕f7 18 ♕f3 ♖b8 19 ♖c7 and as in the main game, the c-file is an important avenue of attack: *Mr. Fritz* is already at "decisive advantage", and indeed White scored the full point in Z.Hracek-Ji.Nun, Pardubice 1999.

14 0-0 ♗e7 15 a4 ♕c4

The queen is just a target here.

16 ♗e3 0-0 17 ♖c1 ♕a6 18 d5! b6

18...exd5 19 ♘f4 recovers the pawn with a substantial advantage; note that Black's light-squared bishop is still not playing.

19 dxe6 dxe6 20 ♕b3

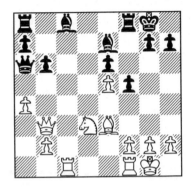

20...b5

This looks like justified desperation, when we consider the alternatives: 20...♗b7 21 ♕xe6+, or 20...♗d7 21 ♖c7 ♖ad8 22 ♖xd7, or 20...♖f7 21 ♘f4. Obviously White wins easily after all three variations, which means Black can't develop his queen's bishop and can't wait either—thus desperation doesn't look too bad!

21 axb5 ♖b8

Black hopes to exchange queens, but then...

22 ♖c7 ♖xb5 23 ♕c2! 1-0

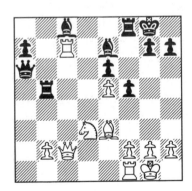

Tal just knocks him out with this move, which wins in all lines; e.g.

23...♖d5 24 ♘f4, or 23...♖b7 24 ♖xc8, or 23...♖e8 24 ♖xa7, or 23...♗d8 24 ♖xc8.

Those are pretty short variations for a Tal game!

Evidently 4...♘d4 can't be recommended—in general Black must prevent e4-e5, at least for one move!

Game 62
M.Adams-A.Zhigalko
European Championship,
Rijeka 2010

1 e4 c5 2 ♘f3 ♘c6 3 ♗b5 ♘f6

Note the Rossolimo move order, instead of our repertoire 3 ♘c3 ♘f6 4 ♗b5. Clearly Black went into this line willingly to try out the 4...♕c7 improvement—unfortunately the rest of the game didn't go as planned!

4 ♘c3 ♕c7

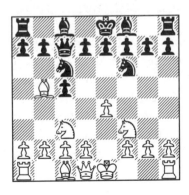

Considered best—Black prevents e4-e5 for the moment—but Adams shows that Black's problems are not completely solved.

5 d3

White surprisingly scores 68% with this modest move: the idea is that White stabilizes his position, and opens a line for his queen's bishop, while keeping the e4-e5 advance in reserve. This constant threat makes it hard for Black to fully equalize.

I think 5 ♗xc6 is premature when one doesn't know Black's central pawn arrangement (in the main game Adams waits until Black commits himself to ...e7-e6 before taking the knight) and now:

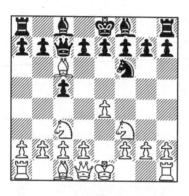

a) 5...♕xc6!? (Black plays for a win and refuses to make any concessions) 6 ♕e2 d5 (very risky, but this does open lines for the black bishops) 7 ♘e5 ♕e6 8 f4 (8 exd5 looks better for White) 8...dxe4 9 0-0 a6 10 b3 g6 11 ♗a3 ♗g7 12 ♗xc5 0-0 13 ♖ae1 b6 14 ♗a3 ♗b7 and Black succeeded in activating both his bishops and went on to win in V.Gashimov-I.Smirin, Calvia Olympiad 2004.

b) 5...dxc6 (the solid move) 6 h3 (here 6 e5 has no effect, as with 6...♘d5

the knight just goes to a good square) 6...e5 (Black blockades the centre) 7 d3 h6 8 b3 ♗e6 9 ♗b2 ♖d8 10 ♘d2 ♗d6 and Black was ultra-solid and made his draw in V.Gashimov-Wang Yue, Elista 2008—though perhaps White could have kept a small edge here with 11 ♘c4 (see the Caruana game given in the note to Black's fifth move).

Another option is 5 0-0, but this can lead to the "maelstrom of forced variations" that we have been trying to avoid;

e.g. 5...♘d4 6 ♘xd4 cxd4 7 ♘d5 ♘xd5 8 exd5 ♕c5 9 c4 a6 10 b4 and we now enter the realm of computer opening analysis, or let's see some crazy moves that only a computer could choose—and not only that, there are 43 games in the *MegaBase* with this insanity, many of them featuring high-rated players and higher-powered computers! Here's one example: 10...♕xb4 11 ♗a4 g6 12 d3 ♗g7 13 ♗d2 ♕a3 14 ♖b1 ♕xd3 15 d6 e6 16 c5 b5 17 ♗c2 ♕c4 18 ♗e4 ♖a7 19 ♗a5 f5 20 ♗f3 e5 21 ♗b6 ♖b7 reaching the kind of

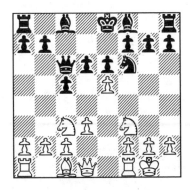

As always, the key break in this variation.

8...♘d7

After 8...dxe5 9 ♘xe5 this centralized knight is worth more than either of Black's bishops.

9 d4

9...d5

Or 9...cxd4 10 ♘xd4 ♕b6 11 exd6 ♗xd6 12 ♘db5 ♗c5 13 ♕g4 and we see the picture of many recent games: Black's light-squared bishop has no legal moves, and the dark squares are cracking.

10 a4 b6 11 ♖e1 h6 12 ♘e2 a6 13 h4 ♗b7

I think Black has to try to open the position at least a little bit, and defend the plus-equals position that arises after 13...cxd4 14 ♘exd4 ♕c7 15 ♗f4. After his actual move, White locks up the centre and Black is stuck in a bad French with an even worse French bishop—presumably not what Black wanted when he played 1...c5!

14 c3 c4 15 a5 bxa5

Black has to weaken his pawns, as after 15...b5 16 b4 ♗e7 (16...cxb3 17 ♗a3 ♗xa3 18 ♖xa3 is a favourable exchange for White: compare either white knight to Black's bad "French" bishop) 17 ♘g3, with the position locked on the queenside, White can gradually prepare an offensive on the kingside, the strong side of his pawn chain.

16 ♖xa5 ♕b6 17 ♖a1

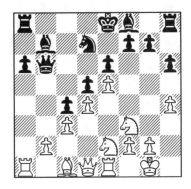

White has won the opening battle: Black has little or no play on the queenside, as the pawn chain is locked and White's sole weakness at b2 is very economically defended. Meanwhile, White stands much better on the king-

241

side with space and good knights. Now watch Adams go to work!

17...a5 18 ♘f4 ♗c6

Black can hardly castle kingside into White's attack: 18...♗e7 19 g3 0-0 20 ♘h2 a4 21 ♕h5 ♗c6 22 ♘g4 ♖fe8 23 ♘xh6+! (White sacs both knights to destroy the black king's pawn cover) 23...gxh6 24 ♘xe6! fxe6 25 ♕g6+ ♔h8 26 ♕xh6+ ♔g8 27 ♕xe6+ ♔h7 28 ♕h6+ ♔g8 29 e6! (there is no defence, despite the two extra pieces) 29...♘f8 (or 29...♘f6 30 ♖e5 and the rook lift finishes matters) 30 ♗f4 ♕b7 31 ♗e5 ♗f6 32 ♗xf6 ♕h7 33 ♕g5+ ♕g6 34 e7 and wins.

19 ♘h2 ♘b8 20 ♕h5 ♗d7 21 ♖e3 ♖a7 22 ♖g3 ♕b3 23 ♕e2 ♗a4 24 ♘h5 ♕c2 25 ♕e1

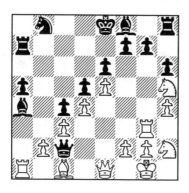

25...♖h7

Very awkward, but other defences allow the knight into f6: 25...♖g8 26 ♘f6+ or 25...g6 26 ♘f6+, with a crushing advantage for White in both variations.

26 ♘g4 ♘d7 27 ♘e3 ♕b3 28 ♗d2 g6 29 ♘f4 ♗e7 30 ♕b1 ♗xh4

One hopes Zhigalko enjoyed his "last meal"!

31 ♖h3 ♗e7 32 ♘xg6!

That's all folks!

32...fxg6 33 ♕xg6+ ♖f7 34 ♖f3 ♗f6 35 ♖xf6 ♘xf6 36 exf6 ♔d8 37 ♖a3 ♕b5 38 ♘g4 ♖ad7 39 ♘e5

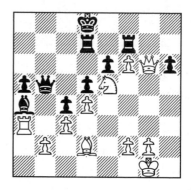

39...♕xb2

No better is 39...♖f8 40 ♗xh6 ♖h8 41 f7 or 39...♖h7 40 ♘xd7 ♕xd7 41 ♖xa4 etc.

40 ♘xf7+ 1-0

After 40...♖xf7 41 ♕xf7 ♕xa3 42 ♕g8+ ♔d7 43 f7 the pawn goes through. This was a very convincing attack by Adams, who gave his opponent no chances after 14 c3.

After the delayed Rossolimo sequence of 1 e4 c5 2 ♘f3 ♘c6 3 ♘c3 ♘f6 4 ♗b5, this line (4...♕c7, monitoring e5) is as good as it gets for the second player, and can be used at a high level. With accurate opening play—6...e5— White can be restricted to a small edge. Nonetheless, White can still play the resulting position for a win, while if

Black takes the slightest step off the correct path, he could face an extremely dangerous long-term attack, as Adams demonstrated.

The reader should note that e4-e5 is always White's big break in these lines. So that brings us to the other version of the Anti-Sicilian that can come about after 3 ♘c3. Black can immediately block the white e-pawn advance by putting his own pawn there—at the cost of the d5-square of course. In my opinion White can easily get some positional advantage against this line, which is the subject of the final three games of this chapter.

Game 63
J.H.Blackburne-J.Heral
Vienna 1873

1 e4 e5

This game reaches the Sicilian through a surprising transposition from the Vienna Game, but first let's take a look at the Sicilian order: 1...c5 2 ♘f3 ♘c6 3 ♘c3 is our basic repertoire, with the aim of avoiding the anti-positional (for both sides) Sveshnikov! Black side Sveshnikov devotee, Dorian Rogozenko, writes as follows in his book: *Anti-Sicilians: A Guide for Black*, referring to this opening position: "White's point is that 3...♘f6 4 ♗b5 leads to a line that is generally considered to favour White" (I agree, as we have seen in the last few games) and

goes on to recommend "the most principled answer, 3...e5." He admits this leaves a permanent weakness at d5, but underestimates, in my opinion, the simple ♘g5 and f2-f4 attack as played by Anand which will be featured in the next game.

I think it's asking a bit much of the black position to take on the weakness at d5 when the white bishop can go directly to c4—it seems that Black will have to suffer for his principles! But first, let's take a look at a very modern game from 1873!

2 ♘c3 c5

It's worth mentioning a line of the Four Knights Game here: 2...♘f6 3 ♘f3 ♘c6 4 ♗b5 ♗d6 is a weird-looking move that has been played about 500 times in the Database, even the mighty Magnus faced it! We'll see something similar in the main game. After 5 0-0 0-0 6 d3 ♖e8 7 ♖e1 a6 8 ♗c4 ♘a5 9 a3 ♘xc4 10 dxc4 (White locks down d5 and enjoys a small advantage, which he converts in a lengthy endgame) 10...h6 11 h3 ♗c5 12 ♗e3 ♗xe3 13 ♖xe3 d6 14 ♕d2 ♗e6 15 b3 ♘d7 16 ♖d1 ♖f8 17 ♕e2 b6 18 ♘e1 ♘c5 19 ♘d3 ♘xd3 20 cxd3 b5 21 d4 exd4 22 ♖xd4 bxc4 23 bxc4 ♕f6 24 ♖d1 ♖ab8 25 ♘d5 ♗xd5 26 cxd5 ♖b2 27 ♕f3 ♕xf3 28 ♖xf3 ♖e2 29 ♖d4 ♖c2 30 ♖a4, it's now clear that Black's pawns are weaker than White's—Magnus converted in another thirty moves or so in M.Carlsen-L.Aronian, Nice (rapid) 2010.

3 ♘f3 ♘c6 4 ♗c4

The bishop gets to this perfect square in one—White owns the weak d5-square. Once again, our Sicilian repertoire route to this key position is 1 e4 c5 2 ♘f3 ♘c6 3 ♘c3 e5 4 ♗c4.

4...♗d6

Maybe this 19th century game inspired Aronian!

4...d6 5 d3 is the modern way, and now 5...♗e7 is correct and will be seen in the next two following. Instead, in a blitz encounter my opponent followed Lasker and developed his king's knight first: 5...♘f6?—but after my reply 6 ♘g5!, he discovered that he had no reasonable way to defend f7, and so resigned: 1-0 T.Taylor-Alexbawtry, Internet (blitz) 2011.

5 d3 h6 6 0-0 b6 7 ♘e2

I would prefer 7 a3, maintaining my strong light-squared bishop, but Blackburne (often known as the Black Death!) also gets the edge this way.

7...♗b7 8 c3 ♘a5 9 ♗b3

Another possibility is 9 ♘g3!? (Magnus-style!) 9...♘xc4 10 dxc4 with a slight edge.

9...g5?!

Correct is 9...♘xb3 10 ♕xb3 ♘e7 with only a slight edge for White, mostly due to the eternally awkward bishop at d6—that square, as we have seen, is a real problem for Black in many variations of the Sicilian.

10 ♘g3 ♕c7 11 ♗c2!

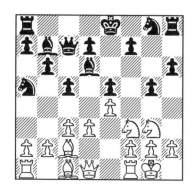

A very modern way of preserving the bishop, which will return to the a2-g8 diagonal later.

11...♘e7 12 ♗e3 ♖c8 13 ♖c1 ♘g6 14 ♘f5 ♘e7 15 ♘g7+!

Black won't castle in this game!

15...♔f8 16 ♘h5 ♘g6 17 ♗b1 ♕d8 18 ♘g3 ♗b8

While I think White could have been more accurate with the early 7 a3 (and Black should have taken the bishop on b3 when he had the chance), after that slight error one could hardly improve on Blackburne's play which, as I said, has a very modern appearance. It's not too soon to say that White has a winning position—but he *must* strike at this moment! After all, Black's last move finally solved the problem of his dark-squared bishop, and he is ready for a central counter—so hit now and hit hard!

19 h3?

Chess is timing, and this is too slow.

19 b4! is a knockout. The black knight on the rim can't retreat normally without losing a pawn, so the c-file must be opened, and then White can use a crowbar on the centre: 19...cxb4 (19...♘c6 20 bxc5 bxc5 21 ♗xc5+ is just a good extra pawn for White) 20 cxb4 ♖xc1 21 ♗xc1 ♘c6 22 b5 ♘a5 (or 22...♘d4 23 ♘xd4 exd4 24 ♗b2 ♗e5 25 ♕a4 and White wins a pawn) 23 ♘f5! ♔g8 (Black can't free himself, as 23...d5 fails to 24 ♘xh6!, picking up a good pawn in view of the latent fork on g5—Black's last move meets this threat, intending 24 ♘xh6+ ♖xh6 25 ♗xg5 ♕f8—but there is a lot more to the White position than a tactical trick) 24 d4! and White has a decisive positional advantage: Black's scattered forces, especially his completely out of play king's rook, can do nothing against White's central assault.

19...d5!

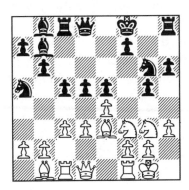

Rogozenko writes: "Often Black can advance his pawn to d5, solving all his problems at a stroke." Indeed! But this did not have to happen.

20 b4

As so often, you see the right move—one move too late!

20...cxb4 21 cxb4 ♖xc1 22 ♕xc1 ♘c6 23 ♘f5 ♘ce7 24 ♘g3 d4 25 ♗d2 ♕d7 26 a3 g4 27 hxg4 ♕xg4

Black has energetically obtained counterplay.

28 ♗a2 ♘f4 29 ♕c4 ♖h7 30 ♘h2 ♕g6 31 ♘f3 ♖g7

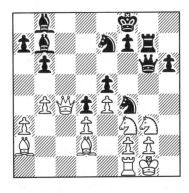

Now even the rook is employed. After White's big mistake on move 19, Black has gradually outplayed his re-doubtable foe, and even if *Fritz* still rates the position as plus-equals, I think Black's activity has taken him to equalizing territory. Evidently Black-burne thought so too—so rather than adapt to the changed circumstance, he tries a bluff.

32 ♗xf4!? exf4 33 ♕xd4

This trick is based on the mate at d8, but Black has a countershot...

33...♘c6 34 ♕d5

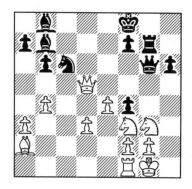

34...♗c7?

After his heroic resistance, with the chance to take the advantage, Black's courage deserts him! Here he could simply have taken with advantage: 34...fxg3 and White has nothing better than 35 b5 gxf2+ 36 ♖xf2 ♗g3 37 ♖e2 (relatively best, as 37 bxc6? ♗xf2+ 38 ♔xf2 ♗xc6 39 ♕d8+ ♗e8 wins for Black, and 37 ♖c2? ♕f6 likewise, due to White's weak back rank) 37...♕d6 38 bxc6 ♗xc6 39 ♕xd6+ ♗xd6 and Black's bishops give him the edge in the ending.

35 ♘h4

Now it's just Black Death!

35...♕g4 36 ♘gf5 f3 37 g3 ♕h3 38 ♘xg7

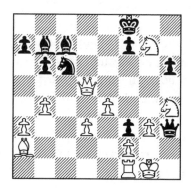

The only *real* mate that is threatened is that of the black king.

38...♘d8 39 ♕f5 1-0

Cruelly logical: White emerges with an extra rook.

Black's 4....♗d6 could not be strategically justified—until Blackburne waited too long!

White players should know their Rogozenko and watch out for Black breaking out of his cramp, as here, with ...d7-d5!

> ## Game 64
> **V.Anand-L.Van Wely**
> Monte Carlo
> (blindfold rapid) 2003

1 e4 c5 2 ♘f3 ♘c6 3 ♘c3 e5 4 ♗c4 ♗e7

Black correctly prevents the immediate ♘g5.

5 d3 d6

Against the alternate move order, 5...♘f6, White plays 6 0-0 (but not 6 ♘g5 0-0 7 f4 which allows 7...d5—the *Dangerous Weapons* "Sveshnikov Gambit"—which may or may not be sound, but it doesn't matter: we are not interested in that "maelstrom of forced variations" and we are especially uninterested in learning long forcing lines in obscure variations that you will face rarely or never!) 6...0-0 7 ♘g5.

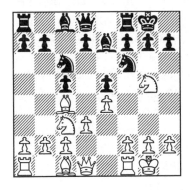

White's fundamental positional idea is to coordinate his splendidly placed light-squared bishop with other attackers. The simplest way to do this is the text followed by f2-f4, which brings two more pieces—the knight and king's rook—directly or indirectly to bear on f7.

Black has three main answers:

a) 7...d6 8 f4 transposes back to the main game.

b) 7...d5 tries to be the "Sveshnikov Gambit" as mentioned above, but doesn't work here as White is safely castled and has no weaknesses: 8 ♘xd5 (even simpler is 8 exd5 ♘b4 9 ♖e1 or

8...♘d4 9 a4 and I can't see any real compensation for the pawn) 8...♘xd5 9 exd5 ♘d4 10 ♕h5 h6 11 ♘xf7! ♖xf7 12 d6!, when White recovered his piece with advantage and went on to win in A.Hellstroffer-H.Rückert, German League 2005.

c) 7...h6 8 f4! (always remember that White is doing the attacking!—not even a direct threat to the knight prevents White from carrying out his positional goal—can you guess Guseinov is in the house?) 8...exf4 (or 8...hxg5 9 fxg5 ♘g4 10 g6 with a tremendous attack) 9 ♘f3 and now Black must decide whether he wants to and to keep his ill-gotten gain or not—essentially we have reached a King's Gambit-type position.

First a give back, then two keepers:

c1) 9...d6 10 ♗xf4 transposes to the next game, where White has some positional advantage.

c2) 9...♗d6 looks like the Blackburne game: after 10 ♘h4 ♔h8 11 ♘f5 ♗e5 12 ♗xf4 White recovered his pawn with advantage in E.Tomilova-L.Figura, Kazan 2003.

c3) 9...g5 (most committal and critical) 10 h4! (as in many variations of the King's Gambit, White must shake Black's rickety pawn structure before he consolidates) 10...♘g4 (the well-known GM Lautier quickly reached a lost position with Black after 10...♘h7 11 hxg5 hxg5 12 g3 fxg3 13 ♕e1 ♔h8 14 ♕xg3 f5 15 exf5 d5 16 ♘xd5 ♗d6 17 ♕g2 ♖xf5 18 ♗d2 ♗f8 and now—instead of 19 ♘xg5 ♖xg5, when heroic defence gave Black a draw in N.Mitkov-J.Lautier, Turin Olympiad 2006—the simple 19 ♘e3! ♖f4 20 ♘xg5! would have won: White is a pawn up and Black's kingside is busted) 11 hxg5 hxg5 12 g3 fxg3 13 ♘d5 ♘f2 14 ♖xf2 gxf2+ 15 ♔xf2 g4 16 ♕h1 (White has a winning attack) 16...♘d4 (or 16...gxf3 17 ♘xe7+ ♕xe7 18 ♗h6 d5 19 ♖g1+ ♔h7 20 ♗xf8+ and mates) 17 ♕h5 ♘xf3 18 ♘xe7+ ♕xe7 19 ♕xg4+ ♔h7 20 ♕h5+ ♔g8 21 ♔xf3 1-0 G.Guseinov-Mi.Richter, Istanbul 2007—Guseinov scores again!

6 0-0

Since you will probably get this line only once in a blue moon, I see no reason to study Kasparov's slower and more complicated alternative here—his plan is to bring another knight to d5 as soon as possible—as the simple main line is good enough for an edge. Nonetheless, I certainly don't want Garry to feel offended by all the Karpov games in this book, so please enjoy the following positional masterpiece: 6 ♘d2 ♘f6 7 ♘f1 ♗g4 8 f3 ♗e6 9 ♘e3

0-0 10 0-0 ♘d7 11 ♘ed5 (there you have it!—White owns d5) 11...♘b6 12 ♘xb6 ♕xb6 13 ♘d5 ♗xd5 14 ♗xd5 ♘b4 15 ♗c4 ♖ad8 16 f4 exf4 17 ♖xf4 d5 18 exd5 ♘xd5 19 ♖f5 ♘c7 20 ♕f3 ♕g6 21 a4 ♘e8 22 ♗e3 b6 23 ♗b3 ♘d6 24 ♖d5 ♕f6 25 ♖f1 ♕xf3 26 ♖xf3 ♗f6 27 c3 ♘c8 28 g4 ♖xd5 29 ♗xd5 ♖d8 30 ♗c4 ♘d6 31 ♗a2 h6 32 ♗f4 g5 33 ♗g3 ♔g7 34 ♔f1 a6 35 ♗f2 ♖c8 36 ♗g3 ♖d8 37 ♔e2 b5 38 a5 b4 39 ♗xd6!! (Kasparov will win the rook and opposite bishops ending with superlative technique) 39...♖xd6 40 ♔d2 ♖d7 41 ♖f5 ♖b7 42 ♔c2 bxc3 43 bxc3 ♖b5 44 ♗c4 ♖xa5 45 d4 ♔g6 46 dxc5 ♗e7 47 c6 ♗d8 48 ♗xf7+ ♔g7 49 ♗d5 ♖c5 50 c4! (Black's rook is locked up—White's advantage is decisive) 50...♗f6 51 ♔d3 ♗b2 52 ♖f2 ♗a1 53 ♔e4 ♔g6 54 ♖a2 1-0 G.Kasparov-V.Babula, Prague (team simul) 2001.

6...♘f6 7 ♘g5 0-0 8 f4

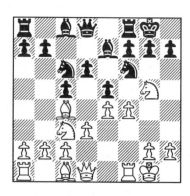

White's fundamental strategic idea: he plays a delayed King's Gambit (without the pawn sacrifice) to get a central pawn majority and kingside play. White scores 62% with this simple plan.

8...♗g4

Rogozenko recommends the line 8...exf4 9 ♗xf4 h6 10 ♘f3 ♗e6, but I don't think Black is equal here—see the next game.

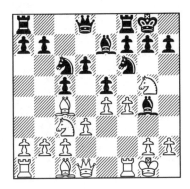

9 ♘f3

The World Champion that Anand dethroned played in even simpler fashion: 9 ♕e1 exf4 (or 9...♘d4 10 fxe5 dxe5 11 ♕h4 h5 12 h3 with a strong attack; and not 11...♘xc2? 12 ♖xf6!, when White wins at once) 10 ♗xf4 ♘d4 11 ♕d2 ♕d7 12 ♗e3 h6 13 ♘f3 ♘xf3+ 14 gxf3 ♗e6 15 ♔h1 ♔h7 16 ♗xe6 ♕xe6 17 ♖ae1 ♕h3 18 ♕g2 (Grind style: White takes his plus-equals into the ending, for even without queens White's central pawn mass gives him the edge) 18...♕xg2+ 19 ♔xg2 a6 20 f4 ♖ac8 21 ♗f2 ♖fd8 22 ♗h4 b5 23 b3 ♘g8 24 ♗g3 ♖d7 25 a4 b4 26 ♘d5 ♖c6 27 ♘e3 ♗f6 28 e5 dxe5 29 fxe5 ♗d8 30 ♘c4 ♗c7 1-0 V.Kramnik-J.M.Degraeve, Senat 2003.

9...exf4 10 ♗xf4 ♘d4 11 ♔h1

Anand "sees" (remember this game is blindfold) that the exchange on f3 does not weaken his king position, but rather opens the g-file so he can attack Black!

11...a6 12 ♕d2

Harmonious! Now the pin is gone and Black is left with positional problems: the d5 hole is still with us, and if he takes on f3, the g-file opens for White as mentioned—but if he doesn't, White has the f-file!

12...b5 13 ♗b3

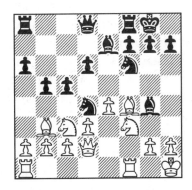

13...♘xb3

13...♗xf3 is a better try: after 14 gxf3 a5 15 ♕g2 g6 16 ♗e3 a4 17 ♗d5

♖b8 18 a3 White has only a slight edge due to the d5-square.

14 axb3 d5

Black regains d5, but loses control of e5—a good illustration of the well-known transition of advantages.

15 ♘e5 dxe4 16 ♘c6 ♕d7 17 ♘xe7+ ♕xe7 18 ♗g5! e3

Black can't take the pawn: 18...exd3 19 ♗xf6 gxf6 20 ♘d5 ♕e6 21 ♘xf6+ gives White a winning attack.

19 ♕xe3 ♕xe3 20 ♗xe3 ♘d7 21 ♘d5

And Anand gets d5 back after all! *Fritz* is at "decisive advantage for White", and this human can't find anything for Black either. The weak pawns on c5 (attacked by the bishop), a6 (attacked by one white rook) and f7 (attacked by the other rook) overstress Black's defence.

21...f6 22 h3 ♗h5 23 ♗f4 ♖a7 24 ♖fe1 ♗f7 25 ♘e7+ ♔h8 26 ♘f5 c4

Desperation, but if Black waits with 26...♔g8 then 27 ♖e7 is paralyzing.

27 dxc4 bxc4 28 b4 ♗g6 29 ♘d6 ♖aa8

29...♗xc2 30 ♖e7 ♖fa8 31 ♗e3 ♖c7 32 b5 a5 33 ♖xa5!, winning, is a pretty

variation.

30 c3 ♘b6 31 ♖a5 h6 32 ♖ea1 ♗d3 33 ♖xa6

We will see more bad bishops unable to defend the queenside in the next main game and notes.

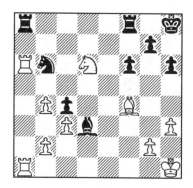

33...♖xa6 34 ♖xa6 ♘d5 35 ♗g3 ♔h7 36 b5 ♖b8 37 ♖a7 ♘e3 38 ♘xc4! ♖e8 39 ♘d6 1-0

Evidently Anand will overlook nothing! Two pawns down against the future World Champion, Black wisely resigns.

Game 65
Wang Hao-Y.Kryvoruchko
World Mindsports Games
(rapid), Beijing 2008

---

1 e4 c5 2 ♘f3 ♘c6 3 ♘c3 e5 4 ♗c4 ♗e7 5 d3 d6 6 0-0 ♘f6 7 ♘g5 0-0 8 f4 exf4 9 ♗xf4 h6 10 ♘f3 ♗e6

Rogozenko's recipe for Black—but does it equalize? I think not, as White maintains a small but persistent space advantage by occupying d5.

11 ♘d5

Best. 11 ♗xe6 fxe6 is weaker as Black has covered d5. White tried a Guseinov-style pawn-cracker, but Black got counterplay on the f-file: 12 e5 dxe5 13 ♗g3 ♘d7 14 ♕e2 ♕c7 15 ♖fe1 ♖f5 16 ♕e4 ♖af8 17 ♕c4 ♕d6 18 ♘b5 ♕d5 19 ♘c7 ♕xc4 20 dxc4 and now—instead of 20...♗d6 21 ♘b5, when White went on to win in M.Tappyrov-M.Barakat, Russian Junior Championship 2004—Black could have obtained the advantage with 20...♘d4!.

Also inferior is 11 ♕e1 d5!, when Black "solved his problems at a stroke" in A.Chibukhchian-A.Anastasian, Armenian Championship, Yerevan 2009.

11...♗xd5 12 ♗xd5

12 exd5 is another option: 12...♘a5 13 ♘h4 ♘xc4 14 dxc4 ♘xd5 15 ♕xd5 ♗xh4 16 ♖ad1 b6 17 ♗xd6 ♗e7 18 ♗e5 ♗g5 19 ♗d6 ♗e7 20 ♗f4 ♗f6 21 c3 ♕xd5 22 cxd5 ♖ad8 23 ♗xh6 ♗xc3 24 bxc3 gxh6, when one sees that the then World Champion has obtained a plus-equals endgame... but his opponent is Peter Leko! Therefore, after some ster-

ling defence by the Hungarian, it becomes apparent that Black's pawn weaknesses are not fatal: 25 ♖fe1 ♖d7 26 c4 a6 27 a4 b5 28 axb5 axb5 29 cxb5 ♖b8 30 d6 ♖xb5 31 ♖e7 ♖bb7 32 ♖xd7 ♖xd7 33 ♔f2 ♔g7 34 ♔f3 ♔f6 35 ♖d5 and a draw was agreed in V.Kramnik-P.Leko, Linares 2003.

12...♘xd5 13 exd5 ♘d4

Rogozenko claims that the alternative 13...♘e5 is equal, but after the obvious 14 ♗xe5 dxe5 15 c4 one sees the legacy of the weak d5-square: White has a protected passed pawn that will plague Black forever. Add in the superior minor piece, and it's no wonder that White scores 84% (!!) from this position in 36 games in the database.

Following are a selection of these wins, including a nice one from our friend Guseinov, who scores in his usual stylish fashion. All the games start with 15...♗d6 16 g4 (to secure the white knight on e4) and then:

a) 16...♕b6 17 ♕e2 ♖ae8 18 ♔h1 ♗c7 19 ♖ae1 ♕d6 20 ♘d2 ♗d8 21 ♘e4 ♕c7 22 ♕e3 (White has a nice bind with the unassailable knight on e4) 22...b6 23 ♖f5 ♗h4 24 ♖e2 f6 25 ♕h3 ♗g5 26 ♕h5 ♖d8 27 h4 ♗f4 28 ♕g6 ♔h8 29 ♔g2 ♕d7 30 b3 a5 31 ♘c3 ♕e8 32 h5 ♕d7 33 ♔f3 ♖b8 34 ♖xf4! (a typical Guseinov positional sacrifice) 34...exf4 35 ♕f5 ♕d8 (here 35...♕xf5 36 gxf5 ♖fe8 37 ♖e6 ♖xe6 38 fxe6 ♖e8 39 ♘a4, winning, shows White's main idea) 36 ♖e6 ♖e8 37 ♘e2 b5 38 ♘xf4 bxc4 39 dxc4 a4 40 ♘g6+ ♔g8 41 bxa4 ♕a5 42 ♕d3 ♖xe6 43 dxe6 ♖d8 44 ♘e7+ ♔f8 45 ♘d5 ♕e1 46 ♕e3 ♕h1+ 47 ♔g3 ♖xd5 48 cxd5 ♕xd5 49 a5 ♔e7 50 ♕a3 ♕e5+ 51 ♔h3 f5 52 ♕f3 fxg4+ 53 ♕xg4 ♕e3+ 54 ♔g2 ♕d2+ 55 ♔g3 ♕e1+ 56 ♔f4 ♕d2+ 57 ♔f5 ♕d5+ 58 ♔g6 1-0 G.Guseinov-K.Haznedaroglu, European Team Championship, Heraklio 2007—there's no point in continuing since 59...♕xa5 (or 59...♕xe6+ 60 ♕xe6+ ♔xe6 61 a6 and Black is out of the square) 60 ♕f7+ ♔d6 61 e7 is just a clean win for White. Guseinov must salivate when he gets these positional grind positions!

b) 16...b5 17 ♘d2 bxc4 18 dxc4 e4 19 ♘xe4

(Black immediately gives up a pawn to activate his bishop, though it's hard to believe in the soundness of such a desperate measure) 19...♗e5 20 ♕e2 (I think this is unnecessarily defensive and gives Black chances: it would be better to return the pawn at once with 20 ♕f3 ♗xb2 21 ♖ab1 with pressure across the board—and don't forget the protected passed pawn at d5) 20...♖b8 21 ♖ab1 ♖e8 22 ♕f3 ♕h4 23 ♘g3 f5 24 d6 ♔h8 (24...♕xg4 puts Black back in the game) 25 gxf5 ♕xc4 26 ♔h1 ♖f8 27 ♕e4 ♕xe4+ 28 ♘xe4 ♖b4 29 ♖fe1 ♗d4 30 d7! (but now the passed pawn has its say, and Black loses material without any counterplay) 30...♖b7 31 ♖bd1 ♖xd7 32 ♘xc5 ♗xc5 33 ♖xd7 ♖xf5 34 a3 ♗b6 35 b4 ♖f4 36 ♖de7 ♖g4 37 ♖7e4 ♖g6 38 a4 ♗f2 39 ♖f1 ♗b6 40 a5 ♗c7 41 ♖g1 1-0 E.Sutovsky-J.Shaw, Gibraltar 2006.

c) 16...g6 (Black wants to gain control of e4 to keep White's knight off that square—but it's not so easy) 17 ♔h1 (to meet 17...f5 with 18 gxf5 gxf5 19 ♖g1+ ♔h8 20 ♘g5! and a winning attack) ♔h7 18 ♖g1 ♕e7 19 ♕e2 ♖ae8 20 ♖ae1 f6 21 ♘d2 ♖g8 22 ♖ef1 ♖ef8 23 ♘e4 (White has complete positional domination, as 23...f5 fails to a similar attack: 24 gxf5 gxf5 25 ♖xg8 ♔xg8 26 ♖g1+ ♔h7 27 ♕h5! and wins) 23...♖g7 24 ♖g3 ♖gf7 25 ♖fg1 ♖g8 26 ♕e3 ♔g7 27 ♖f1 b6 28 a3 ♕d7 29 ♕d2 ♗e7 30 b4 ♖h8 31 ♕c3 ♕c7 32 ♕b2 ♔h7 33 bxc5 bxc5 34 g5! (a well-prepared breakthrough) 34...f5 35 gxh6 ♗h4 36 ♖gf3

☖hf8 37 ♘c3 e4 38 dxe4 fxe4 39 ♘b5 ♕d7 40 ☖xf7+ ☖xf7 41 ☖xf7+ ♕xf7 42 ♕g7+!! (White now wins an accurately calculated ending—as in many of these positions, the black bishop is inferior to the white knight) 42...♕xg7 43 hxg7 ♔xg7 44 ♔g2 ♔f6 45 ♘xa7 ♔e5 46 ♘c6+ ♔f4 47 a4 e3 48 ♔f1 ♔f3 49 ♘e5+ ♔e4 50 a5! 1-0 I.Smirin-M.Parligras, Athens 2007—Black resigned here in view of 50...♗d8 (or 50...♔xe5 51 a6) 51 a6 ♗b6 52 d6 ♔xe5 53 d7 ♔e6 54 d8♕ ♗xd8 55 a7 etc.

Principled, perhaps—equal? Nyet!

14 ♘d2

Now we're down to two games in the database, and White won both of them, the other victim being GM Sveshnikov! One advantage of White's move order (my recommended 3 ♘c3) against a die-hard Svesh player, or even the great Svesh himself, is that he simply *cannot get his opening!*

14...♘b5

Sveshnikov tried 14...♗g5, but after 15 c3 ♘f5 16 ♗xg5 ♕xg5 17 ♘e4 ♕g6 18 ☖f3 ☖ae8 19 ♕a4 b5 20 ♕a6 (even

20 ♕xa7 is possible) 20...☖e5 21 ♕xb5 ☖xd5 22 ☖af1, White won the opening duel and eventually the game in A.Areshchenko-E.Sveshnikov, Moscow 2009.

15 ♕h5

White's advantages include more space, the better bishop, and a target at d6—just plus-equals when you come down to it, but very difficult for Black to defend, especially when he was hoping for strange Svesh counterplay!

15...f5 16 ☖ae1 ♕e8 17 ♕xe8 ☖axe8 18 ♘c4

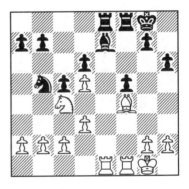

White's advantages become more pronounced in the ending—it's hard to see any counterplay for Black.

18...☖f6 19 ♘a5 g5 20 ♗d2 ♘c7 21 c4 ☖f7 22 b4!

Black was no doubt hoping for 22 ♘xb7 ☖b8 with counterplay, but after this typical break (we also saw this in the Smirin game above) White attacks across the board. Black must either break up his pawns or, as played, let the white knight into his position.

22...b6

22...cxb4 allows 23 ♘xb7 and now that Black has blocked the b-file himself, he has no compensation for the weak queenside pawns. Note how the pawn at d6 often blocks Black's dark-squared bishop from having a meaningful role in the game.

23 ♘c6 ♝f6

After 23...f4 24 ♘xa7 ♜a8 25 ♘c6 ♝f6 26 bxc5 bxc5 27 ♝a5 White also emerges a pawn ahead.

24 ♜xf5

The first pawn drops.

24...♜ef8 25 g4!

This light square bind is, as we have seen, typical of the variation. Black's bishop has nothing to say, while the Chinese GM wins with excellent technique.

25...♚g7 26 ♚g2 ♚g6 27 bxc5 bxc5 28 ♜f3 ♜e8 29 a4 ♜xe1 30 ♝xe1 ♘e8 31 ♜e3 ♘g7 32 ♝g3 ♜b7

Desperation, since the passive 32...♜d7 would only prolong the game

without saving it.

33 ♝xd6 ♜b2+ 34 ♚f3 h5 35 h3 ♜a2 36 a5 ♝c3 37 ♜e2 ♜a1 38 ♝xc5 ♜d1 39 ♝xa7 1-0

Four pawns up is persuasive—Black resigns.

This was a nice win by Wang Hao, though not that difficult. In my opinion Black gives up too much ground in the opening with 3...e5, and White should always get a pleasant edge.

However, in 28 games with this Sicilian repertoire I have never faced 3 ♘c3 e5. I don't think it's much trusted at the IM level or below—though I do note, with all due respect, that 3...e5 is played regularly by super-solid GM Peter Leko (see the note to White's 12th move) and, of 19 games in the database, he has scored, of course, 9½-9½.

I promise that if I play him and he makes a draw with this line, I will not cry.

Chapter Seven
Unusual Second Moves for Black

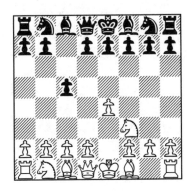

By this point we have covered all the main and most popular variations of the Sicilian Defence, and your repertoire is almost complete. But what if, after 1 e4 c5 2 ♘f3, Black plays something besides the normal 2...d6, 2...♘c6 or 2...e6 - ? The most important of these sidelines are 2...a6 (the O'Kelly), 2...g6 (the Hyper-Accelerated Dragon), 2...b6, and Nimzowitsch's 2...♘f6—and I will cover all of these in this chapter.

As I now know from experience (see the note to move three in the first game below) one *must* be prepared for these offbeat lines, particularly the harmless-appearing O'Kelly. A loss in that variation was my only defeat in the "titled opponents" category!

In general, my recommendation against these subvariations is simply to play commonsense moves that allow Black to transpose back into main lines—but if he insists on his offbeatedness, then just fracture him!

Game 66
A.Karpov-M.J.Franklin
Hastings 1971/72

1 e4 c5 2 ♘f3 a6

The O'Kelly variation, often referred to as a "one-trick pony"—although in the new *Dangerous Weapons* book it is described as "Not Just a One-Trick Pony".

Unfortunately I have to disagree

with the latter, as I checked out the pony and he only knew one trick!

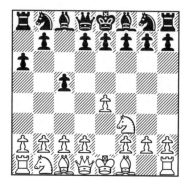

3 c3

Karpov, of course, knows the trick: if White carelessly plays the usual Open Sicilian move 3 d4, Black's seemingly inoffensive pawn move comes into its own: 3...cxd4 4 ♘xd4 ♘f6 5 ♘c3 e5! 6 ♘f3 (6 ♘b3 ♗b4 is similar) 6...♗b4! and Black has a souped-up Boleslavsky Wall structure with his dark-squared bishop outside the pawn chain. I spent a lot of fruitless hours trying to make 3 d4 work as I prepared this chapter—and came up empty. It doesn't work: Black is already at least equal—*don't play 3 d4.*

So much for the trick.

What should one play? Karpov's move is the approved anti-O'Kelly—White enters an Alapin Sicilian where he claims that Black's ...a7-a6 is useless. However, ...a7-a6 is a standard Sicilian move, often useful at some point in c2-c3 variations—and besides, the Alapin is nothing like our main repertoire.

Therefore I am giving both Karpov's line here, and my own personal preference, 3 ♘c3, in the next game.

I came by this preference the hard way, by losing to IM-elect Joel Banawa *before* I had studied the line. In that game I randomly threw out 3 b4?!, knowing only that it had been recommended by GM Gawain Jones in his *How to Beat the Sicilian* book—but my experience and subsequent analysis convinced me that this is a doubtful gambit after 3...cxb4 4 a3 e6 and then:

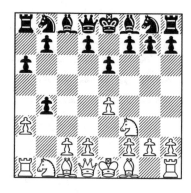

a) 5 axb4 ♗xb4 6 c3 ♗e7 7 d4 d6 8 ♗d3 ♘f6 9 0-0 ♘c6! (correct!—9...♘bd7 10 ♘bd2 0-0 11 ♗a3 with compensation is given by Jones) 10 ♖e1 0-0 11 h3 b5 12 ♘bd2 ♗b7 13 ♘b3 ♖c8 and White had nothing for the pawn in M.Eliezer-F.Badana, Internet (blitz) 2004.

b) 5 d4 b5 6 ♗d3 ♗b7 7 0-0 ♘f6, and one sees that Black is completing his development without hindrance, so White does not have full compensation for the pawn—Black went on to win in T.Taylor-J.C.Banawa, 4th Metropolitan Invitational, Los Angeles 2011.

3...d5 4 exd5 ♕xd5

As pointed out in *Dangerous Weapons*, Black can even play 4...♘f6 5 c4 e6 with a bizarro Icelandic Gambit!

When I saw this I became convinced that, Karpov aside, 3 ♘c3 is the best and most player-friendly move!

5 d4 e6 6 ♗e3 cxd4 7 cxd4 ♘f6 8 ♘c3

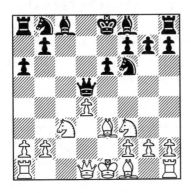

8...♕a5

This doesn't look accurate to me, as Black will always have problems with his exposed queen. Stronger is 8...♕d8, when Black has a solid position, as experience shows: 9 ♗d3 ♘c6 10 0-0 ♗d6 11 a3 0-0 12 ♗g5 ♗e7 13 ♗c2 b5 14 ♕d3 g6 15 ♖ad1 ♗b7 16 ♖fe1 (White could attack immediately, but after 16 ♗h6 ♖e8 17 d5 exd5 18 ♘xd5 ♘xd5 19 ♕xd5 ♕xd5 20 ♖xd5 ♘a5 21 ♖d3 ♘c4 22 ♖e1 ♗f6 23 ♗b3 ♗xf3 24 ♖xe8+ ♖xe8 25 gxf3 ♗xb2 Black had not only defended well, he pirated a pawn too and, after 26 a4 ♗g7 27 ♗xg7 ♔xg7 28 axb5 axb5 29 ♖d5 ♖b8, soon converted in A.Demin-V.Romanko, Kimry 2003; interestingly enough, this game came from a Caro-Kann Panov Attack!)

16...♖e8 17 ♗b1 and now—instead of the too slow 17...♕b6, when Black was outplayed and finally lost in D.Sadvakasov-I.Krush, Miami 2007—the correct 17...b4! cracks open a queenside line with counterplay.

In short, I believe that Black has reasonable chances (with 8...♕d8) in this O'Kelly variation, so in this one case, my personal recommendation is *not* to follow Karpov.

That said, we can now enjoy Karpov's positional mastery one last time, as he takes advantage of Black's inaccuracy.

9 ♗d3 ♘c6 10 a3 ♗e7 11 0-0 0-0 12 ♕c2 ♗d7 13 b4

Karpov is in his element: a plus-equals position where he can manoeuvre—the IQP is not weak, while the black queen is uncertain.

13...♕h5 14 ♘e2 ♘d5 15 ♗d2 ♗d6 16 ♘g3 ♗xg3 17 fxg3!

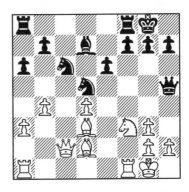

An unprejudiced capture away from the centre, that adds a rook to the attack and increases White's edge.

17...♖ac8 18 ♕b2 f6 19 h3 g5?!

Patient defence with 19...♘ce7 is better, but Black is getting worn down!

20 g4 ♕h6 21 a4!

White has the initiative across the board.

21...b5 22 axb5 axb5 23 ♖fc1 ♖b8 24 ♖c5!

Attacking the b-pawn—and also concealing a typically Karpovian "drop of poison".

24...♘d8 25 h4! ♕g7

The natural 25...♘f4 26 ♗xf4 gxf4 is just a poison pill: White wins with 27 ♖h5!, breaking through to h7, which reveals the second point of 24 ♖c5.

26 hxg5 fxg5 27 ♘xg5

Thus White has won a pawn with attack.

27...♘b7 28 ♖cc1?!

Simpler is 28 ♗xh7+ ♔h8 29 ♖c2 ♘f4 30 g3 ♕xg5 31 ♗xf4 ♕xg4 32 ♖h2 and wins.

As played, Karpov gives the pawn back and actually helps Black for a moment.

28...♘f4 29 ♗xf4 ♖xf4 30 ♘f3 ♕xg4 31 ♗e2 ♘d8?

Here 31...♕g3! is stronger, giving Black some counter-chances with the queen possibly checking on e1 if White gets carried away, while also clearing the fourth rank for the rook.

After Black's actual retrograde move, Karpov regains the initiative, and gives no second chance.

32 ♖c5 ♘f7 33 ♖a3 ♕g7 34 ♖a7 ♗e8

No doubt Black was in time trouble. Clearly 34...♖d8 was necessary, though White is evidently better after something like 35 ♕a1.

35 ♖g5!

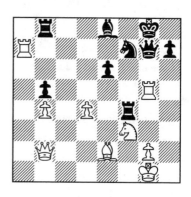

Bang!

35...♕xg5 36 ♘xg5 ♘xg5 37 d5 1-0

You're dead.

All very Karpovian, but Taylor has another idea!

Game 67
S.Brenjo-B.Kurajica
Bosnian Team
Championship 2009

---

1 e4 c5 2 ♘f3 a6 3 ♘c3!

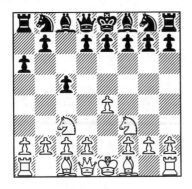

Tossing the ball back into Black's court: now he can easily transpose back into our repertoire lines—but if he tries to stay in O'Kelly, he has trouble.

3...b5

Instead, 3...d6 4 d4 cxd4 5 ♘xd4 ♘f6 6 ♗e2 is our line vs. the Najdorf (6...e5), Dragodorf (6...g6) or Scheveningen (6...e6), while 3...e6 4 d4 cxd4 5 ♘xd4 ♕c7 6 ♗e2 is the similar line vs. the Kan.

4 d4

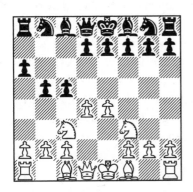

4...e6

Now 4...cxd4 5 ♘xd4 e6 6 ♗d3 reaches the Kan line with an early ...b7-b5 we have already covered (see Games

52-53).

The text looks extravagant to me: this allows White to create a strong wedge in the centre that shuts off the coming fianchetto. However, the O'Kelly in general is about catching White unprepared (I should know, I was caught unprepared!), but it's not necessarily good, except as a transpositional method.

5 d5

White has a lead in development, more space and the better centre—the only advantage Black has is that his opponent may not be familiar with the position.

5...♗b7

No better is 5...b4 6 ♘e2 exd5 7 exd5 d6 8 ♘g3 ♘f6 (or 8...g6 9 ♗c4 ♗g7 10 0-0 ♘e7 11 ♗f4, when White has an advantage in space and a bind on the position) 9 c4 bxc3 10 bxc3 g6 11 ♗e2 ♗g7 12 0-0 0-0 13 ♗f4 ♕c7 14 h3 ♘bd7 15 c4 ♘b6 16 ♕d2 ♖e8 17 ♗d3 ♗d7 18 ♗h6 ♗h8 19 ♕f4 ♗a4 20 ♖ab1 (White has a space advantage on both wings and builds up his attack)

20...♘fd7 21 ♘h5! ♖e7 22 ♖be1 ♖ae8 23 ♘g5! ♘c8 24 ♖e3 ♕d8 25 ♖fe1 f6 26 ♘e6 and GM Tarjan (who would later give up chess to become a librarian) scored with a trademark "all pieces are attacking" assault in J.Tarjan-D.Fritzinger, Aspen 1968.

6 ♗g5

Not mentioned in *Dangerous Weapons*, this developing/attacking move looks strongest, with a clear edge for White.

The same opponent, Joel Banawa, who surprised me with the O'Kelly also got the advantage again against another IM, my perpetual opponent Amanov. The surprised Amanov was only prepared this far and played 6 dxe6, which released the tension and opened the diagonal for the b7-bishop. Chaotic play ensued: 6...fxe6 7 e5 b4 8 ♘b1 ♕c7 9 ♘bd2 ♘h6 10 ♘c4 ♘f7 11 ♗f4 ♗d5 12 ♗d3 ♗e7 13 h4 ♘c6 14 ♕e2 a5 15 ♖h3 ♘d4 16 ♘xd4 cxd4 17 ♖g3 g6 18 ♖g4 ♕c6 19 f3 a4 20 ♗g3 ♗c5 21 ♗f2 ♘h6 22 ♖f4 ♖f8 23 ♕d2 ♘f5 24 ♗xf5 and at this point a draw was agreed in Z.Amanov-J.C.Banawa, 4th Metropolitan Invitational, Los Angeles 2011. However, after 24...♖xf5 Black has an evident advantage: the white knight is hanging, and e5 almost is, so White will have to make serious concessions to get through the next few moves. One possible continuation is 25 ♘d6+ ♗xd6 26 exd6 ♕xd6 27 ♖xf5 (not 27 ♖xd4 as 27...♕h2 is a decisive infiltration, and if White runs, he is

hit on the other side: 28 0-0-0 b3! with a winning attack) 27...gxf5 28 ♗xd4 ♖c8 and Black has all the play.

So good preparation is necessary!

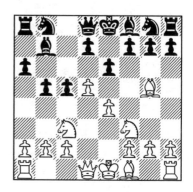

6...f6

A rather ugly self-block, but the alternatives don't look much better:

a) 6...♕a5 7 ♗e2 h6 8 ♗h4 g5 9 ♗g3 ♗g7 10 0-0 (Black's violent play, with knight's pawn advances on each side, has come to nothing against White's centralized development and e4/d5 pawn block—with the idea of getting "something" for his mess of a position, Black takes material and is shortly cut down) 10...b4 11 ♘b1! ♗xb2 12 dxe6 dxe6 13 ♘bd2 ♗xa1 14 ♕xa1 f6 15 ♘c4 (Black could resign now, as White gets two pieces for the rook plus attack, but instead continues until the near spectre of mate convinces him to give up) 15...♕a4 16 ♘d6+ ♔e7 17 ♘xb7 ♘d7 18 ♗d6+ ♔f7 19 e5 f5 20 ♘e1 ♖c8 21 ♗c4 ♕c6 22 ♘a5 ♕b6 23 ♘b3 ♘e7 24 ♕d1 g4 25 f3 ♖hd8 26 ♘d3 ♘d5 27 ♕e1 ♖g8 28 ♔h1 gxf3 29 ♖xf3 ♕c6 30 ♕h4 ♖g5 31 ♖g3 ♘e3 32 ♗xe6+ ♔xe6

33 ♘f4+ ♔f7 34 ♖xg5 ♘f6 35 ♖g7+ 1-0 G.Gras-L.Jiang, Montreal 2010.

b) 6...♗e7 7 ♗f4! b4 8 ♘b1 exd5 9 exd5 d6 (9...♘f6 10 d6, winning, is the point of "losing" a tempo with ♗g5-f4) 10 c4 ♗f6 (after 10...bxc3 11 ♘xc3 White gets a good Shirov-style Benko) 11 ♕c2 ♘e7 12 ♘bd2 ♘g6 13 ♗g3 0-0 14 0-0-0 and it's clear White is better with more space and attacking chances—whereas Black's b7-bishop is not playing, and the one on f6 is going to be hit on the next move by ♘e4. Needless to say, White took the full point in C.K.Pedersen-M.Muse, German League 2006.

7 ♗e3 ♕c7 8 a4 b4 9 ♘b1 f5 10 dxe6 fxe4

If 10...dxe6, then 11 ♘g5 with a strong attack.

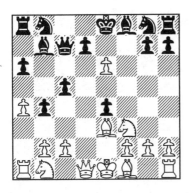

11 exd7+

Not bad, but 11 ♘g5 is even stronger—when GM Kurajica, a specialist in the O'Kelly, is pretty much crushed already in his favourite opening! After 11...♘f6 12 ♘d2 h6 13 ♘gxe4! White sacrifices a piece and

Black has no good answer:

a) 13...♘xe4 14 ♕h5+ ♔d8 (after 14...♗e7 15 ♘xe4 ♗xe4 16 ♕h4+ Black loses in the same way) 15 ♘xe4 ♗xe4 16 ♕h4+ and White recovers his piece with a winning position.

b) 13...♗xe4 14 ♘xe4 ♘xe4 15 exd7+ ♔d8 (15...♕xd7 loses to 16 ♕h5+ ♔d8 17 ♖d1 ♗d6 18 ♕f3 ♖e8 19 ♗d3, while 15...♘xd7 loses to 16 ♕d5—in both cases White recovers material with a huge positional advantage) 16 ♕f3 ♕c6 17 0-0-0 ♗e7 (not 17...♘xd7? 18 ♗d3 and wins) 18 ♗c4 and White has a tremendous attack against Black's permanently uncastled king.

11...♘xd7 12 ♘g5 ♘gf6 13 ♘d2 ♘e5 14 ♘c4 ♗d5

Better is 14...♖d8 15 ♕e2 ♕e7, when Black has chances to hold.

15 ♗f4

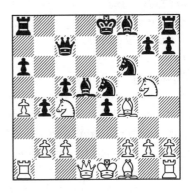

White's advantage is once again clear.

15...♘f3+

After 15...♗xc4 16 ♗xc4 White's bishops are too strong.

16 ♕xf3 exf3 17 ♗xc7 fxg2

Black wins back the piece—clever, but insufficient.

18 ♗xg2 ♗xg2 19 ♖g1 ♗d5 20 ♘b6 ♖a7 21 0-0-0 h6 22 ♖ge1+ ♗e7 23 ♘xd5 ♘xd5 24 ♖xd5 ♖xc7 25 ♘e6 ♖c6 26 ♘xg7+ ♔f7

The game has proceeded logically: White is a pawn up with the better position. Now the *MegaBase* goes haywire and gives the following moves.

27 ♖xe7+?? ♔xe7

Black is now winning, but the database suddenly gives:

1-0 (!)

Obviously this makes no sense, as to believe it requires us also to believe that the IM with White blundered the exchange for nothing, and the GM as Black then resigned in a winning position! Most likely the moves were simply entered wrong. White should of course have played (and possibly did play, though it never made the database) 27 ♘f5 with a winning position.

Going back to the opening, it's clear that Kurajica was fighting for his life after 6 ♗g5.

This concludes my coverage of the one-trick pony. I think it's best not to "refute" it with 3 c3, which may not be possible, but simply to play normal moves (3 ♘c3, 4 d4) and let Black transpose into regular repertoire lines. If Black is stubborn and ignores the centre (allows 5 d5!), then White should get a solid advantage, *if* he knows his stuff. We saw two IMs (Amanov and me) get a loss and a lucky draw against this line because we were *not* prepared—so don't put yourself in that spot!

> ## Game 68
> ## J.Dworakowska-
> ## Kar.Rasmussen
> ## Aarhus 2003

1 e4 c5 2 ♘f3 g6 3 d4 ♗g7

Whenever I have faced this Hyper-Accelerated Dragon, my opponents have always played 3...cxd4 4 ♘xd4 ♘c6, reaching the main lines we have covered by transposition. However, it's also possible to play more riskily with the immediate fianchetto, temporarily sac'ing the c-pawn.

4 dxc5

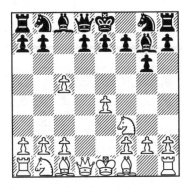

Just take it!

4...♕a5+

After 4...♘a6 White gets the advantage with 5 ♗xa6 ♕a5+ (5...bxa6 6 ♕d5 ♖b8 7 ♘e5 e6 8 ♕d6 is painful) 6 ♗d2 (6 ♘c3 is also good, but the forcing text keeps the pawn and offers to exchange the dragon) 6...♕xa6 7 ♗c3 ♘f6 8 ♕d4 0-0 9 e5 ♘e8 10 ♘a3 ♘c7 11 0-0-0 ♘e6 12 ♕h4 ♖e8 13 ♘g5 ♘xg5 14 ♕xg5 (Black is struggling, a pawn down and cramped) 14...♕e6 and White eventually won after the cautious 15 ♔b1 in F.Urkedal-P.A.Hansen, Oslo 2010—but I don't believe the "threat" to a2 amounts to anything, and White could take advantage of his opponent's complete lack of development with 15 h4! ♕xa2 16 h5, which looks like a winning attack to me.

5 ♘c3!

The problem for the Dragon player is that he is compelled to give up his

favourite piece here.

5...♗xc3+

Evidently forced, as the alternatives are even worse:

a) 5...♘a6 again fails to solve Black's problems: 6 e5 ♘xc5 7 ♗c4 d6 8 0-0 dxe5 9 a3 ♘d7 10 b4 ♕c7 11 ♗xf7+! (beautiful!—eleven moves and Black is crushed) 11...♔xf7 12 ♘g5+ ♔e8 13 ♕d5 ♘h6 14 ♘b5 ♕b8 15 ♘e6 ♘b6 16 ♘bc7+ ♔f7 17 ♘g5+ ♔f6 18 ♘e4+ ♔f5 19 ♘d6+ (it's true that 19 g4+ mates in three, but...) 19...♔f6 20 ♘ce8+ ♖xe8 21 ♘xe8+ ♔f5 22 ♘xg7+ ♔f6 23 ♘e8+ ♔f5 24 ♕f3+ ♔e6 25 ♗xh6 (taking all of your opponent's pieces and ending up a rook ahead is fine too!) 1-0 C.Rivero Ojeda-I.Aguilar Garrido, Catalonian Team Championship 2004.

b) 5...♕xc5 shows the danger of bringing the queen out too early: White attacks with 6 ♘d5 and scores 80% in the database—let's take a look at a couple of crushing White victories:

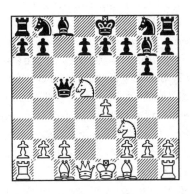

b1) 6...♘a6 7 ♗xa6 bxa6 8 0-0 e6 9 ♗e3 ♕c6 10 ♗d4! f6 11 ♖e1! (White won't retreat and Black can't move!)

11...♕b7 12 c4! d6 13 ♕a4+ ♗d7 14 ♕a3 exd5 15 exd5+ ♔f7 16 ♕xd6 ♗f5 17 ♖e6! (White keeps coming like a charging rhino!) 17...g5 18 ♖ae1 ♖c8 19 c5 ♕c7 20 ♕xa6 ♗xe6 21 ♕xe6+ ♔f8 (21...♔g6 22 ♘e5+ wins the queen or mates) 22 c6 ♘e7 23 ♗c5 1-0 I.Rogers-S.Kümin, Baden 1998. You don't often see +30 on the *Fritz*, but that's how the machine evaluates this one—White's plus is worth about three extra queens!

b2) 6...♕a5+ 7 ♗d2 ♕d8

8 ♗c3 (the typical manoeuvre to exchange the dragon) 8...♗xc3+ 9 ♘xc3 d6 10 e5! (Black's dark squares, in the absence of his king's bishop, are collapsing already!) 10...♘c6 11 ♗b5 a6 12 ♗xc6+ bxc6 13 ♕d4 d5 14 0-0-0 ♕a5 15 e6 f6 16 ♖he1 ♖b8 17 a3 ♕c7 18 ♘a4 ♘h6 19 g4 0-0 20 ♘c5 (utter domination on the dark squares) 20...a5 21 h3 ♖b5 22 c3 ♕a7 23 ♘d7 ♕b7 24 c4 ♗xd7 25 cxb5 ♗c8 26 b6 c5 27 ♕xc5 ♗xe6 28 ♔b1 ♖c8 29 ♕e3 (Black's loose pieces have dropped off the board) 1-0 E.Miroshnichenko-E.Andreev, Alushta 2000.

c) 5...♘f6 6 e5—if you think the previous line was bad, consider this, where White actually scores *90%* in the *Mega*. Even a super-GM like Epishin is simply destroyed here—White is a pawn up and dominates the centre, regardless of Black's reply:

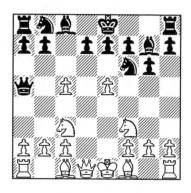

c1) 6...♘g4 7 ♕d4 d6 8 ♗b5+ ♘c6 9 cxd6 ♕xb5 10 ♘xb5 ♘xd4 11 ♘fxd4 ♗xe5 12 h3 ♗xd4 (12...♘f6 13 ♘c7+ ♔d8 14 ♘f3 wins material) 13 ♘xd4 ♘f6 14 0-0 exd6 15 ♖e1+ ♔d7 16 ♗g5 with a decisive queenless attack.

c2) 6...♘e4 7 ♕d4 ♘xc3

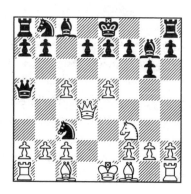

8 ♗d2! (White's point; he refuses to compromise his pawn structure.

8...♘b5 (or 8...♘c6 9 ♕xc3 ♕xc3 10 ♗xc3 b6 11 cxb6 axb6 12 a4 and Black has nothing for the pawn) 9 ♕h4 ♕c7 (9...♕a6 10 a4 doesn't help) 10 ♗xb5 (White has a great attacking development and is at least temporarily up a pawn; even a 2600 GM can't do much with Black—though to Epishin's credit, he avoids losing to a mating attack in 16 moves, as in the other game given in this note, which finished as follows: 10...♗xe5 11 0-0-0 ♗g7 12 ♖he1 e6 13 ♗f4 ♕xc5 14 ♗d6 g5 15 ♖xe6+!!—wins the queen or mates—15...♔d8 16 ♘xg5 1-0 N.Fercec-A.Shahtahtinsky, Nikea 2001) 10...♘c6 11 0-0-0 h6 12 ♖he1 ♘d8 13 ♘d4 e6 14 ♗a4 ♕xc5 15 ♘b5 0-0 16 ♗xh6 f6 17 ♗xg7 ♔xg7 18 exf6+ ♖xf6 19 ♘d6 ♖f8 20 ♕e7+ ♔g8 21 ♘xc8 ♖xc8 22 ♕xc5 ♖xc5 23 ♖xd7 (Epishin gets the queens off—at the cost of two good pawns—and continues to play on hoping for a miracle) 23...b5 24 ♗b3 a5 25 a3 a4 26 ♗a2 ♖e8 27 ♖e3 ♔f8 28 ♖g3 ♖f5 29 ♖xg6 ♖xf2 30 h4 ♖f1+ 31 ♖d1 ♖f2 32 h5 ♔e7 33 ♖e1 ♖ef8 34 ♗xe6 ♖f1 35 ♖g7+ ♔d6 36 ♖d7+ ♔c6 37 ♖dd1 ♖xe1 38 ♖xe1 ♔d6 39 ♗g4 (and the bishop will come to f3, absolutely squelching counterplay) 1-0 J.Shaw-V.Epishin, Groningen 1999. It's certainly rare to see a top GM busted in the opening like that!

In short, by elimination, Black's best chance is to sell his Dragon to come out a dubious pawn up.

6 bxc3 ♕xc3+ 7 ♗d2 ♕xc5 8 ♗d3 d6 9 0-0 ♘f6 10 ♗h6

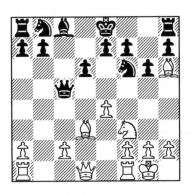

With excellent compensation: White has the two bishops, unopposed dark squares, holes in the enemy kingside and, of course, Black can't castle, at least for the moment. In short, more than enough for the pawn.

10...♘bd7 11 ♖b1 ♘g4 12 ♗g7 ♖g8

Black won't castle kingside in this game—and does he want to castle into White's open b-file on the queenside?

13 ♗d4 ♕h5 14 ♗e2 ♕h6 15 ♗b5 f6 16 h3 ♘ge5 17 ♗xe5 fxe5 18 ♕d5 ♖f8 19 ♘xe5!

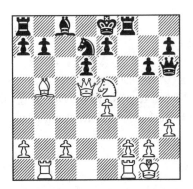

The Polish WGM destroys Black's undeveloped position.

19...dxe5

After 19...♕h5 20 ♘xd7 ♕xd5 (or 20...♗xd7 21 ♕xb7, winning) 21 ♘f6+! is a deadly double check that leaves White a piece up.

20 ♖fd1

White regains the piece and mops up.

20...♖f6 21 ♗xd7+ ♗xd7 22 ♕xd7+ ♔f8 23 ♕xb7 ♖e8 24 ♕xa7 ♕f4 25 f3 ♖c6 26 ♖b8

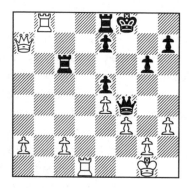

26...♕f7

Not 26...♖xc2? 27 ♖xe8+ ♔xe8 28 ♕a4+ and White picks off a rook.

27 ♕a8 ♖xb8 28 ♕xb8+ ♔g7 29 ♕xe5+ 1-0

Three extra pawns should be enough.

After 3...♗g7 4 dxc5 Black has to suffer to get his pawn back (and is often forced to give up his Dragon), while White gets an easy attacking game.

Game 69
A.Beliavsky-M.Quinteros
Vienna 1986

1 e4 c5 2 ♘f3 b6

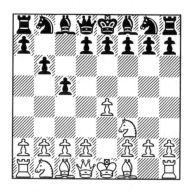

This is much less common than the kingside fianchetto we just examined; the problem is that in most variations of the Sicilian, Black plays a long fianchetto with ...a7-a6 and ...b7-b5, therefore in most variations committing the pawn to b6 is a loss of tempo. White, of course, can get away with this, as in Fischer's famous win over Tukmakov given below—but it's asking a lot of Black's position to go down this road, especially when you add in a slowed kingside development.

Fischer-Tukmakov began 1 b3 e5 2 ♗b2 ♘c6 3 c4 ♘f6 4 e3 ♗e7 5 a3 0-0 6 d3 d5 7 cxd5, when the missing tempo can clearly be seen: after the natural 7...♘xd5 8 ♘f3, Black would like to play ...f7-f5 and ....♗f6—as in various lines of our repertoire—but doesn't have time to make both of those moves as the e-pawn is hanging, and so must defend with something like 8...f6. But just imagine if Black had that extra tempo—say White played 8 h3 f5 9 ♘f3 ♗f6—then Black would have a terrific game. In short, while Larsen's Opening is sound for White, I think 1...b6, and this allied Sicilian line, to be dubious for Black.

Going back to the Fischer game, Black made the awkward recapture with the queen, 7...♛xd5, and after 8 ♘c3 ♛d6 9 ♘f3 ♝f5 10 ♛c2 ♜fd8 11 ♜d1 h6 12 h3 ♛e6 13 ♘d2 ♘d7 14 ♝e2 ♚h8 15 0-0 ♝g6 16 b4!, White made good use of his extra tempo and won stylishly: 16...a6 17 ♜c1 ♜ac8 18 ♜fd1 f5 19 ♘a4 ♘a7 20 ♘b3 b6 21 d4! f4 22 e4 ♘b5 23 ♝g4 ♛f6 24 dxe5 ♘xe5 25 ♝xc8 ♜xc8 26 ♜d5 1-0 R.J.Fischer-V.Tukmakov, Buenos Aires 1970.

3 d4 cxd4 4 ♘xd4 ♝b7 5 ♘c3

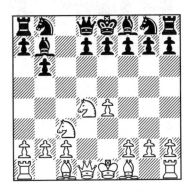

5...♘c6

5...a6 appears to be relatively best, when Black enters a slow Kan without the ...b7-b5 advance. White should get the advantage with our general repertoire lines, as Black is playing almost a tempo down: 6 ♝e2 e6 7 0-0 ♛c7 8 f4 (unlike Tukmakov, White has time here to set up his ideal big centre with attacking chances) 8...♝b4 (8...d6 9 ♝h5 g6 10 f5! gxh5 11 fxe6 with a decisive

attack shows the dangers for Black, who has no kingside development, while White is ready to go!) 9 ♝f3 ♝xc3 10 bxc3 (offering a pawn, but if Black takes it with 10...♛xc3 then 11 ♜b1 offers White great dark-square compensation) 10...♘f6 and now—instead of the premature 11 e5, when Black countered in the centre with 11...♝xf3 12 ♜xf3 ♘e4 and even won eventually in D.Maghalashvili-B.Savchenko, Baku 2009—White should hold e4 with 11 ♛d3, when 11...0-0 12 e5 gives him a big advantage, as 12...♝xf3 fails to 13 exf6 ♝d5 14 fxg7, while after 12...♘d5 13 ♝a3 ♜c8 (not 13...♘xf4? 14 ♛d1, winning material) 14 ♘e2 White retains both bishops and the attack.

6 ♝f4 ♜c8 7 ♘xc6 dxc6

7...♜xc6 8 ♝b5 ♜xc3 9 bxc3 ♝xe4 is *Fritz*'s suggestion to save this mess, though White should of course win after 10 0-0, as Black has no sufficient compensation for the exchange. 7...♝xc6 8 ♝a6 ♜a8 9 ♘d5 is also painful.

8 ♛f3

White naturally keeps the queens on for attacking purposes against Black's undeveloped position.

8...♛d4 9 ♖d1 ♛c5 10 e5!

White already has a decisive positional advantage: Black still has nothing off the back rank on the kingside, and now those pieces will be even harder to get out.

10...♖d8 11 ♖xd8+ ♚xd8 12 ♗e2 ♚e8 13 0-0 f5

13...e6 14 ♖d1 wins easily. Black tries to prevent ♘e4, but is then cramped even more.

14 e6! ♘f6 15 ♖d1

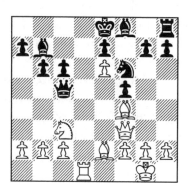

15...♘d5

An amusing mating attack occurs after 15...g6 16 ♗c7 ♘d5 17 ♛xf5!.

16 ♗e5 1-0

After 16...♘xc3 17 ♗xc3 Black can't even move.

It's rare to see a GM defeated so quickly, though Quinteros did not help his own cause. Black should go for the "slow Kan" with 5...a6, but as we saw, even then White gets a clear advantage. Nonetheless, one must take note

that, in the cited game with that line, Black actually won after White misplayed—remember, winning the opening battle does not automatically win the game! Given that note of caution, one can still hardly recommend (or fear) 2...b6.

Game 70
R.J.Fischer-J.Sherwin
US Championship,
New York 1962

1 e4 c5 2 ♘f3 ♘f6

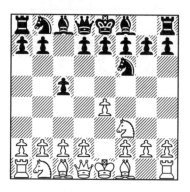

The Nimzowitsch Sicilian: Black tries to provoke White into playing 3 e5, which is an Alekhine's Defence with ♘f3 and ...c7-c5 inserted.

3 ♘c3!

White could rise to the bait: 3 e5 ♘d5 4 ♘c3 e6 5 ♘xd5 exd5 6 d4 ♘c6 7 dxc5 ♗xc5 8 ♛xd5 ♛b6 (8...d6!? is another sharp option) 9 ♗c4 ♗xf2+ 10 ♚e2 and so reach this amazingly complicated main line, with over 200 games in the database! Talk about a maelstrom! Let's watch Spassky wend his way through: 10...0-0 11 ♖f1 ♗c5 12 ♘g5 ♘xe5 13 ♕xe5 (incredibly complicated, as both sides sac madly) 13...d5 14 ♕xd5 ♖e8+ 15 ♔f3 ♕f6+ 16 ♔g3 ♗d6+ 17 ♖f4! (after the natural 17 ♗f4 Black *wins* with 17...♖e3+ which shows just what a crazy mess this is—my feeling is one should never enter such mad complications unless you are thoroughly prepared; but practically, from a human point of view, one can't prepare for every sharp line like this, which you might never face!—in my twenty-eight Sicilian games, I did not face a single Nimzowitsch Variation) 17...♗e6 18 ♘xe6 ♖xe6 19 ♕xd6! (Boris sacs his queen, which is of course completely logical in this insane position, and...) 19...♕g6+ 20 ♖g4 ♖e3+ 21 ♗xe3 ♕xd6+ 22 ♔f2 ♖e8 23 ♖f4 ♖e7 24 ♗b3 ♕e5 25 ♖e1 g5 26 ♖f3 ♔g7 27 ♖d1 f6 28 ♔g1 g4 29 ♗d4 (comes out smelling like a rose!) 1-0 B.Spassky-D.Ciric, World Student Team Championship, Marianske Lazne 1962.

Now if you want to study the fifty years of improvements and-counter improvements to this line—to research and prepare thoroughly for an opening you will probably never face—then be my guest.

But in my opinion we should play just as we did against the O'Kelly: make a natural developing move, stick to our repertoire, and give Black the chance to return to main lines. And if he doesn't—if he insists on staying in the Nimzowitsch—then, just as in the O'Kelly, he runs grave risks.

3...d5

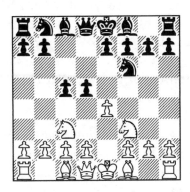

Black chooses "grave risks"! His position can't support such an early counter-attack in the centre.

But he has no choice if he wants to stay in the Nimzowitsch, since other moves return to the main lines we know: 3...♘c6 4 ♗b5; or 3...d6 4 d4 cxd4 5 ♘xd4; or 3...e6 4 d4 cxd4 5 ♘xd4.

4 ♗b5+

White develops with gain of time: simple and strong in Fischer's style.

Alternatively, you could also follow "current theory" and enter *another* long forcing line: 4 exd5 ♘xd5 5 ♗b5+ ♗d7 6 ♘e5 ♗xb5 7 ♕f3 f6 8 ♘xb5 ♘a6 9 ♕h5+ g6 10 ♘xg6 hxg6 11 ♕xh8 ♕d7 12 ♘c3 ♕e6+ 13 ♔f1 ♘ab4 14 ♕h3 ♕xh3 15 gxh3 (and after all this theory—yes, there are still eight games in the database!—the grandmaster doesn't even win against his lower-rated opponent: now that's a waste of study time!) 15...♘c7 16 ♖b1 ♘xc2 (Black has compensation for the exchange) 17 ♖g1 ♔f7 18 d3 ♖d8 19 ♗e3 e5 20 ♖d1 ♘e6 21 ♖d2 ♘b4 22 ♔e2 f5 23 a3 ♘c6 24 ♖dd1 ♘cd4+ 25 ♔f1 ♘f3 26 ♖g3 ♘fd4 27 ♗g5 ♖d6 28 h4 ♖b6 29 ♖d2 ♘b3 30 ♖d1 ♘bd4 31 ♖d2 ♘b3 32 ♖d1 ♘bd4 ½-½ Z.Efimenko-E.Pähtz, Isle of Man 2006. I had to hit the snooze button to get through that one! Now back to real chess.

4...♗d7

4...♘c6 is doubtful, as it leads to doubled isolated pawns for Black: 5 exd5 ♘xd5 6 ♘e5 ♘xc3 7 dxc3 ♕xd1+ 8 ♔xd1 ♗d7 9 ♗xc6 ♗xc6 10 ♘xc6 bxc6 and Black's pawns were weaker than White's pawns—in L.Kotan-T.Jandecka, Tatranske Zruby 2003, White converted 60 or so moves later.

5 e5

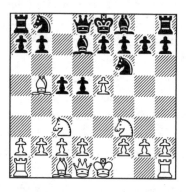

With Fischer's line, you basically just have to know these first five moves: develop rapidly then attack. One sees *Mr. Fritz* is on board with a plus-equals: White has the initiative, but the continuations are non-forcing and one can just *play*. I am sure that even ten years from now, when I face

the Nimzowitsch Sicilian for the first time—I'll still remember these first five logical moves.

5...d4

5...♗xb5 6 ♘xb5 is worse, as White gets a terrific attack with the coming e5-e6 obstructive sac—check out Bronstein's classic destruction below, as well as a miniature from Jakovenko:

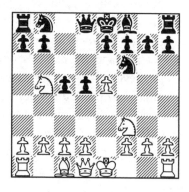

a) 6...♘fd7 7 e6! (this sac is the key to the position) 7...fxe6 8 0-0 e5 9 ♘g5 ♕b6 10 c4 ♘a6 11 d3 g6 12 ♘c3 d4 13 ♘d5 ♕c6 14 ♕f3 ♘f6 15 ♖e1 (Black is already lost, unable to defend his numerous weaknesses) 15...0-0-0 16 ♘f7 1-0 D.Jakovenko-E.Llobel Cortell, Spanish Team Championship 2006.

b) 6...♘e4 can be met strongly by 7 c4 a6 (the natural 7...e6 actually *loses a piece* to 8 ♕a4 ♘d7 9 d3!) 8 ♘a3 dxc4 9 ♕e2 f5 10 ♘xc4 b5 11 d3 with great positional advantage.

c) 6...a6 7 ♘c3 d4 8 ♘a4 ♘fd7 9 e6! (the obstructive sac again, plus Bronstein's tactical genius...) 9...fxe6 10 ♘g5 ♕c7 11 0-0 ♕c6 12 b3 e5 13 d3 ♘f6 14 f4 h6 15 ♘f3 e4 16 ♘e5 ♕c7 17 dxe4 (the pawn is immune due to the check at h5—the game is practically over) 17...♘bd7 18 ♘g6 ♖g8 19 e5 ♘d5 20 c4 ♘b4 21 e6 ♘f6 22 f5 b5 23 ♗f4 ♕c6 24 a3 bxa4 25 axb4 ♘e4 26 ♕f3 (even if Black manages to save his knight, he is still left with two non-playing pieces on the kingside) 1-0 D.Bronstein-J.Saadi, Mar del Plata 1960.

Black can also try 5...♘e4, but then he gets hit immediately with 6 e6! ♗xb5 (or 6...fxe6 7 ♕e2 ♘xc3 8 bxc3 with a powerful bind for the pawn) 7 exf7+ ♔xf7 8 ♘xb5 ♘c6 9 0-0 h6 10 d3 ♘f6 11 ♗f4 a6 12 ♘c3 e6 13 ♘e5+ ♘xe5 14 ♗xe5 ♗d6 15 f4 and White's domination of e5 led to victory in A.Berelowitsch-Y.Afek, Haarlem 2007.

6 exf6 dxc3

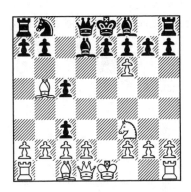

7 fxg7

White can choose to sacrifice a pawn here, though I don't choose to recommend it! 7 ♕e2 cxd2+ 8 ♗xd2 gxf6 9 0-0-0 ♕b6 10 ♗c4 ♘c6 11 ♖he1 0-0-0 12 ♗xf7 (White has recovered his pawn but lost all his positional advantage) 12...e5 13 c3 ♔b8 14 ♘h4 ♗c8 15

♕h5 c4 16 ♗e3 ♗c5 17 ♖xd8 ♖xd8 18 ♕xh7 ♗xe3+ 19 fxe3 ♕c7 20 ♗g6? (20 ♕h5 is better, though now it's Black who has good play for the pawn) 20...♕xh7 0-1 A.Motylev-L.D.Nisipeanu, Rumanian Team Championship 2007—White resigned in view of the coming skewer on the h-file.

7...cxd2+ 8 ♕xd2

Fischer keeps b2 guarded; the queen will move later with tempo.

8...♗xg7

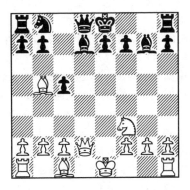

9 ♗d3

This is strong, though White has various other moves (we've avoided the forced variations!). For instance, 9 ♗c4 looks good, pressuring f7, when it's not clear where the black king goes.

Fischer also tried 9 ♕g5 which is not as accurate, though Bobby got the advantage anyway: 9...♗f6 10 ♗xd7+ ♘xd7 11 ♕h5 ♕a5+ 12 ♘d2 ♕a6 13 ♘e4 0-0-0 14 ♕e2 ♕e6 15 ♘xf6 ♕xe2+ (15...♕xf6 16 0-0 ♖hg8 is equal, as Black's attacking chances balance White's superior minor piece) 16 ♔xe2 ♘xf6 17 ♗e3 (now it's just a classic bishop on open board vs. knight set-up) 17...b6 18 ♖ad1 ♖xd1 19 ♖xd1 ♖d8 20 ♖xd8+ ♔xd8 21 ♔f3 (the mature Fischer of 1971 would certainly have won this ending, as he did a very similar one vs. Taimanov in their match; here he allows too many pawn exchanges, and this, combined with Pomar's heroic defence, allows Black to salvage a draw—but desperately defending for hours was presumably not the aim of Black's counter-attacking second move!) 21...♔d7 22 ♔f4 ♘g8 23 c4 f6 24 ♔e4 e6 25 ♗d2 ♘e7 26 ♗c3 ♘g8 27 g4 ♔e7 28 f4 h6 29 f5 exf5+ 30 gxf5 h5 31 ♗d2 ♔d7 32 a4 ♘e7 33 ♗c3 ♘g8 34 ♔f4 ♔e7 35 b4 cxb4 36 ♗xb4+ ♔d7 37 ♗f8 ♔e8 38 ♗d6 ♔d7 39 c5 bxc5 40 ♗xc5 a6 41 ♔e4 ♔c6 42 ♗f8 ♔d7 43 h3 ♔e8 44 ♗c5 ♔d7 45 ♗d4 ♔d6 46 ♗b2 ♔c6 47 ♗c3 ♔d6 48 ♗b4+ ♔d7 49 a5 ♘h6 50 ♗c3 ♘g8 51 ♗b4 ♘h6 52 ♗c3 ♘g8 53 ♔d5 ♘e7+ 54 ♔c5 ♘xf5 55 ♗xf6 ♔e6 56 ♗g5 ♘d6 57 ♔b6 ♔d5 58 ♔xa6 ♔c6 59 ♗d2 ♘e4 60 ♗b4 ♘f6 61 ♔a7 ♘d7 62 a6 ♔c7 63 ♗a5+ ♔c6 64 ♗e1 ♘c5 65 ♗f2 ♘d7 66 ♗h4 ♘c5 67 ♗e7 ♘d7 68 ♗a3 ♔c7 69 ♗b2 ♔c6 70 ♗d4 ♔c7 71 ♗g7 ♔c6 72 ♗a1 ♘c5 73 ♗d4 ♘d7 74 ♗e3 ♔c7 75 ♗f4+ ♔c6 76 ♔a8 ♔b6 77 a7 ♔c6 ½-½ R.J.Fischer-A.Pomar Salamanca, Stockholm Interzonal 1962.

9...♕c7

Pomar, undeterred by his narrow escape above, tried the opening again—was worse again—but this time won! 9...♕b6 10 0-0 ♘c6 11 ♕g5 ♗f6 12 ♕h5 ♖g8 13 ♕xh7?! (central play, as opposed to pawn grabbing, would have kept the advantage: 13 ♖e1 ♘d4 14 ♘xd4 cxd4 15 a3 with an edge) 13...0-0-0 14 ♗f5 e6 15 ♗h3 ♖h8 16 ♕e4 ♖xh3 17 gxh3 ♖g8+ 18 ♔h1 ♘d4 19 ♘xd4 ♗xd4 20 f3 ♗c6 21 ♕e2 ♕b5 0-1 B.Zuckerman-A.Pomar Salamanca, Malaga 1968.

10 0-0 c4

If 10...♘c6 then 11 ♕g5 with a powerful double attack.

11 ♗e4 ♘c6 12 ♕e2

The queen moves with attack, and Black is compromised on both flanks.

12...c3

Nothing else is any better: 12...b5 13 a4 and the black queenside collapses, while after 12...0-0 13 ♕xc4 White is a good pawn up.

13 bxc3 ♗xc3 14 ♖b1 0-0-0 15 ♕c4

White has gained a clear advantage with sound and simple play—no maelstrom!

15...f5

After 15...♗f6 16 ♕xf7 Black has nothing for the pawn.

16 ♕xc3 fxe4 17 ♘g5 ♖hg8 18 ♘xe4

White has won a pawn for basically nothing.

18...♘d4 19 ♕xc7+ ♔xc7 20 ♘g3 ♗c6

Black can't take: 20...♘xc2? 21 ♗f4+ ♔c8 22 ♖fc1 ♗a4 23 ♖b2 wins.

21 ♖e1 ♘xc2

Black has to try to hold in the centre with 21...e5, which contains the trick 22 ♖xe5 ♘e2+!—but White simply answers 22 ♗b2 ♖ge8 23 f3 and stays a good pawn up.

22 ♖xe7+ ♖d7 23 ♗f4+ ♔c8 24 ♖xd7 ♔xd7 25 ♖d1+

Every piece comes in with attack!

25...♔c8 26 ♘f5!

The threat of ♘e7+ (mating as well as forking!) ends matters, if one doesn't count the following spite check!

26...♖xg2+ 27 ♔f1 b6 28 ♘e7+ ♔b7 29 ♘xc6 ♖g4 1-0

After 30 ♘d8+ ♔c8 31 ♘e6 ♖g6 32 ♘d4 White is just a piece up.

Fischer's two games, plus Bronstein's magnificent crush, show what Black must contend with if he insists on his Nimzowitsch Sicilian: basically just a worse position, no matter how you slice it, after White's first five simple moves.

Most likely, should you face this, Black will transpose to regular lines after 3 ♘c3, but if he sticks to his guns, be ready to know two more moves and then just *play* your better position!

Starting with Karpov and ending with Fischer is not so bad—you now have a complete repertoire against the Sicilian!

A Final Word

The main thing I learned from writing this book is that the Sicilian's reputation is far greater than its actual danger. You hear all this nonsense about how you have to be booked up thirty moves, and all the top players have everything memorized, so its far too risky to play the Open Sicilian; you should play it safe with the Closed and hope for an equal position—and yet that image of the Sicilian as some monstrous Hydra is simply not true.

For one thing, if the monster existed in reality as opposed to reputation, I certainly would never have scored 71% against higher-rated opposition! Moving up the scale, Karpov would never have scored like he did—recall that he never, ever lost in the 6 ♗e2 e5 Najdorf, while playing the best in the world and using the same line over and over. Ac-cording to "Sicilian reputation" he would have lost to some "forced variation" somewhere along the road—but that never happened, because the ♗e2 line *does not lead to forced variations!*

Yes, there are "memory variations" in many lines of the Sicilian, but it's easy to avoid them, as my recommended repertoire does. And when I played this way, I found that my opponents (who wore out their brains learning lines I did not play) were disoriented by the fact that they had to think with their own head, and could not rely on forced computer-generated variations. At that point, usually half the battle was won, and I could (most of the time at least!) take care of the other half.

I wish you all good luck with this Sicilian repertoire.

Index of Variations

1 e4 c5 2 ♘f3

Chapter One
The Classical Variation: The Boleslavsky Wall

2...d6 3 d4 cxd4 4 ♘xd4 ♘f6 5 ♘c3 ♘c6 6 ♗e2 e5

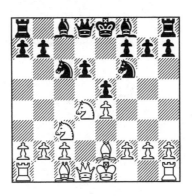

6...g6 – Chapter Two

6...e6 – Chapter Four

7 ♘f3

7 ♘b3 – *15*

7 ♘xc6 – *20*

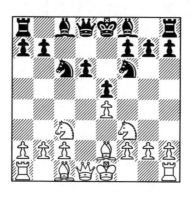

7...h6

7...♗e7 8 ♗g5 ♗e6 9 0-0

9...0-0 – *24*; 9...a6 – *27*

8 0-0 ♗e7 9 ♖e1 0-0 10 h3

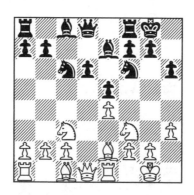

10...♗e6

10...♖e8 11 ♗f1 ♗f8 12 b3 a6 13 ♗b2

13...b5 – *29*

13...b6 – *33*

11 ♗f1 ♘b8 12 b3 a6 13 a4

13...♕c7 – *35*

13...♘bd7 – *37*

Chapter Two
The Najdorf Variation

2...d6 3 d4 cxd4 4 ♘xd4 ♘f6 5 ♘c3 a6 6 ♗e2 e5
7 ♘b3 ♗e7

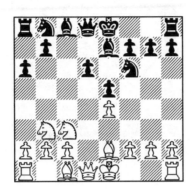

8 0-0

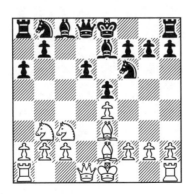

8...0-0 9 g4 ♗e6 10 g5
       10...♘fd7 – *76*
       10...♘e8 – *80*

8...0-0

   8...♗e6 9 f4 – *43*

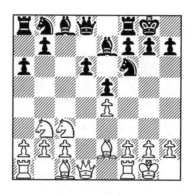

9 ♗e3

   9 a4 – *49*
   9 ♖e1 – *59*
   9 ♔h1
      9...♘bd7 – *69*; 9...♘c6 – *72*

9...♗e6

   9...♕c7 – *55*

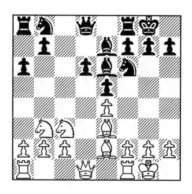

10 f4

   10 ♘d5 – *55*

10...exf4 11 ♖xf4 ♘c6 12 ♘d5

   12...♘e5 – *85*; 12...♗xd5 – *88*

Chapter Three
The Dragon

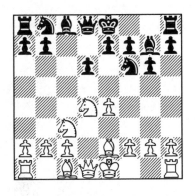

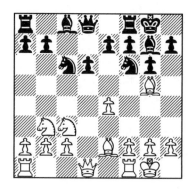

9...♗e6

　　9...a6

　　　　10 f4 – *97*

　　　　10 ♖e1 – *102*

10 ♔h1 a5

　　10...a6 – *91*

11 a4

　　11...♘d7 – *94*

　　11...♖c8 – *106*

Chapter Four
The Scheveningen Variation

2...d6 3 d4 cxd4 4 ♘xd4 ♘f6 5 ♘c3 e6

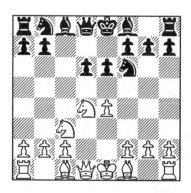

　　5...a6 6 ♗e2 e6 7 0-0

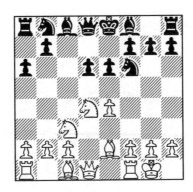

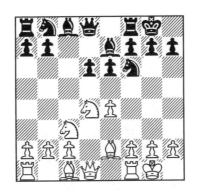

Chapter Five
The Taimanov/Kan Complex

2...e6 3 d4 cxd4 4 ♘xd4

4...♘c6

 4...♘f6 5 ♘c3

  5...♘c6 – 4...♘c6

  5...♗b4 – *186*

  5...♕b6 – *217*

 4...♗c5 5 ♘b3 ♗b6 6 ♘c3 ♘e7 7 ♗f4 0-0 8 ♗d6 f5 9 e5

  9...a6 – *220*

  9...♘bc6 – *225*

 4...a6 5 ♘c3

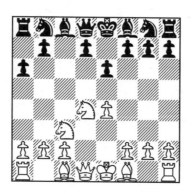

  5...♘c6 – 4...♘c6

  5...b5 6 ♗d3

   6...♕b6 – *200*

5 ♘c3 a6

6 ♗e2 ♕c7

7 ♗e3 ♘f6 8 a3

Chapter Six
No Sveshnikov Allowed

2...♘c6 3 ♘c3

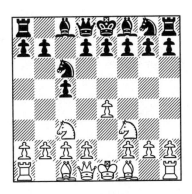

3...e5

Chapter Seven
Unusual Second Moves for Black

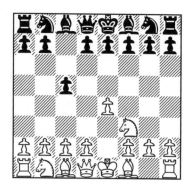

Index of Complete Games